Explorations in Women, Rights, and Religions

Explorations in Women, Rights, and Religions

Edited by Morny Joy

SHEFFIELD UK   BRISTOL CT

Published by Equinox Publishing Ltd.

UK: Office 415, The Workstation, 15 Paternoster Row, Sheffield, South Yorkshire S1 2BX

USA: ISD, 70 Enterprise Drive, Bristol, CT 06010

www.equinoxpub.com

Chapters 1, 3, 5, 7, 9-11, and also parts of the Introduction and of Chapter 12 were first published in Volume 36.2 of the journal *Religious Studies and Theology*
© Equinox Publishing Ltd 2017
First published in book form 2020

© Morny Joy and contributors 2020

All rights reserved. No part of this publication may be reproduced or transmitted in any form or by any means, electronic or mechanical, including photocopying, recording or any information storage or retrieval system, without prior permission in writing from the publishers.

British Library Cataloguing-in-Publication Data

A catalogue record for this book is available from the British Library.

ISBN-13	978 1 78179 838 6	(hardback)
	978 1 78179 839 3	(paperback)
	978 1 78179 840 9	(ePDF)

Library of Congress Cataloging-in-Publication Data
Names: Joy, Morny, editor.
Title: Explorations in women, rights, and religions / edited by Morny Joy.
Description: Sheffield, South Yorkshire ; Bristol, CT : Equinox Publishing Ltd., 2020. | Includes bibliographical references and index. | Summary: "The application of women's rights to the religions of the world have prompted highly contentious debates. This volume explores the many intricate issues raised in such interactions.The chapters in this volume are authored by women scholars of religion from diverse regions of the world, representing a plurality of religions, including indigenous religions. To enrich this already complex undertaking, four philosophers and legal scholars have also contributed. Their chapters help to clarify present challenges and envision innovative possibilities. The volume identifies archaic attitudes involving exclusionary regulations and controversial gender-specific practices. More contemporary impasses, such as individualism, so prevalent in western rights debates, and the unitary model of human rights, where "one size fits all," as promulgated in the west, are also appraised. Current constructive moves, especially expanding the notion of rights to involve relationships, are acknowledged. A primary concern of this volume is that of fostering future such collaborations of women advocates of gender justice"-- Provided by publisher.
Identifiers: LCCN 2019021255 (print) | LCCN 2019981579 (ebook) | ISBN 9781781798386 (hardback) | ISBN 9781781798393 (paperback) | ISBN 9781781798409 (pdf)
Subjects: LCSH: Women and religion. | Women--Religious aspects. | Feminism--Religious aspects. | Women's rights--Religious aspects.
Classification: LCC BL458 .E97 2020 (print) | LCC BL458 (ebook) | DDC 200.82--dc23
LC record available at https://lccn.loc.gov/2019021255

Typeset by CAUFIELD COPYEDITING AND TYPESETTING

Contents

Introduction: Explorations in Women, Rights, and Religions 1
    Morny Joy

1   Sexual Violence, Religion and Women's Rights in a Global Perspective   32
    Louise du Toit

2   Understanding Human Rights from Indigenous Women's Perspectives   47
    Sylvia Marcos

3   Women, Ordination, and a Buddhist Perspective: A Violation of Rights?   65
    Carola Roloff (Bhikṣunī Jampa Tsedroen)

4   Continued Discrimination under the Indian Act   89
    Beverly Jacobs

5   Examining Competing Claims in the Dialogue over Sex Education in Ontario: Women, Rights and Religion   122
    Pamela Dickey Young

6   Women's Rights and Religion: Jewish Style   138
    Norma Baumel Joseph

7   Maria Clara in the Twenty-first Century: The Uneasy Discourse between the Cult of the Virgin Mary and Filipino Women's Lived Realities   155
    Jeane C. Peracullo

8   The Reconstruction of Muslim Women's Property Rights in the Twenty-first Century   172
    Zaleha Kamaruddin

9   Charity and Justice: A Conversation with Evangelical Christian Women Serving Marginalized Populations in British Columbia   190
    Kathryn Chan and Erin Thrift

10	Women, Rights Talk, and African Pentecostalism *Rosalind I. J. Hackett*	207
11	Politicizing Piety: Women's Rights and Roles in the *Tarbiyah* Movement in Indonesia *Diah Ariani Arimbi*	223
12	Women's Freedom of Religion Claims in Canada: Assessing the Role of Choice *Jennifer Koshan and Jonnette Watson Hamilton*	240
13	Women, Rights and Religion in India: Questioning the Tradition *Asha Mukherjee (Dubey)*	260
14	Caring Detachment in Buddhism and Implications for Women's Rights *Suwanna Satha-Anand*	278
	Afterword: Women and Religion in Global and Local Perspective *Paul Bramadat*	295
Index		301

Introduction:
Explorations in Women, Rights, and Religions

> **Morny Joy** is a Faculty Professor in the Department of Classics and Religion at the University of Calgary, Canada. She researches and publishes in the areas of philosophy and religion, post-colonialism and decolonialism, intercultural studies in South and South-East Asia, as well as multiple projects and essays on women and religion. In recent years, she has published three edited books, *Continental Philosophy and Philosophy of Religion* (Springer 2011); *After Appropriation: Explorations in Intercultural Philosophy and Religion* (University of Calgary Press, 2012), and *Women, Religion, and the Gift: An Abundance of Riches* (Springer 2017). In 2011 she was awarded an honorary doctorate by the University of Helsinki for her work on women and religion.

The topic of religion and women's rights raises a myriad of questions and problems. For many of these, there are no clear-cut or easy answers. First of all, there is the question as to which particular religion out of many in the contemporary world is being discussed. Then, women's rights themselves are today a contested area, with strong criticisms coming from many directions, e.g., from religious fundamentalists, post-colonial scholars, and critical theorists. A further major issue that pervades debates on religion and rights derives from a tendency toward essentialism. This often leads to issues involving rights and religions being posed in terms of mutual exclusion. I believe that there is a need to move beyond the resultant polarizations, as they are posited often in the secularized west: whether it be as rights versus religion, as public versus private, or as multiculturalism versus assimilation. However, I also acknowledge that it is indispensable to examine the diverse ways in which the connections between religion and rights have evolved. This volume is an attempt to bring attention to some of the vital issues that still require attention, addressing both convictions that have hardened into intransigent stances and discerning insights advocating positive change.[1] The volume is of an interdisciplinary nature, appealing to the work of women in legal studies and philosophy in addition to scholars of the study of religion.

---

1. Sections of this this essay are revisions of "Women's Rights and Religions: A Contemporary Review," published in 2013 in the *Journal of Feminist Studies of Religion* 29(1): 52–68. Reprinted with permission from the publisher, Indiana University Press.

The Introduction to this edited volume has three sections. The first section reviews early attempts to introduce the concepts of women's rights to religion. It provides a basic overview of developments in the last years of the twentieth century. There were certainly some advances, yet at times there also appeared to be a fraught relationship between women and rights, especially in relation to religion. While there have been many thoughtful and measured evaluations made by women scholars internationally in the disciplines of political science, philosophy, sociology, and legal theory, it has taken quite some time for human rights to be closely examined within the context of religion, especially by women.

In the second section, I acknowledge more recent interventions by contemporary women legal scholars, such as Nicola Lacey and Jennifer Nedelsky. Their work has helped to diminish the resistance and dissension that have informed many of the debates on this topic of rights and religion. One particular matter that needs close attention is the expanding reach of fundamentalist religions,[2] with their attempts the thwart the whole process of women's rights, particularly those concerned with issues of reproduction.[3]

The third section consists of the abstracts of papers presented at a workshop that was held at both the University of Calgary, Alberta, and University of Victoria, British Columbia, in 2016. I would like to express my gratitude to Paul Bramadat who is Professor and Director of the Centre for Studies in Religion and Society at the University of Victoria, for his co-sponsorship and support of this workshop. He has also contributed an Afterword as a summation of his own participation in this event. The astute contributions of the twenty-four invited international scholars are wide-ranging in their scope. They provide further diverse insights of present-day situations, examining this most vital and decisive issues of

---

2. With reference to the use of the term "fundamentalism," I basically follow the definitions of Martin Marty and Scott Appleby in *Fundamentalisms Observed* (1991). However, I do find an absence of reference to the study of women in their various works. Basically, I don't want to restrict my understanding to that designated by a particular species of nineteenth century American Protestantism. Ideally, there are different terms applicable to specific religions to account for this phenomenon, such as Islamist and Hindutva, that would need to be developed in a larger study. For the purposes of this paper, where the main intention is to demonstrate the collaboration of these movements in order to restrict women's further access to rights, I will use the term "fundamentalism."

3. An example of this attitude is the Republican Governor of Alabama, Kay Ivey, recently signing a restrictive law that deems abortion a felony (May 15, 2019). Thirteen other states are in engaged in processes to ratify similar laws.

women, rights, and religions. The final section of the volume consists of the papers presented by the sixteen invited scholars who participated in the workshop. My purpose in undertaking this exercise has been to stimulate further thinking and discussion on these thorny issues. In addition, the hope is to foster future collaborative efforts on the part of both activists and women scholars from disparate backgrounds and disciplines so as to advance awareness of this demanding subject.

International Developments Concerning Women's Rights and Religion

This section should not be regarded as a fully comprehensive study, but rather as a brief introductory survey of certain key events and their consequences that have been crucial in the quest for women's attainment of rights in religions. Its focus is mainly the progress in women's rights as it evolved in the late twentieth and early twenty-first centuries. The movement for women's rights as human rights has a compelling history that attests to women's growing activism and advocacy (Rupp 1998; Jain 2005). These aspects first came to international prominence in 1975, when over 5,000 women attended a conference in Mexico City to celebrate the United Nations (UN) sponsored International Women's Year. From that time, the UN began to promote the interests of women. In December, 1979, the UN General Assembly adopted the Convention on the Elimination of Discrimination Against Women (CEDAW). The worldwide prevalence of violence against women was, from the beginning, one of UN's major concerns. By the time of the UN supported World Conference on Human Rights in Vienna in 1993, this concern had coalesced into the formulation of women's rights as human rights. This achievement featured as an item in the *Vienna Declaration*, which was signed by 171-member nations.

A number of works by women scholars have since chronicled this development and the UN's supportive role in detail. Arvonne Fraser describes how, during three subsequent Women's World Conferences (Copenhagen, 1980; Nairobi, 1990; Beijing, 1995), "Women gradually became a new political constituency" (Fraser 2001, 16). Amrita Basu further describes this development, detailing the consolidation of international women's organizations, at the same time as stressing their local variations (Basu 1998, 4). Her approach to religion, however, was cautious, as she was struck by the global divergences in attitudes to religion. She states:

> The relationship of women to politicized religions is paradoxical and complex. Religious politics have created opportunities for women's activism while simultaneously undermining women's autonomy. Contrary to the

hope of most feminists, women have not always opposed religious nationalist appeals. [...] we are struck by how states, movements, and parties have fallen back on religious – and often gendered – appeals when their legitimacy has foundered. (Basu 1998, 4)

Such an inconsistency also influenced Basu's uneasiness with the growing international influence of the religious right. Her considerable publications, however, provide an expansive documenting over the years of women's movements and their disparities as they continued to confront violence against women and campaign for human rights and civil liberties (Basu 2010, 27).

Fundamentalisms and women's rights

It was at the Beijing World Conference on Women (1995) that the backlash against women's rights was galvanized into action. Fundamentalist elements from a number of religions used the evasive ploy of "tradition" or "culture" to challenge the rights that had been gained thus far by women. The intent was to prevent any further progress, particularly on issues of reproduction. The Vatican was particularly active. It attempted to influence members of the Catholic communities from a number of countries, especially in Central and South America (Bayes and Tohidi 2001, 3). In addition, it made strategic coalitions between Catholic and some strongly conservative countries to support its own position (Bayes and Tohidi 2001, 3). Part of the Vatican's tactics were to argue that human rights for women, especially in the context of gender, was a "western," i.e., colonialist, imposition. From their viewpoint, women's increasing demands for self-determination were decried as nothing less than selfish self-fulfillment. As a result, struggles arose in meetings that attempted to restrict the extension of women's rights in various UN committees. This had been foreshadowed in the earlier refusal of signatory nations to pass a resolution on the implementation of the *Declaration of Elimination of Violence against Women* in 1979, ostensibly on the grounds of protecting religious traditions.

Judith Butler, Professor in the Department of Comparative Literature and the Program of Critical Theory at the Berkeley, Los Angeles campus of the University of California, describes her astonishment when she learned of the machinations on the part of the Vatican in the lead-up to the Beijing Women's Conference: "The Vatican not only denounced the term 'gender' as a code for homosexuality, but insisted that the platform language return to using the notion of sex in an apparent effort to secure a link between femininity and maternity as a naturally and divinely ordained necessity"

(2001, 423). Joan Scott, an American historian and gender theorist, also reported on another occurrence in the United States around the same time, when a sub-committee of the U.S. House of Representatives entertained submissions that warned morality and family values were under attack by "gender feminists" (Scott 1999, ix).

Both the Vatican and fundamentalist Christian religious groups in the States had obviously been made aware of Butler's work examining traditional gender roles in her book *Gender Trouble* (Butler 1990). In their depiction of this threatening situation, the opponents of "gender" insisted that "gender feminists" regarded manhood and womanhood, motherhood and fatherhood, heterosexuality, marriage and family as "culturally created, and originated by men to oppress women" (Scott 1999, ix).

The Vatican's plan, however, did not succeed. The UN did achieve consensus on its use of language and documents, retaining the term "gender" (Butler 2001, 430). In addition, the UN reiterated its commitment to women's rights, especially in relation to sexuality and reproduction. The strategic interventions of the extremely conservative coalition at the UN conference, however, marked the beginning of concerted activity to impede the further passing of progressive motions/conventions at the UN. Fortunately, the UN has not capitulated to their manoeuvres, steadfastly supporting women and their quest for rights.

The charges levelled at supporters of women's rights during the conference declared that religion and rights are resolutely opposed. Many of the anti-rights groups, safeguarded under the umbrella term of tradition, had made reservations, rather than voting for rights-based proposals concerning the status of women. Technically speaking, these reservations meant that such nations were in violation of articles of the UN Charter. Courtney Howland is forthright about this divisive move. She succinctly describes the battle that was taking place, declaring:

> Religious fundamentalism is premised on the notion that religious law takes precedence over all other law and defines, *inter alia*, relations between different religions and between men and women. Thus, some states have argued, in the context of human rights treaties, that religious law takes precedence over international human rights law even when the state has not entered reservations to the treaty on this basis. (Howland 1999a, 616)

In addition, the anti-rights collective mobilized their efforts to include political powers, both nationally and locally. The aim was to dissuade women from claiming their rights not only by applying political and religious pressure, but even by employing tactics of intimidation and force. Anastasia Posadskaya-Vanderbeck documents these disturbing methods in her study where she concludes: "Whether Christian, Hindu, Jewish, Buddhist, or Muslim, political religious movements are taking women's lives, denying or undermining women's education, decision-making, ownership of resources and mobility, and especially controlling women's sexuality" (Posadskaya-Vanderbeck 2004, 187). Such were the subsequent negative effects of this carefully-organized lobby that a number of activists contemplated abandoning the UN as an effective agency for implementing resolutions for women's rights. However, the UN itself has maintained its strong support of women's rights and well-being with its many programs of assistance.

Martha Nussbaum's explorations in religion and women's rights

Another approach that called garnered much attention during this same period, was when, in 1997, Martha Nussbaum published an article entitled: "Religion and Women's Human Rights" (Nussbaum 1997).[4] In this article Nussbaum stated that no system of religious law should be allowed to interfere with the basic rights of citizens. Her particular concern was the situation of women throughout the world where religions have not respected women's rights, that affirm women's equal dignity and the inviolability of their persons. The UN precedents attempted to contest such omissions with their *Declaration of Human Rights*, 1949, and the later promulgation of CEDAW, 1979. For Nussbaum, however, this ongoing neglect and abuse manifested itself in the need to control, even dominate women. This involved specifically matters of sexuality, marriage and divorce and further issues concerning reproduction and custody of children. Since Nussbaum's publication, much heated discussion has ensued about the merits of her political position. One form of criticism was registered by certain postcolonial scholars. The charge was that they viewed equal rights as a "western" or "global north" imposition on women from cultures that are not disposed to adopt such secular values.

In the same year as Nussbaum's work, another article in a similar vein appeared. Susan Moller Okin's article, "Is Multi-culturalism Bad for Women?" (1997). Moller Okin was worried that cultures "that endorse and facilitate the control of men over women in various ways – even informally – limit their capacity to live with human dignity equal to that of men and boys, and to live as freely chosen lives as possible, is severely limited" (Moller Okin 1997, 10). Moller Okin was especially concerned about the

---

4. Over the years, Nussbaum continued to update her explorations in Rights and Religions. See Nussbaum (2016).

way that these practices were still customary when people from such cultures migrate to countries such as the United States.

Okin's short essay provoked an extremely animated discussion. Subsequently, a volume was published with the same name as Moller Okin's essay, "Is Multculuralism Bad for Women," edited by J. Cohen, M. Howard, and M. C. Nussbaum (1999). (A revised version of Moller Okin's paper was included.) There were trenchant observations among the invited responses to Moller Okin's work. One reply alleged that Moller Okin's stark dualism of religion and secularism tended to reinforce existing stereotypes, especially regarding the religious practices and orientations of minority, migrant communities. She was also further criticized by Yael Tamir for her view of culture as a static entity when, in fact, they are constantly changing (Tamir 1999, 52).

In Nussbaum's own response to Okin, she placed particular emphasis on the notion of freedom of religious expression, specifically as it is expressed in the American Constitution. Nussbaum acknowledges the complex and difficult nature of the competing claims of the right to equality of treatment with the right to freedom of religious practice. This results in the constant testing of the limits of toleration in a politically liberal state (Nussbaum 1999, 113). She also admitted that she was in favour of a ruling that such a state – specifically the United States – "would give religion specific deference, on the grounds that minority religions have been especially vulnerable in all societies and are consequently in need of special protection" (Nussbaum 1999, 111).

Yet a question arises as to how congruent is this observation with Nussbaum's earlier remark that religious law should never impede the rights of citizens? It could appear that deference to certain religious practices, which often demand categorical adherence to inflexible laws and tradition, particularly in regard to women, could prove to be extremely problematic. Are such practices to be given deference or be prohibited? This is a fiercely contested area where I believe that there are no easy or immediate answers even in countries such as Canada, where multiculturalism has been an official policy, in contrast to the United States where the metaphor of "melting pot" is preferred.

Such crucial decisions continue to be being painstakingly examined in the secular law courts, and in parliament – at both federal and provincial levels – as well as in public debates. What appears to be at the heart of the present debate is the right of women to equality under the law when this edict appears to be at odds with the right to practice freedom of religion. This is an issue that I believe will be at the forefront of debates in the years to come. It would appear that the time is ripe for concerned scholars of religious studies from many regions of the world, in conjunction with other disciplines, need to bring their insights to bear on this situation. While this might be regarded as primarily a feminist issue, I nonetheless believe that it has serious implications for women of all dispensations.

In turning to the second section of this Introduction, as an illustration of the above dilemma, I will present a case that was prominent in Canada in relatively recent years. It is one concrete illustration of the legal and personal convolutions that can arise in present-day debates.

The debate about introducing Sharī'ah in the province of Ontario in Canada

Although Canada may still regard itself as a multicultural nation, events can still occur that question such a status. On January 17, 2005, Marion Boyd, a former Ontario Attorney General of the province of Ontario, Canada, who had been appointed by the provincial government to investigate whether Sharī'ah law could be introduced in the province, caused something of a stir in the Canadian community. Boyd recommended that Islamic tribunals be allowed to settle family disputes in that province. Was this an example of multiculturalism, within in a liberal democracy, going too far in its deference towards religious diversity? For many women in Canada, including both moderate and liberal Muslims, this seemed to be the case. This decision, however, was not without precedent. Since Ontario's Arbitration Act was passed in 1991, Orthodox Jews, Catholics, and Ismail'i Muslims had used such tribunals to arbitrate family problems, marriage and business disputes. This arrangement was viewed as a way of alleviating heavy caseloads and delays in the civil courts. Boyd's recommendation was not binding, however, and both it, as well as the Act itself, were then submitted to review.

In opposition, there were a number of women's groups who did not appreciate Sharī'ah as conforming with the rights of women to equality under Canadian law. Homa Arjomand, Co-ordinator of the International Campaign against Sharī'ah Courts in Canada, who left Iran in 1989 declared: "The last thing I expected in Canada, the last thing I want, is sharia law. […] Under it, a woman is worth half a man. He can divorce her and she has no rights" (Arjomand 2004). She was supported in her opposition by Alia Hogben, at that time President of the Canada Council of Muslim Women, whose members included Shi'a, Sunni and Sufi Muslim women. Such oppositional groups were of the opinion that The Canadian Charter of Rights and Freedoms supplied sufficient protection for women as equal under the law.⁵ In an Interview, Hogben describes the reaction, "We've had a flood of e-mails from people asking, 'How can we help stop what is so dangerous to Muslim women.'" She further explains: "We believe Canadian women should all live under one law" (Hogben 2004).

Other principal concerns of the Muslim women who disagreed with the implementation of Sharī'ah were about gender bias, especially of the intimidation that could be exerted on recent immigrant women who may not be informed of their rights. There was also unease that such women could also be pressured by family into such arbitration under threat of rejection. Another basic worry was that the arbitration itself, once signed, was compulsory without appeal.

A Canadian professor of law, Natasha Bakht, herself a Muslim, also commented on the situation. In an article, "Family Arbitration: Using *Shari'a* Law" (2004), she expressed her concern that the move to arbitration reflects an attitude on the part of the government to wash its hands of dealing adequately with the status of women in religions – particularly in a time when fundamentalism was increasing. This reflects the fact that courts seemed to be increasingly unwilling to make decisions on matters of religion. In Bakht's view, the state seemed to be reluctant to take responsibility for matters that are considered private.

In her article, Bakht quotes Nicola Lacey: "The ideology of the public/private dichotomy allows government to clean its hands of any *responsibility* for the state of the 'private' world and *depoliticizes* the disadvantages which inevitably spill over the alleged divide by affecting the position of the 'privately' disadvantaged in the 'public' world" (Lacey quoted in Bakht 2004, 22). Bakht feared that such non-regulation by a government amounts to a maintenance of the *status quo*, i.e., "support of pre-existing power relations and distributions of goods within the 'private' sphere" (Lacey quoted in Bakht 2004, 23). She reached this conclusion because, in Canadian law, the burden of proof for a breach of the Charter of Rights and Freedoms is on the person who is making a charge of such a breach. Such an obligation would place many women in an extremely difficult position.

Bakht made another intervention, however, on behalf of those Muslim women who may want to accept arbitration by Sharī'ah. She stated that

---

5. The Canadian Charter of Rights and Freedoms is one part of the Canadian Constitution. It initially came into force on April 17, 1982, and sets out those rights and freedoms that Canadians believe are necessary in a free and democratic society. Any person in Canada – whether they are a Canadian citizen, a permanent resident or a newcomer – has the rights and freedoms contained in the Charter.

one cannot automatically presume that such women are either ignorant or oppressed in making such a choice. To do so would be to "infantilize" Muslim women in discriminatory ways. She further declared: "In fact, making an overly generalized argument regarding women's capacities or experiences homogenizes women and potentially eliminates important differences based on intersecting grounds of oppression" (Bakht 2004, 22). In support of her stance, Bakht quoted from Fareeda Shaheed who posted the following on a network named: "Women Living Under Muslim Law" (WLUML). Shaheed had posted: "WLUML recognizes that living in different circumstances and situations women will have different strategies and priorities. We believe that each woman knowing her own situation is best placed to decide what is the right strategy and choice for her" (Bakht 2004, 22).

Another feminist scholar, Sherene Razack, who, at that time, was a professor of Sociology and Equity Studies in Education at the Ontario Institute for Studies in Education [OISE] at the University of Toronto, provided an insightful analysis.[6] Her principal areas of research were concerned with race and gender issues in the law, and she warned against a strategy that she perceived was all too prominent in the debate. Though Razack conceded that something positive may have resulted from this exercise, in that the "plans of a small conservative religious faction may have been upset" (2007, 27), she believed that there had certainly been a narrowing of focus and attitudes that she understood as damaging for all concerned. This was because destructive dualisms had been reinforced. Razack described such dualisms: "Women's rights versus multiculturalism; West versus Muslims; enlightened Western feminists versus imperilled Eastern women" (2007, 27). From Razack's perspective, such divisions have pernicious consequences, especially when they invoke feminism:

> I argue that in their concern to curtail the conservative and patriarchal forces within the Muslim community, Canadian feminists (both Muslim and non-Muslim) utilized frameworks that installed a secular/religious divide that functions as a colour line, marking the difference between the white, modern, enlightened West, and people of colour, and in particular, Muslims. (2007, 1)

For Razack, in a post 9/11 climate, such a facile distinction served to both "keep in line Muslim communities at the same time that it defuses more radical feminist and anti-racist critique of conservative religious forces"

---

6. Sherene H. Razack is now Distinguished Professor and the Penney Kanner Endowed Chair in Women's Studies. Her research and teaching focus on racial violence. She is the founder of the virtual research and teaching network Racial Violence Hub (RVHub).

(2007, 1). In addition, such a stark division also did not leave any space for negotiation with Muslims for a type of moderate faith-based arbitration that could have resulted from a process of religious and legal interchange. This is what had previously operated in the family court of Ontario for many years in connection with the Catholic, Jewish and Ismail'i cases.

Such diversified views were known to Ms. Boyd before she made her decision. The list of the different groups and individuals whom she consulted, listed approximately 200 people, representing various constituencies. Many people, however, signed a petition supporting a resolution: 04-11-01. This resolution proposed to remove Family Law 186 from the Arbitration Act of Ontario 1991. It also demanded that legal family matters be determined by a secular Family Court, as was the case in the neighbouring province of Quebec. Boyd's anti-discriminatory position did not sway public opinion. Nor was much attention given to Ms. Boyd's statements to the effect that it would not be an unqualified Sharī'ah law that would be applied. After further deliberation, however, in a decision, dated 11 December 2005, Dalton McGuinty, the Premier of Ontario, rescinded the act that had allowed family court proceedings to be judged by religiously affiliated tribunals. The decision did not please everybody, especially other religious groups, besides the Muslims, who had supported the establishment of Sharī'ah courts.

This Ontario decision was ostensibly made in favour of women's equality rights trumping those of freedom of religious practice. But both Government and the courts evaded dealing with the deeper issues that concerned on-going patriarchal practices in contemporary society. Alternatively, they could have proposed a more thoughtful response that instigated an investigation into the power imbalances that continue to exist between men and women in contemporary society, no matter what peoples' allegiances – either secular or religious. More specifically, they could have examined the fact that invariably when religion and rights clash, all too often it is control of women's bodies that is at stake. Ideally, instead of merely confirming entrenched practices and views, such a process could have provided the occasion for a careful examination of the public/private divide where the private element hides many abuses of women to continue. Instead, as a result of this situation, religion and rights are still situated in mutually exclusive domains.

Further complications

At the same time as the opposition to rights from secular and liberal interests, rights came under attack from both postcolonial theorists and critical theorists. Both share similar positions regarding what they viewed as a prevalent form of essentialism that is intrinsic to the human rights platform. They also took issue with western categories and ideals that they viewed as being imposed unilaterally.

Speaking from a postcolonial and critical perspective, Inderpal Grewal had strong reservations about the human rights project.[7] Firstly, she viewed the whole rights undertaking as dependent on a Western linear view of progress. "Human rights is [...] based on linear notions of progress by relying on notions of the South as Other and utilizing North/South inequalities to claim that the North has human rights (with a few aberrations) and the South needs to achieve them" (Grewal 1999, 338). In this connection Grewal also rebuked the assumed "moral superiority" of US global feminism in its operations to save the abused women of the world, disregarding the obvious faults in their own country where rights were concerned (Grewal 1999, 344).

In addition, Grewal charged that the language of women's rights took, as a basis, the western understanding of the individual as the subject of human rights. "The hegemonic forms of Western feminisms [with their emphasis on individual rights] have been able, through universalizing discourses, to propose the notion of common agendas for all women globally, and to mobilize such discourses through the transnational culture of international law that can serve the interests of women globally" (Grewal 1999, 240). This presumed a commonality among all women, so that local political and social anomalies of a structural or institutional nature were overlooked (Grewal 1999, 341–42). Finally, Grewal lamented that, in some countries, the institutions or agencies to which women must appeal for redress are the very bodies that are responsible for the activities that have violated their rights. This alone would seem to defeat the purpose of the exercise.

As a remedial measure, Grewal recommended an approach that paid attention to regional or local contexts and, in particular, the socio-economic, political and cultural conditions that are inevitably interrelated in unique combinations in each locale. As a result, human rights and their violations could never be solely defined or implemented by a Northern generated model – nor by any unreconstructed universal formula, for that matter. Nonetheless, Grewal allowed, despite all her misgivings, that: "To the extent that some women will be able to use the language of universal

---

7. Inderpal Grewal is a Professor in the Program in Women's, Gender, and Sexuality Studies at Yale University. She is also Professor in the Ethnicity, Race and Migration Studies Program, the South Asian Studies Council.

rights and become subjects of the universal regimes, women's rights as human rights could be effective" (Grewal 1999, 351). But she remained wary that, by becoming constituted as a subject in accordance with an international framework, one would be constricted by the regulations of modernity and the nation state.

Grewal, however, did not acknowledge the rebukes that had come from American women themselves, calling their own nation to account for the same attitudes and actions that Grewal herself indicted. Wendy Brown, a critical theorist, and Judith Butler, have respectively criticized America for assuming certain universals that have all the characteristics of essentialist claims in relation to human rights and feminism. Both intensified their rebukes in the light of 9/11. Brown was particularly scathing in her denunciation of the appeal to human rights, with the rhetoric of liberation employed by both Georges Bush and Donald Rumsfeld in the retributive "war on terror" based mainly in Iraq. She declared:

> It is not only that Rumsfeld has co-opted the language of human rights for imperialist aims abroad and antidemocratic ones at home, but that insofar as the "liberation of Afghanistan and Iraq promised to deliver human rights to those oppressed populations it is hard both to parse cynical from sincere deployments of human rights discourse and to separate human rights campaigns from legitimating liberal imperialism." (Brown 2004, 460)

In the face of such distortion of rights, however, Brown pondered how rights could be used in the service of alleviating unjust suffering of other human beings. She observed: "If the global problem today is defined as terrible human suffering consequent to limited individual rights against abusive state powers, then human rights may be the best tactic" (Brown 2004, 461). Yet this statement needs to be put in perspective, particularly in light of the title of her paper, "'The Most We Can Hope For …': Human Rights and the Politics of Fatalism." Brown views rights as only one possible means of redress, allowing that other political remedies may be required to counter the predatory ways of "superpower imperialism" (Brown 2004, 461). From this perspective, human rights are both a limited and limiting strategy. Her final plea is that progressives should try to work towards more that just rights if they are to change the present political regime. Brown's analysis could also provide the basis for a rethinking of women's rights as not simply a means to relieve suffering, but also as a call to engage with the political systems that do not recognize their rights.

There has also been a remarkable change of attitude on this issue in the work of Judith Butler, a critical thinker and debunker of false pretensions to essentialisms of any variety. I have discussed this development in detail elsewhere (Joy 2005), but it bears repetition, for I do think it has pertinence for the issue at hand. In *Bodies that Matter* (Butler 1993), Butler admitted that, in her earlier work, *Gender Trouble* (1990), she may have played somewhat fast and loose with the notion of gender as performance, particularly as it was interpreted as an optional mode of identity that could be assumed at will. She recognized that the physical body was vulnerable to harm and oppression and that claims could be made on its behalf for protection from abuse and violence.

In an article, "The End of Sexual Difference" (2001), Butler takes this a step further. Here, she first acknowledged that gender will always remain a contentious site and needs to be constantly questioned. This is basically because certain conservative if not fundamentalist societies, groups, and religions, in particular, will continue to employ gender not only in a regulative manner but even as invariable and non-negotiable. Aware of the recent inroads that had been made by fundamentalists, however, and the attempts made to reframe, restrain, and even cancel many of the rights that had been hard won by former generations of women, she affirms:

> Although many feminists have come to the conclusion that the universal is always a cover for a certain epistemological imperialism, insensitive to cultural texture and difference, the rhetorical power of claiming universality for, say, rights of sexual autonomy and related rights of sexual orientation within the human rights domain appears indisputable. (Butler 2001, 423)

Butler has also reflected on the nature of the universal and the inevitable problems that arise with its use. In acknowledging that there will always be cultural variables that work against any universal claim, she nonetheless observes:

> This is not to say that there ought to be no reference to the universal or that it has become, for us, an impossibility. On the contrary. All it means is that there are cultural conditions for its articulation that are not always the same, and that the term gains its meaning for us precisely through the decidedly less than universal cultural conditions for its articulation. (2001, 430)[8]

The reclamation of rights, albeit highly qualified, by these two former formidable critics, in the light of present oppositional forces that are mainly motivated by political expediency or religious zealotry, initiated a possibility of rethinking not only the project of rights in relation to women but constructive ways of responding to the hostility of the opponents. For more practical details of different approaches that introduces how rights may be reconceived, and not immediately assume a universal stance, I

---

8. Butler's work has shifted dramatically in recent years, moving in the direction of human vulnerability; see Butler (2016).

will first turn to the work of the British legal scholar Nicola Lacey. In two essays, Lacey succinctly summarizes the effects of feminist theory on law and rights and then provides constructive ideas for their practical implementation.

Re-envisioning rights with Nicola Lacey

Lacey acknowledges that, from a global perspective, one of the most important recent developments is, in her view: "The cross-national and cross-institutional attempt to enact and realize human rights for women, both international treaties and institutions, and in the interpretation of national constitutions and non-legal regimes" (2004a, 479). Lacey nonetheless proposes that there is a need to assess this achievement for both its strengths and weaknesses. In her suggestions for re-evaluation and restructuring, Lacey will introduce constructive critiques for both the conceptualization and institutionalization of rights.

As part of her re-envisioning project, Lacey recognizes that feminist critiques of rights theory have effected "an immanent critique" of liberalism and rights (2004b, 14). She concedes the legitimacy of specific problematic terms, especially those of individualism; of purported gender neutrality; of the public-private distinction; as well as of the limited focus on formal theorizing rather than concrete concerns – e.g., the unjust the distribution of resources. Nevertheless, Lacey does not necessarily believe that rights should be abandoned (2004b, 42). She contrasts the position of those who are critical of rights, mainly women whose rights are basically secure, with those who have only lately obtained access to them. She observes: "Particularly for African Americans in the US and aboriginal groups in Australia and Canada, the recency of their accession to membership of the 'rights community' has generated a keen awareness of its power and of the political problems of a too ready dismissal" (Lacey 2004b, 14).

She then continues by remarking that it is women who come from such backgrounds, especially those from a critical race theoretical background, who have been most vocal if their support to maintain rights, though acknowledging that there is a need to revise them (Lacey 2004b, 42). Lacey is not satisfied in simply making this point in the abstract, as she continues by offering her own practical suggestions for ameliorating the rights framework. She initially surveys the possible contributions of feminist legal theory, noting: "Feminist legal theory has a strong normative, reconstructive and even utopian voice: it engages not only in *analysis* and critique of *current* law, but also in *reformist* or imaginative argument about how law might be otherwise (Lacey 2004b, 42)." She then develops how this can be applied to rights.

Lacey, in the company of all the critics of rights cited in this paper, expresses the need to challenge the obvious ahistorical and seemingly transcendent status of human and women's rights. She also locates the often-invoked tension between universal pronouncements and the required attention to particular local conditions as being at the heart of the rights debate. Lacey then proposes an alternative position, describing rights as having a similar function to that of the feminist immanent critique: "Rights may be seen ... not so much as transcendent, objective, or 'natural,' but rather as an emergent critical force *within* modern societies; as the conscience or superego of modernity, and as a framework within which new political ideals can be articulated" (2004b, 42). In this mode, rights can assume a prospective rather than a regulative role.

At the same time, Lacey takes into consideration the constructive revisions proposed by critical race theorists, such as the African-American scholar, Patricia J. Williams (1991). Such critical analysts argue for an imaginative reconstruction of rights, exploring innovative concepts such as collective rights, practices of affirmative action, group rights and other procedures, such as class actions. Lacey's approach also supports innovations that respond to the unfavorable appraisals of individualism.

In this connection, Lacey herself recommends the work of Jennifer Nedelsky, whose work explores the notion of rights as relational (1993, 1–26). Lacey appreciates Nedelsky's effort as one of "the most promising developments in contemporary feminist and critical legal theory" (2004b, 52). Nedelsky herself, in attempting to bring a more communal sense to rights, observes: "For example, as lawyers know, property rights are not primarily about things, but about people's relation to each other as they affect and are affected by things" (1993, 13). It does need to be appreciated that in this context, insofar as rights are viewed as structuring relations, they are not necessarily contingent on one's existing relationships (Nedelsky 2011, 315). Understood in this way, what rights can establish are different forms of intersubjective relations. Such an approach, according to Nedelsky, could help ameliorate the emphasis on both individualism and confrontation, which still remain prevalent (1993, 14). Lacey also applauds other benefits implied by this approach, especially that of rights implying relationships.

> All rights [...] express a certain view of relationships: all rights affect power relations, and create responsibilities as much as selfish claims. If we put this aspect of rights at the forefront of our thinking, and in particular if we abandon the idea that the paradigm rights are propriety rights which consist in the power to exclude others, we can gradually reconstruct our rights culture towards a model of democratic dialogue and accountability. (Lacey 2004b, 52–53)

Such a conception of rights and its openness to constructive interchange could drastically alter the manner in which the earlier depictions of religions and rights has been handled, often in an exclusionary and even hostile manner. Nedelsky herself enlarges on the way this alternative relational culture could result if it includes a requisite precaution. Specifically, this would imply consideration of and respect for the different constituents and contexts that are involved.

> Even apparently simple prohibitions [...] or guarantees [...] require interpretation and are thus amenable to a relational approach. A relational approach would shift the mode of analysis in those contestations, yielding better understanding of the core issues, more apt arguments, and, sometimes, different results from the more individualistic approach. But, in part because the relational approach does not entail a subordination of the individual to the collective, there will not be any less protection for individual rights [...] nor any tendency to abandon basic rights. (Nedelsky 2011, 77)

Nedelsky is also aware that such an approach also demands a heightened awareness or self-reflection on the part of the persons involved in such a complex undertaking:

> In most instances, I think this will also entail the perspectives of those engaging in the local practices that are in dispute. And conversely, the effort to shift those practices will be most effective when local practitioners can see some value by taking into account in their own judgments, the perspectives of international human rights advocates. (2000, 279)

In *Law's Relations* (2011), Nedelsky meticulously analyzes the many objections that other feminist theorists could propose to her position, as she realizes that not all will agree with her proposals.[9] Her summation of the benefits of a relational approach, however, speak to the issue that has been at the heart of this paper.

> When people realize the complex interpenetration of law, rights, and relations, they can take on the questions of how the law should be used and what kinds of things state power is well suited to organize. These are not small questions. But, of course, the relational approach does not itself create these puzzles, It points to the inadequacy of categories, such as public versus private, individual rights versus the public good, or state versus the market, as tools for analyzing them. The relational approach helps reveal the ways law has helped create the problems to be solved. (Nedelsky 2011, 379)

---

9. Chapter 8 in Law's Relations is a virtual compendium of the most vehement of these objections (2011, 307–379). What is at the heart of Nedelsky's position, however, is not only the restructuring of the law and state power, though this is not negligible, but the cultivation of humanity and a commitment to the enhancement of the quality of human life.

In this manner, Nedelsky, with the notion of law as relational, introduces an alternative perspective that could radically change legal approaches. While such expansions of the notions of rights could undoubtedly bring about welcome revisions to certain western understanding of rights and the mode of their application, for Nicola Lacey herself there remains one other major concern that needs to be considered. She invokes the very strong existent link in legal work between thought and practice (Lacey 2004b, 42). Lacey is concerned that, in rights talk, too much time is spent on theoretical wrangling. This occurs at the expense of acute attention to the obstacles that hinder implementation of even the best of theories. Lacey worries that:

> At the level of institutionally reconstructive projects, we encounter perhaps the most intractable questions faced by feminist theory: philosophical and moral questions about the shape and genesis of the values involved, political questions about building necessary alliances, practical questions about the operation of interlocking social institutions in different parts of the world. (2004a, 483)

To remedy this situation, Lacey believes that what is needed is a more nuanced understanding of the interfaces involved in the operations of social institutions. This requires the gathering of much more data of a "sociotheoretic" nature. Such research would assist in more precise knowledge of material conditions and the manner in which specific institutions operate/ co-operate in their local contexts (Lacey 2004a, 483). This is because, as Lacey appreciates, the contemporary major challenge in relation to rights lies in the fact that "the institutional complexity of the world – the subjectivities – itself presents possibilities for, as much barriers to, change. These possibilities can only be approached if feminist research is informed by adequate general social theoretic understandings" (Lacey 2004b, 29).

It is in the context of endorsing such in-depth knowledge of institutional interaction that Lacey makes a particularly pertinent remark. This is to the effect that further insights are required regarding the specific way that legal institutions are involved with economic, religious, and cultural institutions (Lacey 2004a, 481). She continues by lamenting the existence of certain disciplinary barriers, of a contingent yet forceful nature that, unfortunately, continue to prevent interdisciplinary alliances (Lacey 2004a, 481). Her recommendations of a needed dialogue between both researchers and activists also introduces the need for cooperative interdisciplinary research from scholars in a number of fields. And it is here, I believe, that scholars from the study of religion in its various guises could be of immense assistance.

There are many perspectives that feminist scholars in religion employ within their studies; as the study of religion is inherently interdisciplinary. These include that of textual analysis, hermeneutics, sociology, psychology, history, philosophy – and more recently, law and politics. Their contributions to the vision that Lacey encourages could prove invaluable. They are, I also believe, sorely needed. But little has yet been done in a concerted way.

There has been excellent work by individual scholars on the subject of rights and religion, in the early twenty-first century, such as those by the late Lucinda Peach (2002a; 2002b), Winifred Fallers Sullivan (2005), as well as a number of contributions to the fine edited volume by Courtney Howland (1999b); Amy Whitney and Carolyn Evans (2006); Alison Boden (2007); and Lori Beaman (2008; 2017). The time has come for developments that could be gleaned from the innovative suggestions in the ground-breaking work of Lacey and Nedelsky about rights as relation. These insights could then be incorporated into contemporary research in ways that would both deepen and enrich the study of women, rights, and religion.

Observations

At this stage I would like I would like to offer two observations expressed by inspiring women scholars as ways that religion and rights could be reconsidered, and that speak to the issues discussed in the course of my essay. One approach, taken by Mahavi Sunder in an article, "Piercing the Veil," advises women to claim their rights in the face all forms of religious oppression. Her description of those who participate in the movement is as follows:

> These individuals reject the binary approach of the Enlightenment, which forces individuals to choose between religious liberty (on a leader's terms) in the private sphere and equality (without a normative community) in the public sphere. Rather they articulate a vision of human flourishing that requires freedom *within* the context of religious and cultural community. This vision includes not only a right to equal treatment in one's cultural or religious community, but also a right to engage in those communities on one's own terms. (Sunder 2005, 268)

I can discern in Sunder's strategy a position of renegotiation for women who find themselves in religious traditions that are today resorting to fundamentalist dictates and trying to silence those of a moderate inclination, let alone the progressive voices of women. Sunder then continues to describe the modifications that she would like to see. She supports those "Cultural dissenters or individuals within a community [who seek] to modernize, broaden, the traditional terms of cultural membership, [and who] challenge the traditional liberal understandings of liberty and equality as premised on a 'thin' theory of the self" (Sunder 2005, 268). She states that liberalism takes too lightly the difficulties of women who cannot easily exit from their religious community, or those who may not wish to. Instead of complete rejection she advocates reform of both religion and rights: "I read in the rise of cultural dissent that human flourishing requires not only a liberty right to normative community, but access to a community free of the fear of discrimination within it" (Sunder 2005, 268). Such a position challenges primarily the traditional western public/private distinction, but it also recognizes the need for a "thicker" understanding of subjectivity – one that would include an expansive version of religion. Certain of Lacey's and Nedelsky's recommendations could prove helpful in this context.

A further insight is provided by Mahnaz Afkhami, a former Minister of State for Women's Affairs in Iran and a veteran activist of thirty or more years, who now lives in the United States. She addresses the dualism that pits individual rights against the community and places them as mutually exclusive:

> We must move beyond the theory of women's human rights as a theory of equality before the law, of women's individual space, or a "room of one's own," to the theory of the architecture of the future society where the universality of rights and relativity of means merge to operationalize an optimally successful coexistence of community and individuality. This architectural theory will point to a dynamic design where broadly conceived human relations evolve with the requirements of the times as they satisfy the needs of both community and individuality. (Afkhami 2004, 66)

It needs to be noted that Afkhami's program contains a proviso that is deemed necessary for its success:

> We must insist that no one, man or woman, may claim a right to a monopoly of interpretation of God to human beings or a right to force others to accept a particular ruling about any religion. The upshot of this position is that women ought not to be forced to choose between freedom and God. The same applies on the part of tradition. (2004, 65)

These statements by Sunder and Afkhami are indicative of contemporary women who do not wish to settle for the status quo, but instead are struggling to express ideas and strategies that could help to move beyond the present impasse. None of their recommendations will be uncomplicated to implement – and they do not necessarily all sit easily together – but they are suggestive of an incentive that holds promise. In one sense, I think such developments will be necessary, for I foresee a time when secular feminists and women scholars from liberal and moderate religious positions, as well as from the different regions and religions of the world, will form strategic coalitions. Such a move will help to moderate the influence of fundamentalist forces and that remain effectively mobilized to obstruct and even to prevent any further advances in the area of women's rights.

Comments on workshop contributions

In the opening chapter, "Sexual Violence, Rights and Religion in Africa," **Louise du Toit** describes how Christian churches in Africa are widely regarded as important Civil Society Organizations (CSOs) with a good record of providing social support roles for the marginalized when they are neglected by states. Such churches are recognized as one of the few CSOs that have kept functioning during armed conflict. They are also widely regarded as having authority and impact. In addition, they support the mainstream, a powerful material resource. Consequently, one could reasonably presume that such churches play an invaluable role in the process of healing and transformation needed by victims of sexual violence in the aftermath of violent conflict. Recent research (Le Roux 2014) has, however, shown that in countries such as Liberia, Rwanda and the Democratic Republic of the Congo (DRC), where violent conflict has occurred recently, these churches do not generally support the vast numbers of victims of sexual violence. Instead, they tend to contribute to women's physical, psychological, and economic hardship and to their ongoing marginalization and stigmatization. The unfortunate reality is that, instead, such churches attempt to bolster patriarchal power both within and outside the church. Du Toit demonstrates that the disquieting consequence of such conduct is that women's rights in such circumstances are not supported but seem to be erased.

Sylvia Marcos, in her chapter, "Understanding Human Rights from Indigenous Women's Perspectives," describes the changes that have evolved during the past twenty years, as she has participated by invitation in meetings of the Indigenous women of the Americas. The First Indigenous Women's Summit of the Americas was a United Nations meeting that took place in Oaxaca, México, in 2002. Since then, the geographical range and political agenda have expanded with the convening of numerous national, regional, and continental gatherings. Here, Indigenous women from the Mesoamerican region of Central America and the Andean region in Peru, Bolivia, and Colombia have participated. Marcos's chapter focuses on the collaborative voices of women of the Americas, quoting extensively from key texts and interviews. Her intention is to help discern how the term "human rights," or the term "my right" can be reconfigured, i.e., "recreated and used" in their declarations. What the Indigenous women are articulating, as Marcos perceives, is a form of decolonial revision. In this context, the gender theory that emerges portrays the practices and demands of Indigenous women for their rights. These are strongly voiced in their own language and determinedly enacted in their struggle for justice. Most importantly, the communities of Indigenous women of the Americas do not view themselves as "individual subjects," but neither do they stand alone, as they stand together and claim their own version of rights.

In her chapter, "Women, Ordination, and a Buddhist perspective: A Violation of Rights," **Carola Roloff**, who is a Buddhist nun (Bhikṣunī Jampa Tsedroen), examines the present debate about the ordination of Buddhist nuns. While she appreciates that non-violence is one of the two main pillars of Buddhism, she is vitally concerned that gender discrimination exists in Buddhism in the West. From a theological perspective, Roloff states that discrimination of women violates the Buddhist principle of non-violence and that it does not fit with the values common in modern societies. Admitting that the authoritative religious texts are ambivalent, Roloff asks how an approach can be made to these texts while considering the differences in the twenty-first century's social context? Her solid training in the Tibetan Buddhist tradition has qualified her to investigate the traditional texts concerning the vexed question of ordination for nuns in the Tibetan tradition. While Roloff would not go quite so far as to say that nuns should be able to claim rights, she is concerned about the prejudice that deems that nuns cannot be ordained, even though the Buddha himself allowed it. She concludes by arguing that the principle of equality must take precedence over religious freedom.

Beverly Jacobs, an Indigenous woman, is an eloquent and passionate advocate for the Indigenous women of Canada and their struggle for recognition and rights. Her chapter, "Continued Discrimination under the Indian Act," graphically describes the destructive effects of the *Indian Act* since its inception in 1876 and of its more recent amendments. Jacobs' assessment is that First Nation peoples of Canada, especially women, have suffered from severe disregard by the Government of Canada. She states that they have experienced major human rights violations that, over the centuries, have impacted negatively on their languages, their culture, and their spirituality. Jacobs has demanded: "How many more sisters and daughters do we have to lose before governments take real and meaningful action?" This appeal refers to the very many Indigenous women who have disappeared or have been murdered. Jacobs details the long and exacting journey that Indigenous women have had to endure in their quest for justice.

Pamela Dickey Young's chapter, "Examining Competing Claims in the Dialogue over Sex Education in Ontario: Women, Rights, and Religion," is a case study that examines the complexities of the intersections of the themes of women, rights, and religion in an educational setting. Dickey Young's case study pays special attention to the public debate over a new sex education curriculum that was implemented in the province of Ontario, Canada, in 2015. She examines certain religious individuals and groups of people who supported (and others who opposed) the proposed sex education curriculum. In this study, women could be found on both sides of the debate, espousing religious reasons for their divergent positions. While religion has been traditionally deemed to be a private matter, in this situation, however, it featured in passionate public disputes. By employing media reports and group websites linked to religious and social media groups as its main source of primary data, Young's paper investigates what, if any, rights to freedom of religion are involved. Further, she describes the presence of articulate women on both sides of the debate that raises complex questions about feminism and the rights of women. Using both feminist and postmodern theories, Young also examines various interplays of power and authority, most of which employ the concept of "rights" to support their claims. Yet diverse understandings of rights are widespread. Young's paper seeks not to solve this conundrum but attempts to explore the competing contemporary ideas of women, feminism, rights, and religion that are at issue in the topic of children's sex education.

Norma Baumel Joseph surveys the situation of contemporary Jewish women in her chapter, "Women's Rights and Religion Jewish Style." She confirms that, in Judaism, the case for individual rights and freedoms is a particularly difficult matter. This is because obligation, as a divine decree, is regarded as mandatory and thus takes precedence over rights. Nevertheless, issues of rights do feature in present-day Jewish women's discussions. Baumel Joseph does acknowledge the progress many Jewish women have made in recent years, expanding their awareness of women's rights and responsibilities. However, in Baumal Joseph's view, there remains one disquieting concern where women's gender equilibrium has thus far not been achieved. This is the issue of divorce, where men still maintain the prerogative of granting a woman a divorce document (*get*). But often this is refused and the woman is left stranded. Baumal Joseph details this discriminatory practice, which she describes as "most reprehensible." She then describes the moves that have been introduced to try and help reduce such injustice. In her conclusion, she implies that it is time for this legal abnormality to be amended by a concerned Jewish intervention.

Jeane Peracullo's chapter, "Maria Clara in the Twenty-first Century: The Uneasy Discourse between the Cult of the Virgin Mary and Filipino Women's Lived Realities," describes the contemporary struggle of women in the Philippines between its ingrained Catholic heritage and Filipino women's more recent development of autonomy. Peracullo explains how, in the Philippines, Mary, as the mother of Jesus, is worshipped by most Catholics. Yet, recently, Mary has also been represented by a satirical character named Maria Clara in imagery that depicts her as a weak or passive woman. This development is indicative of a growing opposition to Mary's dominance. While there are a number of contemporary challenges that now threaten traditional religious devotion, the major one for women is an economic one. Many Filipino women are leaving their families to work abroad in occupations such as nurses and caregivers. These "Overseas Filipino Workers" are thus gaining a sense of independence. This alteration means that they are negotiating new identities and, in the process, are rejecting traditional feminine stereotypes. In Peracullo's view, however, this move could appear doomed unless the women can gain access to an education system that would help them to an understanding of their rights as women. The Catholic Church has not sanctioned this change. Peracullo's chapter, with its careful analysis of contemporary Filipino women's economic advances, adds another dimension to the secular/religious debate concerning women's rights.

Zaleha Kamaruddin is an internationally respected expert in comparative family law. In her chapter, "The Reconstruction of Muslim Women's Property Rights in the twenty-first Century," she suggests recasting property rights as a way of improving the status of women. In her analysis, Kamarudd undertakes an assessment of traditional property rights, which have had a negative impact on the lives of many Muslim women. In her reconstruction of the property rights for women in Islam, Kamarudd identifies certain key areas that require policy decisions to clear the doubts relating to the status of women in Muslim communities. Besides the overwhelming influence of a massive acculturation in matters relating to Muslim women's property rights, her paper identifies the non-grounding of fundamental Sharī'ah principles as one of the major challenges facing Muslim societies. Her paper concludes that, for a more productive society, there is a need to reconstruct Muslim women's property rights by means of undertaking a transformative economic empowerment of women. This would help to prevent avoidable discrimination on the basis of gender. From the very core of economic and also fair distributive principles that are part of Islamic law, such a transformative economic empowerment for women needs to be affirmatively recognized. Kamarudd's study offers an insightful and balanced appreciation of Islamic principles, which she names a "treasure-trove" for women's empowerment in the twenty-first century.

In their chapter, "Charity and Justice: A Case Study of Faith-based Charities Supporting Marginalized Women in Vancouver's Urban Core," **Kathryn Chan** and **Erin Thrift** examine the concept of charity in a number of conservative faith-based religions. They observe that in many religious traditions, the concept of charity is closely related to the concept of justice. Yet, in Vancouver, where a number of faith-based charities have recently sought to declare a commitment to the underprivileged, they do this either by deliberately blurring the traditional lines between a service provider and a beneficiary or by seeking to give political voice to the persons they represent. However, Chan and Thrift also remark that there are significant institutional and regulatory obstacles to these types of "justice-oriented" charitable models. Their paper explores these obstacles through a case study of several faith-based charitable organizations that serve sex workers and marginalized women in Vancouver. The authors examine the ways in which the regulatory environment limits the opportunities of both "service providers" and "beneficiaries" to exercise agency in these organizations. In their conclusion, they consider the implications of such limitations for issues of religious freedom, rights advocacy, and participatory democracy.

Rosalind Hackett's chapter, "The Impact of Pentecostalism on Women and their Rights," assesses the impact on the rights of women of the rapid growth of Pentecostalism in Africa since the 1970s, both within and outside religious communities. Her examples are drawn primarily from Nigeria, Ghana, and Uganda. The diversity of these charismatic, revivalist movements and the varied contexts in which they operate provide the basis of a compelling case study that explores the perduring paradoxes of women's leadership and agency in these predominantly patriarchal religious organizations. Hackett's concern is that they have had a mostly negative impact on women's lives and their access to rights. In her paper, Hackett focuses on the concept of "rights talk," which she regards as providing a productive and inclusive way to approach women's leadership in locally grounded (and often transnationally connected) African Christian communities. The irony of this situation is that many women have succeeded in becoming leaders in these churches. They have also publicly addressed the emancipation of women in varying contexts of gender inequality. But, as Hackett queries, at what cost?

In her chapter, "Women and the Politics of Piety: Women's Rights, Roles and Equality in the *Tarbiyah* (Education) Movement in Indonesia," **Diah Ariani Armbi** describes a relatively recent development. The *Tarbiyah* movement is mainly active on university campuses. Many female activists are part of the movement, but, unfortunately, until Arimbi's paper, there had not been previously any in-depth study undertaken. Arimbi explores the *Tarbiyah* movement, which is viewed as reformist, relying heavily on modern interpretations of Islam concerned with democracy, civil society, human rights, and equality of women. These values, however, are understood somewhat differently from Western notions. For example, the *jilbab* (veil) movement in secular university campuses is taken as a sign of religious freedom. Arimbi's contribution provides insights into this new movement, describing the varieties of women's activities involved. Her analysis will help scholars to understand the ways in which the women members of the movement balance their views on rights and roles, especially those related to the notion of piety. Arimbi's study illustrates how young Indonesian women are nonetheless claiming their rights within a conservative religious framework.

Jennifer Koshan and **Jonnette Watson Hamilton**, who are both professors of law, discuss in their chapter, "Women's Freedom of Religion Claims in Canada: Assessing the Role of Choice," whether religious women's reliance on choice to assist their claims to rights in Canadian courts may interfere with the success of those claims. Canadian courts have interpreted religious freedom under section 2(a) of the *Canadian Charter of Rights and Freedoms* to include a strong element of choice. In reality, however, some religious cases based on choice have not received protection, especially when choices have been viewed as a cause of harm to the claimant or a cause of harm to others. Koshan and Watson Hamilton investigate the case of a Muslim woman, Zunera Ishaq, who successfully challenged a federal government policy that required her to remove her *niqab* during a citizenship ceremony. Zunera Ishaq argued that this policy violated her freedom of religion and right to equality and that it also contravened regulations made under the *Citizenship Act*. Though this case succeeded within the broader context of decisions involving women, religious freedom, equality, and choice, Koshan and Watson Hamilton fear that other claims might not be as successful. They introduce other examples from the feminist literature concerning religious women and choice. These include the relationship between choice, agency, and autonomy; the public/private dichotomy; and individualization. Their conclusion is that a de-emphasis on choice may actually be a strategically more helpful approach for religious women to make rights claims.

In her chapter, "Women, Rights and Religion in India," **Asha Mukherjee** looks at the problems that are layered, on the one hand, in the traditional *dharma* discourse, and, on the other, the modern Indian human rights discourse. She highlights this paradox faced by contemporary Indian women. This is obvious in the urge to change and accept the Western progressive-democratic values, yet, at the same time to be rooted in the past glory of Indian society. As a result, there is the struggle for "social justice," as interpreted within the tradition(s). In addition, the category of the "Indian women" is found equally problematic due to the complexity of the social and pluralistic structures involved. This can often lead to futile exercises for women's rights activists. Nonetheless, Mukherjee describes what she considers to be some success stories in the recent past. Her article emphasizes both the need for a reinterpretation of "liberal pluralism" in an Indian context and the necessity of eliminating the entrenched patriarchal world-view of Indian society.

Suwanna Satha-Anand's chapter, "Caring Detachment in Buddhism and Implications for Women's Rights," undertakes an exploration of the meanings of "care" and "detachment" as significant elements of Buddhism. She observes that, despite its seemingly limiting force for women's liberation, caring is a core value that defines various key relationships in human co-existence. On the other hand, detachment is an illustration of spiritual liberation in Buddhism. As such, these two aspects of human experience would seem to cancel each other out. In this final chapter, Satha-Anand undertakes to illustrate and investigate "caring detachment" in Buddhism by exploring and analyzing the ways in which the Buddha deals with two cases of women who are in deep and extreme sorrow. These are the cases of Paṭācārā, the mad and naked woman who lost all her family members in one day of storm and torrential rain, and Kisā Gotamī, the mother who cannot come to terms with the fact that her dear son had died. It is argued that, for the Buddha, detachment does not cancel out caring. In these two cases, the Buddha shows great compassion with his positive engagement in the emotional turmoil of Paṭācārā and Kisā Gotamī, while simultaneously instructing them on a path out of the entrapment of deep and extreme sorrow. Satha-Anand further examines the implications of these Buddhist narratives for cultivating care and, at the same time, as respecting human dignity.

Conclusion

All of the above chapters bear witness to the many problems that still beset women as they strive to achieve equality both within their respective religious domains and in society itself. These diverse investigations of different religious traditions and regions of the world, while clarifying both the obstacles and the possible steps forward, are also indicative of women's determination to strive for recognition of their long-denied rights. At the same time, Satha-Anand's narratives also call attention to the need for a form of discerning discourse that could help to construct a bridge where even a dialogue between rights and Budhhism could be realised.

The chapters provide a vast range of topics, questions, and manifold issues that provoke, challenge, explain, and invite responses. This project does not presume to provide solutions to the dilemmas and disparate divisions that are obvious in certain of the cases described in the volume. It does, however, hope to alert readers of this volume to the difficulties that continue to disrupt possible constructive amendments. It also provides insights into situations where productive activities have accomplished changes in attitudes and practices. Nonetheless, the interactions of women, rights, and religions continue to remain a volatile mixture that cannot easily be brought to a satisfactory conclusion. The struggles and resistance continue, but women from various sites in the world are today finally beginning to find both solace and some satisfaction with the gains they have achieved.

References

Afkhami, Mahnaz. 2004. "Rights of Passage: Women Shaping the Twenty-First Century." In *The Future of Women's Rights: Global Visions and Strategies*, edited by Joanna Kerr, Ellen Sprenger, and Alison Symington, 56–68. London: Zed.

Arjomand, Homa. 2004. Quoted by Linda Hunt, in "Ontario Shari'a Tribunals Assailed," The Toronto Star, May 22.

Bakht, Natasha. 2004. "Family Arbitration Using Shari'a Law: Examining Ontario's Arbitration Act and its Impact on Women." *Muslim World Journal of Human Rights* 1(1): 1–24. https://doi.org/10.2202/1554-4419.1022

Basu, Amrita. 1998. "Appropriating Gender." In *Appropriating Gender: Women's Activism and Politized Religion in South Asia*, edited by Patricia Jeffrey and Amrita Basu, 3–14. Abingdon: Routledge. https://doi.org/10.1086/490548

———. 2010. "Introduction," *Women's Movements in the Global Era, The Power of Local Feminisms*, edited by Amrita Basu, 1–28. Boulder, CO: Westview.

Bayes, Jane H., and Nayereh Tohidi. 2001. "Introduction." In *Globalization, Gender and Religion*, edited by Jane H. Bayes and Nayereh Tohidi, 1–15. London: Palgrave Macmillan. https://doi.org/10.1007/978-1-137-04378-8_1

Beaman, Lori. 2008. *Defining Harm: Religious Freedom and the Limits of the Law*. Vancouver: University of British Columbia Press. https://doi.org/10.1017/s0829320100009819

———. 2017. *Deep Equality in an Era of Religious Diversity*. Oxford: Oxford University Press.

Boden, Alison L. 2007. *Women's Rights and Religious Practice: Claims in Conflict*. London: Palgrave Macmillan.

Brown, Wendy. 2004. "'The Most We Can Hope For…'?: Human Rights and the Politics of Fatalism." *South Atlantic Quarterly* 103(2–3): 451–463. https://doi.org/10.1215/00382876-103-2-3-451

Butler, Judith. 1990. *Gender Trouble: Feminism and the Subversion of Identity*. Abingdon: Routledge.

———. 1993. *Bodies that Matter: On the Discursive Limits of "Sex."* Abingdon: Routledge.

———. 2001. "The End of Sexual Difference?" In *Feminist Consequences: Theory for a New Century*, edited by Elisabeth Bronfen and Misha Kavka, 414–434, New York: Columbia University Press. https://doi.org/10.7312/bron11704-015

———. 2016. "Rethinking Vulnerability and Resistance." In *Vulnerability in Resistance*, edited by Judith Butler, Zeynep Gambetti, and Leticia Sabsay, 12–27. Durham, NC: Duke University Press. https://doi.org/10.1163/15692086-12341320

Fraser, Arvonne S. 2001. "Becoming Human: The Origin and Development of Women's Human Rights." In *Women, Gender and Development Rights: A Global Perspective*, edited by Marjorie Agosín, 15–64. New Brunswick, NJ: Rutgers University Press. https://doi.org/10.2979/nws.2003.15.2.225

Grewal, Inderpal. 1999. "'Women's Rights as Human Rights': Feminist Practices, Global Feminism, and Human Rights Regimes in Transnationality." *Citizenship Studies* 3(3): 337–354. https://doi.org/10.1080/13621029908420719

Hogben, Alia. 2004. Quoted by Susan Bourette. In "Can Tolerant Canada Tolerate Sharia?" *Christian Science Monitor*. 10 August. https://www.csmonitor.com/2004/0810/p01s03-woam.html.

Howland, Courtney W. 1999a. "Women and Religious Fundamentalism." In *Women and International Human Rights Law*, edited by Kelly D. Askin and Dorean M. Koenig, 533–621. New York: Transnational.

———, ed. 1999b. *Religious Fundamentalisms and the Human Rights of Women*. New York: St. Martin's Press.

Jain, Devaki. 2005. *Women, Development, and the UN: A Sixty-Year Quest for Equality and Justice*. Bloomington: Indiana University Press.

Joy, Morny. 2005. "Gender and Religion: A Volatile Mixture." *Temenos* 42(1): 7–30.

Lacey, Nicola. 1993. "Theory into Practice: Pornography and the Public/Private Dichotomy." *Journal of Law and Society* 20: 93–113. https://doi.org/10.2307/1410114

———. 2004a. "The Constitution of Identity: Gender, Feminist Legal Theory, and the Law and Society Movement." In *Blackwell Companion to Law and Society*, edited by Austin Sarat, 471–86. Oxford: Blackwell. https://doi.org/10.1002/9780470693650.ch25

Lacey, Nicola. 2004b. "Feminist Legal Theory and the Rights of Women." In *Gender and Human Rights*, edited by Karen Knop, 13–55. Oxford: Oxford University Press.

Moller Okin, Susan. 1997. "Is Multiculturalism Bad for Women? When Minority Cultures Win Group Rights, Women Lose Out." *Boston Review* 22: 2–28.

———. 1999. "Is Multiculturalism Bad for Women?" [Revised]. In *Is Multiculturalism Bad for Women?*, edited by Joshua Cohen, Matthew Howard, and Martha C. Nussbaum, 106–114. Princeton, NJ: Princeton University Press. https://doi.org/10.1515/9781400840991-017

Narayan, Uma. 1997. *Dislocating Cultures: Identities, Traditions, and Third World Feminism*. Abingdon: Routledge. https://doi.org/10.4324/9780203707487

Nedelsky, Jennifer. 1993: "Reconceiving Rights as Relationship," *Review of Constitutional Studies/Revue d'études constitutionnelles* 1(1): 1–26.

———. 2000. "Communities of Judgment and Human Rights." *Theoretical Inquiries in Law* 1(2): 245–282.

———. 2011. *Law's Relations: A Relational Theory of Self*. Oxford: Oxford University Press.

Nussbaum, Martha C. 1997. "Religion and Women's Human Rights." In *Religion and Contemporary Liberalism*, edited by Paul Weithman, 93–137. Notre Dame, IN: University of Notre Dame Press. https://doi.org/10.2307/2585511

———. 1999. "A Plea for Difficulty." In *Is Multiculturalism Bad for Women?* In J. Cohen, M. Howard, M. C. Nussbaum, editors, 105–144. Princeton, NJ: Princeton University Press. https://doi.org/10.1515/9781400840991-017

———. 2016. "Women's Progress and Women's Rights." *Human Rights Quarterly* 38(3): 589–622. https://doi.org/10.1353/hrq.2016.0043

Peach, Lucinda. 2002a. *Legislating Morality: Pluralism and Religious Identity in Lawmaking*. Oxford: Oxford. University Press.

———. 2002b. "Human Rights Law, Religion, and Gender." *The Global Spiral, Metanexus Views*. http://www.Metanexus.net/magazine/tabid/68/id/6004/Default.aspx

Posadskaya-Vanderbeck, Anastasia. 2004. "International and Post-socialist Women's Rights Advocacy: Points of Convergence and Tension." In *The Future of Women's Rights: Global Visions and Strategies*, edited by Joanna Kerr, E. Sprenger, and A. Symington, 186–96. London: Zed Books.

Razack, Sherene. 2007. "The Sharia Law Debate in Ontario." *Feminist Legal Studies* 15: 3–32. https://doi.org/10.1007/s10691-006-9050-x

Rupp, Leila J. 1998. *Worlds of Women: The Making of an International Women's Movement*. Princeton, NJ: Princeton University Press. https://doi.org/10.3138/cjh.33.3.504

Scott, Joan. 1999 [1988]. *Gender and the Politics of History*. New York: Columbia University Press.

Sullivan, Winifred Fallers. 2005. *The Impossibility of Religious Freedom*. Princeton, NJ: Princeton University Press. https://doi.org/10.1016/j.religion.2006.07.001

Sunder, Mahavi. 2005. "Piercing the Veil." In *Just Advocacy? Women's Human Rights, Transnational Feminisms, and the Politics of Representation*, edited by Wendy Hesford and Wendy Kozol. New Brunswick, NJ: Rutgers University Press.

Tamir, Yael. 1999. "Siding with the Underdogs," In *Is Multiculturalism Bad for Women?*, edited by Joshua Cohen, Matthew Howard, and Martha C. Nussbaum, 47–52. Princeton, NJ: Princeton University Press. https://doi.org/10.1515/9781400840991-007

Whitney, Amy, and Carolyn Evans, eds. 2006. *Mixed Blessings: Laws, Religions, and Women Rights in Asia-Pacific Regions*. Leiden: Brill.

Williams, Patricia J. 1991. *The Alchemy of Race and Rights*. Cambridge, MA: Harvard University Press.

1

Sexual Violence, Religion and Women's Rights in a Global Perspective

Louise du Toit is Associate Professor in the Department of Philosophy at Stellenbosch University, South Africa. She was a Fellow at the Stellenbosch Institute for Advanced Study (2017) and at the Center of Theological Inquiry, Princeton (2018). In 2019 she will an IAS Benjamin Meaker Visiting Professorship at the University of Bristol Law School. She has published widely on sexual violence, including *A Philosophical Investigation of Rape* (Routledge 2009) and, with Jonathan O. Chimakonam, co-edited *African Philosophy and the Epistemic Marginalization of Women* (Routledge 2018).

Introduction

In her 2014 PhD study on The Role of African Christian Churches in Dealing with Sexual Violence against Women: The Case of the DRC, Rwanda and Liberia, Elisabet le Roux (Le Roux 2014, 201–204), concludes that in these three post-conflict African states, neither governments and states, nor international security and peacekeeping bodies, nor various CSOs, including the churches, manage (or even try) to create a culture of accountability for war and post-war rape. Le Roux's research participants widely echo the sentiment of gynaecologist for Panzi Hospital's center for survivors of sexual violence in Bukavu in the Democratic Republic of Congo (DRC), doctor Neema Rukunghu. Linking the post-war child rapes in communities with the legacy of war rape, Rukunghu says men do not rape because they believe sex with a virgin girl may bring them wealth or cure them of disease (while they may in fact believe these things); instead, "they do it because they know that there is no prison waiting for them, no death penalty. They know they can get away with it" (Baker 2016). Not only, Le Roux finds, are there no legal consequences for rape, but equally there are no social sanctions, and no strong condemnation emanating from the influential religious leadership.

In all three countries Le Roux found that the churches "have a good record of effectively filling roles usually associated with the state." Moreover, the vast majority of people in these countries (up to 90%) are affiliated to at least one of these churches and "consider them to have authority and social impact [...] and the ability to influence behaviour, facilitate social change, and provide societal solidarity and cohesion," and importantly, they have often been instrumental in fighting for social justice. She thus hypothesizes that they can play a key role in addressing sexual violence – both in preventing and remedying the phenomenon at grassroots level – and most of her informants underwrite this view. Allowing for important differences between the different contexts – for example the direct involvement of the Catholic Church in Rwanda in the genocide – Le Roux however found on a general level that the African Christian churches in all three these countries at the very least do not address the problem of sexual violence. In fact, she found that churches "vary from non-involvement (and a form of lethargy) to active promotion of sexual violence against women" (2014, 197). Most churches indirectly promote male sexual violence through their patriarchal teachings, all-male leadership structures, and most damagingly, in their overtly censuring responses to sexual violence survivors.

These churches play a key role in silencing and stigmatizing congregation members who are such survivors. They do not openly discuss or critique sexual violence against women. In this, Le Roux claims, the churches "largely reflect community attitudes, beliefs and practices in their opinions and treatment of sexual violence survivors" (2014, 197). The furthest most churches will go in acknowledging the problem is through providing support in the form of food and clothing when survivors become destitute. They fail utterly to engage with the root causes of sexual violence. By silencing, shaming and stigmatizing the victims of male sexual violence, the churches largely reflect the attitudes of society, which includes blaming the victim. Husbands also often adopt or replicate this attitude, regarding a raped spouse as an immense threat to their own masculinity, to which they then 'justly' respond with violence and abuse of their own. Also, children who are suspected to be products of rape are very often actively shunned, neglected, beaten and/or raped. By punishing sexual violence survivors, these churches, Le Roux argues, "enforce their [sexual] beliefs and values – such as the importance of virginity, chastity, purity, monogamy, etc."; by stigmatizing them, churches "reinforce their own power as in-group and create greater social cohesion amongst church members [...] [through] othering survivors," thus reinforcing "patriarchal constructions of women, men and sex." Importantly, women also join in: the female leader of the Rwandan Mother's Union explained to Le Roux that they teach women "to be humble before their husbands, to obey them" (2014, 199). In other words, although these churches wield enormous formative power in their local communities and even nationally, and even though they have at times played important roles voicing social critique, they are largely either passive, or silent, when it comes to sexual violence.

Le Roux's own understanding of this situation includes the patriarchal nature of the sub-Saharan African cultures in which they are embedded, coupled with a kind of hyper-masculinity, "characterised by [sexually] violent and callous attitudes towards women" (2014, 201), driven by the militarization of masculinities during the recent and ongoing armed conflicts in these regions. Drawing on other studies, for example one done in Liberia, Le Roux views the high rates of sex crimes as indicative of "the persistence of hyper-masculinity within the country [...] eleven years after the war" (Jones *et al*. qtd. in Le Roux 2014, 202). On top of the constant threat of sexual violation, women fear the stigma and discrimination which invariably follow on the violation. Survivors are labelled and stigmatized as "deviant" and "other," which leads to further discrimination and even further sexual and other forms of violence visited upon them (Le Roux 2014, 202). Le Roux sees the churches as thereby replicating state and other CSO responses that seek to protect patriarchy, and she ascribes the stance to the patriarchal nature of the Christian churches themselves. She claims: "Truly engaging with sexual violence against women would mean that the patriarchal structure of society, culture and church will have to be dismantled, and this would mean a loss of power for [the] men [leading the churches]" (Le Roux 2014, 202).

While I largely agree with Le Roux's understanding, I wish in this article to extend the scope of analysis. In the first place, I would point to the racist-colonial assumptions that feed into an overly narrow and potentially spectacularizing focus on sexual violence on the African continent. Problematizing the sexuality of the African man as predatory (either essentially and biologically or in terms of his static and a-historical "patriarchal" culture) and of the African woman as pure victim figures as a consistent trope in European empire building. As Elizabeth Philipose cautions, feminist analyses must be vigilant not to sustain "assumptions about the racial and national hierarchies central to international legal systems and meanings." From the perspective of colonial history, she argues, feminists should become more conscious of the extent to which "the contemporary practice of naming war crimes and spectacular violence is both a racialized and a racializing enterprise that reflects gendered and sexualized assumptions about the perverse sexuality of the Other" (2009, 198).

In the second section, I follow Joseph Conrad in linking the "heart of darkness," sexual violence in the DRC, with the heart of darkness of and in London, one of the centres of the European empire. I do this by claiming that sexual violence against women in the DRC, figured in western media as one of the global depths of human depravity, cannot be de-linked from western economic interests in that region. For African Christian churches in the Congo to denounce and address the root causes of this form of violence, they have to not only stand up to their own cultures, societies and governments, but they must also stand up to the much more powerful neo-colonial interests and constitutive influences of western powers in the region. In line with the argument of Philipose, one may say that western powers economically active in the Congo have a lively interest in the portrayal of African men as sexually deviant, as well as in the social destabilization that accompanies large-scale sexual violence perpetrated against African women and girls. One may thus arguably speak of western and African patriarchies colluding. In this second section I therefore wish to thoroughly problematize the Enlightenment narrative that would have us believe that if only the light of western-style human rights could shine into the darkest heart of Africa, all will be well with her women.

Thirdly and finally, I draw attention to the systemic failure of western secular liberalism to protect women against sexual violence. This time around, I locate another "heart of darkness" in and of empire, and this time on the North American continent. My main claim in this section of the article is that the globally dominant institutions and cultural constructs facilitate the subjugation of women through ostensibly private but widespread sexual violence. Following thinkers like Heberle and Boulous Walker, I moreover diagnose the dominant institutions of our time – including the corporation, the state and the church – with a masculine psychosis which projects evil and instability onto the feminized other, while at the same time exempting itself of the possibility of evil-doing. This il-logic or rationale of a fragile and threatened victim-perpetrator also underlies the logic of human rights, the systematic othering of 'evil' violence and the justification of one's own, 'legitimate' violence. In the same way, this dynamic of dominant modern masculine subject-formation underpins the intimate violence of the individual rapist or batterer, the anguished violence of the husband of the rape survivor, the victimization of rape victims by churches, and the structural violence of the neo-colonial corporation.

The spectacular violence of the racialized other

I referred above to the Time Magazine article on war rape in the DRC (2016), and Dr Rukunghu's despair in response to the devastation that she sees every day. The same article features the story and even a photograph of seven-year-old Kanyere Neema, who was left paralysed after being gang-raped by armed men in the region. It is exceptional for the world (read: western world, or the world as created by the western media and disseminated around the globe) to learn the name and face of a victim of sexual violence in the Congo, if we bear in mind that during 2011, for example, 1,150 women were raped daily in the DRC. Recall that Dr. Rukunghu looks to the government and law enforcement agencies to put a stop to the sexual violence, and suggests that perpetrators commit these crimes purely because they are not prevented or deterred from doing so through a stronger force. Although a magazine article normally does not do justice to the nuances of a person's perspective, her comments might nevertheless be construed as implicitly pointing to a problematically essentialized understanding of African male sexuality. Not even scholars and other professionals from the African continent are immune to the wide circulation of reductionist, distorting stories that problematize in essentializing ways the sexuality of men of non-western and non-European descent. Again, Philipose is instructive when she says that "spectacular," especially sexual, violence against women comes to the attention of global audiences in a way that displays a "persistent pattern." In our contemporary neo-colonial times, these images and narratives "reflect a colonial pattern in that the narrative of violence against women recurs throughout Euro-colonial imaginaries as evidence of the inferiority and backwardness of Native men and women, and as a racializing trope" (2009, 177). She argues that the threat presented by the black rapist body has been a central image in the colonizing–civilizing mission of European imperialism, and that "rape stories [about the dark rapist] tend to emerge [historically] at moments of political instability" and (nationalist) resistance to the imperium. Throughout colonial and neo-colonial times, stories about rape have acted as triggers and justifications for often violent, military "intervention, occupation and other kinds of legalist civilizing missions" (Philipose 2009, 177).

Phillipose traces the work of Carl Schmitt and Antony Anghie, who both argue that the origins and logic of international law have always worked to exclude non-European (non-white) nations from sovereign statehood and self-determination (2009, 183). Anghie argues that two types of national sovereignty were created in the aftermath of the Second World War: (i) the "sovereignty inherent to European powers, thought to reflect their essential civilized nature" and (ii) the "second-tier and contingent sovereignty granted to non-European states after decolonization and the decline of the European imperial order" (qtd. in Philipose 2009, 183) In terms of this two-pronged logic, second-tier states have to continually demonstrate their "civilized nature" to a European audience, failing which, all kinds of intervention and external structuring (including economic, military, and social) are seen as justified. I suggest it is within this global political context that questions about the role of Christian churches on the African continent should be located. There is massive investment in maintaining the basic hierarchical opposition (endlessly symbolically reinstated and repeated, circulated through powerful media and international and humanitarian legal bodies), between the civilized "Us" of the white nations and the uncivilized "Them" of non-white nations. This pervasive constitutive relations between Us and Them, and the extent to which the "Us" shapes the often inhumane material living conditions and limit the possibilities for action of the "Them," are systematically denied, repressed and ignored.

Linking different hearts of darkness

When thinking about the reluctance of Christian churches in the DRC to unequivocally take the side of rape victims, what needs to be considered is the role played on the African continent, to this day, by the US's Helms Amendment of 1973. This Amendment prevents American assistance funds from going to programs that also provide abortions, and most international humanitarian medical organizations rely in some part on US funding. The Christian-patriarchal nature and influence of the American superpower is neither neutral nor innocent; it plays out in often devastating ways on the war-ravaged bodies of women and girls in the nightmares that are African armed conflicts. Even when then President Barack Obama was petitioned in July 2015 by "a consortium of fifty-six international human-rights, legal, medical and religious groups from twenty-two countries […] to issue an Executive Order affirming the rights of female war-rape victims to comprehensive medical care, including abortion, under the Geneva Conventions," Obama refused (Baker 2016). This is only one of the ways in which the heart of darkness located in the US's Christian-patriarchal and racist power complexes throws its deep shadows over the African continent, contributing to the plight of the most vulnerable of her inhabitants, war rape victims.

Another, even more pertinent example, pertains to the June 2014 Global Summit to End Sexual Violence in Conflict, held in London and chaired by UN special envoy for refugees Angelina Jolie and UK Foreign Secretary William Hague (see https://www.gov.uk/government/topical-events/sexual-violence-in-conflict). It was the biggest, highest-profile global meeting ever on this topic, with 1,700 delegates, 123 country delegations and seventy-nine Ministers attending. The aim was to address impunity for, and change global attitudes to, sexual violence as a weapon of war. Apart from the formal proceedings, there was a fringe event open to the public. Security was handled by the multi-national security company G4S on behalf of the British Foreign Office. This company refused entry into the public fringe event to a group of Congolese rape survivors and activists, and Rape Crisis women (Westmarland 2014). The reason was that the women carried placards saying: "No end to rape without the end to war," and they petitioned William Hague to listen to the voices of Congolese women and of civil society who repeatedly say that the main cause of sexual violence in the Congo is the economic war for illegal exploitation of its wealth. Their posters highlighted the known fact that the UK does business with Ugandan, Rwandan and Congolese heads of states – all former armed rebels – and that multinational companies directly or indirectly sponsor armed groups. The current DRC conflict principally centres on a struggle for control over the country's rich mineral resources, which include 80% of the world's colton ore, which is in huge demand in the manufacture of microchips. The UK is heavily involved in this resource struggle: it both sells and manufactures items that are made with DRC resources. It also donates huge amounts of overseas aid to Rwanda and Uganda, who in turn support violent militia groups and private security companies known for the widespread rape of women and girls (Westmarland 2014).

How ironic that the voices of the most affected group – a group of women from the DRC comprised of sexual violence victims and activists – were not allowed into the London conference, not even into the fringe event. The reason can only be that these women did not repeat the demonization of African sexuality – and who should know better than these victims and activists? Instead of problematizing African sexualities and ostensibly "uncivilized" cultures, they broke the colonial logic by instead pointing an accusatory finger at the western superpowers who still scramble for the riches of the DRC. They thereby destabilized the region, funding rebel and other armed groups, paying private security companies to intimidate local communities, and in general, turning a blind eye to the devastation, even as they reap the financial benefits. These women, by implication, refuse to see the ravaged and paralysed body of Kanyere Neema simplistically as the result of African sexual depravity (the comforting view ostensibly endorsed by the rest of the Global Summit). They see in her scars also the clear traces of western greed and violent neo-colonial interference, racial-sexual othering, and of global patterns of injustice.

When making these points, I would not detract from the agency of African men within the situation; clearly those directly and indirectly involved in these situations have much to account for. In the very least, one would expect for some of the internal African rhetoric on the need for decolonization and resistance to neo-colonialism, to be directed towards an inversion of the familiar colonial tropes of black male rapist relentlessly exploiting black female victim. One would expect movements pushing for the explicit celebration of African female sexuality as intrinsically valuable, as a way to directly dismantle colonial projects in which African women feature as expendable and un-grievable, even in some contexts as "unrapeable" (see, e.g., Gqola 2015). Yet, these dimensions of decolonization have not yet been forthcoming, and so we must ultimately see neo-colonial sexual dynamics as a collusion between African and non-African male elites, even if the former have limited options. We see that they tend to go for short-term gains instead of resisting colonial logic and building sustainable African communities, centred on restoring the dignity and sexual integrity of the African woman. They thereby gain individually, but further entrench the second-tier status of African so-called sovereign states, when they appear "depraved" while doing the dirty work of the imperial powers. The African Christian churches seem deeply complicit here. They retain the colonial-imperial depiction of African sexuality as depraved, but split this notion off from the male subject and project it purely onto the female scapegoat who gets punished for being a victim of male sexual violence. They are thus firmly embedded in the nested power constellations of the post-colony (African patriarchies nested within western commercial interests, nested within western imperial interests) and repeat the dehumanizing gestures toward African women that are inherent in all of these constellations. As indicated, relatively powerful African women often also align themselves with these forces, which should remind us that a feminist and a decolonizing stance are acquired, political stances, not biologically determined positions.

Delving deeper

I tried to show above that the inaction and complicity of the local churches cannot be viewed in isolation from the DRC survivors being silenced in London. It would thus be more accurate to argue that the excesses of sexual violence that we see on the fringes of empire do not stand outside of the very logic of empire itself, confronting it with something completely alien and incomprehensible (as its own ideological self-image would have it). Instead, they comprise systemic excesses and abuses spun out from within its own dark heart. To bolster this argument, let us briefly consider Jennifer Nedelsky's important contribution. She shows convincingly that the political unwillingness to protect women and children against sexual violence lies not only on the peripheries, representing the breakdown of liberal values and human rights where the power of empire is weakest.

Instead, she argues that sexual violence is rather embedded in the heart of this globally dominant liberal project. She explains this by arguing that a central trait of the liberal state and its, what she calls, "separative" understandings of the self and its rights, entail that it structures the relations of men, women and sexuality in such a way that it "insulates men from responsibility for violence and thus [sustains] patterns of inequality of power and respect between men and women" (220). Her work should be read together with Pateman (1988), Kroeger-Mappes (1994) and others who have realized that appeals to women's rights in the liberal polity have not reduced levels of sexual assault against women.

In an illuminating comparison with racist violence, segregation and apartheid in the American South, Nedelsky follows Robert Cover's analysis of racist violence. In both these forms of violence the widespread "terror" was largely privately perpetrated, and yet "was an essential part of a social and political system in which one group was kept subordinate [...] neither simply individual criminal violence nor state perpetrated," but something in between (Nedelsky 2011, 213). Rather, the control through fear or terror of a whole section of the population is deeply embedded in the culture and fabric of liberal, secular, western society, and moreover sanctioned by state officials as well as by cultural and religious (mainly Christian) leadership (although not technically by the law). This state of affairs thus entails a complex system of oppression which requires neither conscious ideology nor state organization for its survival. Nedelsky quotes Judith Herman's indictment of American law:

> The legal system is designed to protect men from the superior power of the state ... but not to protect women or children from the superior power of men. It therefore provides strong guarantees for the rights of the accused but essentially no guarantees for the rights of the victim. (2011, 218)

The typical sex laws of liberal states thus "shape relations of power and responsibility between men and women by insulating men from legal accountability for violence," especially for sexual violence perpetrated against women (Nedelsky 2011, 223). Put differently: "The cruelty of private sexual violence is not institutionalised, but a great deal of male impunity for that violence is" (Nedelsky 2011, 228). Clearly, this structural situation is not that much different from what we encountered in the DRC, Rwanda and Liberia, in terms of Le Roux's study. Also here, religious leadership fails to strongly and publicly intervene, and male impunity for sexual violence is rife. Clearly, the dominant institutions of the (neo-)liberal global order, on the face of it, take the side of the male perpetrator of sexual violence and turn a blind eye to the damages inflicted on mostly female victims. In the light of the history of colonialism and its lingering structuring effects regarding the global order, I suggest that it is important to emphasize the similarities, overlaps, complicities and concrete, material links between the sexual violence perpetrated and tolerated (and sometimes scandalized) in the peripheries and the sexual violence alive (yet mostly hidden) in the centre of the global political orders. Feminists should be alert to the complicities and continuities, instead of being drawn into artificial and ideologically distorted frameworks that spectacularize sexual violence in the margins and gloss over sexual violence emanating from the centre, in order to bolster and sustain global relations of domination.

In the final part of this article I briefly explore my sense that the culturally embedded, and globally-dispersed tolerance towards perpetrators of sexual violence against women cannot be simply explained in terms of an Enlightenment narrative. By this I mean that it would be naïve to presume that the light of reason has just not illuminated the minds of decision-makers yet, that there has been an innocent oversight, and that all that feminists need to do is to insist on the full humanity of women and to ask / require / demand that the full reach of human rights be extended to them. Philipose's arguments should alert us to the ways in which sexual violence perpetrated against women, both actual rape and rumours of rape, are always already cynically appropriated in the service of agendas other than strictly feminist ones, which would quite simply put an end to such violence. Inspired by Jacqueline Rose's siren call in Women In Dark Times (2014, ix), in which she cautions that feminists must not be blinded by the gleaming corridors of day-light power, I want to delve deeper into the tenacity of the phenomenon of sexual violence against women. Rose thinks it crucial for feminists "to make [our] way into the darker spaces of the world," in order to "[rip] the cover from the illusions through which most deadly forms of power sustain and congratulate themselves." Even as some women rightly ascend to these corridors and claim their place in the world, feminists should also "burrow beneath the surface [of this world] to confront the subterranean aspects of history and the human mind" (Rose 2014, ix).

Read together, the feminist analysis of authors Michelle Boulous Walker and Renée Heberle provide one possible entry into the dark recesses of the dominant masculine psyche which not only seems to allow for, but even to feed off sexual violence perpetrated against women. I agree with Meredith Turshen's (2016) insight into the "political economy of rape," whereby the sexual subjugation of women yields economic benefits to men, and other similar analyses. At the same time, I would claim that purely instrumental (i.e. day-light) explanations of sexual violence will always fall short.

This is simply because, no matter how much military or economic sense it makes to control women and their labour through fear of rape, there will always be countless instances of rape that do not fit neatly into such forms of rationally calculated action. Moreover, I argue here that a more psychological explanation of sexual violence also adds value when it comes to understanding larger male-dominated collectives, and their complicities in perpetuating sexual violence against women.

Renée Heberle, Jacqueline Rose, Nick Mansfield, Michelle Boulous Walker and others, draw our attention to the internal tensions, paradoxes and complexities of (modern) masculine subjectivity. These are tensions and contradictions, they suggest, that have become so intense that the dominant modern masculine subjectivity as such obtains an undercurrent of sexual violence. Rose writes about honour killings as a symptom of "how the sexuality of women can provoke a patriarchal anguish which knows no limits in the violent lengths it will go to assuage itself" (2014, xi). Against this anguish, expressed in acts of hatred against women, daylight reason, human rights and modern liberal institutions are no match. Let me make clear from the start that what is at stake here is a specific, dominant, masculine psychic formation and structure. In her turn, Boulous Walker argues that a certain central psychosis "constitutes the parameters of so-called normal masculine identity." Freud sees psychosis as a "disturbance in the relations between the ego and the external world" (Boulous Walker 1998, 15) and as not so much a loss of reality as a substitute for reality. Boulous Walker locates a typical masculine psychosis in the prevalent western foreclosure of the mother and the desire to replace the mother as the ultimate creative force and as the place of origin. Moreover, she argues that for the Freudian psychotic, "the ego vanishes because it is no longer anything but the other's thoughts" (Boulous Walker 1998, 15), thus the ego of the psychotic dissolves, and thereby the subject's condition becomes passively dependent on the Other. For Freud, psychosis differs from neurosis in degree; the psychotic more and earlier than the neurotic, loosens the relation to reality and then actively refashions an alternative reality peopled with phantasmatic elements. For Boulous Walker, one of the key aspects of this psychotic refusal of reality has to do with male foreclosure, displacement or erasure of the maternal body as the concrete origin of the male self. Thus arises the appropriation by the male subject of the mother's procreative ability in the hallucination of his own ability to give birth to himself. One might also say this particular psychosis is characterized by an unrealistic erasure of the material and emotional dependence on others which is constitutive of the human condition. The active expulsion of the maternal body in its reproductive capacity from the symbolic sphere is pervasive in most dominant religions, in the western philosophical and socio-political tradition, and elsewhere. In many religious traditions, female sexuality is the symbol par excellence of the profane and the abject pollutant which threatens the total symbolic order.

"These Women, They Force Us to Rape Them" is the title of a 2006 article by Helen Moffett which appeared in South Africa, quoting a taxi driver who had been interviewed by a journalist. The driver was explaining how he and some friends would drive around on weekends looking for women who were looking them in the eye, who were cheeky and "clearly did not know their place," and whom they would subsequently abduct and gang rape. Instead of simply reading this astonishingly passive self-understanding of rapists as the most insidious form of bad faith, as most feminist scholars tend to do, Heberle suggests, by implication, that we need to take them seriously, in one sense, at least. These are apparently naïvely honest reports by men who talk about their experience of raping. Heberle argues that there is indeed a systematically reactive quality to male sexual violence, born from anxiety and fear of dissolution of the self, and based on the fragility and sense of external threat built into the very logic and dynamics of dominant masculine-subject, "masochistic" models (2009, 133). She thereby challenges the common assumption that sexual violence is a simple expression of male dominance.

These men are not real victims, so much must be clear. Yet victimhood, self-sacrifice and lack (and a need for and expectation of suffering and pain) are the stuff that their identities are built upon. This is the case, she argues, because they share in the paradox of "willed submission" for the sake of state control of, and protection against, the basic untrustworthiness of the self and others (127). Thus, Heberle explains:

> The [masochist] masculinist subject [...] invents his other that the terms of [social; or should we say sexual-social?] contract protect against. It is the figure of woman, or, indeed, any feminized other, that most threatens this condition of possibility for masculinity and becomes the target for reactive forms of punishment (2009, 141; comments mine).

This is presumably the case because women are excluded from the social contract and men are constantly threatened with similar exclusion, but also because women are ironically, structurally, exempted from the anxieties of this particular subject position. The "self-imagined victim" is particularly dangerous, because the "violence he inflicts is [...] intractable, founded as it is in his reactive identity which assumes the moral rightness of all actions taken in its defence" (141). Consider moreover that "women are in the most danger of suffering an acute battering incident [and murder] when they try to leave the abuser or become pregnant" (141). The most cruel, vicious and violent of batterers act, behave and speak as if they are themselves the victims of those whom they batter (141).

Conclusion

Nedelsky states furthermore that in our symbolic order, the dominant order of the globalizing and globalized western world, "the feminine (whether in men or women) – with its different approach to power and relationship – is itself a target of violence, and that violence pervades [dominant] culture" (204). It is thus precisely the ways in which the feminine is always already (violently) excluded from the social contract and thus exempted from the constitutive anxieties of the 'citizen,' that turn her into the simultaneously resented and threatening other. Nel Noddings further explains in *Women and Evil* (1989) that the central strategy of western culture towards the universally human potential for evil is to expel it from its own self-image and to project it outwards onto a demonized other – this "blameless" or self-purifying logic of scapegoating happens both on an individual and a collective level. Importantly, like Heberle, Nedelsky notices in this psychological move to project evil onto women (and other others) and particularly onto their sexuality, a manoeuvre which leads to a complete failure of compassion, and finally a collapse of the ethical (similar to the colonial encounter), when it comes to violence aimed against women's sexualized bodies. The consistent projection of evil, threat, and of a destabilizing, uncontrollable and external, opposing force onto female sexuality (as onto black skin), for Nedelsky fits in with the mainstream American picture of the view of rights as boundaries that are erected in order to protect the essentially fragile and vulnerable self.

The very angst-ridden unpredictability of the human heart and of sexual desire, with their far-reaching consequences for both personal and collective identity (re-)production and maintenance, are projected onto women's sexualized / sexuate bodies. Nedelsky states that these rights understood as boundaries "feel desperately necessary to the separative self to keep the threatening others at bay – a task whose impossibility only fuels the desperation" (2011, 207). There is thus a deep symbiosis between western rights talk and its fear of the evil it has always already projected onto the foreign "other."

> The anxiety of the separative self is thus a combination of the projection onto others of what seems dark, dangerous, and unacceptable within oneself and the (related) sense that the security hoped for from walling off others is in a constant state of failure. That failure [moreover] is inevitable because of the fact of human interconnection and is exacerbated by the real threats domination provokes. (Nedelsky 2011, 207)

From these diagnostics, it becomes clear the othering of both women and non-Europeans through the demonization of their sexuality is central to the self-constitution of the dominant masculine western subject and its justifications of its own violence, always already construed as passive, defensive, reactive and born from victimhood rather than originally aggressive or autochthonous. Recall that Heberle also speaks about the necessary failure of the masculine psychotic project of safeguarding itself through the construction of an alternative reality. She emphasizes how dangerous this kind of psyche is, precisely because it perceives itself above all as vulnerable, helpless, and determined from the outside. The emptying out of the ego is thus an emptying out of the self as locus of emotional, moral, and other forms of control. This is also how the domination of western empire functions: the sovereign western subject is constitutionally unable to see the terms of its own violence as such. As Heberle puts it: "victims need no rationalisation for the reactive forms of violence they impose on those who threaten their coherence as selves" (2009, 138).

Finally, then, it is my contention that the failure of African Christian churches to speak out against sexual violence and to address its causes, should be read on one level as in conformation with global patterns, especially patterns emanating from the centre of the global order. If the churches were to take the side of the victims here, they would become a truly decolonizing force, thereby provoking the angry backlash not only of male elites within their communities who reap the benefits of collaboration with interfering neo-colonial powers, but also of those neo-colonial powers themselves. Hitherto, clearly this was seen as too high a price to pay by a highly influential social force on the continent. On another level, however, not limiting this analysis to instrumental, day-light reasoning, African Christian churches should also be considered as heirs of the psychosis of western masculine subject-formations. It is this psychosis which demonizes female sexuality and pre-emptively lashes out against women's ostensibly destabilizing force. As a result, these churches are thus included in the modern masculine brotherhood of 'dangerous victims' so aptly diagnosed by Heberle and Boulous Walker.

References

Baker, Aryn. 2016. "The Secret War Crime." *Time Magazine*. March. http://time.com/war-and-rape/

Boulous Walker, Michelle. 1998. *Philosophy and the Maternal Body: Reading Silence*. Abingdon: Routledge.

Gqola, Pumla Dineo. 2015. *Rape: A South African Nightmare*. Auckland Park, SA: Jacana.

Heberle, Renée J. 2009. "Rethinking the Social Contract: Masochism and Masculinist Violence." In *Theorizing Sexual Violence*, edited by Renée J. Heberle and Victoria Grace, 125–146. Abingdon: Routledge. https://doi.org/10.1111/j.1555-2934.2011.01157.x

Kroeger-Mappes, Joy. 1994. "The Ethic of Care vis-à-vis the Ethic of Rights: A Problem for Contemporary Moral Theory." *Hypatia* 9(3): 108–131. https://doi.org/10.1111/j.1527-2001.1994.tb00452.x

Le Roux, Elisabet. 2014. "The Role of African Christian Churches in Dealing with Sexual Violence against Women: The Case of the DRC, Rwanda and Liberia." Unpublished PhD dissertation. Stellenbosch University, Stellenbosch, South Africa.

Mansfield, Nick. 2000. *Subjectivity: Theories of the Self from Freud to Haraway*. Sydney: Allen and Unwin.

Moffett, Helen. 2006. "'These Women, They Force Us to Rape Them': Rape as a Narrative of Social Control in Post-Apartheid South Africa." *Journal of Southern African Studies* 32(1): 129–144. https://doi.org/10.1080/03057070500493845

Nedelsky, Jennifer. 2011. "Violence against Women: Challenges to the Liberal State and Relational Feminism." In *Law's Relations: A Relational Theory of Self, Autonomy, and Law*. 200–230. Oxford: Oxford University Press. https://doi.org/10.1093/acprof:oso/9780195147964.003.0006

Noddings, Nel. 1989. *Women and Evil*. Berkeley: University of California Press.

Pateman, Carole. 1988. *The Sexual Contract*. Stanford: Stanford University Press.

Philipose, Elizabeth. 2009. "Feminism, International Law, and the Spectacular Violence of the 'Other': Decolonizing the Laws of War." In *Theorizing Sexual Violence*, edited by Renée J. Heberle and Victoria Grace, 176–204. Abingdon: Routledge. https://doi.org/10.1111/j.1555-2934.2011.01157.x

Rose, Jacqueline. 2014. *Women in Dark Times*. London: Bloomsbury.

Turshen, Meredeth. 2016. *Gender and the Political Economy of Conflict in Africa: The Persistence of Violence*. Abingdon: Routledge.

United States Department of Justice. 2013. Criminal Victimization in the United States. https://www.bjs.gov/content/pub/pdf/cv13.pdf.

Westmarland, Nicole. 2014. "Not all messages about rape were welcome at Hague and Jolie's sexual violence summit." *Durham University News*. Comment and Opinion. 16 June. Durham University. http://www.dur.ac.uk/news/allnews/thoughtleadership/?itemno=21476

2

Understanding Human Rights from Indigenous Women's Perspectives

Sylvia Marcos is founder and a senior researcher of the Seminario Permanente de Antropologia y Genero at the Institute for Anthropological Research (IIA), Universidad Nacional Autonóma de Mexico (UNAM). She researches and writes on Gender and Women's Issues in ancient and contemporary Mexico, and is committed to indigenous movements throughout the Americas She has been a Visiting faculty member at Harvard University, Visiting Professor of Mesoamerican Religions and Gender at Claremont Graduate University, Union Theological Seminary NY, and other international universities. Dr. Marcos is the author of many books and articles, including: *Taken from the Lips: Gender and Eros in Mesoamerican Religions* (2006) and *Indigenous Women and Decolonial Cosmovision* (2014).

Introduction

The movement of indigenous women in the Americas, through their organizations and political associations, has issued documents containing declarations, plans of action, demands, and proposals to rework the traditional concept of human rights. An analytical reading of some of these key texts has emerged from the main meetings during these last years. It is based both on their understanding of themselves as women in a context of gender relations and, at the same time, as belonging to a collectivity that encompasses communal values and practices. Within these notions of indigenous communities [*pueblos originarios*], women do not stand alone and neither do they perceive themselves as "individual subjects."

If we are to listen and comprehend the demands of indigenous women regarding their "rights," it is a challenge to be able to recognize and perceive the complex re-conceptualizations of the term. This essay reviews some of indigenous women's statements and documents that help to discover how the term "rights," or the phrase "my right," is reconfigured in the declarations proclaimed by organizations of indigenous women. To interrogate the stability of meanings assigned to the term "human rights" by listening, participating, and recording their own voices, non-indigenous people can come to a better understanding of how the term is recreated and used in their own political and social practices. They say, for example, "It is time to act, and time to grab our right with our hand [agarrar con nuestra mano el derecho]."[1]

In the social space that they occupy, indigenous women are placed at the intersection of multiple identities: Gender, race, ethnicity, and class. They contribute significantly to the reformulation of a new world that is more just, and that critically examines not only their role as poor, indigenous women, but also questions the role and power structures of the neoliberal state. They are gradually transforming the meanings of "human rights" within their own struggles as indigenous women.

In the analysis that follows, I highlight the voices of organized indigenous women in the Americas by quoting extensively from key texts and interviews. There, it can be discovered how the internal logic of their speeches, while not always explicit, transforms the language of human rights and redefines it. In analyzing this redefinition, we find some main axes around which they formulate their struggle for social justice. Among them, we find a unique vision of the concept of gender; a defense of their indigenous spirituality; and a revision of responsibilities and rights within their communities.

For the last twenty years, I have been participating in and closely linked to indigenous women's social and political organizations. Always by their invitation, I have been a part of many meetings. This has been a privilege that allows me to do a "hermeneutics of orality" recording not only their words, but trying to uncover the philosophical context by which we can understand the deepest meanings and the ontological dimensions of their struggles for justice.

The main countries in Latin America where these meetings have been held and from which its documents have emerged are Mexico, Guatemala, Nicaragua, Ecuador, Colombia, Chile, Peru, and Venezuela. National, regional, and continental reunions have taken place where indigenous women collaborate and make their statements from the Mesoamerican region in Central America as well as the Andean region in Peru, Bolivia, and Colombia.

In the declaration, "Building our History," from the National Meeting

---

1. Fragmento de discurso de la mujer autoridad de la JBG del CCRI. [Part of the speech given by a woman leader of the Clandestine Indigenous Revolutionary Committee of the Zapatista Army of National Liberation], Caracol de Morelia, 8 de marzo de 2009. See: enlacezapatista.ezln.org.mx/sdsl-en/ (Sixth Declaration of the Selva Lacandona).

of Indigenous Women, Oaxaca, México, in 1997, the indigenous women state:

> Indigenous women form an important part in the development of our peoples and of the country;
>
> That the rights of women, and in particular, of indigenous women, are not recognized by the Constitution;
>
> That the right to parity and equity constitute part of the demands that we presented at the meeting on Indigenous Rights and Culture in San Andres, Chiapas;
>
> That we seek to change Article 27 of the Constitution to allow women the right to inherit land. (29)

The ideas and practices of gender relations in the different indigenous communities began to interact intensively with the proposals that emerged from the Zapatista revolutionary movement in 1994. For some indigenous people, belonging to independent organizations, Zapatismo opened the possibility of new expectations by broadening their perspectives and expressing their demands and aspirations in the language of rights. It was this language of rights that allowed them to communicate with other organized women, despite class and ethnic barriers. More recently, there is a broad movement of indigenous women of the Americas that is constantly growing, and that now transcends even national boundaries.

This movement has been the organized by the women themselves, who have figured out ways to express their demands in the context of their own communities, seeking to challenge and transform those traditional practices that negatively affect them. They also affirm their wish that indigenous normative systems [*usos y costumbres*] be recognized, as well as the autonomous governance in their communities. In this regard, what needs to be respected is that it is the women of the indigenous communities themselves who make these decisions that are incumbent upon them in their own spaces. It is here that they manage to verbalize their most heartfelt demands regarding participation, equity, and a life free from violence. For these reasons, they consider it is important to discuss their traditions and customs, analyzing which of them they will determine to nurture and recover, and also which they will determine to discard. A human rights perspective features as central to this task, as is confirmed in the following statement.

> [T]he human rights framework expands social justice issues beyond the relatively narrow focus of civil rights, which seek only to punish the guilty. Human rights provide a broader perspective of social justice by combining civil and political rights with social, economic, and cultural rights. A

human rights perspective on the problem of domestic violence, for example, considers the right to live free of violence together with the right to health, housing, education, and employment. In addition, the human rights perspective is built at the intersection of gender, race, language, religion, national origin, and a variety of additional factors. (Engel 2006, 1)

The human rights framework, in the opinion of the same author, is helpful because it provides:

> a broad framework of social justice based on ideas of equity and dignity, and the aspiration to attain its universal application. In essence, this is a morally based claim on the idea that equity and dignity are international ideas, shared by others. The universality of this claim provides a very powerful moral attraction. The perspective from a social movement implies that civil and political rights are inseparable from the social, economic, and cultural. (Engel 2006, 1)

Importantly, the "universality" of this claim has been gradually channelled and re-created from below by women who come from different cultural contexts. These cultural contexts are often based on a "formation of a subject that is not necessarily aligned with the conception of the European Enlightenment's notion of individual empowerment" (Mahmood 2005, x) Rather, this "re-semanticization" (Hernandez 2004, 3), expresses specific characteristics that are part of the Mesoamerican cultural universes.

Foucault (1981) and Bakhtin (2011) have argued that every discursive act implies a dialogical process, i.e., an answer to the discursive act that preceded it. In this way, a discourse (in our specific case, of human rights) only exists in the context of prior discourses and is in dialogue with them. In this way, although discourse is influenced by prior discourses, there is simultaneously a re-formulated and new discourse that will serve as a base for those that will follow later. In relation to the discourse of rights, this implies that its origins as "Western," or as a product of capitalist neo-liberal philosophy *does not determine its potentialities* when discourse is adopted and used in a *dia-logical* way. Quite often, these new meanings, which arise from the practice of dialogue, question and critique the original discourse that preceded it.[2]

A subversive redefinition

This adoption of the dialogic language of "rights" by indigenous women has produced a profound change in its meanings. The notion of a free, rational, individual, rights-bearing subject who holds ideals of equality

---

2. For a discerning discussion, see Tarcila Rivera and how she reconceptualizes, in a dialogical way, the discourse on human rights. (2004, 12).

and freedom, according to the tenets of globalized urban worlds, does not seem to reflect what indigenous women mean when they use the term.

These alternative perspectives of the rights of women who claim the indigenous cosmovision as a space of resistance, are also being transnationalized by a continental movement of indigenous women that has its most visible face in an instantiation of an international coordination called *Enlace Continental de Mujeres Indigenes* [Continental Network of Indigenous Women] (Hernández 2004, 3; see also Clifford 2013 for discussion of such movements).

To illustrate these developments, documents, declarations, and demands presented at several meetings will be cited, such as: the Continental Encounter of Indigenous Women, which took place in Quito, Ecuador (1995); the First Summit of Indigenous Women of the Americas, Oaxaca, México (2002); the Fourth Conference of the Continental Network of Indigenous Women, Lima, Peru (2004); the Third International Forum of Indigenous Women, New York (2005); the Encounter of Zapatista Women with Women of the World, La Garrucha (Zapatista autonomous territory) (2007); the First Continental Summit of Indigenous Women of Abya Yala,[3] Puno, Bolivia (2009); the Second Continental Summit of Women of Abya Yala, Cauca, Colombia (2013); and "The Zapatistas and the '*ConSciences*' for Humanity," Chiapas, México (2017).

In these locations, as is the case with so many other gatherings, declarations, proposals, and demands have been issued by means of a collective consensus. This accumulation of texts is interconnected to and interdependent with broadly based indigenous movements' achievements. The discourse of human rights, however, has endowed these documents with a new moral language and legal framework to help orchestrate their demands.

The Declaration of the Third International Forum of Indigenous Women, which took place in New York City in 2005, states:

> We maintain that the advance of the human rights of indigenous women is tied inextricably to the struggle to protect, to respect, and for the fulfillment of the rights of our peoples as a whole, and our rights as women within our communities at national and international levels. We recommend – in relation to the third report of the UN Permanent Forum of Indigenous Peoples – that themes having to do with women be transversal throughout United Nations. (NA)

---

3. Abya Yala is the self-selected term that indigenous peoples of the Americas today have chosen to call the lands and territories invaded and colonized by Europe that were/are called Central and South America.

While demanding rights for their own gender specificities, these women do not forget that they also form part of a larger collectivity – that of other indigenous peoples. This helps to contextualize, in a heightened way, the collective priorities of their demands.

As researchers, Maria Teresa Sierra (2001) and Ana María Garza (2000) have indicated, the Zapatista project has meant, for many indigenous women, an opportunity to question "bad customs" and to speak about rights. These include the right to make decisions concerning their own bodies; their rights to health; and their rights to education. Other rights confirm their sharing in the decision-making of the family, and that couples are co-responsible for domestic tasks and childcare. In addition, there is opposition to structural violence, both institutional and domestic. Further rights comprise the right to be respected, to work and receive fair remuneration as well as their need to be affirmed as co-producers within the household. Finally, their rights to participate in their communities and organizations, especially political organization, are confirmed.

Tarcila Rivera, who is a Kichwa leader of the Continental Network of Indigenous Women and current Executive Chairwoman of the International Forum of Indigenous Women (FIMI), announced: "We believe that indigenous peoples who keep alive the concept of gender from our own sources, must make an effort to ensure that this concept is consistent with the daily reality in our respective societies" (Rivera 2004, 11).

For indigenous women today, their tasks are many. This is because their demands, as described above, have introduced innovative reforms. Each step of their rewording of "rights" or "democratization" that occurs in the daily interactions between genders, or in their finding of new perspectives, has consequences. Today, to speak of such rights is a common occurrence for the women in everyday life. This, however, marks an expansion into areas where they need to request certain prerogatives that were previously ignored.

Comandanta Rosalinda, from the Ejercito Zapatista de Liberacion Nacional, said at a recent meeting at Caracol de la Garrucha, Zapatista territory on October 17, 2017: "[L]as mujeres tenemos el mismo derecho que los hombres." [We women have the same right as men.] This same language of "rights" has legitimized women's spaces and opened other possibilities within the indigenous movement more generally. However, women also state:

> [W]e cannot assume that they [indigenous women] simply pass through a linear route without conflict, toward the broadening of the rights of indigenous women. […] The path has been complex, full of roads walked and retraced – as well as abandoned – alliances, confrontations, negotiations,

and no easy consensus. In an atmosphere permeated by such profound differences, it can hardly be thought that a social movement can eliminate these obstacles so easily. Neither can one think that the aspirations of women are the product of a community of pre-given interests dictated by biological, natural characteristics. (Garza 2000, 139)

Tarcila Rivera also examines the situation:

[I]t is very difficult to find relations of equity and respect because foreign influence, extreme poverty, marginalization, and the patriarchal forms of relationship in dominant societies generate violence. Men learned these negative forms very quickly, adopting them for themselves. These attitudes created privileges, individualisms, and domestic violence. Western religion also played an evangelizing role, leading us to believe that we came from the rib of man, and thus owe him our obedience. (2004, 12)

Another indigenous woman explains a constructive way forward:

Our rights as indigenous women find the space for their resolution in the recognition of the autonomy of indigenous peoples, as a most democratic form, starting in our person, from our house to the community to the people, and synthesized in the State.[4]

Women's critique of forms and mechanisms of exclusion

In the Third National Indigenous Congress, held in Nurío, Michoacán, in 2001, with the Zapatista Comandantas present, women from thirty indigenous peoples expressed their demands and interests in guaranteeing gender rights and of participating in their communities and tribes (Sierra 2001: 19). In addition to their own demands as women, they proposed universal indigenous demands such as specifically gendered social actors, while, at the same time, as members of particular communities. Their leadership in this Congress left a lasting impression.

The prominent role of indigenous women has produced many other examples, e.g., that of the Mayan women in Guatemala, who, when the indigenous peoples' human rights were violated under dictatorial regimes, organized immediately to denounce to the world these abuses and violations. Quechua women of Peru,[5] have also raised their voices to denounce

---

4. Ms. "Propuesta de las mujeres indígenas en la fundación del CNI", Congreso Nacional Indígena, [Proposal of the indigenous women in the foundation of the CNI, National Indigenous Congress], Mexico City, 8 al 12 de octubre, 1996.

5. There are variations in both names of groups of Indigenous peoples and languages due to the specificities of local customs and language uses – e.g.quechua, kichwa. There are ethnological differences in several communities of the area belonging to South American Andean region as to

the disappearance of family members in times of violence in the Andes. Indigenous migrants, located in urban *barrios*, have initiated the organization of neighborhoods and give political status to formerly banned spaces, such as popular eateries. In the case of Nicaragua, the Misquito people participated in the revolution to defend the right of indigenous peoples in general, and the struggle for autonomy specifically.

As Tarcila Rivera has observed:

> In the last five years, it has been up to us to clarify things among us. Being certain that fighting for our people also means helping diminish the differences and privileges between members of the indigenous community; making it so that our male leaders understand that it is necessary to recapture a balance in relations between all of us; and that speaking about and working on improving the capacities of indigenous women does not mean dividing the organization, as it has often been said to us, but rather, to become mutually stronger and to unite the collective struggle. (2004, 15)

In another diverse experience, however, this time in Zapatista territory, Shannon Speed tells about a woman, "Rosalína," to whom she posed the classic question that often confronts feminist struggles on the political left: "Do the men suggest that women's rights must wait because they are a distraction from the main goal of the struggle?" (Speed 2008: 130). 'Rosalína,' an indigenous woman from Nicolas Ruiz Community in the highlands of Chiapas, was reflective. She waited a moment before answering her rhetorical question. "I think the opposite is true. It was through the organization that we began to organize, that we began to become conscious of our rights as women" (Speed 2008, 130). Another woman added: "Some men are more *consciente* (enlightened) than others, […] but they also know that a community, to advance, must work as a collective, men and women. That's why they supported us." (Speed 2008, 130).

In Xoxocotla, a Nahua community in the State of Morelos, México, a young woman, Yoloxóchitl Severiano, an activist in the Council of Thirteen Peoples in Defense of the Earth, Water, Air, said: "Everyone must do their part. If everyone did the exact same thing, it would not be achieved" (Marcos n.d., research notes). In this way, she expressed the constraints and amplifications of a struggle for women's rights when they are concurrently immersed in the collective. When both rights and responsibilities are assumed by the community as a whole, the results will inevitably be both interactive and configured by the gender "difference."

---

how they name themselves as a people.

From indigenous women: Particularities of gender concepts

The executive summary on "Gender from the View of Indigenous Women," the declaration produced by the First Summit of Indigenous Women of the Americas (*Memoria* 2003), demonstrates the search for a necessary bridge between all the diverse types of struggles within the women's movements. Using the concept of human rights, certain commonalities can be recognized; especially those related to the struggle against gender violence, but nonetheless, certain differences may also be observed.

Misunderstandings between Global North feminism and the demands issuing from the expansive movement of indigenous women are often understood by the indigenous women as products of ethnic and class differences. On the feminist side, a large fissure appears due to the misunderstandings of indigenous conceptions of gender.

In a personal letter that Tarcila Rivera sent to me in April 2004, she asked that I take part in the Fourth Meeting of the Continental Network of Indigenous Women that would take place in Lima Peru. She believed that my participation would "help to remove prejudices about this concept of gender, if I spoke "on our indigenous ways of understanding it." As is well known, multiple theorizations on gender construction have been proposed largely by the Global North's feminist and intellectual tradition on the topic of gender in the past fifty years. Some of these theories are not applicable to indigenous peoples.

To begin with, if gender – to put it simply – is defined as the cultural construction built on sexual difference, it would be necessary to include highly sophisticated and variegated theories that present, in great detail, all the cultural domains that modify the particularities of the perceptions of human beings, beginning with the body, "the biological." The division between sex and gender as mutually exclusive categories would need to be debated – and this would mark only the beginning. It is accepted in various indigenous communities that what defines a being as feminine or masculine is not their genitalia (their biological sex), but the way in which they interact in their community, including the social interactions within family milieu, i.e., according to their gender. As a result, in these milieus, the difference and definition between men and women begins with gender and not with anatomy or sex (Moore 1994, 24).[6]

What I would like to emphasize here is the reason why indigenous women often express some discomfort and sometimes reject proposals

---

6. For a more extensive development of this theme, see Marcos (1996; 2006).

for "gender justice." It occurs when these demands are made from the philosophical and practical contexts of urban women's theoretical gender concepts. References to the document, "Gender," from the Summit of Indigenous Women of the Americas in the city of Oaxaca, 2002, can provide clues as to the way they locate themselves in their relationships with the men of their communities. This will also help us to understand how to respect their priorities and their specificities.

Gender, in the indigenous worlds of Mesoamerica, is primarily conceived within the framework of a concept of duality, as distinct from Western notions of dualism. The entire universe is governed in these terms: male and female are regarded as complementary. In claiming, as part of their rights, the right to be guided by the manner in which their worldview conceives of gender, indigenous women reveal the place from which their struggles emanate: "Duality as a theory exists in our cosmovision and in our customs. But sometimes in practices, there are situations where only the man decides. [...] The media, schools, and many other elements have influenced this principle, living duality is a bit shaky now."[7]

Duality is the symbolic space that indigenous women intend to recover and revitalize, instead of adopting the urban women's gender framework and their demands. Indigenous women are very active, re-conceptualizing all the customs and practices that undermine women's dignity, e.g. violence of any kind; the obligation to marry for family arrangements; contempt for their condition as women. As Comandanta Esther decried defiantly at the venue of the Chamber of Deputies in 2001: "From the moment that we are girls, they (in certain traditional places) believe that we are worthless." But this assessment, as the lesser valued pole in a duality, does not correspond to their ancestors' philosophical background, nor to their plans for contemporary survival. Indigenous women recognize the mode of duality and demand to be placed in a relation of complementarity with men.

This alignment introduces another major confrontation with those forms of feminism that seek to establish a rigid equality. Such a model is based on an idea of human rights as conceived from an individualistic philosophy, i.e., one that centers itself on the rights of the individual subject. This legal subject is considered to be an independent being, rather than an interdependent being, as one is in the indigenous villages. In this context, an interconnection exists and it constitutes a collective ideal, not only between a man and a woman, but also among the larger groups, such as

---

7. "Género" ["Gender"], *Primera Cumbre de Mujeres Indígenas de América*, [First Summit of Indigenous American Women]. December 2002.

the extended family, the community, and even beyond, as with all natural beings.

It is within this cosmovision that indigenous women are constructing and restoring their rightful roles in the world. They proclaim:

> We Zapatista women, we are exercising our right and freedom to participate in our autonomous government of rule by obeying [*mandar obedeciendo*].
>
> We saw that it is a space, for us as women, for the construction of a new society.[8]

For these indigenous women, gender equity is conceived of, and referred to, as a "balance" between two opposites: the feminine and masculine. This "balance," or equilibrium, momentarily stabilizes the polarities and its extremes.

What becomes apparent in reviewing the discourses that have emerged from the indigenous women's struggles, is a challenge to design a comprehensive itinerary that re-conceptualizes both the term "human rights" and of "gender relations." This is apparent in the following encounter:

In the Encounter of Zapatista Women with Women of the World, at the Caracol of La Garrucha in December 2007, we heard women express themselves in the following phrases:

> We can walk together as *compañeros* and *compañeras*;" "that we have respect for both for men and women";
>
> That we have respect for both men and women";
>
> Struggle alongside them";
>
> Let us have unity;" "let us walk together";
>
> Our struggle is not only for us, the indigenous women, but for all the indigenous and non-indigenous peoples";
>
> I, as a little girl, have a right to everything";
>
> I turn nine years old on January 8, 2008"; as a little girl, I have the right to do what I like." (Marcos n.d., research notes)

Another relevant document, the "Mandate" of the First Continental Summit of Indigenous Women of Abya Yala (2009) reads: "On the basis of the cosmological principles, and taking as a premise that our cultures are the cradle of values and are based on balance, harmony, reciprocity and complementarity."[9] These dimensions and re-elaborations become

---

8. *Preguntas a las Ciencias y las ConCiencias*, CIDECI, San Cristobal de las Casas, Chiapas, Mexico. December 26, 2016.

9. NA, Mandato de la Primera Cumbre Continental de Mujeres Indígenas de

discernable in this lengthy movement of reflections and revisions that are continually undertaken, managed, and directed by the women from indigenous communities.

Comandanta Esther, in her own words, expressed the intention of the EZLN (Zapatista Army of National Liberation):

> We also want to say to men that they should respect our right as women. [...] But we are not going to ask as a favor, rather, we are going to oblige them to respect us. Because many times the mistreatment that we women receive doesn't only come from the wealthy exploiters. [...] So then we say loud and clear that, when we demand respect for women, it's not only a demand we make of the neoliberals, it is also something we are going to compel of those who struggle against neoliberalism and say they are revolutionaries, but in their house they act just like [George W.] 'el Bush.'[10]

A further statement that reflects the ideals of the movement can be found in one of the final documents of the First Summit of Indigenous Women of the Americas, Oaxaca, México, 2002, which stated: "It is important to move beyond rhetoric to the practice of our cosmological values, from the personal, the family, the community, and in our own organizations" (*Memoria* 2003, "Resoluciones de las mesas de trabajo," 42–45).

The defense and recovery of indigenous spirituality

The indigenous peoples of Abya Yala are also claiming the right to live and express their own spirituality. This claim refers to what United Nations documents refer to as "cultural rights." It is related to those rights that have extended the scope of "human rights."

Spirituality has been generally associated with the Christian religious sphere, and particularly. Catholicism, especially in Latin America. The spirituality claimed by the indigenous peoples is spirituality in its "indigenous" dimension. It is a "spirituality that is not a religion," as Mexican indigenous women affirmed in their response to the bishops of the Episcopal Commission on Indigenous Peoples, issued during the First Summit of Indigenous Women of the Americas (*Memoria* 2003, "Respuesta a la Conferencia Episcopal," 287–288). It is a spirituality that frequently disassociates itself from Catholic beliefs, although sometimes it visibly preserves its images, devoid of their original significance and newly re-signified.

Spirituality, thus conceived, demands the recovery of those sacred

---

Abya Yala [Declaration of the first meeting of the Indigenous Women of Abya Yala. Puno], Bolivia. May 30, 2009.

10. Address presented at a meeting of "La Via Campesina: International Peasants Movement." Cancún, September 2003.

spaces that were destroyed and vandalized by the Spanish and Portuguese conquistadors, colonists and violent catechists who arrived in these lands. For example, during the First Summit of Indigenous Women of the Americas, in Oaxaca, México, 2002, it was determined that the summit open with a ceremony in the ancient sacred city of Monte Alban, in the same state of Oaxaca.

At this gathering, more than sixty indigenous groups of women – Zapotecas, Mixes, Mixtecas, Chontales, Tzotziles, Tzeltales, K'iche's, Kaqchikeles, Q'eqchi's, Poqomames, Tzutujiles, Popti's, Chorti's, Mames, Achi'is, and Q'anjobales – from twenty-eight organizations and several communities of Oaxaca, Chiapas, and Guatemala, united in their diversities, cosmovisions, needs, work experiences, and hopes for justice and dignity, have collectively expressed their decisions:

> We are recovering and strengthening ancestral practices and the spirituality of our peoples.
>
> We are promoting an identity-based development based on the cosmovision of indigenous peoples.
>
> Indigenous spirituality is not a matter of the church, of personal devotion, or of individual beliefs. It is something that unifies and identifies communities; it is what gives them cohesion. It is what is retrieved from the ancestors; that which gives meaning to their political and social struggles. It is absolutely not institutionalized religion. (*Memoria* 2003, 42–45)

The Mandate of Abya Yala also makes the following demands:

> To respect our sacred places and the administration of them by our peoples;
>
> To rescue the people's indigenous cosmovision so as to keep alive spirituality and culture;
>
> To safeguard our worldview so that it be not turned into folklore by states and corporations.

Other declarations were also included in the resolutions that resulted from the work committees and appeared in *Gender from the Perspective of Indigenous Women*. It stated: "We urge the organizations of indigenous women to deepen, analyze, and socialize proposals on how to address the gender perspective from the cosmovision of indigenous peoples and to direct our actions across common parameters" (*Memoria* 2003, 44).

Demands for Trans-cultural/Trans-national Justice

The demands of indigenous women for their "rights" refer not only to indigenous norms within indigenous regulatory systems, but, in addition, their aim for such access to be assured within the jurisdiction of the State. This would include official systems of health, education, etc., based on a foundation of non-discrimination and respect (Sierra 2001, 19). This final reflection is an important one.

At the same time, indigenous women, from their condition as native peoples, appeal to their own internal indigenous regulatory systems. These bodies also struggle for the implementation of the Indigenous and Tribal Peoples Convention 169, which concerns the rights of their indigenous communities.[11]

An important and recent contribution is the theorization that has emerged from the indigenous women's reflections is that concerning the rights of "Mother Earth," especially of territory. As is well known, indigenous women are frequently associated symbolically with the earth. Groups of Mayan women in Guatemala refer to, and struggle for, the defense of "my body, my territory," merging their female bodies with the earth, respected as a feminine element that gives life. The symbolic wealth of this merger of body/territory is outside the scope of this study, but I mention it to point out some of the theoretical re-conceptualizations that the indigenous women have introduced, inspired by their epistemic and cosmological roots.

The indigenous women's demand for the right to "inherit the land," has been regarded as a somewhat confusing demand for many years. Was the demand to inherit the land only claimed as an individual subject? What about the demand for collective rights to the land and thus to territory?

In an interview at the end of 2016, Tarcila Rivera introduced a new proposal to promote the "empowerment" of indigenous women in connection with the possession of the land. She made an important clarification and annotation to the deliberations on the drafting of UN documents on the rights of women, such as the Convention on the Elimination of all Forms of Discrimination against Women (CEDAW).

> For women, it would be individual rights *over land*, but for us indigenous women, we prefer the recognition of collective rights *to land*, to the territory. And then from there, individual rights *over land* shall be determined. [...] Therefore, it must be about both collective rights to the land, and individual rights over the land. (Rivera 2016)

Rivera then further refined this statement:

> [T]hrough experience of this reality (individual rights over land), this would increase the vulnerability of women to lose their lands. Their hus-

---

11. Convenio 169: Sobre Pueblos Indígenas y Tribales en Países Independientes [Indigenous and Tribal Peoples Convention], 1989. http://www.ilo.org/public/spanish/region/ampro/lima/publ/conv-169/convenio.shtml

bands can pressure them to relinquish them, and they can easily be harassed to sell them because they are individual landholders. But if land is held under a collective possession regime, where individuals are protected within the collective, then they would, more securely, preserve their rights to land. (2016)

In addition to the practical details spelled out in the defense of land rights, what can also be discerned in Rivera's proposal is a theoretical contribution, implied and inscribed in the concept of the "simultaneity" of both rights: individual and collective (Marcos 2013). It is a response that combines and does not discard either of these two rights, and proposes a solution to the interminable discussions in the contentious dialogues that occurred between feminist activists and the broad movement of indigenous women. There is a demand for both of these two rights at the same time, which bell hooks has similarly theorized in her methodological proposal of "positionality" (Marcos 2013).

Joan Carling, a Filipino indigenous woman, also explains how individual rights *over land* and collective rights *to land* are interdependent and go together as a "pair." Further, Carling is able to adjust the terminology theoretically to illuminate their similarities, while, at the same time, their differences (see Rivera 2016).

Indigenous women are also creating a new collectivity, and they are reformulating and challenging their respective states to meet many of their international commitments, such as the Inter-American Convention on the Prevention, and Eradication of Violence against Women.[12] All the women of Mexico and of the world are joining together to demand the right to a life free of violence, and that violence against women be considered as a human rights violation.

As a specific illustration of this, the "Pronouncement of Women of Chiapas against Government Repression in San Salvador Atenco" (in the State of México) reads:

To all women prisoners and to all wounded women, and to all disappeared women, we say:

We will not abandon you!

We also want to say that when we women denounce the violence against us, the authorities and those who have power do not help us, or they hide or minimize it, which is why we are not surprised that women who have been detained tell us that they were raped and the authorities deny it. They always do that […]

---

12. Convención de Belem do Pará, Brasil, June 1994.

Women *compañeras*: We are with you because in Chiapas we know what women suffer when there are killings and repressions.[13]

In this way, the women of Chiapas constitute a nexus that both facilitates and expands the possible priorities of indigenous peoples. They are building a wide bridge towards multiple societal groups, toward all women, and especially toward the dispossessed. They are a link and a re-creation of another collectivity that begins with them, both from below and on the left – where the heart is – to incorporate us all. In Zapatista speeches, we now often hear words of inclusion, e.g., "to indigenous and non-indigenous women, to indigenous and non-indigenous peoples." In a concrete example of this, at the Fourth National Indigenous Congress in San Pedro Atlapulco, Estado de México, 2006, the Mazahua indigenous delegates offered fifty of their own group in exchange for ten women prisoners in the city of Atenco.

As innovative as this attitude that emerges from their struggles may be, the indigenous women, however, do not cease to emphasize the re-evaluation of their own particularities: "The important thing about the new times," said a Rarámuri, woman from the state of Chihuahua, "is that we have begun to appreciate our traditional customs again" (Bellinghausen and Chávez 2006, 6).

Conclusion

I would like to end my paper with a quotation from the *Declaration of the Second Summit of Women of Abya Yala*, which had its final session on November 15, 2013, in Cauca, Colombia:

> That the exercise of the rights of indigenous women begin by empowering ourselves of our lives and of our bodies, rejecting every form of violence. […]

> That the realization of *Buen Vivir* is based on the reconstruction of complementarity between women and men, and with all the beings that inhabit the territory […]

> That States be held responsible for ensuring individual and collective rights recognized at the national and international levels, while respecting the autonomy and the self-determination of the people. (NA)

---

13. "Pronunciamiento de mujeres indigenas de Chiapas ante la agresión a las mujeres de Atenco", [Pronouncement of the Indigenous Women of Chiapas against the Aggression of the Women of Atenco]. December 2006. San Cristobal de las Casas, Chiapas.

Acknowledgement

I would like to acknowledge sincerely the generosity of the indigenous women who have allowed and supported me in my attending their meetings. It has been a privilege to listen and document – when that is possible – their discourses, demands, oral presentations, and official declarations. I have participated in many congresses where the remarkable strength and purpose of these women is manifest in their claims for rights and justice. As a witness to their proceedings, I have employed an ethnohistoric approach, which allows me to document their verbal presentations as well as have access to their official pronouncements. (Certain statements may not be available as references, as they were circulated at meetings as leaflets, and were not published). Finally, I hope that I have been able to convey the deeply dynamic process that I have witnessed as these determined women have engaged in their pursuit for justice.

References

Bakhtin, Mikhail. 2011. *Las fronteras del discurso*. Buenos Aires: Las Cuarenta.

Bellinghausen, H., and S. Chávez. 2006. "Hoy Atenco ¿mañana quién? preguntan los indios" *La Jornada* (7 May): 6.

"Building our History." 1997. *Cuadernos Feministas* 1(2): 29–31. National Meeting of Indigenous Women. Oaxaca, Mexico.

Clifford, James. 2013. *Returns, Becoming Indigenous in the Twenty-First Century*. Cambridge, MA: Harvard University Press. https://doi.org/10.1002/ocea.5108

Engel, S. 2006. Ponencia magistral [Keynote address]. Congreso de Antropología Jurídica. October. Oaxtepec, Morelos.

Foucault, Michel. 1981. "The Order of Discourse." Inaugural lecture, Collège de France, 1970. In *Untying the Text: A Post-Structuralist Reader*, edited by Robert Young, 51–78. Abingdon: Routledge.

Garza, Ana Maria. 2000. "Autoridad consenso y género." *Memoria* (México) 139: 28–33.

Hernández, Aída. 2004. "El Encuentro Continental de Mujeres Indígenas, Quito, Ecuador, 1995." Presentación de la Primera Conferencia del Enlace Continental de Mujeres Indígenas, Lima, Perú. https://doi.org/10.1016/s0188-9478(16)30016-0

Mahmood, Saba. 2005. *Politics of Piety: The Islamic Revival and the Islamic Subject*. Princeton, NJ: Princeton University Press. https://doi.org/10.7202/015997ar

Mandato de la Primera Cumbre Continental de Mujeres Indígenas de Abya Yala, 2009. 30 May. Puno, Bolivia.

Marcos, Sylvia. 1996. "Pensamiento Mesoamericano y categorías de género: un reto epistemológico" *La Palabra y el Hombre*. Xalapa: Universidad Veracruzana. https://doi.org/10.25009/lpyh.v0i45.2627

———. 2006. *Taken from the Lips: Gender and Eros in Mesoamerican Religions*. Leiden: Brill.

———. 2013. *Mujeres Indigenas Rebeldes Zapatistas*. Mexico: Eon.

"Memoria." 2003. *Primera Cumbre de Mujeres Indígenas de las Americas* [*First Summit of the Indigenous Women of the Americas*]. Mexico: Fundacion Rigoberta Menchu.

Moore, Henrietta. 1994. *A Passion for Difference: Essays in Anthropology and Gender*. Bloomington: Indiana University Press.

Rivera, Tarcila. 2016. "Objetivos de Desarrollo del Milenio y Mujeres Indígenas, Conversación con Tarcila Rivera Zea, Presidenta Ejecutiva del FIMI y Joan Carling, recién nombrada integrante de la Junta directiva del FIMI." *Foro Internacional de Mujeres Indigenas (FIMI), ONU, Boletin annual*. https://doi.org/10.18356/170c64f5-es

———. INFO@IIWF www.fimi-IIWF.org

Sierra, Teresa. 2001. "Conflicto cultural y derechos humanos: en torno al reconocimiento de los sistemas normativos indígenas," *Memoria* (México) 147: 15–21.

Speed, Shannnon. 2008. *Rights in Rebellion*. Stanford: Stanford University Press.

Via Campesina: International Peasants Movement. 2019. https://viacampesina.org/en/

3

Women, Ordination, and a Buddhist Perspective: A Violation of Rights?

Carola Roloff (Bhikṣuṇī Jampa Tsedroen) is Visiting Professor for Buddhism in the Academy of World Religions of the University of Hamburg (endowed docentship until 2025). She studied Tibetology and Classical Indology with a focus on Buddhist Studies in the Asia-Africa-Institute of the University of Hamburg (M.A. 2003, PhD in 2009). Her current focus in research and teaching is "Buddhism and Dialogue in Modern Societies". Other research topics include gender-religion interactions in Buddhism and their significance in social dialogue processes.

Introduction

By taking women's ordination – a main gender issue debated in Buddhism – as an example, I reason why discrimination against women in religion not only violates women's human rights but also basic Buddhist principles such as non-violence.[1] I question whether from a Buddhist perspective religion and rights are two mutually exclusive terms, and then discuss two areas of tension: A tension between religious and secular law on the one hand and a tension between religious freedom and gender equality on the other. Based on this, I analyze how the dynamics of these areas of tension and gender issues could become a driving force for interreligious dialogue and for dialogue between religions and secular societies.

In many world religions, women are discriminated against and treated as second-class citizens – Buddhism does not constitute an exception. This will be demonstrated in the context of the Buddha's teaching, on the one hand, and of contemporary societies, on the other hand. A special focus lies on the compatibility of Buddhism with the Universal Declaration of Human Rights and the Constitution, the so-called Basic Law, of the Federal Republic of Germany.

Human rights play an important role in this postmodern world. Therefore religions are called upon to take a stance on it. Although the term

---

1. I am extremely grateful to Monika Deimann-Clemens and Morny Joy for their support in editing.

"human rights" is not part of the Buddhist vocabulary, the basic idea of human rights is not alien to Buddhism (Schmidt-Leukel 2010; Tsedroen 2010; Roloff 2015).

Women's ordination: A main gender issue in Buddhism

In the fifth century B.C.E., in India, Mahāprajāpatī Gautamī, the Buddha's foster mother, was the first woman worldwide to be ordained. Today, more than 2,500 years later, women's ordination is one of the main gender issues debated in Buddhism. From the eleventh/twelfth century onwards, full ordination of nuns, comparable to women's priesthood, was either lost or never transmitted to the countries outside India. Today, three main strands of Buddhism are practised: Theravāda Buddhism, East Asian Buddhism (including Zen), and Tibetan Buddhism. Nuns' ordination was only preserved in East Asian Buddhism, mainly in China, Korea, and Vietnam. But even there, gender equity is not fully reflected in the leadership of Buddhist institutions. This stands in stark contrast to the assumptions cherished by large parts of the West: That Buddhism fits best with democratic principles and modern life. By now. Western Buddhist circles had begun to realize that with the transfer of Buddhism to the West, almost imperceptibly an ancient hierarchical model of social structure is also seeping through. This is that in classical Buddhist hierarchy women are subordinate to men. Devout Buddhists believe that only if this principle of seniority and gender subordination is followed, the Buddhist community will be in harmony and the teaching of the Buddha will be ensured. This implies that every attempt to question this hierarchy – for example, by requiring gender equality – is regarded as a threat for the harmony of the Saṅgha and a risk for the very survival of Buddhism.

When the context changes: Buddhism coming to the West

More and more Western Buddhists reject these role allocations and call for a change. A hierarchical model based on seniority and gender that disparages women as second-class beings, is neither in accordance with the ideals of European enlightenment, nor with the *Universal Declaration of Human Rights*. This declaration recognizes "the inherent dignity and […] the equal and inalienable rights of all members of the human family" as "the foundation of freedom, justice and peace in the world" (United Nations 1948).

Due to globalization, issues such as full ordination for nuns, and gender equality in religion have been discussed not only in the West, but also in Asia. Thus, the rising of the International Buddhist Women's movement in the 1970s/1980s finally led to the restoration of the Buddhist nuns' order in Sri Lanka, where it had died out in the eleventth/twelfth century. The first ordinations of Sri Lankan women took place in a Taiwanese Buddhist Temple in Los Angeles in 1988. Next followed the first women's ordination in Sarnath, India, in 1996, involving native Sri Lankan monks from the Mahābodhi Society. Since the 1998 Bodhgayā ordination, which entailed a significant variant in the ordination procedure,[2] the order of Buddhist nuns (*bhikṣuṇī* in Sanskrit, *bhikkhunī* in Pāli), has definitely gained momentum, and subsequent *bhikṣuṇī* ordinations have been conducted in Sri Lanka itself. This was the starting point, since the legal validity of the ordinations has been largely accepted (*cf.* Anālayo 2013).

Despite strong resistance from a number of conservative Buddhist monks, a similar movement started in Thailand and Burma and also among Tibetan-Buddhist communities in India. Although the number of fully ordained nuns is small compared to the number of fully ordained monks, it is constantly growing. But most Buddhist communities are still structured according to gender and seniority. Thus, adaptation is badly needed. This process involves legal, political, social, and psychological aspects. More egalitarian models, ones better suited to democratic standards, are needed.

Thailand: Women's ordination forbidden

An alliance of state and church working hand in hand against women's rights can be illustrated by the following example. In 1928, the Saṅgharāja, the head of the Buddhist monks' order in Thailand, had issued an order forbidding all Thai monks from giving ordination to women (Dhammananda 2010, 150). By now, at least a hundred fully ordained nuns, in Thailand referred to as *bhikkhunīs*, however, are spread over twenty provinces nationwide; nevertheless, the Supreme Saṅgha Council still claims that the lineage of Theravāda nuns has died out. On 29 November 2014 Ven. Dhammananda, a former professor of philosophy and women's studies at Thammasat University and abbess of a Buddhist convent, organized a *bhikkhunī* ordination on the Koh Yor Island in Southern Thailand. A few days later, on 11 December, the Thai Supreme Saṅgha Council reiterated that all monks in Thailand must follow the Saṅgharāja's order issued in 1928. They even announced that, in cooperation with the

---

2. The Bodhgayā ordination was followed by a daḷhīkamma, a formal act performed by Theravāda *bhikkhus* "reinforcing" that the bhikkhunīs, who had received ordination from the East Asian Dharmaguptaka school first, have now gained the recognition of belonging to the Theravāda school of which they wish to be part.

Ministry of Foreign Affairs, a decree would be issued enacting that monks who wish to come to Thailand to perform an ordination ceremony need the Saṅgha Council's written permission. This provoked criticism, even from mem¬bers of the National Reform Council (NRC), who blamed the Supreme Saṅgha Council for "violat[ing] religious freedom, a fundamental human right" (Thip-Osod 2014).

It is important to note that here we are not only confronted with a dispute concerning the interpretation of the *Vinaya*, the ancient Buddhist monastic law, but also concerning the local secular basic law, ensuring religious freedom for women. The *Vinaya* is one part of the threefold Buddhist canon (*Tripiṭaka*). For two and a half thousand years, it has provided the legal norms for the life of the Buddhist community. Thus, for Buddhism, law and religion are closely linked. The decree of the Thai Saṅgha Council is neither in accordance with the *Vinaya* nor with the Thai secular law – but it is still in effect.

Religion, women and power structures

Another question that has bothered me for a long time is: How can women reach their goals if those who hold the positions of power in the respective religions; that is, men, are backed by largely *male*-dominated political entities and refuse to discuss religious matters on an equal footing with those affected? I think we need more interdisciplinary cooperation in the field of gender and religion in order to learn from each other's success stories and to develop effective strategies. In this way, gender issues could not only become a driving force for interreligious dialogue but also for joint action, provided that political governments take their legal responsibility seriously and protect women from all kinds of discrimination, including religious ones.

It is alarming that in Europe, even after observing some progress, we are still encountering stagnation and setbacks. During a meeting at the Council of Europe in Strasbourg in 2016, I participated together with the senior Tibetan Buddhist nun, Ven. Tenzin Palmo, in a side-event: "Are religions a place of emancipation for women? Progress and setbacks." During the main session, Agnes von Kirchbach, a German theologian and pastor of the United Protestant Church of France said:

> Today, the greater part of the historical Protestant churches in Europe also entrust more important leadership functions to women, for example the office of a bishop. But none of these decisions was made without difficulties, and significant disparities still exist. An example: The Lutheran Church of Poland has not yet opened women's access to ordained ministry the way men are able to practice it. [And] the Latvian Lutheran church decided

in June 2016 to ban women's further access to the same offices as men. (Council of Europe 2016)

From 1999 on, there had been permanent discussion in the Council of Europe about including the study of religions in its educational remit. This overall wish was implemented after the 9/11 attacks when religion became an integral part of the Council's educational program and of the public discussion.

Another possibility would be that political institutions create a neutral space for publications and dialogue on questions such as: What are the concrete reasons for women being partly excluded from equal sharing of religious leadership positions?[3]

Religious freedom and gender equality or, in short, religious freedom and equal rights for women, are not only anchored in the Charter of Human Rights, but – at least in Germany – also laid down in Articles 3 and 4 of the German Basic Law (Basic Law 2019).

Rights and religion: Two mutually exclusive terms

The work of Morny Joy (2008), the Canadian scholar of religions, made me especially aware that tensions particularly arise when the women's right to equality is not consistent with the practices of that religion. Gender equality in politics, business, and society worldwide are still not self-evident. Religions are jointly responsible. Joy has recorded that the Vatican has concurred with Islamic conservatives when it comes to the definition of women's rights (2008, 194).[4]

---

3. As Adrian Loretan, a lawyer for state church-law and expert on comparative constitutional law and religion, points out: "In state law (state church right) the exclusion of women from the consecrated offices and thus of all-important leadership functions of the church is a discrimination on the basis of sex" (2010, 221; translation mine). Stella Ahlers states: "Already earlier, W. Rüfner spoke of the possibility of the Catholic priestess by virtue of European law, even though he himself considered this an 'abstruse' and unrealistic example of the indirect impact of European law on church life" (2005, 151; translation mine). And Loretan with reference to the missing women's ordination in the Roman Catholic Church even adds: "How binding are the constitutional principle of gender equality and the principle of non-discrimination on grounds of sex for the state? This question will still have to be decided by state courts in Germany, Switzerland, Brussels (European Court of Justice) and Strasbourg (European Court of Human Rights), but a lawsuit has not yet been filed, although K. Sahlfeld and individual lawyers consider it desirable" [226] 2010, 219; translation mine).

4. The Vatican's machinations and interference, etc., especially with conservative Muslims, more specific as to the actual event have been discussed by Joy in

The restriction of women's rights is often justified by the protection of women's "dignity" in terms of religion, without specifying what it refers to. The Vatican, by the way, has not yet ratified the *Universal Declaration of Human Rights*, stating that it acknowledges human rights only insofar as these are in accordance with the doctrine of the Catholic church.[5]

This problem became particularly significant in the framework of the Vienna Declaration on the Elimination of Violence against Women of 1993 (United Nations 1993; United Nations 1979). Although it should actually be a matter of course, it was noted that women's rights are an inalienable and indivisible aspect of universal human rights and in no way could be relativized with reference to cultural and traditional mores. Acts of violence against women – including physical and sexual violence in the household and the family – were explicitly condemned as human rights violations.

The human rights debate is primarily about the justification of the universality of human rights in the context of increasing presence of different cultures, religions, and ideologies in postmodern societies. It also entails evaluating how to enforce its critical claim against ancient traditions, if necessary. Put simply: Does religion allow religious individual self-determination, or is there no other choice left than to turn away from one's religion if it violates important principles such as gender equality? On 4 October 2005, the Parliamentary Assembly of the Council of Europe adopted a resolution that reads: "States must not accept any religious or cultural relativism of women's human rights" (Council of Europe 2005, Resolution 1464 no. 6).

From a feminist theory perspective, Christine Koggel observes: "Just as second-wave feminists could be charged with assuming the perspective of privileged white women, Western feminism more generally could be charged with assuming the perspective of privileged white women in dominant countries and cultures" (2011, 554).

This challenge to mainstream feminism may have led to important developments such as the theory of intersectionality, which holds that descriptions of women's inequalities and injustices need to be placed within a complex network of intersecting kinds of oppression. Koggel states: "Women are not only women; gender intersects with one or more

---

a paper she gave first in 2004 in Helsinki and then published with the Finnish journal, *Temenos* (2006, 17–18).

5. In the Encyclical *Pacem in Terris* ("Peace on Earth") Ceming sees an official acceptance of human rights by the Catholic Church (2010, 73). But it reads: "It is right to obey God rather than men" (II, 51). See also IV, 143–144.

facts of race, class ethnicity, disability, sexual orientation, age, and so on" (Koggel 2011, 554). She does not, however, include religion. Yet I believe that it is not only possible but imperative to integrate the category of "religion" into the concept of intersectionality.

Although Koggel herself does not include religion, she thinks that the future lies in a "coalition building around specific issues and causes and not in what it means to be a woman or a feminist" (558). This means that patterns of commonalties need to be acknowledged. At the same time, historical and cultural variations need to be recognized within the overarching impact of global factors and economic globalization itself. In this context, however, we should be aware that religion has always been a significant factor not only in history but in all cultures. We cannot ignore it. As Ursula King already pointed out in 2005, there is still a harmful "double blindness;" that is, most contemporary gender studies, whether in the humanities, in social sciences, or in natural sciences, remain extraordinarily "religion blind," whereas far too many studies in religion are still quite "gender blind."

In my view, politics also suffers from this double blindness with regard to gender in religion. By trying to keep "neutral," political organizations maintain patriarchal religious structures and indirectly support structural inequity against women. During the already-mentioned side-event at the Council of Europe, for example, a group of Jewish women from Eastern Europe criticized the organizer for having – due to budget reasons – invited a (local) male religious representative to speak on their behalf. The next day, at a workshop on gender equality, it turned out that their suspicions were right. The only official Jewish representative, a rabbi and member of the Chabad Lubavitch, stated that men and women are different in nature. Because of this difference, women were quite capable in organizing the parish but unable to lead rituals. Similarly, the permanent representative of the Holy See to the CoE stressed, that in the Christian vision, the human being, as male and female, exists irreducibly different, one from another. The fact that the Catholic Church reserves the priesthood exclusively for men has to be similarly understood. In the natural, as well as in the supernatural, order, roles are definitely not interchangeable.

From a Buddhist perspective, this means that, for gender reasons alone, women do not have the freedom to publicly manifest their religion in practice and observance.

Before returning to this point, let me briefly comment on the term "gender equality" from a Tibetan Buddhist perspective and then explain in a nutshell which Buddhist teachings the idea of women's human rights can be based on.

A brief comment on the term "gender equality"

In Tibetan circles, in the religious context, I personally speak only about "equal opportunities" (Tib. *go skabs gcig pa* or *go skabs 'dra mnyam*) and not about "equal rights" or "equality" of women. Why? There have been allegations that religion and politics are being confused when talking about equal rights for men and women in religion. Women seeking full ordination or monastic academic titles have been accused of no longer seeking religious goals. They are charged with striving after purely secular ideals, such as fame and glory, which contradict monastic mores. But why should Buddhist women be blamed for expecting the same opportunities enjoyed by Buddhist men in following the spiritual path towards liberation? The Tibetan *lam rim* teachings ("Stages of the Path") speak of a precious *human* birth, not of a precious female or male birth. Such a distinction between men and women would be seen as an obstacle on the way to liberation.

The Tibetan translation of "human rights" in modern Tibetan is *mi'i thob thang*, lit. "that which falls to a human being's (*mi'i*) share." Although in Modern Tibetan the term *thob thang* is used for "right(s)," the second basic meaning is "status," rank, social position. Literally *thob thang* means a value or privilege (*thang*) that is obtained (*thob*). Similarly to the rest of the world, in Tibetan society, words such as *thob thang 'dra mnyam* ("equal rights") or *bud med thob thang* ("women's rights") are only used in the secular, not in the religious, context. So if you speak about rights in the context of religion, you need to know how to frame it. The same goes for the translation of the term "human rights' values," i.e., the values that are associated with "human rights."

Values that support the idea of human rights in Buddhism

In Buddhism, there are several values that attest to the basic idea of human rights: The dignity of the individual, for example, and the equality of all human beings and therefore also the idea of gender equality. In relation to gender justice or gender equality, I want to take three of them as an example:

1. The Buddhist principle of equality and the Buddha nature of all beings
2. Universal responsibility
3. The equality of all human beings: Buddha's rejection of the caste system and his explicit acknowledgement of women's potential for enlightenment

I will mainly concentrate on the first of these, the Buddhist principle of equality.

1. The Buddhist principle of equality and the Buddha nature of all beings

In the West, about two centuries ago, Buddhism became part of mainly Judeo-Christian dominated societies where nowadays gender equality is taken for granted – at least theoretically. Thus, we must ask how gender equality is understood from a Buddhist perspective and how far it is taken into consideration within Buddhist institutional structures. Can Buddhist women participate equally in preserving, teaching, and representing their religion? No. Do they have equal access to religious leadership positions? No. Can they independently observe all of the obligatory rules and rituals? No.

In Buddhism, in general, there is no technical term for "justice"[6] or "injustice." When dealing with human coexistence, one can therefore only rely on the term "equanimity" because the Buddhist mental training in love, compassion, sympathetic joy, and equanimity includes *all* sentient beings without exception, irrespective of their gender, nationality, or religious affiliation.

The understanding of the Buddhist concept "Equanimity or Lack of egocentricity"[7] (Skt. *upekṣā*, Pā. *upekkhā*), plays a key role in contemporary societies. It should not only be understood as a peaceful state of mind. Equanimity has the potential to be interpreted according to secular values, and thus encourages Buddhists to become socially engaged. This would involve taking active responsibility and care for others and fighting other forms of discrimination and inequality.

One may object, stating that such reasoning can be explained as an attempt by white Western feminists to influence or patronize Asian Buddhists with Western ideas. My emphasis on equanimity, however, derives from my personal experience of living Buddhism in Asia. The first conclave of the "International Buddhist Confederation" in Delhi (India) in September 2013, for example, adopted *"equanimity"* as an argument for demanding equality of women in Buddhism (Roloff 2014, 250). In December 2013, the renowned Thai reformer Sulak Sivaraksa, referring to the Thai Saṅgha Council's stance on women's ordination, mentioned above, asked somewhat polemically: "Is their opposition [...] based on the Dhamma and the Brahmavihāras,[8] or are they acting out of jealousy and

---

6. Sallie B. King, "Buddhism does have a theory of natural justice in the concept of karma" (2005, 2003).
7. I intentionally avoid the translation as "impartiality" here because the term implies neutrality. Advocating justice, however, means not remaining impartial but to take the side of those oppressed.
8. The Brahmavihāras, also known as the Four Divine States or the "Four

ignorance?" (International Network of Engaged Buddhists 2014). This remark reveals that equanimity is also cited by Asian Buddhists in the context of gender equality.

From a Buddhist Mahāyāna point of view, it should be supplemented here that in the *Perfection of Wisdom Sūtras* (Skt. *Prajñāpāramitāsūtras*), a genre of Mahāyāna Buddhist scriptures, wisdom is called the "mother of all Buddhas." Iconographically, the female *bodhisattva* Prajñāpāramitā embodies the completion of highest wisdom and knowledge. Already in early Buddhism, the Buddha taught the same path to *nirvāṇa* for women and men. With the advent of early Mahāyāna in the first century B.C.E. all beings are said to equally possess "Buddha nature" (Skt. *tathāgathagarba*), the potential to become a Buddha. In this regard, all human beings are equal, whether female or male. Buddhists of all traditions agree that the nature of the mind is the same for all, regardless of race, color, sex, language, religion, political ideology, nationality, social origins, property, birth status, or other distinctions. Sometimes sentient beings are born female and sometimes male. The concept of evolution from a lower form as a woman to a higher form as a man does not exist. In short, from a Buddhist philosophical point of view, gender difference is not a question of mind but of body, and, like all other natural attributes, gender lacks inherent reality.

2. Universal responsibility

Another important term, based on equanimity, is "Universal Responsibility." This term was coined by H.H. the Dalai Lama in 1989 when he received the Nobel Peace Prize in Oslo.

"Universal Responsibility" is for him the key to human survival and the best foundation for world peace. He defines it as a sense of human interrelatedness, solidarity, and sympathy, which goes beyond all national borders. He reminds us that we are all members of one large human family. In Buddhist terms of "dependent origination," we are all related to each other. If we change ourselves, the world changes. Peace starts within oneself. From this, it follows that we have a moral obligation to get involved for the common good. Thus, you may understand Universal Responsibility as a kind of Buddhist liberation theology, or, as we call it: Engaged Buddhism.

Immeasurables" (Skt. *Catvārya–pramāṇāni*, Pā. *catasso appamaññāyo*) are a set of four Buddhist virtues and the according meditation practices to develop the mental attitudes of love, compassion, sympathetic joy, and equanimity.

3. The equality of all human beings: Buddha's rejection of the caste system and his explicit acknowledgement of women's potential for enlightenment

Article 1 of the *Universal Declaration of Human Rights* states that all human beings are born free and equal in dignity and rights (United Nations). This is not without problems, especially when it comes to the dignity of women from the perspective of religions. As Perry Schmidt-Leukel (Schmidt-Leukel 2010, 44) points out, one has to recall the numerous instances where a legally restricted status of women is justified by an alleged specific womanly dignity. Therefore, he suggests that, within the context of justifying human rights, dignity should be restricted sharply to the dignity of free individual agency and self-determination. It should be left precisely to the individual woman to determine how she understands her dignity. Just as the term "human rights" is lacking, the term, "human dignity," cannot be found in Buddhist canonical texts. The idea, however, can be tracked. The Buddha did not adopt the caste system into which he himself was born, but said, for example:[9]

> One is not an outcaste by birth, by birth one is not a priest (*brahmin*), by deeds one becomes an outcaste, one becomes a priest (*brahmin*) by deeds. (*Sutta Nipāta* 1.7, verse 142)

The Buddha did not intend to create two new castes, a caste of men and a caste of women. This clearly shows that he accepted the principles of human equality and dignity of the individual. At the time of the Buddha, everyone could join the Buddhist community, irrespective of the caste he or she belonged to. The hierarchy in both the order of monks and the order of nuns follows the principle of seniority, i.e., the age of service as a fully ordained monk or nun in the order, and not the social status.

Furthermore, the Buddha explicitly acknowledged women's potential for enlightenment. "From the viewpoint of early Buddhist texts, women just as well as men can reach the final goal" (Anālayo 2016, 79). When the monk Ānanda asked the Buddha whether women can attain arhatship, the fourth and last stage in religious development, equivalent to *nirvāṇa* or *mokṣa* (liberation), the Buddha clearly stated: "They can attain it" (Anālayo 2016, 78, 185). The Buddhist canon is full of stories of women who, during the lifetime of the Buddha, became female *arhats*.

But what about the value of men and women? Are they equal or of equal value? This leads us to the question of the role of women and the question of women's human rights violations in contemporary Buddhist societies.

---

9. *Na jaccā vasalo hoti, na jaccā hoti brāhmaṇo, kammanā vasalo hoti kammanā hoti brāhmaṇo.*

Women's human rights violations in contemporary Buddhist societies

1. The ambivalent Attitude toward Women in Buddhism

The role of women and their potential is depicted as controversial in Buddhist literature, especially in present-day traditions of Buddhism. Even though the Buddha had confirmed that women can attain arhatship, the source texts and exegesis are ambivalent.[10] So it is not surprising that there are Buddhist women making aspirational prayers to be reborn as a man (Dalai Lama XIV. 1988, 36). This is due to the fact that the different traditions build up on different text collections in different languages. Not every source has been translated into all the relevant languages. But all traditions agree that enlightenment, whether for man or for woman, is solely attained through the practice of ethics, concentration, and wisdom.

According to the Buddha, a Buddhist community is only complete when it includes monks (Skt. *bhikṣus*, Pā. *bhikkhus*), nuns (*bhikṣuṇīs*), laymen (Skt./Pā. *upāsakas*) and laywomen (Skt./Pā. *upāsikās*). Therefore, the establishment of the nuns' order is canonical and present in the *Vinaya*s of all traditions. This documentation includes full ordination of women, teaching the Dharma and ritual observance. Nevertheless, over the centuries, the social position of women has been very limited.

Although each canon tells the story of the foundation of the nuns' order differently, the core is as follows: The foster mother of the Buddha Mahāprajāpatī and 500 women in her retinue, asked the Buddha several times for admission in the order, until he finally agreed, influenced by his favourite disciple Ānanda. But Mahāprajāpatī had to accept the eight *gurudharmas*, a set of eight rules that directly address monk-nun relationships and interaction, and subordinate the nuns to the monks. One of these states that even if a *bhikṣuṇī* is fully ordained for a hundred years, she should speak kind words, praise him, rise up, put her palms together and show respect to a *bhikṣu* who has just been ordained that day. Mahāprajāpatī, the first "Buddhist feminist," requested the Buddha to replace this with the principle of seniority regardless of gender. The Buddha, however,

---

10. Even today, many Buddhists are convinced that rebirth as a woman is inferior. *Cf.* Bapat (1970, 211 [10]): "Out of these two sexes, the male sex is superior, the female sex is inferior," or Pabongka (1999, 365): "We could not have found a better rebirth than the present one, except those of us, who have not been reborn as a man." See also Anālayo (2014) on karma and female rebirth as well as Anālayo (2009) on women's inabilities.

refused, explaining that adherents of non-Buddhist sects would not greet women at all.[11]

Thus, the Buddha, as depicted in the Vinaya, did subordinate women to men, but this has to be understood in the context of the prevailing customs and traditions in ancient Indian societies. In terms of caste system, he swam against the stream, but women were cross-class; that is, in each caste subordinated to men. This meant they were under the protection of their father, brother, or son, unless they were prostitutes. Accordingly, the order of nuns was finally put under the "protection" of the order of monks. A revolutionary for his time, the Buddha *did* found an order of nuns. But even this order, although acknowledged canonically, is controversially interpreted.

Today, the customs have changed and mutual respect is required, so now the rule should be interpreted accordingly. Actually, in contemporary communities of all three main strands of Buddhism, we already find examples of a respective change in the daily practice of local communities. Some *bhikṣus* ask senior *bhikṣuṇīs* to go first or even bow to them in return. Yet these are still exceptions.

In East Asian Buddhism, where higher ordination for women still exits, the eight *gurudharmas* still carry weight. In Taiwan, for example, nuns recite them at the end of each of their bimonthly confession ceremony (Skt. *poṣadha*). Some contemporary Taiwanese Buddhist feminists, however, demand their abolition. The most radical attempt documented is that of the Taiwanese nun Ven. Chao Hwei. Together with her disciples, Chao Hwei supports "efforts by the government and NGOs to work toward gender equality in Taiwan." In 2001, during the opening ceremony of a conference, Chao Hwei first read the eight *gurudharmas* out and then tore them up (DeVido 2010, 107).

Whether the *gurudharmas* were established to protect women or to entrench power, today, they are largely experienced as discriminatory.[12] In many places, especially in Asia, nuns sit still behind monks, walk behind

---

11. D 6 (*'dul ba*), da, 121a1-b1. *Cf.* Gyatso (2010, 43 note 17); for the Pāli Vinaya cf. Hüsken (1997, 347, 359).
12. Ute Hüsken has shown (1997, 480, 330–333) that, not only the gurudharmas, but the entire set of Vinaya rules (*prātimokṣa*) disadvantage nuns compared to monks. Nevertheless, from an academic theologian's point of view, for practitioners the larger set of *prātimokṣa* rules for nuns may be interpreted as "the more rules, the more merit" (Tib. *bsod nams*, Skt. *puṇya*), thus being an advantage to achieving the spiritual goal rather than a disadvantage. From a Buddhist nuns' perspective, the main problem is found in the eight gurudharmas, not in the prātimokṣa.

monks, and receive food and accommodation after them. They are clearly second-class monastics.

From a monastic legal point of view, however, one of these eight *gurudharmas* is indispensable in order to revive the nuns' order, namely *gurudharma* 1. This gives women permission to receive all stages of women's ordination from monks when no community of nuns exists – starting with the going forth,[13] and reaching all the way up to the higher ordination. This reading, which we find in the Tibetan canon as well as in the respective ancient Sanskrit manuscript, obviously presents a very early formulation of this *gurudharma*, when the nuns' order had not yet come into existence.[14]

2. Feminist hermeneutics: How to approach ambivalent texts

A hermeneutical question needs to be raised asking how to approach such ambivalent authoritative religious texts while considering the twenty-first century's different social context. It is not helpful to apply a radical mode of hermeneutics that simply rejects uneasy passages. What we need is a hermeneutic of liberating tradition, taking the liberation of the oppressed as the norm by which texts are re-read/re-told.

Elisabeth Schüssler Fiorenza (1984) offers a model of four-stage feminist interpretation we can build on: (1) The hermeneutic of suspicion, (2) the hermeneutic of proclamation, (3) the hermeneutic of remembrance, and (4) the hermeneutic of creative actualization. The hermeneutic of suspicion encourages readers to keep in mind that the religious texts and their interpretations are androcentric and serve patriarchal functions. The hermeneutic of proclamation emphasizes the texts that are supportive of women. This hermeneutical strategy, however, can result in ignoring other texts that can be interpreted in a harmful, violent, or oppressive way. For such texts, we need a strategy of rebuttal or a contextual rectification. This could be part of the hermeneutic of remembrance or re-membering, a historical reconstruction of those things that give hope and inspiration to women. As Schüssler Fiorenza explains in *Wisdom Ways: Introducing Feminist Biblical Interpretation* (2001), "texts and information must be contextualized in their variegated cultural and religious environments and reconstructed not only in terms of the dominant ethos but also in terms of alternative social movements for change." The hermeneutic of creative

---

13. Skt. *pravrajyā*. This means to leave home to live the life of a Buddhist renunciate.
14. For further details, see Tsedroen and Anālayo (2013); *cf.* Jyväsjärvi (2011, 193), and Tsedroen (2016).

actualization means to take what one can learn from the religious texts to recreate or re-envision what it means be a woman in the respective tradition today.

In Buddhism, we find different interpretations that have an impact on daily practice. Social reality often stands in direct contradiction to fundamental religious principles such as nonviolence. Consequently, not only the interpretation, but also the practice can be contrary and even contradictory: Thus, for example, you can witness monks and nuns in Tibet, Myanmar, and Cambodia demonstrating in support of human rights. This means, in the case of human rights violations (including the area of religion), that the nuns and monks themselves rely on the Charter of Human Rights as an authority (2009, 137). But when the question of gender equality in religion is at stake, women are asked not to mix religion and politics.

Nonetheless, Asian Buddhist women increasingly demand equal opportunities for themselves and protest against injustice. It is striking, however, that they largely avoid referring to human rights or calling themselves feminists. Some even distance themselves explicitly from these terms. At the Hamburg "International Congress on Buddhist Women's Role in the Saṅgha" in 2007, there was a remarkable incident. Some Tibetan nuns stated they were not interested at all in obtaining full ordination, while others disagreed. Some European nuns even refused to discuss human rights in a religious context, while others insisted on their observance. The positions, whether in the East or West, are divergent.

3. Women are demanding equal opportunities and protest against injustice

In 2011, exiled Tibetan women established the ACHA Tibetan Sisterhood initiative, which among other things opposes domestic violence. The social pressure not to make such abuses public is immense and requires a lot of courage (Tsering 2014). Women's rights are being violated in all countries. Buddhist societies have been no exception.

For example, in Tibetan Buddhist institutions, all of the leading offices are held by men. Until recently, there have not been any female monastic academic titles equivalent to *geshe* (Tib. *dge bshes*, lit. "friend of virtue, spiritual guide") or *khenpo* (Tib. *mkhan po*, lit. "teacher, preceptor"). In addition, classes in Buddhist philosophy, even at the Central Institute of Higher Tibetan Studies in Sarnath, India, are taught only by monks. After almost thirty years of effort, this, however, is now changing. In 1987–1988, several education programs for Buddhist women have been established in various Asian countries. Now, we are harvesting the fruits of these tremendous development efforts.

In 2016, in Tibetan Buddhism, for the first time in its history, the first twenty nuns successfully passed all the necessary exams after more than twentyyears of studies. On 22 December 2016, they received the academic title of a *geshema*, comparable to a Doctorate in Tibetan Buddhist philosophy/theology, from H.H. the Dalai Lama. Furthermore, in 2005 at a meeting of the *Tibetan Nuns' Project*, twenty novices from eight Tibetan nunneries decided to pursue their efforts to follow through with women's higher ordination. On 19 August 2016, *Buddhistdoor Global* posted an interview with H.H. the Karmapa, the head of the Tibetan Karma Kagyü tradition, who said: "We would like to start the process of reviving the bhikshuni ordination next year – first within the Kagyu lineage. We had hoped to begin this year, but it didn't work out, so we will try to begin next year" (Butet 2016). "History in the Making: The First Step Toward Full Ordination for Tibetan Buddhist Nuns" indicates that as of March 2017 the process has indeed started (Karmapa 2017).

The situation is very different in Korea, where nuns teach Buddhism at universities alongside monks and lay scholars. In contrast, gender distinctions are still found in the Vietnamese and Chinese traditions, as is shown by the different colours of their robes. Changes, however, are under way. The Australian Saṅgha Association, for example, has included gender equity in its statutes. For the United States and Europe, the course is not yet settled. However, all countries to which Buddhism has spread have ratified not only the *Universal Declaration of Human Rights* of 10 December 1948, but also the *Convention on the Elimination of All Forms of Discrimination against Women*, adopted in 1979.

By now, it should have become clear that there is a double tension, a tension between religious and secular law, on one hand, and a tension between religious freedom and gender equality, on the other.

Two areas of tension: The tensions between religious and secular law and between religious freedom and gender equality

In summer 2016, the University of Münster, Germany, published a study on "Integration and Religion as seen by People of Turkish origin in Germany," based on a survey of 1,200 ethnic Turks. Almost half of them agreed with the statement: "It is more important to obey religious laws than state laws."[15]

---

15. See Figure 12 on page 14 here: http://www.uni-muenster.de/imperia/md/content/religion_und_politik/aktuelles/2016/06_2016/study_integration_and_religion_as_seen_by_people_of_turkish_origin_in_germany.pdf

In contrast, in 2008, on the occasion of the Sixtieth Anniversary of the *Universal Declaration of Human Rights*, the Dalai Lama wrote:

> Mere maintenance of a diversity of traditions should never be used to justify violations of human rights. Thus, discrimination against persons of different races, against women, and against weaker sections of society may be traditional in some regions, but if they are inconsistent with universally recognized human rights, these forms of behavior should change. The universal principle of the equality of all human beings must take precedence. (Dalai Lama 2008)[16]

What does this mean when applied to women in religions? The Basic Law for the Federal Republic of Germany says in Article 3 [Equality before the law]:

> (2) Men and women shall have equal rights. The state shall promote the actual implementation of equal rights for women and men and take steps to eliminate disadvantages that now exist. (Basic Law 2019)

There is no mention that the area of religion constitutes an exemption. In my view, if one accepts human rights as being universal, these rights must also be in effect in the field of religion. It is in this context that a discussion should be launched about the question: Is it possible to build on the forces between the two areas of tension, i.e., religious and secular law, and religious freedom and gender equality, to gain momentum for interreligious dialogue?

It would seem that the statement: "No one should be discriminated against because of his/her gender," should apply, in particular, in the field of religion, and thus set an example on ethics. Human rights are universal and indivisible and must always be realized in their entirety. And a Basic Law, like that of the German constitution, reflects fundamental rights. In Germany, these rights have become an integral part of the canon of values. If religions want to be credible, they cannot lag behind the minimal global consensus of human rights.

This also applies to parts of Asia. Sallie King (2009, 141), for example, states that the superiors of the Cambodian Buddhist Saṅgha have decided

---

16. That equality between men and women should take precedence over religious customs and traditions matches with a clear conclusion taken by the UN Commission on Human Rights on 5 April 2002, resolution 2001/42, E/CN.4/2002/73/Add.2, "Study on the Freedom of Religion or Belief and the Status of Women from the Viewpoint of Religion and Traditions." Paragraph 30 of the Report of the Special Rapporteur states: "There can be no compromise in that respect, since, without this common denominator, there can be no credible system for the enduring protection of human rights in general and those of women in particular. For the full text see: http://www.ohchr.org/EN/Issues/FreedomReligion/Pages/Annual.aspx

that the population needs instruction in basic moral principles, stressing, in particular, teachings on the five lay precepts laid down by the Buddha, and on human rights. The five lay precepts are: Not killing, not stealing, no sexual misconduct, not lying, and no intoxication.

With reference to the tension mentioned above between religious freedom and gender equality, the European Court of Human Rights (ECHR) came to a landmark ruling on 15 January 2013 (see also the European Parliament's LGBTI Intergroup). This proclaimed that freedom of religion is an individual right: "It is emphatically not a collective right to discriminate against LGBT [Lesbian, Gay, Bisexual, and Transgender] people, women, or people of another faith or life stance. The court showed conclusively that the principle of equality and equal treatment cannot be circumvented with a simple reference to religion."

Conclusion: Gender issues could become a driving force for interreligious dialogue and for dialogue between religions and secular societies

From an academic theological perspective, a self-critical questioning of religious practice is needed. It is the responsibility of theologians to speak up when the traditional interpretation of the fundamental principles of their religion does not adequately respond to the requirements of a new context. Deviations and shortcomings should be critically reflected upon, common practice be questioned, and requirements for a positive change – and thus the survival of our religious traditions – highlighted. Theologians of the different world religions, depending on the local secular context and also the global religious context, should demand equal participation of all human beings, regardless of gender and sexual orientation.

The dilemma arises where religions, both globally and locally, lag behind human rights – in democratic societies; thus falling short of observing the fundamental rights by subordinating women to men. Many women are denied equal participation in the religious life, in study as well as in practice, especially when it comes to the performance of rituals.

Hamideh Mohagheghi, an Islam theologian and lawyer, originally from Teheran, recalls that the Koran "in the religious beliefs, principles and rituals [...] makes no difference between the sexes" (2011, 179–180). Nevertheless, "in some places equal participation of women" was difficult. She also speaks of the Islamic principle of self-reliance and stresses (Mohagheghi 2011, 191–192): "The rethinking and restructuring in Muslim societies requires the participation of women in theological discourses."

Katajun Amirpur goes a step further. She envisages the possibility of reconciliation between "Islam and Democracy, Islam and Human Rights" (2011, 212). At the same time, she points out that in Europe one does not have to legitimize everything Islamic, but many Muslim women would seek a way "how to remain authentic – that is, Islamic – but also become equal." She demonstrates (201) that Islamic feminism, as a theoretical direction, has long been established and can be recorded as a successful movement in many Islamic countries. At the same time, she points out that many women's rights activists in the Islamic world still "prefer not to be called feminists."

In the Christian context, Volker Kuester (2011, 75) makes similar observations: "Third World theologians, […] make […] use of the theoretical tools of feminist theology, where it appears to them useful for the analysis of their culture. They equally repudiate paternalisation by their male colleagues, as well as othering by Western feminists."

In Judaism, feminist theology seems similarly advanced as in Protestantism. Thus, the female rabbi Eveline Goodman-Thau (2011, 217) ascertains:

> In religion as well as in the general feminist revolution we are in the third phase: Today women are not only fighting for rights; they have long known that rights are never given, but only taken. They also do not perform endless discussion about the roles they like to play, if they would just get the permission. Now it comes to the rules of participation: Women are no longer willing to participate, if they cannot determine the rules of the game by themselves, or have at least a say.

The Roman Catholic Church is also making progress. On 3 June 2016, Pope Francis decided to raise the celebration of a memorial of St. Mary Magdalene to the dignity of a liturgical feast. And soon after that, he surprised observers by creating a commission to study whether women can be ordained as deacons (Vatican Radio 2016).

It is striking that Morny Joy, describing the extraordinary range of meanings of the term "gender" in a concluding reflection on normativity, already in 2006, made a very similar observation, which in my view is of utmost importance. She states:

> In Indonesia and Thailand, I came across two similar instances where the term "gender" was being used in markedly reformative ways. At a conference in Yogyakarta, Java, I chaired a panel on "Feminism in Islam." One of the women participants, who was involved in teaching women's studies at a local college, was using the word "gender" as an effective replacement for the term "feminism." (The latter term is unwelcome in Indonesia because of specific designations of feminism that identify it only with the

radical form of Western feminism.) In Thailand also, where I interviewed government policy makers, as well as Buddhist nuns, on the situation of women, the word "gender" was also being used in a very deliberate way as an alternative to feminism. In particular, it was being used to argue for "gender balance" in the representation of women in the civil or public service. It also figured prominently in government documents that detailed a programme to combat sexual violence against women. It is obvious that women from these countries, as well as in the UN, have adopted the word "gender" as a substitute, not for radical feminism, but for what, in North America and Europe, would be viewed as the basic liberal feminism of equality. (2006, 19)

It seems that gender equality in the religions will become one of the most important topics for theologians in all religions, thus establishing grounds for a contextual, critical, and constructive dialogical theology.[17]

To undertake such a change or transformation, change cannot only come from the secular, legal side, but also from the religious side. Textual evidence must come from the direct and original source: The authoritative religious texts themselves. Many men and women, with deeply engrained conservative patterns of behaviour will resist change and attempt to justify their beliefs and actions referring to the authoritative texts. Thus, it will be necessary to appeal to the repository of the very texts themselves, and to dismantle erroneous views, by means of hermeneutics, in order to promote progress. In this process, it is the cultural approach that will need to be transformed, not only the canonical texts. Yet all such interpretations, whether local or global, will require to be both contextual and dialogical if they are to be accepted and the goal achieved.

From the political side the state should promote the actual implementation of equal rights for women and men and take steps to eliminate disadvantages that now exist. The religious sphere should not be an exception when it comes gender equality. The principle of equality must take precedence over religious freedom.

---

17. The term "Dialogical Theology" has to be understood programmatically. To develop a dialogical theology is the aim of a five-year interdisciplinary project at the Academy of World Religions of the University of Hamburg, which started in 2013. The first results have been published in an anthology (Amirpur *et al.* 2016). Our research encompasses the Christian, Islamic, Jewish, Buddhist, Hindu, and Alevi traditions. We understand dialogical theology as a content-based dialogue on essential themes relevant to contemporary societies as well as a reflection of dialogue trying to describe its constitutive elements and conditions theoretically.

References

Amirpur, Katajun. 2011. "Islamischer Feminismus." In *Unbeschreiblich weiblich? Neue Fragestellungen zur Geschlechterdifferenz in den Religionen*, edited by Christine Gerber, Silke Petersen, and Wolfram Weiße, 195–213. Berlin: LIT.

Ahlers, Stella. 2005. *Gleichstellung der Frau in Staat und Kirche – ein problematisches Spanunngsverhältnis*. Religionsrecht im Dialog 2. Münster: LIT.

Amirpur, Katajun, Thorsten Knauth, Carola Roloff, and Wolfram Weiße, eds. 2016. *Perspektiven dialogischer Theologie: Offenheit in den Religionen und eine Hermeneutik des interreligiösen Dialogs*. Religionen im Dialog 10. Münster: Waxmann.

Anālayo, Bhikkhu. 2009. "The Bahudhatuka-sutta and its Parallels. On Women's Inabilities." *Journal of Buddhist Ethics* 16: 136–190. http://www.buddhismuskunde.uni-hamburg.de/fileadmin/pdf/analayo/Bahudhatuka.pdf.

———. 2013. "The Legality of Bhikkhuni Ordination." *Journal of Buddhist Ethics* 20: 310–333.

———. 2014. "Karma and Female Birth." *Journal of Buddhist Ethics* 21: 109–53.

———. 2016. *The Foundation History of the Nuns' Order*. Hamburg Buddhist Studies 6. Bochum: Projektverlag.

Thip-Osod, Manop. 2014. "SSC faces fire for female monk ban. Reform trio back female ordination." *Bangkok Post*. 16 December. https://www.bangkokpost.com/thailand/general/450083/ssc-faces-fire-for-female-monk-ban

Bapat, P. V. 1970. *Samantapāsādikā. Shan-Chien-P'i-P'o-Sha: A Chinese Version by Saṅghabhadra of Samantapāsādikā*. Bhandarkar Oriental Series 10. Poona: Bhandarkar Oriental Research Institute.

Basic Law for the Federal Republic of Germany. 2019 [1949]. *Federal Law Gazette*. Part III, classification number 100-1. 28 March. https://www.gesetze-im-internet.de/englisch_gg/

Brodbeck, Karl-Heinz. 2008. "Buddhismus und die Idee der Menschenrechte." In *Wege zu Menschenrechten: Geschichten und Inhalte eines umstrittenen Begriffs*, edited by Hamid R. Yousefi, Klaus Fischer, Ina Braun, and Peter Gerdsen, 155–175. Nordhausen: Bautz.

Ceming, Katharina. 2010. *Ernstfall Menschenrechte: Die Würde des Menschen und die Weltreligionen*. München: Kösel.

Council of Europe. 2016. "Are Religions a Place of Emancipation for Women? Progress and Setbacks." Conference of INGOs of the Council of Europe. Strasbourg. 21 June. https://www.annenegre.com/egalit%C3%A9-equality-expert/seminar-colloque/women-and-religion/

Dalai Lama XIV. 1988. "Eröffnungsvortrag S.H. Dalai Lama." In *Töchter des Buddha: Leben und Alltag spiritueller Frauen im Buddhismus heute*, edited by Karma L. Tsomo, 25–39. München: Diederichs. https://doi.org/10.3726/978-3-653-02896-6/12

DeVido, Elise A. 2010. *Taiwan's Buddhist Nuns*. Albany, NY: State University of New York Press.

Dhammananda, Bhikkhunī. 2010. "A Need to Take a Fresh Look at Popular Interpretations of the Tripiṭaka: Theravāda Context in Thailand." In *Dignity & Discipline: Reviving Full Ordination for Buddhist Nuns*, edited by Thea Mohr and Jampa Tsedroen, 149–160. Boston: Wisdom. https://doi.org/10.1163/15728536-05800058

Goodman-Thau, Eveline. 2011. "Ethos und Eros im Judentum." In *Unbeschreiblich weiblich? Neue Fragestellungen zur Geschlechterdifferenz in den Religionen*, edited by Christine Gerber, Silke Petersen, and Wolfram Weiße, 215–239, Berlin: LIT.

Gyatso, Janet. 2010. "Female Ordination in Buddhism: Looking into a Crystal Ball, Making a Future." In *Dignity & Discipline: Reviving Full Ordination for Buddhist Nuns*, edited by Thea Mohr and Jampa Tsedroen, 1–21. Boston: Wisdom. https://doi.org/10.1163/15728536-05800058

Hüsken, Ute. 1997. *Die Vorschriften für die Buddhistische Nonnengemeinde im Vinaya-Piṭaka der Theravādin*. Monographien zur Indischen Archäologie, Kunst und Philologie 2. Berlin: Dietrich Reimer. https://doi.org/10.1163/000000099124993518

Jackson, Robert. 2014. *Signposts: Policy and Practice for Teaching about Religions and Non-Religious World Views in Intercultural Education*. Strasbourg: Council of Europe. https://doi.org/10.5559/di.25.1.11

Jyväsjärvi, Mari J. 2011. "Fragile Virtue: Interpreting Women's Monastic Practice in Early Medieval India." Doctoral dissertation, Harvard University.

Joy, Morny. 2006. "Gender and Religion: A Volatile Mixture." *Temenos* 42(1): 7–30.

———. 2008. "Women's Human Rights in the Context of Religious Studies." In *Svensk religionshitorisk årsskrift 2006–2007*, Volume 15, edited by M.-L. Keinänen, 181–199. Göteborg: Svenska samfundet för religionshistorisk forskning.

Karmapa XVII, Ogyen Trinley Dorje. 2017. "History in the Making: The First Step Toward Full Ordination for Tibetan Buddhist Nuns." 11 March. Monlam Pavilion, Bodhgaya.

King, Sallie B. 2005. *Being Benevolence: The Social Ethics of Engaged Buddhism*. Honolulu: University of Hawai'i Press.

———. 2009. *Socially Engaged Buddhism*. Honolulu: University of Hawai'i Press.

Koggel, Christine M. 2011. "Global Feminism." In *The Oxford Handbook of World Philosophy*, edited by J. Garfield and W. Edelglass, 549–561. Oxford: Oxford University Press. https://doi.org/10.1093/oxfordhb/9780195328998.001.0001

Küster, Volker. 2011. *Einführung in die Interkulturelle Theologie*. UTB 3465. Stuttgart: Vandenhoeck & Ruprecht. https://doi.org/10.1163/1572543x-12341255

Loretan, Adrian. 2010. *Religionen im Kontext der Menschenrechte. Religionsrechtliche Studien 1*. Zürich: Theologischer.

Mohagheghi, Hamideh. 2011. "Gleichberechtigte Teilhabe der Frauen." In *Unbeschreiblich weib¬lich? Neue Fragestellungen zur Geschlechterdifferenz in den Religionen*, edited by Christine Gerber, Silke Petersen, and Wolfram Weiße, 177–94. Berlin: LIT.

Pabongka and C. Wellnitz. 1999. *Befreiung in unseren Händen*. München: Diamant.

Roloff, Carola. 2014. "Interreligious Dialogue in Buddhism from a Gender Perspective." In *Religions and Dialogue: International Approaches*, edited by W. Weiße, K. Amirpur, A. Körs, and D. Vieregge, 245–281. Religions in Dialogue, Series of the Academy of World Religions 7. Münster: Waxmann. https://doi.org/10.1353/jkr.2014.0006

———. "Menschenrechte im Buddhismus im Spannungsfeld zwischen Religionsfreiheit und Geschlechtergerechtigkeit." In *Religionen-Dialog-Gesellschaft: Analysen zur gegenwärtigen Situation und Impulse für eine Theologie im Plural*, edited by K. Amirpur and W. Weiße, 207–32. Religionen im Dialog 8. Münster: Waxmann. https://doi.org/10.1007/978-3-531-90773-4_14

Schmidt-Leukel, Perry. 2010. "Buddhism and the Idea of Human Rights. Resonances and Dissonances." In *Buddhist Approaches to Human Rights*, edited by Carmen Meinert and Hans-Bernd Zöllner, 41–61. Bielefeld, Germany: transcript. https://doi.org/10.1086/663786

Schüssler Fiorenza, Elisabeth. 1984. *Bread not Stone: The Challenge of Feminist Biblical Interpretation*. Boston: Beacon. https://doi.org/10.1177/004057368504200313

———. 2001. *Wisdom Ways: Introducing Feminist Biblical Interpretation*. Maryknoll, NY: Orbis.

Tomalin, Emma. 2006. "The Thai Bhikkhuni Movement and Women's Empowerment." *Gender & Development* 14(3): 385–397. https://doi.org/10.3362/9781780440217.004

Tsedroen, Jampa. 2010. "Women's Rights in the Vajrayāna Tradition." In *Buddhist Approaches to Human Rights*, edited by Carmen Meinert and Hans-Bernd Zöllner, 195–210. Bielefeld: transcript. https://doi.org/10.14361/9783839412633-010

Tsedroen, Jampa. 2016. "Buddhist Nuns' Ordination in the Mūlasarvāstivāda Vinaya Tradition: Two Possible Approaches." *Journal of Buddhist Ethics* 23: 165–246.

Tsedroen, Jampa, and Bhikkhu Anālayo. 2013. "The Gurudharma on Bhikṣuṇī Ordination in the Mūlasarvāstivāda Tradition." *Journal of Buddhist Ethics* 20: 743–74.

Tsering, Dechen. 2014. "Keine Gewalt gegen Frauen! Tibeterinnen werden aktiv." *Tibet und Buddhismus: Vierteljahresheft des Tibetischen Zentrums e.V., Hamburg* 28(3): 32–35.

4

Continued Discrimination under the Indian Act

> **Beverly Jacobs** is from the Mohawk Nation of the Haudenosaunee Confederacy, Bear Clan. She is an alumna and now assistant professor at the Faculty of Law, University of Windsor, Ontario. She obtained a Master's degree in Law at the University of Saskatchewan in 2000 and an Interdisciplinary PhD (Indigenous Legal Orders, Aboriginal Rights Law, Indigenous Wholistic Health and Indigenous Research Methodologies) from the University of Calgary in 2018. Dr. Jacobs has been an activist and was the president of the Native Women's Association of Canada from 2004 to 2009. Her passionate defence of Indigenous women, who are historically and currently being discriminated against under the *Indian Act* with its sexist and racist policies, is at the heart of her chapter – graphically describing their continued oppression.

Introduction

The amendments to the *Indian Act* over the past forty-four years have done very little to assist First Nations women and their children in their fight to reclaim their identity and their connections to their ancestry. The Act, originally enacted in 1876, has had a few amendments since that time. In 1982, the Constitution Act of Canada was legislated and with it came the Charter of Rights and Freedoms so the federal government was designated to remove any discrimination in all of its legislation. This included the *Indian Act*. The amendments following were in 1985, commonly referred to as Bill C-31 as well as C-3 in 2011 and S-3 in 2017. These amendments have resulted in many heated and disturbing conflicts amongst First Nations people,[1] including First Nations women and their

---

1. As noted in the *Constitution Act* of 1982, an Aboriginal person is defined as a First Nations, Inuit, or Métis. This article focuses on the people who are mostly affected by the *Indian Act*, mostly First Nations women and her descendants. The *Indian Act* defined First Nations people as "Indians;" however, many First Nations people refer to themselves as being members or citizens of their specific First Nation (Mohawk, Cree, Ojibway, Maliseet, Mik'maq, and so on). The term First Nations will be used interchangeably with "Indian" when making specific reference to the *Indian Act*.

children who have been directly affected by the sexually discriminating sections of the Act. This chapter provides a historical overview of the Act, its origins and its inherent racist and sexist policies. As well it discusses those amendments affecting First Nations women and her descendants, specifically the registration and membership provisions that continue to discriminate against First Nations Women and her descendants who are both male and female.

Historical Overview

Pre-Confederation

The early history of the tripartite relationships between Indian nations and the Crown in British North America during the stage of displacement can be described in terms of three phases in which first protection, then civilization, and finally assimilation were the transcendent policy goals. Although they may appear distinct from each other, in fact, these policy goals merge easily. They evolved slowly and almost imperceptibly from each other through the nineteenth century when the philosophical foundations of the *Indian Act* were being laid. (Royal Commission on Aboriginal People 1996).

The *Indian Act* originated in the British policies of the 1850s, before the enactment of the *Indian Act* and prior to the *British North America Act* of 1867. The definitions of membership to an Indian band in 1850 did not discriminate based on gender. For example, the definition of an "Indian" in the Act for the Better Protection of the Lands and Property of the Indians in Lower Canada of this period read:

> V. And for the purpose of determining any right of property, possession or occupation in or to any lands belonging or appropriated to any Tribe or Body of Indians in Lower Canada, Be it declared and enacted: that the following classes of persons are and shall be considered as Indians belonging to the Tribe or Body of Indians interested in such lands:
>
> First — All persons of Indian blood, reputed to belong to the particular Body of [sic] Tribe of Indians interested in such lands, and their descendants.
>
> Secondly — All persons intermarried with any such Indians and residing amongst them, and the descendants of such persons.
>
> Thirdly — All persons residing among such Indians, whose parents on either side were or are Indians of such Body or Tribe, or entitled to be considered as such.
>
> And

Fourthly — All persons adopted in infancy by any such Indians, and residing in the Village or upon the lands of such Tribe or Body of Indians, and their descendants. (Act for the Better Protection 1850, 42)[2]

It is interesting to note that the purpose of this particular Act was to determine who held the rights of property and who had the right to possess or occupy any lands belonging to the Tribes or Indians in Lower Canada. The legislation did not distinguish between male and female registrants.

Gender discrimination began in 1857 with the British Parliament's creation of its civilization and enfranchisement policies through the Gradual Civilization Act.[3] Under this Act, the definition of Indian status came to be defined through the male head of the household. The Act contained many references to "any such Indian of the male sex" in section 3 and "any male Indian" in section 4. In its preamble, it defined the meaning of enfranchisement as "desirable to encourage the progress of Civilization among the Indian Tribes […] and the gradual removal of all legal distinctions between them and Her Majesty's other Canadian Subjects, and to facilitate the acquisition of property and of the rights accompanying it."

For example, an Indian man who could be legally registered as an Indian was automatically enfranchised if he "was not under twenty-one years of age, [was] able to speak, read and write either the English or the French language readily and well, and was of good moral character and free from debt." Enfranchisement happened automatically under these circumstances, which meant that not only was the Indian man enfranchised but so were his wife and children. At that point, they were no longer considered Indian persons. This Act also provided that widows or female lineal descendants of enfranchised men could marry a non-enfranchised Indian man and become a member of his tribe. This meant that the woman, although entering the marriage as an enfranchised individual, would no longer be enfranchised once married. Her status as an Indian would be defined through her husband.

During the pre-Confederation and the initial period of these British policies, changes to the traditional roles of First Nations women changed and their connections to their traditional territories became non-existent once they were forced to identify their status through First Nations men. If a woman married a First Nations man and he decided to become enfranchised, she and her children were forced to become enfranchised. If a

---

2. Act for the Better Protection of the Lands and Property of the Indians in Lower Canada, 13 &14 Vict., c. 42, 1850.

3. *An Act to Encourage the Gradual Civilization of the Indian Tribes in this Province*, 20 Vict., c. 26, 1857.

woman married a non-First Nations man, she lost her status and was considered to be non-First Nations and was forced to leave her home community.

In the *Corbiere* case, the Supreme Court of Canada made an excellent comment on this pre-Confederation period and the patriarchal notions that were embedded in the legislation during this period:

> [I]n the pre-Confederation period, concepts were introduced that were foreign to Aboriginal communities and that, wittingly or unwittingly, undermined Aboriginal cultural values. In many cases, the legislation displaced the natural, community-based and self-identification approach to determining membership — which included descent, marriage residency, adoption and simple voluntary association with a particular group — and thus disrupted complex and interrelated social, economic and kinship structures. Patrilineal descent of the type embodied in the *Gradual Civilization Act*, for example, was the least common principle of descent in Aboriginal societies, but through these laws, it became predominant. From this perspective, the *Gradual Civilization Act* was an exercise in government control in deciding who was and who was not an Indian.[4]

Post-Confederation

In 1897, the passing of the *British North America Act* gave the federal government the authority to govern "Indians and lands reserved for Indians" under section 91(24). Two years later, in 1869, an Act for the *Gradual Enfranchisement of Indians*[5] was passed and provided that any Indian woman marrying any other than an Indian man as well as the children of such a marriage would no longer be considered Indians. It also provided that an Indian woman who married an Indian man from another band would no longer be registered under her own band but under her husband's band. The children of this marriage would belong to their father's band. As a result of the patriarchal notions of this legislation, many First Nations peoples who were once matriarchal (for example, the Haudenosaunee and Mik'maq) and followed the lineal descent of the women were forced into following a foreign process in order to determine their identity with and their connections to traditional territories.

The first *Indian Act* of 1876 was a compilation of existing legislation and British policies regarding Indians. The foundations of gender discrimination and enfranchisement within the *Indian Act* were laid through the

---

4. *Corbiere v. Canada*. Minister of Indian and Northern Affairs, [1999] 2 S.C.R. 203 at para. 86.
5. *An Act for the Gradual Enfranchisement of Indians and the Better Management of Indian Affairs*, 32–33. Vict. C. 6, 1869.

earlier British Indian policies of patriarchy, civilization and assimilation, as noted above. With the 1876 Act, the notion that the status of an Indian was determined through Indian men was reinforced. It is important to note the definitions of a non-treaty Indian, an enfranchised Indian, a status Indian and a "person" according to this Act in order to understand the membership provisions. A "non-treaty" Indian meant any person of Indian blood who belonged to an "irregular band" or who followed the Indian mode of life, "even though such person be only a temporary resident in Canada." An "enfranchised Indian" meant any Indian, his wife or unmarried child, or any unmarried man, who received a letter patent granting him in fee any portion of reserve land. A "status Indian" meant "any male person of Indian blood belonging to a particular band, his children and any woman who is or was lawfully married to him." The term "person" meant an individual other than an Indian. In this context then, Indians were not considered persons. These notions of identity, combined with enfranchisement, would have profound influence on First Nations peoples, especially women.

An Indian man could pass his status on to any woman, whether she was a First Nations woman or a non-First Nations woman. It also meant that even if the man and woman divorced, these women—Indian or non-Indian—would maintain their Indian status. Furthermore, if an Indian woman married a non-status man, she and her children would no longer be considered Indian. This occurred even if she married a First Nations man who lived in the United States, because Native Americans were considered to be non-status. These rules had deleterious effects on the Haudenosaunee and other Nations who had members living on both sides of the border. Illegitimate children were excluded from the membership of the band unless the band consented to the distribution of band monies to the families for more than two years.

The Act also provided that a female "half-breed" was not entitled to be registered as a status Indian unless she was the widow of an Indian or the widow of a half-breed who was already admitted into a treaty. In most cases, unless under very special circumstances, the superintendent general or his agent had the power to determine whether or not a "half-breed head of a family" be counted as an Indian or be admitted into any Indian treaty.

Through the Act of 1876, many First Nations peoples lost control over their own identities, specifically First Nations women and their children because they were forced to completely disenfranchise themselves and disassociate themselves from their home communities. Despite the fact that there were minor amendments made to the *Indian Act* in 1951 and 1970 (as noted in the sections below), gender discrimination against First

Nations women continued. Even the 1985 Amendments, which were designed to eliminate gender discrimination in the Act, have not done so, in fact, the Amendments have caused a tremendous amount of conflict and continue to maintain control over who is and who is not a "status Indian."

1951 and 1970 amendments

Amendments regarding membership were not made to the *Indian Act* until 1951, which further entrenched the definitions of enfranchisement and membership and gave greater controls over First Nations identity to the federal government. For example, an Indian man (whether single or married) could have voluntarily applied for enfranchisement. He would no longer be considered an Indian under the law. If a married Indian man applied and if it was the opinion of the Minister of Indian Affairs that he was twenty-one years old, was capable of assuming the duties and responsibilities of citizenship and capable of supporting himself and his dependents, then "the Indian and his wife and minor unmarried children" were enfranchised. If the husband and wife were separated and living apart when the husband applied for enfranchisement, the wife and children were not included in the enfranchisement. However, if the Governor in Council was satisfied that the wife was back together with her husband, she and her children were enfranchised. A woman who married a person who was not an Indian was automatically enfranchised as of the date of marriage. The point of this assimilationist policy is well expressed by the Supreme Court in *Corbiere*:

> The enfranchisement provisions of the *Indian Act* were designed to encourage Aboriginal people to renounce their heritage and identity and to force them to do so if they wished to take a full part in Canadian society. In order to vote or hold Canadian citizenship, status Indians had to 'voluntarily' enfranchise. They were then given a portion of the former reserve in fee simple, and they lost their Indian status. At various times in history, status Indians who received higher education, or became doctors, lawyers or ministers were automatically enfranchised. Those who wanted to be soldiers in the military during the two World Wars were required to enfranchise themselves and their whole families, and those who left the country for more than five years without permission also lost Indian status.[6]

Patriarchal notions were also re-entrenched in the 1951 amendments. This fact was pointed out in the report of the Aboriginal Women's Action Network (AWAN) of Vancouver (Huntley and Blaney 1999), which argued that sexual discrimination against Native women existed in section 11 of the amendments. The section "dictated that if Native women had children

---

6. *Corbiere*, note 4 at para. 88.

with non-status or non-Native fathers they would not be eligible for status, yet Native men were not restricted in this way and their children could be registered at their request." Furthermore, the amendments had introduced the "double-mother" clause which meant that "if a child's mother and paternal grandmother were non-status or non-Indian, the child lost status at the age of 21" (Huntley and Blaney 1999, 7). A detailed description of this "double-mother rule" was provided by Mary Eberts, in which she described the amendment to the 1951 *Indian Act* as:

> the first and only pre-1985 imposition on what had previously been the male progenitor's untrammelled ability to confer Indian status on children born inside marriage. This rule provided that persons born "of a marriage" entered into after the 1951 Act came into force lost Indian status upon attaining 21 years if both their mother and their paternal grandmother had acquired status through marriage to an Indian. Up until age 21, they were fully Indian. A "double mother" Indian male under 21 could confer status on any of his children born before he turned 21, and they would not lose it when their father lost his. (Eberts 2010, 19)

Eberts provided a clear example of how the double-mother rule works, indicated in Figure 1 below:

Brother #1	Brother #2
Marries status woman	Marries non-status woman, gives her status ("mother #1")
Son A derives status from father	Son B derives status from father
Son A marries non-status woman, gives her status	Son B marries non-status woman, gives her status ("mother #2")
Son of A derives status from father Son of A passes status to his children	Son of B has status only until 21 because of double mother rule
Son of A passes status to his children	Son of B can pass status only to children born before he is 21

Figure 1. Status father and mother: Brother #2 and his descendants are affected by the double mother rule (Eberts 2010, 20).

Section 11 (c) of the 1951 *Indian Act* provided that a person is entitled to be registered if he is "a male person who is a direct descendant in the male line of a male person" who is entitled to be registered (*Indian Act*, S.C. 1951, c. 29, s. 11(c). Further entrenched patriarchal notions of the *Indian Act* were confirmed by the Supreme Court of Canada in 1983 in which "the out-of-wedlock son of an Indian male was entitled to registration under this provision. Daughters born out of wedlock to a male Indian would not be registered, a situation not repaired" (Eberts 2010, 21n7). until the 1985 *Indian Act*, known as Bill C-31, which will be detailed later on.

Section 12 of the 1951 *Indian Act* "provided that the child could be registered as an Indian unless the Registrar was satisfied that the father of the child was not an Indian" (Eberts 2010, 21n7). A further amendment to the *Indian Act* was made in 1956 to allow for a change in this section and to allow the Band to "protest the addition of the child's name to the Band list, forcing an adjudication by the Registrar on the question of whether the father of the child was a non-Indian. If no successful Band protest occurred, the child would be registered" (Eberts 2010, 21).[7]

The 1951 *Indian Act* also provided that a woman who lost her status upon marriage to a non-Indian was also liable to be involuntarily enfranchised by Order-in-Council issued under s. 109(2) of the *Indian Act* (Eberts 2010, 22).[8] Her minor children would also be enfranchised with her even if they were born prior to the marriage (Eberts 2010, 21).

Twenty years later, sexual discrimination provisions reappeared in the 1970 amendments to the *Indian Act*, but this time they were disputed in *Lavell and Bedard* at the Supreme Court of Canada.[9] The case was brought forward by Jeanette Corbiere-Lavell and Yvonne Bedard, who were both registered Indians and band members of their respective communities. As a result of their marriages to non-Indian men, they were no longer considered members of their communities, were deleted from the Indian registry and were exiled from their homes. Both argued that section 12(1)(b) of the 1970 *Indian Act* should be rendered inoperative by section 1(b) of the Canadian Bill of Rights because it denied them equality before the law by reason of sex.[10] As Kathleen Jamieson explains it: "their argument was

---

7. Eberts is citing *An Act to amend the Indian Act*, S.C. 1956, c. 40, s. 3, adding a new 1(a) to s. 12 of the 1951 Act.
8. Eberts is citing the *Indian Act*, S.C. 1951, c. 20, s. 109(2).
9. *A. G. Can. v. Lavell: Issac et al. v. Bedard*. 1973, 38 D.L.R. (3d) 481.
10. It is necessary at this point to consider *s.* 12(1)(b) in the context of sections 11 and 12 as follows:
    s. 11(1) Subject to section 12, a person is entitled to be registered if that person is:
    (a) on the 26th day of May, 1874 [...] considered to be entitled to hold, use or enjoy the lands and other immovable property belonging to or appropriated to the use of the various tribes, bands or bodies of Indians in Canada;
    (b) is a member of a band;
    (c) is a male person who is a direct descendant in the male line of a male person described in paragraph (a) or (b);

eloquent in its simplicity: that the *Indian Act* discriminated against them on the basis of race and sex and that [...] the Bill of Rights prohibiting such discrimination should override the sections of the *Indian Act* which discriminated against them as Indian women" (Jamieson 1978, 86).

In his decision in *Lavell and Bedard*, Mr. Justice Ritchie of the Supreme Court of Canada held:

(1) that the Bill of Rights is not effective to render inoperative legislation such as *s.* 12(1)(b) of the *Indian Act*;

(2) that the Bill of Rights does not require federal legislation to be declared inoperative unless it offends against one of the rights specifically guaranteed by *s.* 1, but where legislation is found to be discriminatory, this affords an added reason for rendering it ineffective;

(3) that equality before the law under the Bill of Rights means equality of treatment in the enforcement and application of the laws of Canada before the law enforcement authorities and the ordinary Courts of the land,

---

(d) is the legitimate child of
   i) a male person described in (a) or (b); or
   ii) a person described in paragraph (e);
(e) is the illegitimate child of a female person described in paragraph (a) (b) or (d); or
(f) is the wife or widow of a person who is entitled to be registered by virtue of paragraph (a), (b), (c), (d) or (e).
(2) Paragraph 1(e) applies to persons born after the 13th day of August, 1956.

s. 12(1) The following persons are not entitled to be registered, namely,
   (a) a person who
       i) has received or has been allotted half-breed lands or money scrip,
       ii) is a descendant of a person described in paragraph (i),
       iii) is enfranchised, or
       iv) is a person born of a marriage entered into after the 4th day of September, 1951 and has attained the age of 21 years, whose mother and whose father's mother are not persons described in paragraph 11(1)(a), (b) or (d) or entitled to be registered by virtue of paragraph 11(1)(c), unless, being a woman, that person is the wife or widow of a person described in section 11, and (b) a woman who married a person who is not an Indian, unless that woman is subsequently the wife or widow of a person described in section 11.

and no such inequality is necessarily entailed in the construction and application of *s.* 12(1)(b).[11]

The majority of the Supreme Court of Canada thus ruled that Indian women were not being discriminated against. Despite this heart-breaking decision for First Nations women, Jeanette Corbiere-Lavell persisted and worked even harder to make this small change in the *Indian Act*. She stated that "women have to take the lead going into the new millennium. They should rely on their traditions, their role models and their teachings. It is important to persist, not to be deterred from the goal of protecting the children, their future and the community" (Corbiere-Lavell 1999, 35).

As noted by Patricia Monture-Angus, the decision in this case was very hard to understand and did not make sense. In her response to the decision, Monture-Angus provides this evaluation:

> The best I can do at explaining what the Chief Justice said was to direct you to look at who is being discriminated against. Look at all Indians. All Indians are not being discriminated against. The men are not being discriminated against. Therefore, there is no discrimination based on race. Look at women […] All women are not being discriminated against because this does not happen to all White women. Therefore there is no gender discrimination. The court could not understand that this pile of discrimination (race) and that pile of discrimination (gender), amount to more than nothing. The court could not understand the idea of double discrimination. Double discrimination is not an acceptable category of equality. Grounds of discrimination are listed as separate entities. (Monture-Angus 1995, 136)

In following Monture-Angus's line of argument, I believe that the Supreme Court of Canada was not willing to take the leap at that time to support First Nations women, and I agree with the obvious: that these women were being discriminated against based on their race and gender. As a result of this decision, Indian women who had lost their status upon marrying non-Indian men had no further recourse to the courts in Canada.

This is why Sandra Lovelace took her case to the United Nations Human Rights Committee in 1977 ("*Lovelace v. Canada*" 1981, 158). A Maliseet woman from the Tobique First Nation in New Brunswick, Lovelace had lost her Indian status when she married a non-Indian man, in accordance with section 12(1)(b) of the *Indian Act*. As a result, she and her son were denied access to education, health and housing benefits. In protest, Lovelace

> moved back to her reserve and pitched a tent on band land because she had no other place to stay. Because of the controversy around her fight, her

---

11. *A. G. Ca. v. Lavell: Issac et al. v. Bedard* 1973. 38 D.L.R. (3d) 481.

tent was burned to the ground. The struggle for public support led her to occupation of the band office, which was also later burned down. Leaders were not supportive: they told her to go back to where she came from and asked her what she was trying to prove. (Lovelace 1999)

At the United Nations, Sandra Lovelace argued that the discriminatory section of the *Indian Act* violated four articles of the International Covenant of Civil and Political Rights, namely:

> Article 23(1), which provides for the protection of the family; Article 23(4), which requires the equality of spouses in marriage; Article 26, which provides for the right to be equal before the law and to equal protection of the law, and protection against discrimination, and; Article 27, which provides for the right of individuals belonging to minorities to enjoy their culture, practice their religion, and use their language in community with others of their group. (Bayefsky 1982, 245)

The Committee made its decision on July 30, 1981, focusing on whether Article 27 had been violated. In doing so, it agreed that "Sandra Lovelace, because she is denied the legal right to reside on the Tobique Reserve, has by that fact been denied the right guaranteed by Article 27 to persons belonging to minorities, to enjoy their own culture and to use their language in community with other members of their group" (*"Lovelace v. Canada,"* para. 132).

The Committee understood "persons belonging to the minority" as meaning "those persons who are born and brought up on a reserve, who have kept ties with their community and wish to maintain those ties" (Bayefsky 1983, 251). Although the Committee noted that Article 27 did not guarantee the right to live on a reserve, it was of the opinion that "the right of Sandra Lovelace to [have] access to her native culture and language 'in community with the other members' of her group, has in fact been and continue to be interfered with, because there is no place outside of the Tobique Reserve where such a community exists" (*"Lovelace v. Canada,"* para 15). The Committee therefore found that Canada's *Indian Act* did violate Article 27 of the Covenant on Civil and Political Rights.

Despite this finding and despite the arguments made by Yvonne Bedard and Jeanette Corbiere-Lavell and by the Native women's lobby groups that emerged after these cases were decided, Canada's Parliament made no attempt to amend the *Indian Act*. As Monture-Angus states:

> The legal advancement of the position of all women in Canada has been based on the struggle by Indian women for Indian women. The result of the struggle advanced by Indian women is the betterment of the legal position for all women. Indian women, however, walked away with nothing tangible, Indian women still had section 12(1)(b). (Monture-Angus 1995, 137)

The 1985 amendments: "Bill C-31"

Amendments to the *Indian Act* were made in 1985 to bring the Act "into accord with the Canadian Charter of Rights and Freedoms to ensure equality of treatment to Indian men and women" (Isaac 1999, 570). Equality rights are defined in section 15(1) of the Charter. The 1985 amendments to the *Indian Act* are commonly known as Bill C-31. There were three fundamental principles to the amendments: (1) to eliminate discrimination from the *Indian Act*; (2) to restore Indian status to individuals who may have voluntarily or involuntarily lost their status; and (3) to give First Nations control of their membership (Indigenous Foundations 2009).

Despite these amendments, there is still a requirement under the *Indian Act* to define who is and who is not entitled to be registered as a status Indian. The Registrar at Indigenous and Northern Affairs Canada (INAC) makes the final determination of their entitlement. The only difference now is that First Nations communities have the chance to control their membership by creating their own membership codes, which has also become a contentious issue. I now turn my attention to the issues of registration and membership and how they affect First Nations women and their children.

Registration and registrar's control

Bill C-31 is the amendment to the *Indian Act* in 1985 that pertains to registration of a status Indian: those who are entitled to be registered or entitled to Indian status are now registered under section 6(1) or 6(2) of the *Indian Act*. This basically means that all registered Indians are "Bill C-31" Indians, not just those who have been reinstated as status Indians (NWAC 1986).

The amendments themselves are not so clear cut, but instead have created confusing subcategories of status. For example, there are six subsections under section 6(1): 6(1)(a), (b), (c), (d), (e) and (f). As a bit of background, I will briefly describe each of these.

Section 6(1)(a) applies to those who were already registered under the previous provision of registration of the *Indian Act* (that is, section 11). Section 6(1)(b) applies to those individuals who are members of bands newly created by government. Section 6(1)(c) refers to the reinstatement of status for those who lost status through sections 12(1)(a) and (b), 12(1)(b) and 109 of the previous *Indian Act*. Section 6(1)(c)(ii) refers to the reinstatement for life of those who lost their status at the age of 21 due to the "double mother rule." Prior to 1985, if both mother and grandmother gained status through an Indian man, they only had status until the age of 21. Section 6(1)(c)(iii) refers to the reinstatement of status to those Indian women who were involuntarily enfranchised as a result of marrying a non-Indian man, as well as any or all of her children from a former union who were involuntarily enfranchised due to that marriage. Section 6(1)(d) refers to the reinstatement of status to those men and well as their wives and unmarried children who were "voluntarily" enfranchised. Section 6(1)(e) applies to those persons who were enfranchised as a result of living outside Canada for more than five years without the consent of the Indian Agent as well as those who became enfranchised as a result of becoming a lawyer, doctor, clergyman or upon receiving any degree from a university. Section 6(1)(f) refers to the reinstatement of children whose parents are entitled to be registered under any subsection of section 6, whether or not their parents are alive. In addition, section 6(2) refers to the reinstatement of status of children, only one of whose parents is entitled to be registered under subsection 6(1)(a) to (f).

Furthermore, section 7 provides two categories of persons who are not entitled to be registered as status Indians: non-Indian women who gained status through marriage under the old section 11(1)(f) and non-Indian women who lost this status for any reason and children of these women whose fathers are non-Indian. There were exceptions added to this section, which guaranteed that the Act would protect women and children who were entitled to status at birth.

When Bill C-31 was first introduced, many First Nations women and their families were quite excited about the possibility of reclaiming their status. However, when they encountered the bureaucratic process of INAC, it became quite apparent that registering would be very difficult. For example in order to determine eligibility for reinstatement, applicants had to produce various types of documentation to "prove" who they were and who their ancestors were. Sometimes, it was difficult to find proof of ancestry, either because the records never existed or because church records had been lost or destroyed in fires.

In many instances, it took two to three years to go through this process. For example, one woman interviewed for the report prepared by Aboriginal Women's Action Network (AWAN) reported that she submitted an application with all of the required documentation for registration on July 10, 1986. INAC received it on July 18, 1986, but she did not hear from them until August 14, 1989—three years later! (Huntley and Blaney 1999, 21). It was noted by another interviewee that INAC did not automatically cross-reference applications from members of the same extended family, even if they all registered at the same time. Each individual person was required to submit her own information. In some cases, the time span in responding to each individual from the same extended family also varied. (Huntley and Blaney 1999, 22) First Nations women also felt that there was no process to assist them with the application and registration process. Another AWAN interviewee commented:

> I don't think that there was any group anywhere that represented the needs of the First Nations People who lost their status. They more or less floundered. And there is nowhere for them to go to. My mother lost her status, she is illiterate. How would she know where she could go to get the help? Because at every turn that she ever had, she had a hard time dealing with government agencies. If it wasn't for my sister helping my mother get her status back, then the rest of us, quite likely, would not even have it. She had problems with her birth certificate and her marriage certificate. It was a big problem. (Huntley and Blaney 1999, 23)

Another issue that affects both male and female reinstated members under Bill C-31 is the process of the registrar's decision when determining the status of a particular member. Many members who are entitled to be status Indians are appealing the registrar's decisions by arguing that they should be registered under specific subsections of section 6 of the 1985 *Indian Act*. In some cases, the registrar makes decisions arbitrarily. For example, a case that clearly illustrates how this has occurred appeared before the British Columbia Court of Appeal.[12] The registrar had removed Christine Joyce Marchand, a woman of First Nations ancestry, from the register. Her registration history began in 1972, when she married a member of the Okanagan First Nation and registered as a member of that Nation; she registered under what was then section 11(1)(f) of the 1970 *Indian Act*. In 1984, she divorced and married a non-member, immediately notifying the department of her remarriage. Her name remained on the band list until 1996, when she was advised by the registrar that it had been removed.

Marchand's name was on the register immediately prior to April 17, 1985, thereby conferring her status under section 6(1)(a). The Crown, however, was arguing that the word "validly" should be included in the section, but the court said there was no basis for this. The court held that if Parliament had intended to restrict registration then it would have done so in Bill C-31 and it would have made it clear in the legislation. The court was unwilling to allow the registrar to start a roving commission to determine whether someone had Indian status. It would lead to too much uncertainty and would give rise to concerns of discriminatory and arbi-

---

12. *Marchand v. Canada*. Registrar, Indian and Northern Affairs. 2001. 2 C.N.L.R. 106. BC Court of Appeal.

trary treatment. The court found that Marchand's name should remain on the Indian registry.

Second-generation "cut-off" rule

It is also important at this point to review the second-generation "cut-off" rule of the 1985 *Indian Act* amendments, which imposes a new rule for all second-generation descendant, that is, section 6(2) Indians. Those persons and their children (the first generation) who lost their status through the old enfranchisement provisions of the *Indian Act* are to be reinstated. In order for the second generation to have status, both parents have to have status under section 6(1) or 6(2) or at least one parent has to have status under section 6(1). For example:

> If only one parent has status under section 6(1), the first generation child will have status under section 6(2). If that child marries another status Indian, their children (second generation) will have status under section 6(1)/f). On the other hand, if the first generation child has a non-Indian spouse, their children will not be registered. (*McIvor* 2009, 9)

An example of this issue was brought to the Federal Court as a class-action law suit by Connie Perron and her son Michael Perron.[13] Connie Perron lost her status when she married a non-Indian man, and her sons were not granted status because of this. When her sons were grown, they married non-Indian women and as a consequence her grandchildren did not have Indian status. Perron regained her status under section 6(1)(c) of the 1985 *Indian Act*, and her sons regained their status under section 6(2). However, her grandchildren, despite being raised on the Tyendinaga reserve and learning the Mohawk culture and language, were not granted status.

Meanwhile, Connie Perron's brother married a non-Indian woman and both became registered status Indians under section 6(1)(a) of the 1985 *Indian Act*, as did their children. Even though her brother's children married non-Indian partners, the grandchildren retain their status under section 6(2).

The consequence of the second-generation cut-off rule is that, unlike Connie's brother, "Connie and Michael cannot transmit Indian status to their descendants. Rather than removing the sex-based discrimination in the *Indian Act*, Bill C-31 merely added to the discriminatory consequences of section 12(1)(b) of the 1951 Act by also discriminating against her children and grandchildren" (paragraph 65). Michael's children will

---

13. *Connie Perron et al. v. Attorney General of Canada.* 1992. Statement of Claim under Class Proceedings Act.

not be able to live in the community once they become independent of their father. If their parents separate or divorce and Michael's wife has custody of them, the children will not be permitted to live on the reserve. Connie's grandchildren will never be able to inherit the family's on-reserve property (Huntley and Blaney 1999, 48).

The second-generation cut-off rule has been termed the Abocide Bill (Daniels 1999) as well as generational genocide (Wilson 1998). What this means is that a status Indian could eventually die off if the parents who are status Indians do not keep track of who their children marry and if the parents do not advise the children who they need to marry in order to maintain their status.

Membership

As noted earlier, one of the principles of Bill C-31 was to give First Nations bands the choice of controlling their own membership. This meant that membership into a particular First Nation became separate from being registered as a status Indian. It did not necessarily mean that a status Indian was a member of her or his particular band nor did it infer that being a member of a particular First Nation granted status. "If a band's rules do not match Federal rules regarding status, an individual accepted as a member of a band may not be accepted by the Government as a status Indian. Similarly, loss of band membership does not mean loss of status." (NWAC 1986, 27).

Following the introduction of the 1985 amendments, all bands had until June 29, 1987 to decide whether or not they were taking control of their membership. According to section 10 of the 1985 amendments, those bands that did choose to control their own membership, a process had been set in place for this to happen. According to section 13.1, if bands chose not to control membership, the federal status rules would continue to apply as long as a majority of electors consented that control of the band list would be left with the Department of Indian Affairs and that the decision to do so was provided to them in writing. This decision did not prevent a band from assuming control of its band list in the future (section 13.1(3)). Furthermore, a band could initially choose to control its own membership but then decide to return control to the Department of Indian Affairs. If a band did decide on this process, it became the responsibility of the department to maintain the band list. The government's rules rather than the band's would then apply.

The Native Women's Association of Canada pointed out an important fact about the membership rule:

It is important to note that a band that takes control of membership can either include or exclude all those 'conditionally' entitled. Again, though, it is important to keep in mind when the band assumes control. If this is before June 28, 1987, the band can validly exclude all the conditionally entitled. After June 28, 1987, the band may not exclude anyone who, immediately before that date was entitled to band membership. (NWAC 1986, 17)

Those who were "conditionally entitled" were mostly the women and their children who were applying for reinstatement of their status. June 28, 1987, was an important date to those who had to register as a conditional member. Bands who took control of their membership prior to this could validly exclude those people. As noted by the Native Women's Association of Canada:

Bands are permitted to shape their own membership codes, and there is no requirement for these codes not to discriminate against Bill C-31 reinstates. There is essentially no oversight mechanism for these codes, and it is very difficult to access them. In addition to these flaws, the separation of status and Band membership penalizes those Bands which do wish to be inclusive: the federal government allocations to Bands cover only status Indians, so that a Band which includes in this membership the non-status spouses and children of reinstates must care for them out of the funds provided for those Band members who are status Indian. (NWAC, year unknown)[14]

This creates further divisions between families and explains the source of some of the conflict. Parliament may have believed it deleted those sections of the *Indian Act* that discriminated against women, but instead it added even more sections that are discriminatory. One of the most controversial issues with respect to the membership sections of Bill C-31 is that First Nations women are bringing cases forward and asserting that their right to determine their own membership is not being upheld by the bands. This has happened because once they are reinstated, they are denied membership by their respective bands that have developed their own membership codes that exclude "reinstated women."[15]

---

14. Ms. Eberts is a litigation lawyer who focuses on equality rights and Charter litigation. She was counsel for the Native Women's Association of Canada, which had intervener status in the *Twinn* case.

15. See, for example, *Noade v. The Blood Tribe Chief and Council*. October 24, 1995. Federal Court of Canada, Trial Division, Notice of Motion, File No. T-2243-95; *Elizabeth Courtoreille v. Walter Twinn et al.* July 25, 1996; *Krahenbil et al. The Queen et al.* January 24, 1996. Federal Court of Canada, Trial Division, Statement of Claim, File No. T-131-97; *Poitras v. Walter Twinn, The Council of Sawridge Band, The Sawridge Band and Canada*

One prominent example of this is the Sawridge Band in Treaty Eight Alberta. The Sawridge Band has been involved in litigation related to aspects of Bill C-31 since 1987.[16] Initially, representatives from the Sawridge Band, Ermineskin Band and the Sarcee Band challenged Bill C-31 due to the belief that only First Nations have the right to determine their own citizenship. The bands felt that once a First Nations woman married a First Nations man from another community, then she must move to her husband's reserve. They believed that "the woman must follow the man." As a result, women and their children could not access what was rightfully theirs from their own communities. The Federal Court found against the bands for a multitude of reasons, suggesting that First Nations had lost the right to determine their citizenship as a result of the *Indian Act*. The Federal Court of Appeal overruled this decision based on the bias of a Federal Court trial judge and sent the case back to trial. It has taken a number of years, but the Sawridge Band has now refiled the case, which will be heard in 2005 at the Federal Court.

Since the initial case was rejected, the Sawridge Band has tried other tactics to deny membership to reinstate women. It devised an extremely lengthy application form, which asked many unrelated questions about membership. During this time, the band only reinstated members of the Twinn family,[17] while other women were denied membership. Ultimately, these women brought a case to the Federal Court challenging the application from and requesting their reinstatement. Many of these women were elderly and one woman died while waiting to be reinstated. In December 2003, Justice Hugessen, of the Federal Court Trial Division, ordered that the Sawridge Band reinstate the eleven "acquired right" women until the Sawridge Band's initial case is heart.[18]

Another struggle that is facing First Nations women and their children who are reinstated to band membership and Indian status is the distribu-

---

(Indian Affairs), September 4, 1998. Federal Court of Canada, Trial Division, Court Number T-2665-89; *Gilbert Anderson et al. v. The Attorney General of Canada*. October 9, 1996. General Notice of Motion, T-2224-96; *Huzar et al. v. The Queen and the Sawridge Band*, July 20, 1995. Federal Court Trial Division, T-1529-95; *Prince et al. v. The Queen, the Province of Alberta and the Sucker Creek Band*. October 17, 1991. Federal Court of Canada, Trial Division, T-2642-91.

16. *Sawridge v. Canada* 1995, 4 C.N.L.R. 121 (F.C.T.D.).
17. The late Walter Twinn was the Chief of the Sawridge Band at the time of the initial case in 1987. He stayed in power until his death in October of 1997. During this period, the late Chief only reinstated his sisters, who had regained their status under Bill C-31.
18. *Sawridge Band v. Canada* (T.D.) 2003, FCT 347.

tion of per capita shares of the bands to which they belong. For example, in 1987, the Garden River Band of the Ojibways received a land-claim settlement and distributed a portion of the settlement to its members on a per capita basis (i.e., the average per person).[19] When the shares were distributed to band members, the band leadership deducted from the shares belonging to "reinstated women" the amount of money that the band had given to these women when they were enfranchised and forced to leave their communities. When the women were reinstated, the band was entitled to recover this money if the payment had exceeded $1,000.00. However, none of the women had been paid an amount over $1,000. So, as a result, the women did not receive a fair share of the per capita payments; instead, they were penalized for monies that they never received.

Therefore, in 1992, a group of women and their children brought a class-action law suit representing members of their class (that is, all of the women reinstated to and entitled to membership and all of their respective children). They argued that they were denied an equal per capita distributive share of the land-claim settlement monies. They also argued against the band's decision that their children were ineligible to receive a portion of the per capita shares. Administrative backlogs with the DIA in the processing of their applications meant that the children had not yet been reinstated when the per capita shares from the land-claim settlement were distributed. Even though the children would be reinstated eventually, the band determined they were not eligible. Thus the delays in reinstatement interfered with the children's entitlement to their shares. To add insult to injury, the band made a distinction between these women's children and those children born to unmarried Indian women who had never been enfranchised and had never lost their status or band membership. These children did receive their shares of the land-claim settlement.

The trial court dismissed the claims made by the women and their children; they in turn appealed this decision to the Court of Appeal for Ontario. At issue was whether the band had breached its duty as a trustee to act impartially by deducting the enfranchisement payments from the women and their children's portion of the land-claim settlement. However, the Court of Appeal found that the band had established an express trust through which to make per capita payments and, that as a trustee, the band was obligated to treat all beneficiaries impartially. By deducting amounts received by the women on enfranchisement and not deducting from other members who owed money to the band, the band was discriminating against the women. Full shares should have been advanced to them.

---

19. *Barry v. Gordon River Band of Ojibways* 1997, 33 O.R. (3d) 782.

The band also knew that the children would have been reinstated eventually. The court concluded that all of the women and their children were entitled to a payment of an equal distributive share without any deduction of any kind. This was a very successful "win" for the women and their children, yet it was a disappointment that they had to take their case to court for what was rightfully theirs in the first place.

What is most difficult in these cases is the fact that although bands are given "control" over membership, some bands are still discriminating against a group of band members: those women and their children who have been reinstated under Bill C-31. The real issue at hand in First Nations communities is about identity and how members of a certain community can determine their identity. Traditionally and culturally, membership was always determined by First Nations women. In order to be true when returning to cultural way and customs, each First Nations must ensure that the women are included in the decision to determine membership.

Unstated paternity

A difficulty faced by single mothers wishing to register their children as status Indians was the requirement of submitting proof of First Nations paternity of their children. Prior to 1985, the *Indian Act* held a rebuttable presumption that illegitimate children of Indian women whom were fathered by Indian men were entitled to register as Indians. In *Gehl v Canada (Attorney General)*, Lynn Gehl challenged section 6(1)(f) of the *Indian Act* and the Proof of Paternity Policy adopted by the Registrar (2017, 133–134). The argument was founded on an infringement of section 15 of the Charter by discriminating descendants of illegitimate children of Indian women based on sex.

In cases where a father or grandparent is not identified upon registration of a status Indian, INAC held the discretion to deny an application. This led to children and grandchildren not receiving status even though their father or grandfather might have status. Between the years of 1985 and 1999 up to 13,000 children born from mothers who held s. 6(2) status were unable to pass on status to their children because of unstated paternity (Gehl (2017, 133–134). The requirement of paternal lineage causes grave invasions of privacy and creates difficult and risky situations for First Nations women especially in cases where woman have been raped or were victims of domestic violence. The Proof of Paternity Policy allows for the Registrar to hold a hearing or consider other evidence where documentary proof is not available due to confidentiality or personal safety of the mother and child. Unfortunately, the process itself frustrates the remedial objectives of Bill C-3.

Gehl initially applied for registration in 1994 upon her grandmother receiving s. 6(1)(f) "full" Indian status. Accordingly, Gehl's father acquired status under s. 6(2) which he could not pass to his daughter as Gehl's mother did not have status. The Registrar declined Gehl's application as Gehl's paternal grandfather's signature was missing from her father's birth certificated nor was his Indian status documented elsewhere. As well, the Registrar did not take into consideration evidence demonstrating five generations of Gehl's Indigenous lineage.

An initiative by the Anishinabek Nation, amidst Gehl's proceedings, brought temporary hope for Gehl for an opportunity to receive Anishinabek citizenship. In 2007, the Grand Council of the Anishinabek Nation endorsed a resolution to develop Anishinabek citizenship law based on the lineage of one parent (2017, 141). This would allow a mother alone to pass on citizenship to her child. Unfortunately, the one parent lineage provisions were removed from the code. This was due to the discrepancies in the proposed citizenship code and the *Indian Act* over funding given to First Nations based on the number status Indians in their nation (Gehl 2017, 146).

Gehl's case was eventually heard by the Superior Court of Justice in October 2014. Justice Stewart, like the Registrar, dismissed Gehl's appeal on the grounds of unstated paternity. The Ontario Court of Appeal overturned the Superior Court of Justice's decision granting Gehl status under section 6(2) in April 2017. Justice Sharpe declared that the Registrar's failure to consider the equality-enhancing values and remedial objectives of the *Indian Act*'s 1985 amendments in communion with the burden placed on Gehl to prove the something that was impossible to prove was unreasonable (2017, 53n37).

Amendments following Gehl were addressed in Bill S-3, *An Act to amend the Indian Act in response to the Superior Court of Quebec decision in Descheneaux c. Canada (Procureur Général)* (Gehl 2017, 53n37)[20]. regarding unknown or unstated paternity and will be further discussed after a review of the Descheneaux case further on in this chapter. The bill received Royal Assent on December 12 2017 and states:

> 5(6) If a parent, grandparent or other ancestor of a person in respect of whom an application is made is unknown – or is unstated on a birth cer-

---

20. Bill S-3, An Act to amend the Indian Act in response to the Superior Court of Quebec decision in Descheneaux c. Canada (Procureur general), 1st Sess, 42 Parl, Canada (assented 12 December 2017).

tificate that, if the parent, grandparent or other ancestor were named on it, would help to establish the person's entitlement to be registered – the Registrar shall, without being required to establish the identity of that parent, grandparent or other ancestor, determine, after considering all of the relevant evidence, whether that parent, grandparent or other ancestor is, was or would have been entitled to be registered. In making the determination, the Registrar shall rely on any credible evidence that is presented by the applicant in support of the application or that the Registrar otherwise has knowledge of and shall draw from it every reasonable inference in favour of the person in respect of whom the application is made.

The amendment suggests a more fluid approach will be taken by the Registrar regarding unstated paternity if credible evidence is available. It further provides that a reasonable inference in favour of the applicant shall be drawn by the Registrar. At face value, it appears that the burden of proof placed on First Nations women to demonstrate the paternity of their children has lessened. To the contrary, the provisions lack a shifting of focus by parliament to protect the safety of First Nations women whom cannot disclose the identity of their father's or children's fathers. Rather than minimizing the discriminatory impacts of historical sexism, the amendment perpetuates a greater focus on the Registrar's discretion.

Clearly, there are a number of injustices that continue to face First Nations women under Bill C-31 and Bill S-3. The Native Women's Association of Canada (NWAC) and the Aboriginal Women's Action Network (AWAN) provided concrete recommendations to address these issues and to lobby for much-needed changes to the amendments. These recommendations included a legal review of the discrimination that still exists in Bill C-31 that would include the full participation of First Nations women in the decision-making process of legal reform and policy change. Both NWAC and AWAN recommended that both the second-generation cut-off rule and the proof of paternity required by single mothers be abolished, and that advocacy and education on all issues affecting Bill C-31 be carried out. Finally, they strongly argued the launching of a challenge at the international level to argue that the effects of section 6(2) of the 1985 Indian Act are nothing less than human rights violations (Huntley and Blaney 1999, 75).

As noted by Martin Cannon, there are three new types of discrimination as a result of the 1985 Indian Act: "inequalities of Indian status, discrimination toward unmarried or unwed women, and the development of Canadian case law concerning Aboriginal citizenship rights…It is the children born to women—not to men—before 1985 who face ongoing legal assimilation under section 6(2)" (Cannon 2013, 36).

Post-McIvor Amendments

Sharon McIvor, a lawyer and activist from the Lower Nicola Band in British Columbia, and her son, Jacob Grismer brought a case before the British Columbia Supreme Court[21] in 2000 and was finally decided in 2007.[22] With respect to the discrimination against herself she argued that if she were a man, she would be entitled to be registered as an Indian, as would her spouse, prior to 1985 and therefore registered under Section 6(1(a). Her child would therefore be entitled to be registered as he would have been a status Indian prior to 1985 and thus, her son would also be registered under Section 6(1)(a). Because she was a woman, however, McIvor's spouse was not entitled to be registered and therefore neither was her child. They argued that Bill C31 and the amendments to the 1985 Indian Act "maintained a discriminatory effect between the descendants of Indian men and Indian women" (Indigenous Bar Association 2017, 5).They also claimed that the 1985 Act violated sections 15 and 28 of the Charter and breached international human rights law, including the *International Covenant on Civil and Political Rights* (1967), Discrimination (1966), the *International Convention on the Elimination of All Forms of Discrimination Against Women* (1981) and the *Convention Against Torture and other Civil Inhuman or Degrading Treatment or Punishment* (1984).

The British Columbia trial court found that the 1985 Indian Act was discriminatory on the basis of sex and marital status. Justice Ross concluded:

> that s. 6 of the 1985 Act violates s. 15(1) of the Charter in that it discriminates between matrilineal and patrilineal descendants born prior to April 17, 1985, in the conferring of Indian status, and discriminates between descendants born prior to April 17, 1985, of Indian women who married non-Indian men, and the descendants of Indian men who married non-Indian women. I have concluded that these provisions are not saved by s. 1. (*McIvor* 2009, para 343n45)

She held that Section 6 of the 1985 Indian Act was of no force and effect "insofar, and only insofar, as it authorizes the differential treatment of Indian men and Indian women born prior to April 17, 1985, and matrilineal and patrilineal descendants born prior to April 17, 1985, in the conferring of Indian status" (*McIvor* 2009, para 351). This meant "that Indian women born before April 17, 1985 and previously registered under

---

21. *Sharon Donna McIvor et al. v. The Registrar, Indian and Northern Affairs Canada.* Statement of Claim, September 20, 2000, filed in the British Columbia Supreme Court.
22. *McIvor v The Registrar, Indian and Northern Affairs Canada* 2009 BCSC 827 [*McIvor*].

s. 6(1)(c) could now register under s. 6(1)(a) and the descendants of these women born before April 17, 1985 could also register under s. 6(1)(a)" (IBA 2017, 6n46). Canada appealed this decision just one week after it was delivered (Cannon 2013, 32n43).

The BC Court of Appeal upheld the decision of the trial judge (*McIvor* 2009, 153); however, the scope of the decision only applied to the claims of Sharon McIvor and her son, Jacob Grismer and held a narrower view of discrimination as follows:

> The 1985 legislation violates the Charter by according Indian status to children:
>
> (i) who have only one parent who is Indian (other than by reason of having married an Indian).
>
> (ii) where that parent was born prior to April 17, 1985, and
>
> (iii) where that parent in turn only had one parent who was Indian (other than by reason of having married an Indian).

This applies if their Indian grandparent is a man, but not if their Indian grandparent is a woman (*McIvor* 2009, 54). As noted by the Indigenous Bar Association,

> in their application of whether the identified discrimination is saved by s. 1 of the Charter, the Court found that the discrimination could be justified as it served to preserve the rights of those subject to the Double Mother rule, which were vested prior to the 1985 Indian Act. The Court goes on, however, to rule that the infringement does not minimally impair the equality rights of McIvor and Grismer as the 1985 Indian Act improves the status of an already advantaged group in providing rights beyond greater than they possessed prior to 1985. (*supra* n46 at 6)

The BC Court of Appeal declared that Section 6(1)(a) and 6(1)(c) to be of no force and affect and suspended the declaration for one year "to allow Parliament time to amend the legislation to make it constitutional" (*McIvor* 2009, 161n51). Eberts stated that:

> The Court of Appeal decision is a deep disappointment. The decision is badly reasoned, and fails even to apply successfully its own constricted comparator group test and standard for assessing whether discrimination has been established. There can be no doubt that its errors in reasoning come from a panicky desire to achieve a narrow result that can be more easily managed by the government. (2010, 40n7)

McIvor and her son appealed the Court of Appeal decision; however the Supreme Court of Canada dismissed the appeal.

In the Spring of 2010, the federal government presented Bill C-3, Gender Equality in Indian Registration Act, which received Royal Assent in

December 2010 and came into effect January 31, 2011. The new amendments added s. 6(1)(c.1) to the 2011 Indian Act, "which permits eligible children and grandchildren of women who lost status as a result of marrying a non-Indian man to apply for Indian status" (IBA 2017, 6–7n46).

> 'upgrades' the status of children of women who had married non-Indigenous persons and regained their status in 1985 from s. 6(2) status to s. 6(1) status. Therefore, the grandchild of a woman who had lost her status upon marrying out and then regained the status in 1985, now enjoys s. 6(2) status (unless their other parent is a status Indian, in which case they are registered under s. 6(1) (IBA 2017, 7).

The following are the specific 2011 amendments to the 1985 Indian Act and grants entitlement to registration as follows:

1) Any person that was registered or entitled to be registered immediately prior to April 17, 1985;

2) Any person whose mother lost status as a result of marriage under provisions related to marrying out dating from the 1951 *Indian Act* through 1985, or under former provisions of the *Indian Act* related to the same subject matter;

3) Any person whose father is or was, if deceased, not entitled to be registered under the *Indian Act* in effect since the creation of the Indian Registry in the 1951 Act, or was not an Indian as defined in the pre-1951 *Indian Act*;

4) Any person who was born on or after the date the mother lost Indian status but before April 17, 1985 – individuals born after that date are entitled to registration only if their parents married prior to it (note: individuals born to common law parents after April 17, 1985 will be entitled to register under s. 6(2); and

5) Any person who had or adopted a child on or after September 4, 1951 with a person who was not entitled to be registered on the day the child was born or adopted (IBA 2017, 7)

The following sets out the criteria that is required by INAC to apply for status after the Bill C-3 Amendments:

- the applicant's grandmother lost her entitlement to registration as a Status Indian as a result of marrying a non-Indian;
- one of the applicant's parents is/was entitled to be registered pursuant to subsection 6(2) of the *Indian Act*; AND
- the applicant, or one of his/her siblings of the same entitled to be registered parent, was born on or after September 4, 1951.[23]

---

23. Canada. Indigenous and Northern Affairs Canada. 2011 Indian Act Amendments – Gender Equity in Indian Registration Act Application for

- it must be noted that despite these 2011 amendments, discrimination continues for those descendants of female Indians who lost their status through provisions of the pre-1985 of the Indian Act.

Post Bill C-3 amendments

Descheneaux v Canada (Attorney General) dealt with discrimination against females who lost their status through *pre-1985* provisions which *McIvor* did not address. Because Bill C-3 did not go far enough to address gender-based inequality and lent itself to systemic discrimination, the outcome of *Descheneaux* was the enactment of more amendments to the *Indian Act* through Bill S-3, *An Act to amend the Indian Act in response to the Superior Court of Quebec decision in Descheneaux c. Canada (Procureur général).*[24]

The plaintiff, Stéphane Descheneaux, had only 6(2) status and his children could not be registered because of his marriage to a non-Indian. Descheneaux's position was that he was deprived of 6(1) status because of sex discrimination (2016, 55n60). His grandmother lost her status after marrying a non-Indian and, as a result, his mother had no status at birth and also went on to marry a non-Indian. Descheneaux was born before the 1985 Indian Act and was thus born without status. Although his grandmother regained Indian status under 6(1)(c) of the 1985 Act and his mother obtained 6(2) status, Descheneaux still did not have status (Descheneaux 2016, 56).

Following the amendments arising out of *McIvor*, Descheneaux's mother obtained status after meeting the conditions under 6(1)(c.1). Descheneaux, however, did not directly benefit from this provision since his mother had married a non-Indian and she was not entitled to register either at birth or before her marriage (Descheneaux 2016, 57). Descheneaux was able to benefit indirectly under his mother's 6(1)(c.1) status and received status under 6(2) (Descheneaux 2016, 57). Descheneaux would have been entitled to 6(1) status if his Indian grandmother had been a male. Descheneaux argued that Section 6 of the *Indian Act* violated the equality guarantee set out in Section 15(1) of the *Charter*. He argued that it created discriminatory differential treatment between grandchildren of an Indian woman who married a non-Indian man and grandchildren of an Indian man who

---

Registration and Secure Certificate of Indian Status. https://www.aadnc-aandc.gc.ca/eng/1309980394253/1309980447982

24. Bill S-3, *An Act to amend the Indian Act in response to the Superior Court of Quebec decision in Descheneaux c. Canada (Procureur general)*. First Session, Forty-second Parliament, Canada (assented 12 December 2017).

married a non-Indian woman. The outcome of the treatment affected the capacity to pass onto their children the right to be registered (Descheneaux 2016, 58).

Descheneaux went on to further argue that this distinction based on the sex of the Indian grandparent is discriminatory because it perpetuates stereotypes surrounding Indian women (Descheneaux 2016, 59). The discrimination upheld the idea that the identity of Indian women and their descendants has less worth or value than that of Indian men and their descendants. Discriminatory treatment, as section 6 of the Act is interpreted and applied, is contrary to the *Charter*.

Other issues dealt with in this case involved plaintiffs Susan and Tammy Yantha whom were illegitimate daughters born out of wedlock (Descheneaux 2016, 171). The discrimination concerned the differential treatment in the ability to pass on status depending on whether the child was female or male. Indian women could not pass on status unless their child's father is a status Indian while Indian men in similar circumstances could (Descheneaux 2016, 172).

Ultimately, the Court was of the view that paragraphs 6(1)(a), (c), and (f) and subsection 6(2) of the Act infringed on the plaintiffs Descheneaux and Susan and Tammy Yantha's right to equality enshrined in the *Charter* and, as a result, the Act discriminated against them by not allowing them to be registered with a status equivalent to 6(1) (Descheneaux 2016, 152–153). The Court declared paragraphs 6(1)(a), (c) and (f) and subsection 6(2) of the Act in operative because they unjustifiably infringed section 15 of the *Charter* (Descheneaux 2016, 244–245).

Although this case further enshrined amendments to the Indian Act, the systemic discriminatory aspects of the Act still exist. As noted by Mary Eberts and Kim Stanton:

> The structural barriers that continue to prevent large sectors of society from attaining substantive equality cannot be removed by piecemeal individual cases. This is so even if we assume that the main job of removing systemic discrimination will ultimately be done by the legislature; the legislature will benefit from the specific guidance of the court on the *Charter* implications of the systemic discrimination found to have occurred. (Eberts and Stanton 2018, 4)

Eberts and Stanton highlighted Justice Masse's guidance in her thoughtful reasons:

> Judges hear only one specific dispute and are privy only to what is adduced and argued before them. They are not in the best position to grasp all of the implications of the laws and their potentially discriminatory effects […] (Descheneaux 2016, 237n57)

When Parliament chooses not to consider the broader implications of judicial decisions by limiting their scope to the bare minimum, a certain abdication of legislative power in favour of the judiciary will likely take place. In such cases, it appears that the holders of legislative power prefer to wait for the courts to rule on a case-by-case basis before acting, and for their judgments to gradually force statutory amendments to finally bring them in line with the Constitution. (Descheneaux 2016, 239)

Following the *Descheneaux*, Bill S-3 was introduced in the Senate in 2016 and received royal assent in 2017. It proposed amendments to provisions of the *Indian Act* to no longer violate the equality provisions of the Charter.

A list of the amendments from Bill S-3 are as follows:

Paragraph 6(1)(c.2)

This paragraph deals with the "cousins issue" identified in *Descheneaux* and corrects the differential treatment in obtaining and passing on status between first cousins of the same family regardless of the sex of the Indian grandparent (where grandparent married a non-Indian prior to 1985)

This paragraph entitles status to children of persons that obtained entitlement under paragraph 6(1)(c.1) as a result of Bill C-3 arising from the outcome of *McIvor*

Paragraph 6(1)(c.3)

This paragraph deals with the "siblings issue" identified in *Descheneaux* and corrects the differential treatment in passing status between male and female children whose parents were not married at the time of birth

Paragraph 6(1)(c.4)

This paragraph arises from *Descheneaux* and provides that grandchildren and great-grandchildren are entitled to registration if they have one parent entitled or deemed entitled to registration under paragraphs 6(1)(c.2) or 6(1)(c.3), and if their other parent is not entitled to registration, or, if no longer living, was not entitled to registration or not Indian at that time of their death

This paragraph seeks to correct great-grandchildren and grandchildren status affected by either the "cousins" or "siblings" issue.

There is continued criticism of Bill S-3. Shanké Sarkhanian stated:

This legal reform may institute equitable change, but misses the greater democratic concern that this change would occur within a colonial structure. I acknowledge, however, that in the upcoming second phase to enact these amendments, the Government of Canada plans to engage in a 'collaborative process' with Indigenous peoples 'to examine the broader issues surrounding Indian registration and band membership.' This initiative demonstrates a decolonized accountability to law, as it holds potential for Indigenous groups to voice concerns and for the Government of Canada to acknowledge Indigenous laws and ways of being to take next steps. Section 35(4) of the Constitution Act, 1982, for instance, could be given more substantive influence over questions of gender equity in realizing Indigenous rights, beyond issues of status. The legitimacy of the Indian Act ultimately remains questionable. (2018, 14)

Sarkhanian recognized that "in order to make this legal reform reconciliatory in nature, those moral values should extend to recognize the values encompassing Indigenous Legal Traditions" (2018, 15).

United Nations Human Rights Committee

Sharon McIvor and her son Jacob Grismer filed a petition to the United Nations Human Rights Committee in November 2010 (United Nations 2019). They, as the authors, concluded in their petition that inequality persists and Bill S-3 did not change this. McIvor argued that she continues to be confined to inferior and stigmatized section 6(1)(c) status and is neither able to hold section 6(1)(a) status nor pass that status to her child (United Nations 2019, para 5.25). The authors requested the UN Human Rights Committee to find that they are entitled to be registered under section 6(1)(a) of the Indian Act. The sex discrimination persists, as McIvor's brother is eligible for full section 6(1)(a) registration status for himself that he can transmit fully to his children and grandchildren—which McIvor, as a woman, cannot (United Nations 2019, para 2.7).

In its decision, the Committee said that Canada is obliged to remove the discrimination and ensure that women and their descendants are granted Indian status that they can transmit on the same grounds as men. The Committee went on to say that:

> 3.6 The discrimination embodied in section 6 of the Indian Act is not pursuant to an aim which is legitimate under the Covenant, objective and reasonable. The authors disagree with the Court of Appeal's finding that preserving acquired rights was a legitimate goal justifying creation of different tiers of status. Preservation of the full status of those registered under section 6(1)(a) would in no way be diminished by extending that same registration entitlement to others. (United Nations 2019, para 3.6)

> 3.7 The continued discrimination embodied in the 1985 Act results in the authors' being denied full status under section 6(1)(a). Sharon's brother and his children, in contrast, are entitled to that status. As a result, his grandchildren are entitled to status, and can transmit status to their children. The effect of the sex-based status hierarchy will thus continue for generations. (United Nations 2019, para 3.7)

The decision from the UN represents an important support for changing gender discrimination under the *Indian Act*. The UN Committee gave Canada 180 days (from its decision on November 1, 2018) to report back on the measures taken to address the issue. We await Canada's response.

Conclusion

When Parliament enacted Bill C-31, Bill C-3 and Bill S-3, its intention was to eliminate sexual discrimination in the *Indian Act*. First Nations women, their children and their grandchildren are, however, still being discriminated against because of their gender. In some cases, they were being denied membership or were being denied service on-reserve because they were labelled "Bill C-31 women." As noted by AWAN,

> The most pervasive long-term effect [of Bill C-31] appears to be the division of community [...] The community has been divided along gender lines with women receiving the brunt of discrimination; with respect to identity by degrees of "Indianness" which have produced stigmatization and racism; with respect to allocation of resources, which has created competition and nepotism; and finally, with respect to the exclusion of future generations from their birthright. (Huntley and Blaney 1999, 49)

Many First Nations women and their children are demanding that the courts recognize just how the whole of section 6 of the *Indian Act* continues to discriminate on the basis of gender and that such gender discrimination be read out of the Act. As a result of this continued gender discrimination, many First Nations women, their children and their grandchildren are still fighting for what is rightfully theirs – a home and a community.

There have been many powerful First Nations activists and advocates who are impacted by the Indian Act and who have fought long and hard against the Canadian government to make and to enforce changes. First Nations women like Jeanette Corbiere-Lavell, Yvonne Bedard, Sharon McIvor, Lynn Gehl as well as advocates Stephane Descheneaux, Susan and Tammy Yantha have battled it out in the court system to ensure their rights were upheld. Another strong advocate for change on behalf of First Nations women came from Pam Paul (now Pam Montour), formerly of the Atlantic Policy Congress of First Nations Chiefs. In considering how traditional approaches used to determine band membership can be detrimental to women, she recommended that "the Micmac and Maliseet First Nations should examine thoroughly the traditional methods of identity determination and incorporate these methods into a modern system of registration" (Paul 1999). These traditional methods of identity determination also exist within the Haudenosaunee peoples as well as the Gitxsan Nation in British Columbia through matrilineal descent. In following this line of argument, membership should be an issue about self-determination. This was recognized in Article 33 of the *United Nations Declaration of the Rights of Indigenous Peoples* (UNDRIP):

1. Indigenous peoples have the right to determine their own identity or membership in accordance with their customs and traditions. This does not impair the right of Indigenous individuals to obtain citizenship of the States in which they live.

2. Indigenous peoples have the right to determine the structures and to select the membership of their institutions in accordance with their own procedures. (2007, Article 33)

In May 2016, the Minister of Indigenous and Northern Affairs anounced Canada is now a full supporter, without qualification, of UNDRIP (Indigenous and Northern Affairs Canada 2017). This should be enough impetus for all First Nations to declare their own identity or membership according to their Indigenous legal orders.

Acknowledgements

The original version of this article was commissioned by the Aboriginal Legal Services of Toronto for its national roundtable discussion on Bill C-31 (Jacobs 2005). I would like to thank Research Assistants Erin Merriweather, third year law student and Irma Shaboian, second year law student at the Faculty of Law, University of Windsor, who assisted with the updated research to this chapter.

References

Act for the Better Protection of the Lands and Property of the Indians in Lower Canada [1850]. 13 &14 Vict., c. 42.

Bayefsky, Anne F. 1983. "The Human Rights Committee and the Case of Sandra Lovelace." *Canadian Yearbook of International Law* 20: 244–266. https://doi.org/10.1017/s0069005800002265

Cannon, Martin. 2013. *Revisiting Histories of Legal Assimilation, Racialized Injustice, and the Future of Indian Status in Canada*. Volume 5, Moving Forward, Making a Difference. Manitoba: Thompson Educational.

Corbiere-Lavell, Jeanette. 1999. "Keynote Presentation." Presented at the Equality for All in the Twenty-first Century: Second National Conference of Bill C-31 Report. 14–16 May. Ramada Inn and Conference Centre. Edmonton.

Daniels, Harry. 1999. "Abocide Bill." Presented at the Equality for All in the Twenty-first Century: Second National Conference of Bill C-31 Report. 14–16 May. Ramada Inn and Conference Centre. Edmonton.

Descheneaux v Canada (Attorney General), QCCS 3555, [2016]. 2 CNLR 175.

Eberts, Mary. 2010. "*McIvor*: Justice Delayed – Again." *Indigenous Law Journal* 9(1): 15–46.

Eberts, Mary and Stanton, Kim. 2018. "The Disappearance of the Four Equality Rights." *National Journal of Constitutional Law* 38(1): 89–124.

Gehl, Lynn. 2017. *Claiming Anishinaabe: Decolonizing the Human Spirit*. Regina: University of Regina Press.

Huntley, Audrey, and Fay Blaney. 1999. *Bill C-31: Its Impact, Implications and Recommendations for Change in British Columbia—Final Report*. Vancouver: Aboriginal Women's Action Network.

Indigenous Bar Association (IBA). 2017. "Bill S-3 *An Act to Amend the Indian Act (elimination of sex-based inequities in registration)*. http://www.indigenousbar.ca/pdf/ibc_bill_S-3.pdf [IBA]

Indigenous Foundations. 2009. "Bill C-31." First Nations and Indigenous Studies, University of British Columbia. https://indigenousfoundations.arts.ubc.ca/bill_c-31/

Indigenous and Northern Affairs Canada. 2017. *United Nations Declaration on the Rights of Indigenous Peoples*. https://www.aadnc-aandc.gc.ca/eng/1309374407406/1309374458958

Isaac, Thomas. 1999. *Aboriginal Law: Cases, Materials and Commentary*. Saskatoon: Purich.

Jacobs, Beverly. 2005. "Bill C-31." In *Feminism, Law, Inclusion. Intersectionality In Action*, edited by Gayle MacDonald, Rachel Osborne and Charles Smith, 175–199. Toronto: Sumach.

Jamieson, Kathleen. 1978. *Indian Women and the Law in Canada: Citizens Minus*. Ottawa: Advisory Council of the Status of Women.

Lovelace, Sandra. 1999. "Keynote Presentation." Presented at the Equality for All in the Twenty-first Century: Second National Conference of Bill C-31 Report. 14–16 May. Ramada Inn and Conference Centre. Edmonton.

"*Lovelace v. Canada*." 1981. *Human Rights Law Journal* 2.

McIvor v Canada (Registrar, Indian and Northern Affairs) [2009]. British Columbia Court of Appeal.

Monture-Angus, Patricia. 1995. *Thunder in My Soul: A Mohawk Woman Speaks*. Halifax: Fernwood.

Native Women's Association of Canada. 1986. *Guide to Bill C-31: An Explanation of the 1985 Amendments to the* Indian Act. Toronto: Native Women's Association of Canada.

———. n.d. "Aboriginal Women's Rights are Human Rights *Canadian Rights Act* Review." https://www.nwac.ca/wp-content/uploads/2015/05/2000-NWAC-Aboriginal-Womens-Rights-Are-Human-Rights-Research-Paper.pdf

Paul, Pam. 1999. "The Politics of Legislated Identity. The Effect of Section 6(2) of the *Indian Act* in the Atlantic Provinces." A report prepared for the Atlantic Policy Congress of First Nations Chiefs. 28 September. Amherst, NS.

Royal Commission on Aboriginal People. 1996. *Report of the Royal Commission on Aboriginal Peoples*, vol. 1, *Looking Forward, Looking Back*. Ottawa: Ministry of Supply and Services Canada.

Sarkhanian, Shanké Melanie. 2018. "Decolonizing Accountability to Law: Reforms Concerning Indigenous Peoples in the Post-TRC Period." *Journal of Parliamentary and Political Law* 12: 425.

United Nations. 2007. *United Nations Declaration of the Rights of Indigenous Peoples*. General Assembly. Sisty-first Session. 7 September. A/61/L.67. https://doi.org/10.1163/ilwo-iiiq14

United Nations Human Rights Committee. 2019. *Views adopted by the Committee under article 5(4) of the Optional Protocol, concerning communication No. 2020/2010*, 124th Session. UN Doc CCPR/C/124/D/2020/2010. http://fafia-afai.org/wp-content/uploads/2019/03/CCPR_C_124_D_2020_2010_28073_E.pdf

Wilson, Jack. 1998. "A Sociological Analysis of Bill C-31 Legislation." MA Thesis, Department of Sociology, University of Saskachewan.

5

Examining Competing Claims in the Dialogue over Sex Education in Ontario: Women, Rights and Religion

Pamela Dickey Young is Professor and Interim Director of the School of Religion, Queen's University, Kingston, Ontario. Her research interests concern the intersections of religion, sex, gender and public policy. Her current research project (with Heather Shipley, University of Ottawa) studies "Religion, Gender and Sexuality among Youth in Canada." Selected publications include: *Religion, Sex and Politics: Christian Churches and Same-Sex Marriage in Canada* (Winnipeg: Fernwood Publishing, 2012) and *Women and Religious Traditions,* Third edition, edited with Leona Anderson (Oxford: Oxford University Press, 2015).

Introduction

In this article, I will examine some of the forces at play due to the introduction of a new sex education curriculum in the province of Ontario. The article examines the recent debate over sex education in Ontario through the lenses of women, rights and religion. It seeks to problematize all three lenses as well as to show how the three categories intersect. It also endeavours to expose some of the power dynamics in the debate. It suggests that we need to find better ways to interrogate religion in the public sphere than either simply accepting or condemning its presence.

The context of the Ontario debate

In 2015, the province of Ontario implemented a revised Health and Physical Education curriculum which included materials on education about sexuality (Human Development and Sexual Health). The previous curriculum dated to 1997. Dalton McGuinty, Liberal Premier of Ontario, had set out such a new curriculum in 2010, but he quickly withdrew it when there was a storm of protest, some of it from individuals and groups purporting to represent religion.

When the (slightly revised) curriculum was reintroduced under the leadership of Premier Kathleen Wynne and then-Education Minister Liz Sandals, there were also protests that either invoked religion specifically or were seen to be connected to religion. It is important to note, that the province's Roman Catholic School system was consulted during the writing of the curriculum. It agreed to implement the curriculum in the publicly-funded Roman Catholic School system where the Institute for Catholic Education (ICE) was tasked with providing supplementary materials to help deliver this curriculum consonant with Catholic values. "In Catholic schools, Ontario's new HPE curriculum is an opportunity for parents and teachers to talk to students about a distinctively Catholic view of human life, sexuality, marriage, and family" (ICE 2015).

The curriculum, especially for Grades one through eight, includes material that some parents and others saw to be age-inappropriate or contrary to the religious beliefs of certain groups of people. The curriculum is not particularly prescriptive. It seeks to provide children with the information they need to make healthy choices about sexuality among other things. Much of it provides guidelines for discussions and issues that children might raise. For example, in grade six teachers are expected to teach about the changes that happen during adolescence. They are not *required* to teach about masturbation as some opponents of the curriculum say. Rather, they are given prompts to help deal with questions as they arise. On the question of masturbation, the prompt does include the following: "Exploring one's body by touching or masturbating is something that many people do and find pleasurable. It is common and is not harmful and is one way of learning about your body" (Ontario 2015a, 175). There is clearly a point of view here, that masturbation is both common and not harmful. But the curriculum does *not* teach children to masturbate.

This paper will not engage in much detail about the specifics of sex education in Ontario. Rather, it will examine certain facets of the debate through the lenses of women, religion and rights. It will raise questions about power and authority, agency, voice, and freedom of religion.

In Ontario, school policies are bound by the provisions of the Ontario Human Rights Code, which prohibits "discrimination on any of the following grounds: race, colour, ancestry, place of origin, citizenship, ethnic origin, disability, creed (e.g., religion), sex, sexual orientation, gender identity, gender expression, age, family status, and marital status" (Ontario. Ministry of Education 2013, 4). Further, "all publicly funded school boards are required to develop, implement, and monitor an equity and inclusive education policy that includes a religious accommodation guideline" (Ontario Ministry of Education 2013, 3).

In addition, some school boards permit parents to request that their children be excluded from some of the content of the new Health and Physical Education Curriculum if they have religious objections. However, they needed to make that request in writing. After the curriculum was introduced, some schools were also permitted to modify the curriculum slightly in the face of parental objections, e.g., using such terms as "private parts" rather than specifically labelling body parts (Rushowy 2016).

It is also important to note that the vast majority of Ontario parents surveyed in 2013 (94%) either agreed or strongly agreed that schools should provide sexual health education There was no appreciable difference between parents of children in public schools and parents of children in Catholic schools in this regard (see McKay *et al*. 2014, 161, 165). McKay et al. also discovered that most parents felt competent and comfortable talking to their kids about sex (McKay *et al*. 2014, 162).

The place of religion in the debate

One of the big issues in studying "religion" in a debate like this is figuring out what counts as "religion" and who gets to speak for "religion." There is a temptation to adopt an easy classification. Media stories began with sentences like: "For Catholic and evangelical Christians, as well as for orthodox Jews and Muslims and assorted other religions who take a doctrinal line on their respective faiths, the restraint of sexual conduct within codified moral bounds is the cornerstone of the good society" (*National Post* 2015). But in such a telling, so much of the variety of religion is left out. And in this recent debate, the public focus, for a number of reasons, was focussed on the vocal objections of some Muslims and, to a slightly lesser extent, some Christian parents.

Before I enumerate some of the positions in the debate, I want to problematize easy characterizations of religion on two grounds:

1. Religion, especially lived religion, is highly variable. So, for example, when the *National Post* lumped all Catholics or Muslims together, it did a vast disservice to the variety of positions within these groups.

2. How do we know when we are talking about "religion," and how do we know when other cultural or social issues are at play? Is opposition to the new curriculum based (only) on religion or might it (also) be based on such grounds as recent immigration or ethnic/community identity?

In addition, when some parents protested the new sex education program in Ontario on the grounds of religion, that does not take into account for the legions of parents in Ontario who are also religious but who did not protest. As will become evident below, some Christians and some Muslims did protest, but most did not. Then, if we link this fact to McKay's research that finds that 94% of Ontario parents want sex education in schools, this means that the most religious parents in Ontario, however religion is construed, also support sex education in schools. "Religion" does not have a single opinion on sex education, nor does "Christianity" or "Islam."

Secondly, it is notoriously difficult, some would say impossible, to separate "religious" influences from other cultural influences. The centre of what the press called the "Muslim" protest against the Ontario sex education curriculum, Thorncliffe Park in Toronto, is also a school with a significant number of new immigrant families. Yet the stories reported were not about how recent immigrants protested. This fact raises the question as to why this protest was characterized primarily as a religious issue.

I will definitely elaborate more on this topic below, i.e. that many of the parents who did protest or did ask for accommodations cited Islam (Selley 2015; Zaheer 2015; Marfatia 2015) as a reason. And I have no doubts as to the earnestness of their claims. But as scholars of religion, we do need to remember that religion, all religion, is a matter of interpretation and that there is great cultural, geographic and temporal, as well as individual, variance on what is claimed in the name of any one religion. In addition to who protested in the name of Islam, there were also groups and individuals who were Muslims supporting the new curriculum. These included the group *Muslims for Ontario's Health and Physical Education Curriculum* as well as sex educators, Sameera Qureshi (Islam 2015) and Sobia Ali-Faisal (n.d.) and school principal, Jeewan Chanicka (2015). It is also important to note that the sorts of protests made by Muslim parents were very similar in content to the protests made by conservative Christian groups, in particular, those issues associated with Charles McVety (Warmington 2015).

An Environics poll in 2016 found that only 3% Canadian Muslims considered sex education in schools as one of the most important issues facing Muslims in their community. But this same study also found that, in 2016, homosexuality was more of a "hot button" issue for Muslims than for most other Canadians. In the recent survey of Muslims in Canada, 36% of Muslim respondents answered that "homosexuality should be accepted by society" and 43% said "homosexuality should not be accepted by society," whereas (80% of Canadians as a whole think homosexuality should be accepted by society) (Environics 2016). These figures are evidence that there does seem to be more division among Muslims on this specific topic than there are more generally in Canadian society. This may well have informed some Muslim opinions on the sex education debate in Ontario.

But it also needs w to be remembered that Canadian society as a whole moved slowly on opinions of homosexuality in the 1980s and 1990s. Further, it is clear that Muslim respondents do not speak with one voice on this topic.

In 2010, the storm of religiously based protest against the introduction of a new sex education curriculum came mostly from conservative Christian individuals and groups (Shipley 2015). In 2015, there were very few protests from Christian groups and none from official denominational voices. Some conservative Protestant and Catholic individuals and groups (such as Charles McVety of Canada Christian College and the Institute for Canadian Values; or the Campaign Life Coalition) were vocal opponents and engaged in fear-mongering (see, e.g., Warmington 2015). Nevertheless, the vast majority of even conservative Christians seems to have been content to embrace the idea that the curriculum was not going to change. They then accepted that it was their responsibility to provide their children with the values they wanted them to have, as well as to engage in dialogue with schools about those particular religious values.

Another important question was: How was religion itself invoked in this debate? The examples I will use here refer to Christianity and Islam, because these were the religions most often mentioned. Those who protested most against the revisions to the sex education curriculum invoked religion as a matter of rules about sexuality (Marfatia 2015; McVety [see Warmington 2015]; Campaign Life Coalition 2015). In these cases, specific religions were understood as static purveyors of a singular opinion and opponents of the curriculum did not want their children exposed to points of view that, in their view, contradicted that opinion.

Religion was also invoked as a source of values. In this case, those who were religious understood it to be their job to inject religious values into the debate in a variety of ways Generally, this was by emphasizing the idea that parents needed to be clear about their own religious values so that children would understand what they were taught about sex (and everything else) in that light. The Catholic school system in Ontario has a huge advantage in this approach because they can do this formally through school curriculum. But some conservative Protestants and some Muslims have come to an approach where they are content to have the curriculum taught to their children and they plan to supplement that curriculum with their own distinctive religious values (see, e.g., ICE2015, EFC 2015, Ali-Faisal n.d.).

Sometimes, it seemed that for the most Ontario parents who would consider themselves religious, religion was not a huge issue in this debate. They wanted their children to learn about sex in school and they did not see that the revised curriculum clashed with their religious values.

Gender in the debate

On the face of it, both women and men seemed to be well-represented in the debate. Both the Premier and the Education Minister (Liz Sandals at the time) were women. Many of the organizers of protests were women. Many of the Muslims and Christians (and of course others) supporting the curriculum were women.

How was gender invoked in this debate?

One of the interesting things about gender in this debate was that, because it is a debate about schooling and education, women were both permitted and expected to be centrally involved, at least as far as their own children were concerned. Many of the objections to the curriculum were couched in the language that parents are the first and primary educators of their children and that they should be able to set the course of that education (see, e.g., the Catholic group, Parents as First Educators; the Evangelical Fellowship of Canada 2015; Parents against Ontario Sex-Ed Curriculum; Thorncliffe Parents Association). In particular, women referred to their status as mothers to support why their point of view should be paramount (see, e.g., CBC 2015a). Women, together with their children, were prominently featured in the protests.

There was, however, something of a gender divide when it came to "official" expertise. So, although moms were the experts or co-experts for their own families, many of the "real" experts were men. This showed up in a number of ways, and not only on the part of those who were themselves conservatively religious. For instance, when TVO's Steve Paikin devoted a program to a discussion of Islam in relation to the curriculum, he invited 2 imams for the discussion as presumed "experts" in Islam. Although the author of a book on how to talk to your Muslim child about the new sex-ed curriculum is a woman, she prominently noted that she passed the book by a number of imams for their approval (Marfatia). Virtually all of the self-appointed spokespersons for conservative Christianity were men. This emphasis on male experts, however, should not simply be attributed to the patriarchal influence of religion. I suspect the media continually keep calling on people like Charles McVety for "Christian" comment on matters to do with sex because they know they will get an extremely emotional, right wing and therefore "newsworthy" opinion about what Christians purportedly think.

Part of my point here is that the patriarchy of some versions of religion was reinforced by forces outside the specific religious group or individual.

If religious "experts" were those whose opinion was seen as most important, and if conservative religious traditions and groups had mostly male "experts," then both the media and other social forces played a major role in re-inscribing the patriarchy of religion.

Another way that women were specifically invoked in this debate was in the way in which Ontario's female premier, Kathleen Wynne, was sometimes portrayed. Because she is openly lesbian, she was the object of *ad feminem* attacks that portrayed her as having a radical, sex-crazed, pro-gay agenda (see, e.g., Institute for Canadian Values 2015; Vox Cantoris 2015). In this, we can see at work one of the primary issues that many opponents had with the new curriculum. They saw it as somehow "promoting" homosexuality, which they found to be abhorrent to their religion and they linked this directly to Wynne's own lesbianism. In this context, there were a lot of conflicting power dynamics at work. Although most opponents of the curriculum couched their comments about Wynne's agenda with assurances that they were not homophobic, sometimes this homophobia was thinly veiled (see, e.g., CBC 2015b). Undoubtedly, it was easier to publicly criticize Wynne because she is a woman and therefore not in the usual role of "expert" and because she was already suspect for her sexuality.

Rights

Part of the context for the debate over the new curriculum were the official documents of the Canadian Charter of Rights and Freedoms and the Ontario Human Rights Code. Both The Charter and Human Rights Code guarantee freedom of religion and non-discrimination on the basis of religion, as well as freedom from discrimination on the basis of sex, sexual orientation or gender identity.

In discussions of parental rights to absent their children from sex education classes they found objectionable, the province made it clear that students could not be exempted from teaching about the antidiscrimination clauses in these documents. Each school board has its own policies and procedures for how that works. Usually requests must be made in writing and are decided on the basis of the specific case at hand. For example, the Toronto District School Board says in part:

- The Board will take reasonable steps to provide accommodation to individuals who state that a specific part or parts of the curriculum of the revised curriculum [*sic*] limits and/or prevents their ability to learn or participate based on their religious beliefs and practices.

- Students will not be permitted to opt-out of specific lessons or classroom discussions about gender identity or sexual orientation. As a public school board, it is important to foster greater understanding by students about these topics and to promote a learning environment that is consistent with the protections against discrimination found in the Ontario Human Rights Code and with the values embodied in the TDSB's Equity Foundation Statement. (TDSB 2015)

The rights of religious parents here were seen as specific and individual rights. Such a practice was in keeping with the pervasive view in Canada (evidenced in many Court decisions) that religion is a private matter requiring private accommodations. The TDSB asserted that "Religious accommodation in the TDSB is carried out in the larger context of the secular public education system" (TDSB 2015).

And yet schools in Ontario, however diverse, are still subject to the hegemonic Christian-influenced forces that underlie them (and indeed there is still a specifically religious publicly funded Catholic school system). And it is true that it is easier for the more liberally religious to see their values line up with the so-called "secular" values of the Ontario school system. Although this article in no way intends to solve the issues raised, it does want to point out that in a clash of "rights" the school system has opted for certain "rights" over others. This raises a question that I will discuss below, about whether rights discourse is the best way to frame such controversies.

It is difficult to make a discernment here about whether, and how religion was impacting women's rights in this case, but I will make a couple of comments. It does seem that conservative understandings of both Christianity and Islam, probably fostered in part, in the case of Islam, by recent immigration, underlay much of the protest against the sex education curriculum. In terms of leadership, the front-line conservative voices were those of both men and women.

Many, myself included, believe that women are differentially affected if they do not have access to factually correct and comprehensive sex education. Studies show that those without comprehensive sex education are much more likely to have unprotected sex (and therefore be susceptible to pregnancy and disease) because they are often totally unprepared for the possibility of sex (see, e.g., Stanger-Hall and Hall 2011). The stigmas on women who do not conform to gendered understandings of appropriate sexual conduct are many, especially in communities that have strongly gendered expectations to begin with (for some examples, see Wiesner, 2000; Sanjakdar 2012; Page *et al.* 2012). Some of these strongly gendered expectations are anchored in religious interpretations that proclaim and enforce strict gender binaries including in some cases the separation of boys and girls, men and women (Marfatia 2015; McVety [see Warmington

2015]; Campaign Life Coalition 2015).

Misinformation

The whole debate over sex education was, unfortunately, sensationalized by the media. When Steve Paikin invited 2 imams to comment on Islam and the new curriculum, the tag line was "A Clash of Cultures" (TVO 2015). Both imams presented fairly conservative but informed and reasoned opinions about Muslims and sexuality. As noted above, both "experts" (as chosen by the media) were male. This whole idea of a clash of cultures fuels an already prevalent idea in Canada that "Muslims" are neither "us" nor like "us." Further, although the media focussed on conservative Christians in 2010, it focussed on Muslims in 2014–2015. Such othering of Muslims both paints a false picture of the range of Islam and invites speculation that "they" are not truly Canadian. Thus, it appears that Muslim assertions of religious rights are not as important as those on which "we" all agree. Never mind that, for example, in the debate over same-sex marriage, "we" did not all agree and those who mostly disagreed, at least vocally in the media, and who claimed the need for the protections of religious freedoms, were conservative Protestant Christians and Roman Catholics (Young 2012).

The opposition to the curriculum mostly claimed to be grassroots (see Thorncliffe Parents Association Facebook page), yet certain themes in the opposition kept arising. The main theme of the opposition was that students would be taught about various body/sexual matters too soon. Yet some of these themes were not based on careful reading of the curriculum, but on a desire to inflame opposition by sensationalizing what the curriculum did *not* say. Misinformation was spread about the curriculum, including things such as that teachers would teach students how to masturbate or encourage anal sex. Many of these themes were found in McVety and may well have had their substantial genesis there, even though they were later used by other groups (Warmington 2015).

One of the crucial ideas put forward by those who opposed the new curriculum was the idea that parents should be the primary sex educators for their children and, indeed, that parents had the right to determine what education their child received. McKay *et al.*,'s study finds that Ontario parents considered themselves knowledgeable and comfortable enough to provide sex education for their children (McKay *et al.* 2014, 165). But as he notes, and as other studies find, what parents said is not necessarily what they did, especially with regard to in-depth discussions. Sobia Ali-Faisal's research indicated that Canadian Muslim parents, for example, do not talk to their children about sex (n.d., 15 September). Both Tabatabaie and Zain Al-Dien found that Muslim parents did not really understand the sexual realities of their children's lives and also that Muslim adolescents really wanted appropriate sex education (Tabatabaie 2015; Zain Al-Dien 2010). My own research on Canadian youth between the ages of eighteen to twenty-five suggested that most young adults, regardless of religious background, did not think their parents talked adequately to them about sex (Young 2018). Most of the 486 young people in my study learned more about sex from their friends and the internet than from their parents, although it might console parents to know that parents were a significant source of sexual values.

The majority of respondents to my study (60%) indicated that religion should changes its views of sexuality to keep up with the time. In other words, although they were conscious of, and took seriously the sexual values of their parents, many of them thought that religiously inspired sexual values needed to and could be updated.

Analysis

We know from feminist analysis that power is always gendered, but in the religiously motivated debate over Ontario's sex education curriculum, power was complexly gendered. Although the two top government figures in the debate were women, sometimes these women, especially lesbian premier Kathleen Wynne, were the target of gendered and homophobic commentary, which the media was only too happy to report. Women were sometimes spokespersons in the name of religion, but they often deferred to the "greater" authority of men.

Because the debate was about education, women were both permitted and expected to have opinions. The "mom" factor is somewhat ambiguous. While it gives women prominence, it also places them squarely in contexts where women are supposed to have at least some power and authority – parenting and early religious teaching. In addition, the rhetoric about parents as first educators was not only espoused by parents but also by others such as religious officials (e.g., McVety, various imams) who had a stake in a particular outcome that was not just about parental self-determination.

In this debate there was also the relatively silent power of the province's publicly funded Roman Catholic school system that already had agreed to the curriculum, in part because it could also control the teaching of that curriculum through official means. Thus, Ontario continues to privilege a certain form of Christianity officially in the face of growing religious diversity.

As presented in the media, this debate was largely "created" by Muslim parents and others who objected to the new curriculum. There were also a few media stories about objectors from other religious groups (Hune-Brown 2015), but the overall thrust was to portray Muslims as conservative and "non-Canadian." If one hearkens to the recent debates over hijabs and niqabs in various Canadian contexts, one can see how very gendered the debate is, playing itself out over an idea that Muslim women (and now their children) needed to be "liberated" from old ways of thinking or that women and their children needed to protected and controlled.

Feminist thinking has come to embrace the notions of intersectionalities and plural feminisms. It has also begun to reckon with the idea that not all women want the same things (see, e.g., Mahmoud 2006). Any feminist analysis of this debate needs to take account of the fact that there are a lot of women, whom we can't simply dismiss as "unenlightened," who want something different for their children than the majority of Ontarians wants.

Further, in this debate, a hierarchy of rights was created when the province and some of its various school boards declared that although children could be removed from teaching about sex when parents objected to the content, there were limits to that. Those limits were seen to be imposed by some of the non-discrimination clauses of the Charter and the Ontario Human Rights Code. Thus, at least *prima facie*, the right to non-discrimination on the basis of sexual orientation was seen by the Ontario government as more important than the right to non-discrimination on the basis of religion.

In the Toronto School Board's policies, for example, religious accommodation was seen largely in terms of accommodating religious practice (TDSB 1999; 2011). As important as this item is, it fails to recognize the full extent of the practice of religion in some peoples' lives and the way it impacts on value-formation. A more complete understanding of religion would lead to a better understanding of the points of view of religious persons even if one disagrees with those points of view.

Rights language is important. It is especially important that people are treated equitably in relation to government processes. Yet feeling included is also important. If Muslim parents removed their children entirely from public schooling, as many in Toronto have, in favour of private schools or home schooling, the "rights agenda" is thwarted (Csanady 2016). Studies have shown that second generation Canadians view both religion and sex differently from their immigrant parents (Beyer and Ramji 2013; Zain

Al-Dien 2010). From my own research with eighteen to twenty-five year olds I have discovered that for most the values of one's religion of origin are far more important than the specific rules. By making this discussion only or primarily about rights, the many ways in which individual religious and sexual identities are molded and re-molded, are lost from sight. And, crucially, the students, those in whose name this whole matter is being disputed, also disappear.

Conclusions

This debate over the Ontario sex education curriculum was an excellent example of the complexity of the three categories women, religion and rights. No one and no group fits in a single place. The debate was an interesting case study in intersectionality. The place of women in the debate was multiple: women in official power, immigrant women, women who have varying views on what religion is and what it requires, women who feel included and women who feel rejected.

Religion, likewise, was multifaceted and cannot be reduced to simple naming of traditions like Christianity or Islam. Religious and non-religious women were variously placed in the debate and religion played many different roles. Not all religious people invoked religion when discussing the sex education curriculum.

Religion was profoundly public in the debate over sex education in Ontario and yet we have not figured out well in Canada how to take account of religion when it spills over into public life. Perhaps we can take some hints from the development of LGBTTQI rights. In the first Trudeau era, Canadians became, on the whole, content to not investigate in depth what happens in the bedrooms of the nation, as long as it did not spill out into the streets. And yet, once it did spill over, Canadians had to reckon with LGBTTQI claims for public space and recognition. That has happened, and there is no going back. In my opinion, this needs to be done for the sake of religion, not just for the assumed and pseudo-established Protestant and Catholic Christianities, which are now largely read as "secular" anyway, but because religion needs to be engaged robustly. As Canadians, we need to be prepared to talk about differences of values. And we also need to see how those differences are internal to religious traditions as well as between religions or between religions and other cultural forms. If religious rights mean anything then we have to debate and interrogate religion rather than fear its covert forms.

Rights are complex and sometimes official systems need recourse to rights to sort out what to do and whom to privilege when groups are, as groups, disadvantaged. Sometimes the only way to mobilize change is to use rights discourse. But rights discourse often assumes that we are in a single category, say, "Muslim" and looking for rights on that basis. Yet we are always simultaneously involved in several categories. Identity is complex (see, e.g., Sharma 2006; Collins *et al.* 2010). Nevertheless, inclusion is also important and much more work needs to be done on the inclusion of religion in public life than what is being presently done in the province of Ontario and in Canada more broadly.

What I hope this article does, then, is not to answer a question but to problematize the discourse of rights and religion and to indicate the ways that debates need to be carried on simultaneously at the level of rights and at the level of local contextual details.[1]

References

Ali-Faisal, Sobia. n.d. "Writing about Health, Culture, Society and Psychology." https://sobiaalifaisal.com/page/2/

Beyer, Peter, and Rubina Ramji. 2013. *Growing Up Canadian: Muslims, Hindus, Buddhists*. Montreal and Kingston: McGill-Queen's University Press.

Campaign Life Coalition. 2015. "Ontario's Radical Sex Ed Curriculum." http://www.campaignlifecoalition.com/index.php?p=Sex_Ed_Curriculum

Canadian Broadcasting Corporation. 2015a. "Ontario Sex-ed Dispute: Why 1 Mother Will Keep Her Kids Home." 9 September. http://www.cbc.ca/news/canada/toronto/sex-education-ontario-curriculum-1.3220454

———. 2015b. "Ontario Sex-ed Protest 'Unlike Anything I've Ever Experienced,' Principal Says." 1 October. http://www.cbc.ca/news/canada/toronto/ontario-sex-ed-protest-1.3251799

Chanika, Jeewan. 2015. "A Muslim Principal on Ontario's New Sex Ed Curriculum." 28 February. *Muslim Link*. http://muslimlink.ca/in-focus/opinions/newsexedcurriculum

Collins, Dana, Sylvanna Falcon, Sharmila Lodhia, and Molly Talcott. 2010. "New Directions in Feminism and Human Rights." *International Feminist*

---

1. In 2018, the new Conservative government in Ontario under Premier Doug Ford scrapped the 2015 Health and Physical Education curriculum and mandated a return to a 2010 curriculum, including a document on sexual health from 1998. A subsequent court challenge in February 2019 determined that, although this change back to an earlier curriculum was not a violation of Canadian Charter rights, teachers could exercise a good deal of discretion in deciding how to deal with sexual consent, naming of body parts, sexual and gender identity, etc., things that were explicitly discussed in the 2015 curriculum. The Conservative government has promised a revised curriculum in the fall of 2019, but there is no clear sense of how such a curriculum will deal with those topics that seem most to offend Ford supporters.

Journal of Politics 12 (3–4): 298–319. https://doi.org/10.1080/14616742.2010.513096

Csanady, Ashley. 2016. "One in ix Ontario Parents Considered Pulling Kids from School over New Sex-ed Curriculum: Poll." *National Post*. 3 June. http://news.nationalpost.com/news/canada/canadian-politics/one-in-six-ontario-parents-considered-pulling-kids-from-school-over-new-sex-ed-curriculum-poll

Environics. 2016. Survey of Muslims in Canada 2016. http://www.environicsinstitute.org/uploads/institute-projects/survey%20of%20muslims%20in%20canada%202016%20-%20final%20report.pdf

Evangelical Fellowship of Canada. 2015. "Ontario's Revised Health and Physical Education Curriculum (2015)." http://www.evangelicalfellowship.ca/ef.ca/si/revised-ontario-curriculum-letter-writing

Hune-Brown, Nicholas. 2015. "The Sex Ed Revolution: A Portrait of the Powerful Political Bloc that's Waging War on Queen's Park." *TorontoLife*. 3 September. http://torontolife.com/city/ontario-sex-ed-revolution/

Institute for Canadian Values. 2015. "Stop the Wynne-Levin Sex-Ed Program." http://canadianvalues.ca/ICV/stopcorruptingchildren/?page_id=2452.

Institute for Catholic Education. 2015. *A Parent's Guide to Understanding Family Life Education in Catholic Schools (and How It Connects with Ontario's Revised Health and Physical Education Curriculum)*. http://iceont.ca/resources/parent-resources/health-physical-education-resources/

Islam, Sanam. 2015. "Breaking the Taboo: Why a Calgary Therapist is Teaching Muslims to Talk about Sexual Health." *Muslim Link*. 20 November. http://muslimlink.ca/in-focus/breaking-the-taboo-muslims-sexual-health

Mahmoud, Saba. 2006. "Agency, Performativity and the Feminist Subject." In *Bodily Citations: Religion and Judith Butler*, edited by Ellen T. Armour and Susan M. St. Ville, 177–217. New York: Columbia University Press.

Marfatia, Farrah. 2015. *How to Talk to Your Muslim Child about Topics in the Ontario Ministry of Education's Health Education Curriculum*. Self-published.

McKay, Alexander, E. Sandra Byers, Susan D. Voyer, Terry P. Humphreys, and Chris Markham. 2014. "Ontario Parents' Opinions and Attitudes towards Sexual Health Education in the Schools." *Canadian Journal of Human Sexuality* 23(3): 159–167. https://doi.org/10.3138/cjhs.23.3-a1

Muslims for Ontario's Health and Physical Education Curriculum. https://www.facebook.com/MuslimsforOntariosNewHealthPhysCurriculum

National Post. 2015. "The Parents' Sex Ed Rebellion." View section. 6 October. http://news.nationalpost.com/full-comment/national-post-view-the-parents-rebellion-to-sex-ed

Ontario. Ministry of Education. 2013. Policy/Program Memorandum No. 11. 23 April. https://edu.gov.on.ca/extra/eng/ppm/119.pdf

Ontario, 2015a. *The Ontario Curriculum, Grades 1–8; Health and Physical Education.* http://www.edu.gov.on.ca/eng/curriculum/elementary/health1to8.pdf

Ontario, 2015b. *The Ontario Curriculum, Grades 9–12, Health and Physical Education.* http://www.edu.gov.on.ca/eng/curriculum/secondary/health-9to12.pdf

Page, Sarah-Jane, Andrew Kam-Tuck Yip, and Michael Keenan. 2012. "Risk and the Imagined Future: Young Adults Negotiating Religious and Sexual Identities." In *The Ashgate Research Companion to Contemporary Religion and Sexuality*, edited by Stephen Hunt and Andrew K. T. Yip, 255–270. Farnham, UK: Ashgate. https://doi.org/10.18352/rg.10190

Parents against Ontario Sex-Ed Curriculum. n.d. https://www.facebook.com/Parents-Against-Ontario-Sex-Ed-Curriculum-1620174608211662/home

Parents as First Educators. n.d. https://www.facebook.com/pafe4/

Rushowy, Kristin. 2016. "Toronto School Offers Sanitized Sex-ed Amid Parent Concern." *Toronto Star.*

Sanjakdar, Fida. 2012. "Probing the Boundaries: How Religion and Sexuality Are Negotiated within Islamic Educational Institutions." In *The Ashgate Research Companion to Contemporary Religion and Sexuality*, edited by Stephen Hunt and Andrew K. T. Yip, 157–172. Farnham, UK: Ashgate. https://doi.org/10.4324/9781315612836

Selley, Chris. 2015. "Muslim Community Taking the Lead in Latest Rounds of Ontario Sex-Education Protests." *National Post.* 5 May. http://news.nationalpost.com/news/canada/muslim-community-taking-the-lead-in-latest-round-of-ontario-sex-education-protests

Sharma, Jaya. 2006. "Reflections on the Language of Rights from a Queer Perspective." *IDS Bulletin* 37(5): 52–57. https://doi.org/10.1111/j.1759-5436.2006.tb00302.x

Shipley, Heather. 2015. "Challenging Identity Construct: The Debate over the Sex Education Curriculum in Ontario." In *Religion and Sexuality: Diversity and the Limits of Tolerance*, edited by Pamela Dickey Young, Heather Shipley and Tracy Trothen, 97–118. Vancouver: University of British Columbia Press. https://doi.org/10.3138/utq.85.3.329

Stanger-Hall, Kathrin F. and David W. Hall. 2011. "Abstinence-Only Education and Teen Pregnancy Rates: Why We Need Comprehensive Sex Education in the U.S." *PLoS ONE* 6(10): 1–11. https://doi.org/10.1371/journal.pone.0024658

Tabatabaie, Alireza. 2015. "Childhood and Adolescent Sexuality, Islam, and Problematics of Sex Education: A Call for Re-examination." *Sex Education* 15 (3): 276–288. https://doi.org/10.1080/14681811.2015.1005836

Thorncliffe Parents Association. n.d. https://www.facebook.com/thorncliffeparents/info/?entry_point=page_nav_about_item&tab=page_info

Toronto District School Board. 1999. "Equity Foundation Statement." http://www2.tdsb.on.ca/ppf/uploads/files/live/102/200.pdf

———. 2011. "Guidelines and Procedures for Religious Accommodation." http://www.tdsb.on.ca/Portals/0/HighSchool/docs/Guidelines%20and%20Procedures%20for%20Religious%20Accommodations.pdf

———. 2015. "Revised Health and Physical Education Curriculum." http://www.tdsb.on.ca/highschool/yourschoolday/curriculum/healthandphysicaleducation/revisedhealthandphysicaleducationcurriculum.aspx

TVO. 2015. "Sex Ed and Islam." http://tvo.org/video/programs/the-agenda-with-steve-paikin/sex-ed-and-islam

Vox Cantoris. 2015. "Ontario's Lesbian Premier's Perverted Sex Education Agenda." http://voxcantor.blogspot.ca/2015/01/ontarios-lesbian-premiers-perverted-sex.html

Warmington, Joe. 2015. "New Sex Ed curriculum under fire." *Toronto Sun*. 3 February. http://www.torontosun.com/2015/02/23/new-sex-ed-curriculum-under-fire

Wiesner, Merry E. 2000. *Christianity and Sexuality in the Early Modern World: Regulating Desire, Reforming Practice*. Abingdon: Routledge. https://doi.org/10.4324/9781315787350

Young, Pamela Dickey. 2012. *Religion, Sex and Politics*: *Christian Churches and Same-Sex Marriage in Canada*. Winnipeg: Fernwood. https://doi.org/10.18352/rg.9177

———. 2018. "Informal Sex Education: Forces that Shape Youth Identities and Practices." In *Critical Pedagogy, Sexuality Education and Young People*, edited by Andrew Yip and Fida Sanjakdar, 149–166. New York: Peter Lang. https://doi.org/10.3726/b11365

Zaheer, Javd, 2015. "People Determined to Fight for Rights, Oppose and Reject Bad Policies and Leaders." 10 May. *Hamari Web*. http://www.hamariweb.com/articles/article.aspx?id=60625

Zain Al-Dien, Muhammad M. 2010. "Perceptions of Sex Education among Muslim Adolescents in Canada." *Journal of Muslim Minority Affairs* 30(3): 391–407. https://doi.org/10.1080/13602004.2010.515823

6

Women's Rights and Religion: Jewish Style

Norma Baumel Joseph teaches in the Department of Religions and Cultures of Concordia University, Montreal, where her teaching and research areas include women and Judaism, Jewish law and ethics, and women and religion. She is an Associate of the Institute for Canadian Jewish Studies. Norma was also the founding co-director and currently associate director of the Azrieli Institute for Israel Studies. Two of her recent publications are: "T'beet: Situating Iraqi Jewish Identity through Food." In *Everyday Sacred: Religious Lives and Landscapes in Quebec*, edited by Hillary Kael (2007), and "Food, Gift, Women Gift-Givers: A Taste of Jewishness." In *Women, Religion and the Gift: An Abundance of Riches*, edited by Morny Joy (2017).

Introduction

Feminist critical approaches to religions have often been marked by a Western hegemony, discrediting traditionalists with sweeping claims of women's oppression and suppression. But much is lost in this universalist and absolutist position. Current approaches embracing diversity and cultural particularities open a door to considering auspicious heritage patterns. In this frame of reference, rights may not be the language appropriate for a universal application or for a constructive critique.

The Jewish take on rights and responsibilities

The Canadian Charter of Rights and Freedoms is a useful document principally in terms of women's proposed self-determination. It has been used successfully in the courts and in public policy situations to clarify and promote gender parity. Yet some translations of this document suggest subtle shifts of meaning and application. Attention to these various translations yields consideration of cultural diversities inherent in our multicultural context, concerns that should have been at the forefront of our legal development.[1]

---

1. I raised this issue at a similar event in Quebec (Joseph 2006).

For example, the official Hebrew document of the Montreal Charter uses provocatively different words. Parsing the distinctions depicts an attention to cultural diversity and a thought-provoking application for feminist concerns. The Hebrew translation, which claims consonance with the United Nations (UN) and Canadian charters, is titled the Montreal Charter of Rights and Obligations. Using the word "obligations" clarifies the attentiveness in the document to the Jewish community's exceptional focus. As Morny Joy (2013) has written, the notion of "rights is both a limited and limiting strategy."

In Judaism, the case for individual rights and freedoms is arguably a complicated matter. The legal issues are often presented within a rabbinic tradition that frequently argued against the language of purely personal freedom. God had to be at the centre of the conventions of rights and responsibilities. From that perspective, humans are responsible to God so that God manages it all, and one could not argue against God's determination, could one? Additionally, the classical conservatism within the tradition contended that the configurations of rights and freedoms must be presented within a communal framework, thereby eliminating the purely personal form. Finally, even in the modern period of rampant individuation, Jews were suspicious of feminist claims for equality. Opinions about women's rights and freedoms may have been easily accepted on a philosophical level, but socio-politically, in all sectors, women did not easily attain concrete privileges of representation or leadership. Nonetheless, many Jewish women did feel that they were indeed freely choosing their place in a community of equals. They did sense that their roles were valued and cherished. They did not consider themselves oppressed or victimized and were unwilling to accept feminist versions of their religious or traditional oppression. They shied away from outside criticism that often appeared to them to come from a place of anti-Semitism. Furthermore, Jewish women were not willing to allow outsider women to proclaim their rights or freedom requirements. This format did not appear to be feminist liberation. In the twenty-first century, feminist scholars have acknowledged and recognized the authenticity of this reproach.

Yet, away from the glare of outsiders, within the Jewish community, issues of women's rights and participation are nevertheless pervasive. The context should be carefully extrapolated so that the discussion rests on concrete legal and socio-political bases. As has been noted, Judaism as a legal entity focuses most clearly on the issues of obligations. Jewish legal doctrine sees all Jews not as entitled citizens, but as entities commanded by God, free to be obligated.² The applicable Hebrew word is *mitzvah*, poorly translated as "good deed" when it actually means "commandment." Thus, the Jewish community's translation might be an opportunity, not to dismiss a traditional legal standard as regressive and oppressive (though it might be that), but rather to present a case study through which we can examine an alternate path of women's full emancipation; i.e., the path to women's full participation and recognition may differ from one culture to another.

Thus, from a feminist critical perspective, much of Judaism's admittedly problematic conception of "woman" would be restructured if women were to be considered fully obligated instead of ritually exempt in particular categories.³ To be fully obligated would then render the legal and ritual distinctions between men and women null and void. Fully obligated women become full Jews, uniformly and practically included in the covenantal community and therefore functioning as ritually equal to men. One clarification is necessary. Women are and always were fully Jewish. As is abundantly clear from the genealogical factum, one is a Jew if one's mother is a Jew. In other words, Jewishness is passed on through the maternal lineage. Obviously, then, women are Jews: Full Jews. There is no hesitancy or imbroglio. Furthermore, female Jews are part of the divine covenant established at Sinai: Again no impediment, no impurity, and no gender distinction here.⁴ But since there are ritual exemptions that lead to ritual exclusions or prohibitions, many read this as clear indication of women's second-class citizenship. Fully obligated corrects for the ritual imbalance and, thus, establishes equilibrium in communal participation and leadership. But is this sufficient?

Two problems

Two acute questions persist. One is whether this type of change of perspective is possible. The other, perhaps more pressing, is whether such a legal conception would solve all the issues of discrimination or gender disequilibrium. Addressing the latter is the intent of this paper.

---

2. In this sense Genesis 1:27 is taken seriously to mean that men and women are created equally in the image of God: Equally obligated to God.
3. The list of ritual exemptions is short: fourteen. But the consequences are extensive. See Biale (1984); Joseph (2005).
4. There are commentaries about men being commanded to stay away from women at Sinai (Exodus 19:15), but whatever it meant in terms of sexual prohibition, it did not mean that women were not there at the mountain participating in revelation.

Confronting the first question simply and briefly, as a feminist and as a Jew, I would say that women must be considered full-obligated Jews today. I know there are sociological and psychological barriers. But given the vast changes already experienced in all sectors of the Jewish world, it is more than possible to change the communal perspective. The issue of equality on the table is not a matter of the absence of difference in nature or physicality. Feminist Jews, as far as the situation has been defined, are not claiming identicality. Equality and equivalence are not issues of androgyny or removal of all distinctions. In fact, recognizing diversity in gender identity is gaining recognition and convention. Rather the problematic is existential and theological equivalence.

The problem persists in a legal tradition that created discrepancies of status and practice and is over two thousand years old. Changing it would be fundamental, and certainly the Jews of a *haredi* (ultra-pietistic) persuasion argue against all change. They perceive gender roles as biblically defined and permanent. Yet shifts are possible and have been taking place. Over time and in response to varying conditions, rabbinic opinion and decisions pertaining to community and personal praxis have been altered to include women and give them a wider range of spiritual expression – even in the most ultra-pietistic communities.

One critical example of the above point is found in association with Torah (Bible and Talmud) study from which women were either exempt or prohibited. Today, women, *especially in the Orthodox community*, have gained entry into this exclusive world. The concomitant change in status and role is slowly overtaking the Jewish world.[5] The reality of women studying and teaching Torah with all its concentrated meanings is shifting the discourse from exempt to obligated. Watching that movement is illustrative of my point.

This shift in perspective on women's participation and obligation is occurring in all sectors of the Jewish world, expanding conceptions of women's rights and responsibilities. Escalating that to an overall impulse of obligation, of all women being obligated, is taking time and courageous leadership. Many assume the recalcitrants are only in the Orthodox world. That is not the case. It is ironically within the Orthodox world that this transformation in Jewish education has taken place. Furthermore, when the Conservative rabbinate began including women in the prayer quorum and synagogue rituals, they erred by not simply declaring women fully obligated Jews. They were afraid of the negative reaction from men and

---

5. Recently, the *Jerusalem Post* began a series of articles on just how much text study has changed Jewish leadership in Israel (Keats-Jaskoll 2019).

from the women who did not want to add more rituals to their daily routine. This left them with some very troubling decisions when it came time to ordain women rabbis. Clearly, the path to modification within a traditional community is challenging, especially when women's rights are involved.

But my main concern resides within the second theme: Is disequilibrium built into the basic fabric of Judaic tradition and praxis, separate from issues of ritual exemptions and obligations. Consideration and demonstration of this problem is exemplified best in the case of Jewish divorce, its laws and practices. I argue that it is explicitly in divorce that all criticism of *halakha* (Jewish law) from a feminist perspective finds its cumulative or symbolic centre. It is here in Jewish divorce that women's rights are trampled most reprehensibly.

Jewish divorce

Jewish divorce, like any other, can be simple or complicated; a release or a tragedy; straightforward or a swindle. It can set people free to resume or reinvent their lives, or it can involve whole families in constant conflicts and harassment. The original intent of rabbinic Judaism was to ensure a tolerable disengagement. Regrettably, the current implementation does not ensure that minimal standard. And, although primarily an Orthodox issue, it also affects many other Jews, especially those living in Israel where all divorces are determined by Jewish law and not civil law.[6] The problem is that, according to biblical law (Deuteronomy 24:1), it is the husband who must initiate a divorce. If he is either unable or unwilling to give her a *get* (Jewish bill of divorce), she cannot ever remarry. Divorce Jewish style can thus become a tool for extortion on the part of the husband and embroil individuals and families in a never-ending cycle of abuse.

Jewish women who do not receive their divorce are known as *agunot* (pl.), chained women. An *agunah* (singular) is a woman who cannot remarry because her husband will not give her a *get* (Jewish divorce). The original talmudic use of the word *agunah* was limited to cases in which the man had disappeared and literally could not act as a legal channel in the Jewish divorce proceedings. Recently, popular usage has expanded the term to apply to all cases of women who are unable to remarry because their husbands will not acquiesce and present the divorce document. Since the rabbinic court cannot authorize the writing of the *get*, and only a man

---

6. There is no civil divorce in Israel. Religious heritage courts mandate marriage and divorce, and all personal status issues.

can initiate the proceedings, problems arise most frequently for women, although the term can be applied to men (*agun*).[7]

To clarify, the biblical account of divorce is found in Deuteronomy, which accepts marital break-ups and establishes a procedure that is at the heart of the problem.

> When a man has taken a wife, and married her, and it come to pass that she find no favour in his eyes, because he has found some unseemliness in her: then let him write her a bill of divorce, and give it in her hand, and send her out of his house. And when she is departed out of his house, she may go and be another man's wife. (Deut. 24:1, 2)

Different Jewish courts have variously interpreted this sentence, but, as applied by Jewish law, the man is the initiator, the actor. Rabbinic law established that there need be no grounds for divorce other than mutual consent; it enforced the structured order of the verse: the male is the active legal principle. He must initiate, author, and give the document to her. She receives it and only then is free to resume control of her life. Hence, the current concern for a Jewish woman's human rights.

Thus, while in most cases Judaism's tolerant acceptance of divorce enables a decent split, in too many situations, this male prerogative becomes the means for extortion, vengeance, and affliction. Certainly, this does not appear to be a biblical ideal. Today, her consent to the divorce is necessary, but the woman is still at the mercy of the man. In the course of the centuries-long development of Jewish law, many improvements have been incorporated into the system in an attempt to limit the man's unilateral power and prevent misery. The rabbis were aware of and sensitive to women's vulnerability.

But today a Jewish divorce still requires a male-authored *get*, a document that a man freely gives to his wife and she must voluntarily accept. Without this document neither partner may remarry, according to classic Jewish law. The Reform movement often relies on local civil divorce courts, avoiding Jewish law altogether. The Conservative movement has empowered its central rabbinic court to intervene and act unilaterally to effect a divorce when there are insurmountable problems. But throughout Israel and in the Orthodox community outside of Israel, the pattern of insisting on the biblical directive has left too many women chained to dead or abusive marriages. And these rabbinic courts do not recognize those of the Reform or Conservative movements.

---

7. In the original process women had no role other than recipient. But around the year 1000 CE, Rabbeinu Gershom issued an edict that a wife had to consent to the proceedings, in that way at least giving her a legal presence and participatory role.

Initially, the individual problem begins with a common enough difficulty, a failed marriage. But Jewish law, which favours marriage and enables divorce, handicaps the female spouse and enables the legal domination of the female by the male. While there are several steps that intervene and require rabbis and court proceedings, only the husband can actually empower the male scribe with the authority to write the divorce document. The three-member male rabbinic court sits as legal authorities, checking that all necessary details are performed according to the law. There are also at least two male witnesses to attest to the proceedings. As the description indicates, the proceedings are all traditional, patriarchal, androcentric, and archaic. Pointedly, the document, the *get*, is the vehicle of the man's rights. In establishing this unilateral power, rabbinic interpretation of the biblical verse, set in motion an abusive system that even they are unable or unwilling to override. The problems for women within this system appear obvious.

Some did use vigorous – even forceful – measures to *persuade* men to *voluntarily* grant the *get*. Over the centuries, rabbinic courts and individual decisors ameliorated elements of the system, but none have ever overturned the structured patriarchy of the court process. Certainly, no one ever declared that either spouse could initiate the proceedings. By leaving the husband as sole initiator, the rabbis gave lawless men lawful power over law-abiding women and denied women recourse to their own rabbinic intervention. It is quite an amazing history. We do have records of individual rabbinic courts going to extreme lengths to insure that women were set freewives a Jewish divorce. Some like Maimonides (twelfth century) ruled that no Jewish wife should ever be like a slave, subjugated to a husband that she could no longer tolerate. There were lists of things that a woman could claim disgusted her about her spouse; items of behaviour, belief, and comportment that she could not live with. These were legal claims she could go to a court and plead her case. Yet, even if the rabbis found her case rightful, they could not settle the matter. They did not have the authority or legislative power to order a divorce. Their task was to summon the male recalcitrant and convince him to voluntarily give her the *get*. So his right of initiator always took precedence and got in the way of justice even if the rabbinic court decreed the woman's pleas were admissible and a divorce justifiable. Rights, justice, and obligations were all lost in this one interpretive trope, and women over the centuries suffered at the hands of male spouses and an absolute patriarchal rabbinic system.[8]

---

8. See Hacohen (2004), Novak (1974), and Shenhav *et al.* (2005).

But wives were not the only victims of this system. If a woman without the requisite *get* did give birth subsequent to the marriage break-up but before a divorce, then those children would be considered *mamzerim* Jews who are not allowed to marry other Jews. They are not illegitimate in the common sense of the term. They are thoroughly Jewish and can fulfill most ritual roles of Jews. But they cannot marry other Jews. The *Mamzerut* – illegitimate – state is a biblical determination and a supposed deterrent against adultery and incest. Both these crimes are actually gender neutral. But the definition of adultery in a polygynous (multiple wives) marriage depends of the status of the wife: Sexual intercourse between a man and a married woman who is not his wife. Thus, if a man does not give his wife a *get* and he has relations with an unmarried woman (even though he is still not allowed to marry her), his subsequent children are *not mamzerim*, illegitimate. Children receive their status from their mothers, legitimate and illegitimate. Thus, procedurally dependent on her husband and on a male rabbinic court, a woman's future children also become pawns in this tug of war as the problem is compounded.

Consequently, the system disadvantages women who cannot escape a bad marriage by limiting her future children and preventing even the children's marriage. The gender disequilibrium builds to a crescendo with the inheritance of status. For the status of illegitimacy is continuous in the female line. If the *mamzer* child is male and he has children, then his children inherit his wife's status and he does not pass his illegitimacy on.[9] But a female *mamzer* passes her illegitimacy on eternally. In the female line, it is a perpetual handicap that can *never* be fixed in rabbinic law. Hence, the concern with this legal gap: If it is not fixed is it because of a basic flaw in Judaism or because of a weakness of resolve in Jewish communities of the world?

It would seem, then, that for Jewish society today divorce constitutes a major moral problem – not because of the increase in numbers,[10] nor because of the guilt of either party, but because of the inequities of the process and the unresponsiveness of the larger community. People no longer

---

9. The issue here is not marriage but passing the status on to future children: A *mamzer* cannot "enter the congregation of the Lord" (Deut. 23:3), meaning that either a man or a woman in that category can only marry another *mamzer* or a convert (*Code of Jewish Law*, Sh. Ar., EH 4:22). There is no remedy other than the fact that the male *mamzer* can marry a female convert and his children will be common Jews (*Code of Jewish Law*, Sh. Ar., EH 4:20). But a female *mamzer* marrying a male convert will pass on the status to her children.

10. In the fifteenth century, approximately thirty per cent of Jewish marriages in parts of Europe ended in divorce (Baumgarten 2009).

married, no longer living together, are still tied to each other. Bound together and yet abandoned. This then raises the question posed initially: Does Jewish divorce especially in its biblical format of constraining women pose unresolvable ethical problems for Judaism?

Solutions

There are many in the Jewish world, rabbinic and lay leaders, who have been working diligently to mend the breach. Partial solutions and communal vehicles are currently being theorized and initiated. Social awareness and educational formats were the first steps. Some organizations took on the task of working quite successfully with individual cases, while others promoted educational formats. Working within both the secular and Jewish systems, activists initiated both civil and *halakhic* Jewish legal remedies.[11] None have intimated that Judaism is unethical; none have agreed that women's rights are eternally damaged. But many have walked away from a Judaic solution. Many have given up hope that this generation of Jewish leaders has the will or fortitude to effect the necessary changes. Nonetheless, some success established the use of prenuptial agreements. Although not a full solution, these documents signed before the marriages are both civilly and Jewishly legal and therefore often useful. They are certainly educational and indicate rabbinic and communal concern.

Canadian examples

In Canada, in the 1980s, the Coalition of Jewish Women for the *Get*, was established for the sole purpose of helping *Agunot*. After a decade of educational advocacy across Canada, activists in Toronto worked out a partial solution within Ontario family law (Syrtash 1992). In 1985, in Quebec, advocates opted to work with parliamentarians on the federal divorce law. By 1990, an amendment to the federal divorce law was enacted. It stated that no person should maintain barriers to the religious remarriage of their spouse that is within their control. This legislation was successful, despite its apparent encroachment on the territory of state/church separation. Its mere existence has reduced the use of extortion in *get* cases and avoided long years of litigation for many women. It is an interesting piece of leg-

---

11. In the spirit of full disclosure, I have been at the forefront of activities to ameliorate the situation for women in Jewish divorce cases, internationally. In Canada, I worked with the Coalition of Jewish Women for the *Get*, which successfully advocated in 1990 the federal Canadian Divorce Act amendment that would ameliorate the situation of Jewish women (Canadian Divorce Act, section 21.1).

islation that has been analyzed (Fishbayn 2008), borrowed, and criticized. It was carefully constructed so as not to violate the Canadian Charter of Rights and Jewish legal concerns.[12] It involves affidavits and court procedures to ensure that the respondent spouse can present a case for non-compliance. So far, in twenty-nine years, no one has successfully argued that they should be allowed to maintain barriers to the religious remarriage of a spouse after a civil divorce. Arguments for one spouse's religious freedom fail to convince when someone is impeding the religious freedom of their ex-spouse.

Often people do not understand how this law does not violate a theoretical church/state separation principle. The concerns over these issues are certainly different in Canada than in other countries. But the attorney general at the time felt that it was important to draft legislation so that no one would use religion to "violate the integrity of the civil process." "A spouse should not be able to refuse to participate in a Jewish religious divorce [...] in order to obtain concessions in a civil divorce" (*House of Commons Debates* 1990). Interestingly, in this instance, the Canadian government took on a citizen's rights protective role. Instead of worrying about separation of church and state, the Canadian justice ministry worried about the misuse of state procedures and the limiting of a woman's freedom to remarry. It also worked with Jewish legal specialist to avoid a clash with religious authorities across the country by making sure there was no conflict in legislative norms. These developments were based on notions that it was the government's duty to protect its citizens from extortion and that the civil divorce was meant to allow a divorced woman to remarry, should she so desire. Thus, the state became a significant partner in ensuring that the charter worked as a protective system even for a religious minority without voiding the authority of that minority's religious leaders or system. For those of us involved at the time, it was quite an experiment in accommodation, multiculturalism, and integration.

There have been additional situations in which Jewish divorce entered the field of Canadian law. Freedom of religion and state intervention was a critical factor in a 2007 case before the Supreme Court: Bruker *v.* Markovitz.[13] Many thought that this case challenged the law of 21.1 just discussed. It explicitly did not, although the Supreme Court justices do discuss it. In the original divorce agreement, the man signed a separate contract stating that he would give a *get*, which he did, although it took

---

12. In effect, the *get* is the mere voiding of a previously entered into contract. The ceremony is a ritual within Jewish law, but it does not require any religious act or worship.

13. See Joseph (2011).

him fifteen years to do so. The female plaintiff then sued for damages.[14] The Supreme Court case directly concerns the complex and ambiguous principles of separation of church and state: Is a contract whose basic provision is a religious ritual act – giving a Jewish divorce – justiciable?

There are, of course, many issues raised by this case and others like it. But for this critique, the main points are vital. It took the Court over one year to produce its judgment. The decision of seven of the justices was that such a contract is justiciable. In other words, the law today is that if a man signs a separate contract that he will give a *get* and he then refuses, the woman can sue him for damages in a court of law.

For many of the activists involved, the real victory was not to be found in the specifics of this case but in the principles invoked both in the Supreme Court decision, as well as in the reasoning associated with the 21.1 divorce amendment. Religious elements do not protect individuals or contracts from judicial scrutiny or litigation. Justice Abella noted that moral obligations could be transformed into civil ones and be enforceable by the courts.[15] The government would not necessarily abandon women when the vehicles of their restrictions were framed in religious rituals or laws, if civil actions were also incurred.

> On the contrary, Parliament manifested a clear intention to encourage the removal of religious barriers to remarriage. Moreover […] the enforceability of a promise by a husband to provide a get harmonizes with Canada's approach to religious freedom, to equality rights, […] The courts are charged with the task of ensuring that citizens are not arbitrarily disadvantaged by their religion.[16]

Admittedly, this is very tenuous legal territory. Both parties can claim religious freedom before the courts. Yet, what has been clarified is that religious freedom claims of one party are subject to limitations when they collide with public rights and interests. Thus, the state can intervene in a

---

14. The case: Stephanie Bruker married Jason Marcovitz in 1969. Divorce was granted in 1981. In 1980, they had negotiated a contract that included (paragraph 12) an agreement to appear before rabbinical authorities to obtain the *get immediately* upon granting the *decree nisi*. The *get* was not given until 1995, despite her repeated requests. Marcovitz v. Bruker, Q.J. No. 13563, R.J.Q. 2482 (Quebec Court of Appeal, 2005).
15. Justice Rosalie Abella, p.32, 20. Bruker *v.* Marcovitz (2007) S.C.J. No. 54 (2007) 3 S.C.R. 607 (S.C.C.) Supreme Court of Canada, Docket 31212, 2007/12/14. http://csc.lexum.umontreal.ca/en/2007/2007scc54/2007scc54.pdf
16. Justice Rosalie Abella, p. 34, 63. Bruker *v.* Marcovitz (2007. Supreme Court of Canada, Docket 31212, 2007/12/14. http://csc.lexum.umontreal.ca/en/2007/2007scc54/2007scc54.pdf

case such as Jewish divorce if one spouse is being extorted or restricted and has previously agreed to negotiate a settlement. One can access civil law to protect individual and minority citizen rights. His freedom of religion must be weighed against hers, and his power over her can be balanced with a civil law procedure. Freedom of religion can be limited if the exercise is harmful to others.

A Jewish solution

It should be obvious to everyone that the genuine solution to the problem of Jewish divorce lies solely within Jewish law. There can be no complete solution without a Jewish legal resolution. Many people – rabbis, legal scholars, and activists – are working towards that end. There are various possible paths such as annulments, forcible divorces, conditional marriages or divorces, empowering rabbinic courts to act when the man refuses, and more. Personally, I would like to see a new structure that enables either spouse to initiate simpler divorce proceedings. But that will not come in my lifetime and who can wait. We cannot in good conscience ask a woman to put her life on hold. Compassionate and concerned individuals must use whatever means are practicable and available. Canadian law emerged able and willing to help its citizens.

But the importance of this decision goes far beyond Jews, women, or Canada. It situates the relationship between church and state where it should be; the secular state has a vested interested in certain ways religion is used and applied. Sometimes the state refuses to allow religious law to operate, as was seen in the Ontario decision to exclude religious courts from acting as arbitrators in family law matters.[17] But at other times and in other cases, the state takes a very active role in welcoming and working with religious educators and legalists. The process depends on a case by case situation with the government deciding what is best for its citizens and in what ways it is mandated to act as protector of its citizenry.

The court followed through on Canada's tradition of multiculturalism. Different people with different faiths and practices can find that the law protects them, recognizing their diverse legal needs. The civil system joined international law makers in extending a protective shield to Jewish women while waiting anxiously for rabbinic law to eliminate the need for it. Finally, the court publicly and officially applied the principle of equity as a Canadian value.

---

17. This is also the law in Quebec.

Agunah activism

Agunah activism highlights the conflicts, fractious identities, and ruptures for many women in the Jewish community. Even in the face of acceptance as individuals and full members of the community, women face the reality of ultimate invisibility or disparity. For many, *agunah* activism presents the clearest and most unambiguous way in which Judaism and feminism collide.

How do we understand a commitment to Jewish law that enables lawless men to tyrannize law-abiding women? How do we adjust to a concomitant acceptance of rabbinic authority, which is defined and legislated by a male elite system that is unable or unwilling to hear women? What do we do with Judaic respect for the law and lawmakers when the law regarding divorce is unacceptable in its treatment of these women? How do we manage a rabbinic authority when it is worse than patriarchal, when it is corrupt? How do we stick to a feminist critique that puts women's experience and needs at centre stage when women are sidelined legally? How do we manage a social activism that is bred legitimately by the biblical commandment to seek justice when the system ignores justice? Finally, how can Jews claim commitment to Torah justice when there is no justice for some?

In trying to decipher the social, ethical, and religious issues embraced by this chaos of divorce, there are a number of caveats that need to be addressed. Solutions come in a variety of forms and suggestions. Not all of those forms are obvious.

1. To discuss religious Jewish feminism and the Jewish divorce process, we have to understand the non-negotiable commitment of many to the *halakha* and its process. Orthodox feminists are not willing to abandon the law or living a lawful life.

2. The law is not intentionally oppressive to women, though undoubtedly at times women suffer because of the law. The rabbis often found ways to interpret and adapt the law so that the community could survive. Rabbis have done this for generations. Rabbinic legislation did redesign biblical law to eliminate slavery and capital punishment. The commitment to justice was pursued. Our question is why have they stopped?

3. As the law preserves its patriarchal character, it retains an inability to correctly hear women. Many maintain this was not always the case.

4. Some rabbis and men are actually "good guys." It is suitable to work with them in partnership.

5. Today, women are Jewish legal scholars, recognized *to'anot* (advocates) in Jewish divorce courts, accepted *yo'atsot* (advisors) in Jewish legal matters. Interpreting and legislating law.

6. Don't blame the victim. Many people say why don't Orthodox women leave the community? If they cannot get a *get*, and if the law is difficult for them, or too patriarchal, why don't they leave? But that, of course, misses the point – both of religion and of feminism. Orthodox Jews are Orthodox because they believe in the tenets of Orthodoxy. They believe in the law; they believe in the integrity of the system. They do not wish to abandon their beliefs, their heritage, and their community, no matter how they feel about a particular element, and no matter that at times they feel abandoned by that system. They have chosen to be practicing *halakhic* Jews. Their choice! And feminism is about choice. It's about the ability of a woman to choose to stay where she is, free to be obligated, and perhaps to want to renovate from within. Feminism is about enabling and supporting women who say, "I am an Orthodox Jewish feminist, I wish to stay inside, and I need you to network with me, be in partnership with me on the difficult issues, not to tell me to leave." We all face that challenge now. It's not theoretical; it's not just practical; it is existential.

Conclusion

As I have claimed,[18] the solution, if there is going to be any solution, has to come from within Judaism. The community may seek remedies elsewhere in terms of social action – vigils in front of this man's business or denial of communal and synagogue honours. But none of these are sufficient. That puts *agunah* activists in a direct path of confrontation with their heritage, with their beliefs, with their community, and with their rabbis.

If the Bible teaches that men and women are created equally before God, how do humans concretize that? It is certainly not evident or accessible in Jewish divorce law as practiced today. This is not just about who the legalists are but rather what the law enables. This specific arena challenges every aspect of a Jewish woman's identity, especially if she is also a feminist. But it challenges every Jew's identity too. It risks one's position in the community.

Alarmingly, this *agunah* issue can also increase anti-Semitism. When I describe the situation truthfully, people in the audience often get up and say, "Judaism is terrible to women. I knew that all along. It's what my priest taught me." Then, I have to live with the fact that my honest assessment of the tradition and the community that I love dearly enables and

---

18. I have written on this subject many times and in many different formats: Joseph (2007; 2009; 2011) and Joseph *et al*. (1997).

promotes distortions and even anti-Semitism. How can I continue? How shall we continue? I cannot sit idly by and watch women suffer. Ironically, I cannot allow the Jewish tradition of justice and righteousness to be diverted. But equally, I cannot besmirch my own heritage. I cannot feed the evils of racism and anti-Semitism. Shall I be silent?

Agunah activism is about doubting and challenging and even contradicting the rabbinic authority we do respect. It is about questioning the very basis of one's own beliefs. It is to engage in an existential ordeal. We claim that Jews must passionately pursue justice as biblically commanded. We proclaim women's rights and unique contributions in Jewish history and law must be recognised. Exceptionally, we acknowledge that there are legal problems: Jewish law needs to be revised or amended or adjusted.

Despite the criticism and activism, I do not believe that Judaism is intrinsically based on a system of legal or purposeful discrimination and injustice. The divorce process was developed by human beings within social and political contexts that did not operate with notions of equity and human rights. We now stand inside a distinctive worldview that would encourage an appreciation of that Torah-based command to seek justice in its fullest perspective. It then is up to this current generation of leaders to apply that justice objective systemically so that no one can wonder: Does this inequity stem from Judaism – from God?

References

Baumgarten, Elisheva. 2009. "Medieval Ashkenaz (1096–1348)." *Jewish Women: A Comprehensive Historical Encyclopedia.* Jewish Women's Archive, https://jwa.org/encyclopedia/article/medieval-ashkenaz-1096-1348

Biale, Rachel. 1984. *Women in Jewish Law: An Exploration of Women's Issues in Halakhic Sources.* New York: Schocken.

Bruker *v.* Marcovitz. 2007. S.C.J. No. 54 (2007) 3 S.C.R. 607 (S.C.C.) Supreme Court of Canada, Docket 31212, 2007/12/14. http://csc.lexum.umontreal.ca/en/2007/2007scc54/2007scc54.pdf

Charter of Human Rights and Freedoms. 2009 [1975]: R.S.Q. Chapter C-12 (Quebec Charter). http://www.cdpdj.qc.ca/en/commun/docs/charter.pdf

Code of Jewish Law. 2010 [1992]. Shulchan Aruch, Even Ha'ezer (Jerusalem: Ketuvim edition), Bar-Ilan University Responsa Global Jewish Data Base (18þ version).

Fishbayn, Lisa. 2008. "Gender and Multiculturalism: The Case of Jewish Divorce," *Canadian Journal of Law and Jurisprudence* 21(1): 71–96. https://doi.org/10.1017/s0841820900004331

Hacohen, A. 2004. *The Tears of the Oppressed: An Examination of the Agunah Problem: Background and Halakhic Sources.* Jersey City, NJ: Ktav.

House of Commons Debates. 1990. (15 February) vol. VI, 2nd session, 34th Parliament (Doug Lewis, Minister of Justice).

Joseph, Norma Baumel. 1984. "Divorce and the Jewish Woman." *Viewpoints* 12: 8.

———. 1994. "Jewish Divorce and Canadian Law." *Ecumenism* 115: 18.

———. 2000. "Agunah." In *Reader's Guide to Judaism*, edited by J. Salkin. Chicago: Fitzroy Dearborn.

———. 2005. "Jewish Law and Gender." In *Encyclopedia of Women and Religion in North America*, Volume 2, edited by Rosemary Keller and Rosemary Radford Reuther., 576–587. Bloomington: Indiana University Press.

———. 2007. "Women in Orthodoxy: Conventional and Contentious." *Women Remaking American Judaism*, edited by Riv-Ellen Prell, 181–209. Detroit: Wayne State University Press.

———. 2009. "Why Do I Need a Jewish Divorce?" Booklet prepared in collaboration with Jewish Women International, at the request of the Ontario Government: Family, Law and Education for Women Committee. Ottawa. This pamphlet, available in five languages, is now distributed across Canada.

———. 2011. "Civil Jurisdiction and Religious Accord: *Bruker* v. *Marcovitz* in the Supreme Court of Canada." *Studies in Religion/Sciences religieuses* 40(3): 318–336. https://doi.org/10.1177/0008429811408213

Joseph, Norma Baumel, Evelyn Bekor Brook, and Marilyn Bicher. 1997. *Untying the Bonds ... Jewish Divorce.* VHS. Directed by Francine Zuckerman. Montreal: Coalition of Jewish Women for the *Get*. This film is accompanied by a guidebook of the same title. Article author acted as participant as well.

Joy, Morny. 2013. "Women's Rights and Religions: A Contemporary Review." *Journal of Feminist Studies in Religion* 29(1): 52–68. https://doi.org/10.2979/jfemistudreli.29.1.52

Jukier, R. and S. Van Praagh. 2008. "Civil Law and Religion in the Supreme Court of Canada: What Should We Get out of Bruker v. Marcovitz?" *Supreme Court Law Review* (2d) 43: 381–411.

Keats-Jaskoll, Shoshanna. 2019. "Women scholars assume the mantle of Jewish leadership," *Jerusalem Post* (Jerusalem, Israel). 28 February. https://www.jpost.com/Magazine/Women-assume-the-mantle-of-leadership-559405

Minnow, M. 1995. "Rights and Cultural Difference." In *Identities, Politics and Rights*, edited by A. Sarat and T. Kearns, 347–366. Ann Arbor: University of Michigan Press. https://doi.org/10.2307/2952381

Novak, D. 1974. *Law and Theology in Judaism.* New York: Ktav.

Porter, J. N. 1995. *Women in Chains: A Sourcebook on the Agunah.* Northvale, NJ: Jason Aronson.

Shenhav, S., S. Aronoff, N.B. Joseph, and S. Weiss. 2005. *Choosing Limits, Limiting Choices* (conference transcript). A conference presented by the Hadassah-Brandeis Institute and the Jewish Orthodox Feminist Alliance (JOFA). Boston, MA, March 13–14.

Syrtash, J. 1992. *Religion and Culture in Canadian Family Law*. Toronto: Butterworths.

7

Maria Clara in the Twenty-first Century: The Uneasy Discourse between the Cult of the Virgin Mary and Filipino Women's Lived Realities

> **Jeane C. Peracullo** is a Full Professor at the Philosophy Department in De La Salle University. She is also the past international coordinator of the Ecclesia of Women in Asia, a forum of Asian Catholic women theologians and pastoral workers. She also serves as a resource person on the Technical Panel for the Master of Arts in Women and Gender Studies for the Commission on Higher Education (CHED). Jeane is currently a Research Fellow of the Center for World and Intercultural Theology at DePaul University, Chicago.

Introduction

The Virgin Mary looms large as the image of a "good" Filipina or Filipino woman in both cultural and religious landscapes in the Philippines. A "good Filipina" imagery points specifically to the weak or passive woman, who is represented by a satirical character named Maria Clara. The Roman Catholic Church reinforces such imagery to highlight the Madonna-Whore dichotomy. However, in the twenty-first century, Filipino women have come to challenge the image of a good woman as weak and passive person. This paper explores the challenges that Filipinas face in their everyday lives, which call for a re-examination of the role of Catholic faith in their lived experiences.

Destabilizing the Stereotypical Image of Filipino Women

A photograph, which appeared in the *Philippine Daily Inquirer* on July 23, 2016, would become the haunting image of the human cost of the present administration's "war on drugs." A grieving woman cradled her slain partner, a rickshaw driver, and a suspected illegal drug peddler, who was killed in execution-style supposedly by vigilante killers. Raffy Lerma, who photographed the haunting scene, named it as "La Pieta," an obvious reference to *The Pieta* by Michelangelo. The then newly-elected President Rodrigo Duterte, in his first-ever State of the Nation Address (SONA) on July 25, 2016, regarded the picture (and the reference to *Pieta*) as "melodramatic." His precise words: "Then there you are, sprawled, and you are portrayed in a broadsheet like Mother Mary cradling the dead cadaver of Jesus Christ. These people, we'll be doing dramatics here."

The mention of *The Pieta* in the historic SONA reveals the power that photographs wield in framing the perceived association of Filipino women to the long-suffering Virgin Mother. Madonna and Child images abound – a fitting image of a loving mother. *The Pieta* provides a magnificent background for a, self-sacrificing and passive mother. These images loom heavily and provide a fitting representation of a loving mother. Indeed, *The Pieta* offers a magnificent impression of a long-suffering mother (Peracullo 2015, 38). What *destabilizes or problematizes* this image however is another image of Filipino women as "empowered" and "highly educated."

Representations of educated Filipino women, bravely and resolutely leaving their loved ones and country behind to work in strange lands as domestic helpers, nurses, caregivers and performers abound in mainstream media. These images are, at first glance, contradictory inasmuch as they represent Filipino women being tied to their traditional roles as mothers and caregivers. Yet, such images are also representations of empowered Filipino women as Overseas Filipino Workers. These images suggest that workers live these contradictions and they negotiate with them, all the while refusing to be held down by stereotypes of what it means to be a woman.

It is notable that the Philippines is ranked highest among all other Asian countries in the World. Economic Forum (WEF) Gender Gap Report for several years. This high rank seems to create an assumption that being a Filipino woman is definitely much better than say, being a Korean or a Japanese woman. Nevertheless, there is dissonance between the WEF Gender Gap Report and the lived experiences of many other Filipino women who are not well-educated, do not have jobs, and do not have access to reproductive health clinics.

The conflict is partly due to the centuries-old representation of the "Virgin Mary" describing who they ought to be, and how they ought to live their lives. The effects of such an idealized representation are manifested in the double-talk that the local Roman Catholic Church makes regarding migrant female workers. The internal conflict with which Filipino women have been struggling holds them back from making authentic choices. As a result, there is a general lack of sustained collective resistance among Filipino women themselves to rally against the continuing production of motherhood that is oppressive. This is possibly why rights have not yet featured in their repertory.

This paper presents the complex journey of modern Filipino women as they embark towards greater access to full participation in the discourse surrounding women, rights and religion. It also offers accounts of resistance against the hegemonic attempts of the Roman Catholic Church to frame their identities and experiences within the totalizing discourse of the "Virgin Mother." These accounts can be observed in several fronts: within the local Roman Catholic Church through the re-claiming of pre-colonial ideas on the nature of God; in the re-imagining of Mary using postcolonial discourse; and from the migrant Filipino workers themselves who, through their sacrifices, allow us re-examine the meaning of re/productive work, *hanap-buhay* (in English, looking for life), in motherhood and care.

Filipino women, human rights and the Catholic church

The 2015 Global Gender Gap Report of the World Economic Forum (hereafter WEF) places the Philippines in the seventh place for its strong showing of female presence in various economic and political areas. The Philippines is the only Asia country in the top ten. The high ranking might not come as a surprise to those who have seen up close how Filipinas, a colloquial term for Filipino women, are highly literate and hardworking. After the historic EDSA revolution in February 25, 1986 that toppled a reviled dictator, the Filipino people have since elected two female presidents. In Southeast Asia, where dictators abound and machismo is a reality, this feat is worth noting. In almost all areas that the WEF considered as key areas to measure gender gaps, Filipinas do much better compared to their male counterparts, except in the area of the human development index.

The Philippines has several laws that pertain to, and are considered to be, highly beneficial to women, such as the Republic Act 10354 or The Responsible Parenthood and Reproductive Health Act of 2012; the Republic Act 9710 or the Magna Carta of Women; the Republic Act 10398 or An Act Declaring November Twenty-Five of Every Year as "National Consciousness Day for the Elimination of Violence against Women and Children"; the Republic Act No. 10361 or Domestic Workers Act; Republic Act 9995 or the Anti-Photo and Video Voyeurism Act of 2009; the Republic Act 9775 or the Anti-Child Pornography Act of 2009; the Republic Act 9262 or the Anti-Violence against Women and their Children Act of 2004; the Republic Act 8972 or the Solo Parents' Welfare Act of 2000; the Republic Act 8505 or the Rape Victim Assistance and Protection Act of 1998.

Moreover, the country is also a signatory to many United Nation treaties on addressing gender inequality and violence against women and children. The first notable international agreement pertaining to women and gender equality that the Philippines ratified in 1981 was the Convention on the Elimination of All Forms of Discrimination against Women (CEDAW), which was adopted by the UN General Assembly in 1979. Since 1981, The Philippines has, over the years, shown institutional commitment to the ideals of the United Nations.[1]

In the 2014 Gender Development Index (GDI) of the United Nations, the Philippines was placed in the Group 1 category of countries that have achieved high scores in areas that were considered, namely: Human Development Index; Life Expectancy; Expected Years of Schooling; Mean Years of Schooling; and Estimated GNI (Gross National Income) per Capita. Again, Filipinas fared better than their male counterparts in all areas except one.

These progressive and advanced laws were promulgated despite the long, hard and bitter fights between Filipino feminists and the Roman Catholic Church. The Magna Carta Law of Women, (the Republic Act 9710), which was signed into law in 2009, saliently underscores in section 8 that "All rights in the Constitution and those rights recognized under international instruments duly signed and ratified by the Philippines, in consonance with Philippine law, shall be rights of women under this Act to be enjoyed without discrimination." Nevertheless, the Catholic Church opposed its ratification. Its objections revolved mainly around provisions that protect women's health, at the same time as maintaining an explicitly anti-abortion approach (Parmanand 2014, 71).

The fourteen-year journey of the Responsible Parenthood and Reproductive Health Act of 2012 (Republic Act No. 10354), promulgated in December 21, 2012, is a testament to a long drawn-out struggle between progressive and liberal sectors in civil society and the Catholic Church. In a 2012 article on the Reproductive Health Bill, I had wondered why the Catholic Church should position itself against a potential law that was anchored in freedom of conscience and autonomy, which are considered to be normative moral standpoints that the Church promotes. I argued for the primacy of autonomy and self-determination in framing a perspective on the reproductive health debate. I had gleaned these insights from the

---

1. However, the country's healthy cooperation with the United Nations is being threatened by the President Dutarte's perception that the UN is meddling in the affairs of the nation when one of the UN rapporteurs expressed her intention of visit to look into the allegations of widespread extra-judicial killings committed by the police as part of the "war on drugs."

experiences of Filipinas who must decide on: a) whether to limit the number of children they have, b) how to space the births, and c) whether to terminate a pregnancy, or d) whether to use contraception. A Filipino mother is a person, a subject entitled to her own autonomy and self-determination. Reproductive rights need to be situated in a framework that recognizes the complexity of women's needs in the sphere of reproduction. I maintained that a truly Filipino feminist perspective on reproductive health debates should be anchored deeply within the lived experience of poor Filipinas who are burdened by caring for multiple children (Peracullo 2012, i).

Maria Tanyag declares that Catholic fundamentalism is partly to blame for the Catholic Church's response against efforts to legislate gender equality in the Philippines. For instance, the Catholic fundamentalist notion of 'pro-life' is rooted in a doctrine that stipulates that sex, which is only valid within the sacrament of marriage, is inseparable from its procreative function (Tayag 2015).

The Virgin Mary, Motherhood and Colonial Discourse

The Virgin Mary image captures both the internal and external dispositions of a chaste Filipina who, if married, follows the natural family planning the Church promotes. Yet, the natural family planning method, also known as the "rhythm method," requires diligence and a keen knowledge of women's reproductive cycle that are simply unsustainable. Faced by mounting challenges from many fronts, foremost of which is economic, it is becoming increasingly difficult for many Filipino women to remain faithful to such an image of a chaste woman whose sexuality is determined solely by its ability to be open to life.

In the 1975 Pastoral Letter, the Catholic Bishop's Conference of the Philippines (CBCP) claims that the Filipinos' widespread devotion to the 'Blessed Mother' has surpassed Catholicism and spilled over into other Christian churches (such as the Philippine Independent Church). The Philippines was under Spanish colonial rule for more than three hundred years. Consequently, Christianity, especially Catholicism, is deeply entrenched in the cultural and religious landscape of Filipinos. US-based Filipino anthropologist Deidre de la Cruz observes:

> Throughout the Spanish colonial period, images of the Virgin Mary proliferated throughout the Philippines, with shrines that bear their names to this day: Our Lady of *Manaoag, Caysasay, Salambao, Turumba,* and *Namacpacan,* to name but a few. By conjoining a singular title (Nuestra Señora, or Our Lady) to sites whose names remain in the vernacular; these shrines monumentalize the colonial encounter. (de la Cruz 2015, 40)

The devotion to Mary, as manifested in countless churches named after her, and in numerous town *fiestas* that are celebrated in her honor every day throughout the country. The sheer number of devotees who ask for her "intercession," in their various prayers and pleas to God, seem to suggest that Mary is seen by her devotees as "Mother God." In the same CBCP 1975 Pastoral Letter, the Catholic bishops warned their members against this tendency to place Mary on the same pedestal as Christ and God the Father, or even put her in a higher rung above them in the divine hierarchy.

In no uncertain terms, the Vatican II Papal Encyclical, *Lumen Gentium: The Dogmatic Constitution of the Church* (1964) has made it clear that Mary, both as a Mother and Virgin, is the archetype of a perfect disciple. For Filipino historian Roland Mactal (2007, 269) this means that all else follows from her example. It implies that she is the mother of God and freely accepted to be so. Mary gave her assent to the Word at the Annunciation, committing herself wholeheartedly to God's will in faith and obedience even up to standing at the foot of the Cross. However, in both the CBCP Pastoral Letter and in *Lumen Gentium*, one could discern vacillations between two Marys: the Mary that is worshipped by the people and the Mary in the dogmatic theologies of the Vatican Curia.

Mary has always been a conflictual figure for Catholic feminist theologians. Elisabeth Schüssler Fiorenza (2013) argues for a critical research on religion from the "inside out." This implies a demanding review, from within the Roman Catholic Church, which would highlight the self-reflexivity involved in doing critical work. Such a critical mode of research about religion that is self-reflexive[2] is apparent in a statement made by Schüssler Fiorenza:

> The discourse on the "Eternal Feminine" or the Cult of True Womanhood, which I have dubbed the discourse on the "White Lady," was developed in tandem with Western colonization and romanticism that celebrated

---

2. An example of self-reflexivity is Noriko Kawahashi's 2013 work on Japanese Buddhist women's reframing of Buddhism in their own terms. This reframing, according to Kawahashi, allows them to speak their own voices, voices that had been rendered silent by a patriarchy intimately bound up in Japanese society and its practice of Buddhism. Kawahashi passionately sets forth an argument that the seeming "silence" of Japanese Buddhist women's voices (which include priest's wives and nuns) is not due entirely to their uncritical embrace of their religion. Some Western feminist scholars' inability to hear past their own ethnocentric framework ironically contributes to these Buddhist women's "muteness." This article critiques two accounts that supposedly define Japanese Buddhist women: 1: The account from patriarchal understanding of Buddhism from Japanese male scholars; 2: The account from feminists, both inside and outside Japan, who doubt the usefulness of religion to Japanese women's emancipation.

Christian white elite European women/ladies as paradigms of civilized and cultured womanhood. This ideology functioned to legitimate both the exclusion of elite wo/men from positions of power in society and church and at the same time to make them colonial representatives who mediated European culture, religion, and civilization to the so-called savages. (Fiorenza 2013, 46)

The cult of Mary, which depends on her being both a mother and a virgin, is an instrument used by colonialists to subdue their subjects. It can be claimed that Filipino women's internalized expectations of a good woman or mother are colonial vestiges that are very deeply burrowed in the cultural psyche of the people. The exception is a few images of a *Filipinized* Mother Mary, which depict her as a very young girl, wearing traditional Filipino dresses, and clutching a cute baby Jesus. Mary's statues and figures, which are found in almost all corners of the Philippines, also depict her to be Caucasian, with narrow nose and blue eyes.

The 1975 CBCP pastoral letter on Marian devotion in the Philippines did not admonish the proliferation of the glaringly colonialist images and statues of Mary, but rebuked believers and worshippers who might have gone overboard, so to speak, in their adoration and devotion to her. Filipino historians are critical of the local Catholic Church hierarchy's positioning as the sole interpreter of religious phenomena and deliverer of "good news." For instance, the EDSA Revolution of 1986, which, according to the local RCC, was a result of "Mother Mary's intervention," is such one example. For local historians, Christianity was "the colonizers" effective instrument of thought control, [and] that is what made the masses submissive (Bräunlein 2016).

In 2005, the Catholic Bishops' Conference of the Philippines issued a pastoral letter on the occasion of the 19th National Migrants' Sunday on February 13, 2005. The theme was, "With Mary, the Migrants and their Families, Find Life in the Eucharist." It was publicized by a large poster (see Figure 1).

The poster clearly positioned Mary as bigger than the world, towards which her compassionate gaze is directed. Just below the globe, a picture of a nuclear family, which is imposed on the Eucharistic cup, can be seen. The letter hopes that,

> The example of Mary, through whose unconditional trust in God the Word was made Flesh, should inspire migrants and their families towards trust in the Lord, the source of true life. Families will therefore endeavor to lead them into a true devotion to the Blessed Mother—a Eucharist, the Bread of Life! It is our prayer and fervent hope that the migrants and their families will work not only for "more bread" but also for the Bread of Life. (CBCP 2005, n.p)

Figure 1. Poster for the Nineteenth National Migrants Sunday.

The letter is the Catholic bishops' plea for Overseas Filipino Workers not to make economics (a reference to the "bread") as the main reason for seeking work abroad. Instead, they ought not to lose sight of that which will nourish them eternally (the Bread of Life).

Harsh economic realities, however, would in time undermine the "Bread of Life." In 2005 alone, the number of Overseas Filipino Workers (OFWs) during the period from April to September 2005 was estimated at 1.33 million. This number is 12.5 per cent more than the 1.18 million OFWs estimated for the period April to September 2004, according to the 2007 Philippine Statistical Authority. In the same period, it was found that women comprised 49.5 per cent of the total number of OFWs, and they tended to be younger, between twenty-five to twenty-nine years old. About ninety-five per cent of the OFWs would belong in unskilled labour category. Not much had changed ten years later, except for the fact that in 2015, women outnumbered men.

In the novel, *Noli me Tangere* (The Social Cancer), Philippine National Hero, Jose Rizal created a character, Maria Clara, to poke satirical fun at the stereotyping of an ideal Filipino woman who was an obedient and dutiful daughter. These were the qualities, which the colonial Spain promoted. The fact that Maria Clara, who was an illegitimate child of a Catholic priest, and had committed herself to marry only for love, seemed to have been lost to many Filipinos. Many read Maria Clara as the quintessential damsel-in- distress who needed a knight to save her. The reality was that she herself was raped by another Catholic priest.

In addition, just like Mother Mary in the Christian faith, the Filipina mother is expected to possess certain qualities such as kindness, piety, obedience, care, and virtue, essentially a sacrificial being who puts God's will above her own needs (Soriano et al. 2015, 4).

The *Lineamenta: The Vocation and Mission of the Family in the Church and Contemporary World*, which was released by the Vatican on December 9, 2014, reinforces these qualities. The document, was a result of the Second Extraordinary General Assembly of the Synod of Bishops, which took place on October 5–19, 2014, in Vatican City. Pope Francis had ordered the public release of the *Lineamenta* to prepare for the Fourteenth Ordinary General Assembly, which was to take place in the following year. The release of the document was presumably to enable the faithful to comment, and perhaps suggest changes to their bishops who would in turn bring them to the synod.

My main concern, however, occurs in the last sentence of paragraph 46, which reads: "Special attention is to be given in the guidance of single-parent families, so that women who have to bear alone the responsibility of providing a home and raising their children can receive assistance."

This last sentence of paragraph 46, which is indicated by a preface named, "special attention," is explicitly essentialist. By equating single-parenthood with women exclusively, the document reinforces gender stereotypes, such as the following: parenthood is ontologically linked with being female. This is a generalization about an extraordinary situation of single parenting, to which, for various reasons (such as accidental pregnancy, abandonment by partner, among others), women are invariably assigned, with or without their consent.

Not Anymore Maria Clara

Filipino theologian Gemma Cruz (2007) argues that to draw from a particular experience of women, helps to reveal multiple oppressions that are only evident when one reflects on the way by which differences in class, race or ethnicity impact on the lives of particular women. She notes, however, that despite constraints, some Filipino women who work as domestic helpers in Hong Kong resist cultural oppressions. This can be observed particularly in areas of sexuality. By coming out, lesbian Filipinas abroad form domestic partnerships with same-sex lovers. These acts of resistance are forms of rejection that are aimed at the cultural mandate that commands Filipinas to marry and have children and admonishes those that who will not follow these directions (2007, 64).

Ruth Mabanglao, a Filipino feminist poet, created a series of "letters" purportedly coming from female migrants in Brunei, Hong Kong, and Japan. The series exposes the cultural double-bind the Filipino women experience in trying to live up to cultural expectations to be good mothers, wives, sisters, and daughters.

In the poem, *Letter from Brunei* (1997), an OFW woman recounts that when she was still at her home in the Philippines, she longed for overseas work that would take her away from her domestic slavery. Perhaps the thought of being literally oceans apart from the family (and country) and all its demands, duties and responsibilities, were too attractive to resist. Or perhaps, the thought of economic independence, of having some time for oneself, erased any fear. In the poem, she only cried at the beginning.

Work as *hanap-buhay* (searching for life)

The United Nations Development Program statement on work states:

> Work enables people to earn a livelihood and be economically secure. It is critical for equitable economic growth, poverty reduction and gender equality. It also allows people to fully participate in society while affording them a sense of dignity and worth. Work can contribute to the public good, and work that involves caring for others builds cohesion and bonds within families and communities. (UNDP 2014, 1)

I do not want to belabour this point any longer. Nonetheless, the local Roman Catholic Church would prove to be the main obstacle to allowing for a truly compassionate turn towards a search for solutions to the problems surrounding migrant female labour. In her reflection on Filipino female migrant workers, Filipino feminist theologian Agnes Brazal wonders why in the papacy of John Paul II and Benedict XVI, the Church teachings continue to implicitly maintain that the man is the primary breadwinner and the woman is primarily responsible for the care of the children at home (Brazal 2010, 38).

In a papal letter, *Laborem Exercens* (14 September 1981), Pope John Paul II observed that:

> It will redound to the credit of society to make it possible for a mother – without inhibiting her freedom, without psychological or practical discrimination, and without penalizing her as compared with other women

– to devout herself to taking care of her children and educating them In accordance with their needs, which vary with age. (John Paul II 1981, 3)

He also emphasized the special role of women as mothers by saying: "Having to abandon these tasks in order to take up paid work outside the home is wrong from the point of view of the good of society and of the family when it contradicts or hinders these primary goals of the mission of a mother" (John Paul II 1981, 3).

Brazal finds these exaltations as unfortunate: "This strong statement from the Church has the effect of putting additional burden of guilt on women who are forced to migrate to earn for their family. Indeed, the care of the children should not be neglected but can only the mother do this? This also reinforces the negative attitude of families and communities toward men who cannot live up to the ideal of men as the primary providers of the family" (2010, 38).

Reimagining Mary for the twenty-first century Filipinas

The Virgin Mary of the hierarchical Roman Catholic Church is exposed in the above paper as a colonial trope to uphold a particularly harmful myth of a "good" woman. However, it turns out that this "good" woman is also both a weak and passive one.

In response to Schüssler Fiorenza's challenge that a self-reflexive, critical stance is helpful in the on-going assessment of the many ways that religion, and in particular, Christianity, informs the lives of Filipino women, some Catholic feminist theologians have embarked on the "reclaiming" act of retrieving. This involves reimagining Mary whose actions, choices and qualities reflect the lived realities of Filipino women. This reflexive questioning that is taking place within feminism is important, and must be viewed by feminists as a positive development insofar as it exposes the implicit ethnocentrism in white feminist theorizing.

Contemporary feminist theology is not immune to this self-reflexive internal critique. Morny Joy, who is a Canadian feminist scholar of religion, herself points out a challenging question that renders any Western feminist articulation in theology as suspect: "In whose voice and on whose behalf do women from Europe and North America and Australia, for example, speak when undertaking projects in religious studies of women from other cultures?" (Joy 2004, 31).

Catholic nun and feminist theologian, Mary John Mananzan (2005) reflects on the ways that Filipinos can integrate both the feminine and masculine aspects of God. Accordingly, this led her to discover that in Philippine history there are no traditions of women goddesses. However, it is significant to note that the word for God, *Bathala*, does not have a sexist connotation. In the primitive Tagalog script, the word "god" is made up of three consonants *Ba-Tha-La*. The first consonant is the first syllable of word *babae* (woman), which symbolizes generation. The third consonant is the first syllable of *lalaki* (man), which symbolizes potency. They are joined by the middle consonant, an aspirated sound, which means light or spirit. The word "god," therefore, means the union of man and woman in light. And when one reads the word backwards, it reads *LaHatBa*, meaning total generation, total creator ("to do," or *creador*). In other words, the concept of god among the ancient Tagalogs was more closely linked with woman; and, when linked with both the concepts of man and woman, there is nuance of union and mutuality, not subordination.

One of the most inspiring images of Mary that I have seen by far is the *Virgen of Balintawak*. According to legend, *Virgen sa Balintawak* appeared in a dream of one of the *Katipuneros* (members of the revolutionary society *Katipunan*, which is a group of freedom fighters) who stayed in a place called *Balintawak* during the time of the revolution against Spain in the 1890s. In the dream, the virgin was with a child named *Katipunero*, who stood by her side shouting "Freedom! Freedom!" while carrying a *bolo* (in English, sword) in his hand. The virgin supposedly gave a warning to the dreamer to the effect that they should act with caution. The *Katipuneros*' eventual decision of staying longer in *Balintawak* saved them from being arrested in Manila. The title *Balintawak* stands for both the name of the dress the virgin is wearing and the actual place where she appeared in a dream (Furusawa 2013, 92).

Furusawa points out that in the countries in Asia which have strong devotion to Mary, such as Vietnam and the Philippines, a reimagined Mary would often wear a local dress. This could be because a national or ethnic dress is considered as the representation of cultural identity in the modern nation state. Accordingly, the local dress, re-created at the time of the birth of the modern nation state, serves as a symbol of the authenticity of its tradition and culture. And, often, images of a woman wearing an ethnic dress function as the symbol of tradition or the metaphor of a nation (Furusawa 2013, 89).

The Wandering Virgin: Our Lady of Caysasay

De la Cruz notes the legend that surrounds the Lady of Caysasay, named after the town of Caysasay, Taal:

> A villager is out doing whatever it is that he does in the everyday course of village life, when he stumbles upon a statue of the Virgin Mary. He

prostrates himself before it, tucks it under his arm, and brings it home. The local priest learns of the discovery and goes to where the image is kept. He, too, kneels in adoration before the image and brings it to the parish church, displaying it there for all to venerate. Then, the strangest thing happens. One day the image disappears from its revered post. Time passes, and on another occasion, another villager is going about daily life, when she stumbles across the same image, resting near the spot where it was originally found. The priest brings it back to the parish, but the little image is willful, and again when no one is looking, it returns to where it was found. The image appears to be saying something, speaking by appearing, speaking without properly saying. What – if anythingn – she is communicating may be contested terrain. Fearing this ambiguity, the priest intervenes, declares the image miraculous, and erects a shrine at that spot. (De la Cruz 2015, 44)

Similarly, the mobility of the *Lady of Caysasay* (she keeps on disappearing) seems to reflect the journeys that Filipino women undertake to be able to work abroad. The experiences of Filipino women who migrate for work are empowering in so far as it underscores mobility and agency. While the cultural impetus of being the primary caregiver in the family is embedded deeply in the consciousness of Filipino women, nevertheless, for Filipinas who migrate overseas to work, or those who opt not to marry, or to be childless, the ability to make that choice reveals an independent streak. This streak, however, is glaringly missing or suppressed in the Virgin Mother Mary/Maria Clara imagery. The Lady of Caysasay, however, moves around, and often times, ordinary Filipinos (fisherman, village girls) stumble into her in places where they live and work.

Conclusion

In this paper, the conflation of the images of the Virgin Mary with Maria Clara is shown to be unhelpful for Filipino women. In reality, Filipino women are neither weak nor passive. This is confirmed by many international economic indices that put the Philippines in the top tier of nations that have lessened the gender gap over the decades since studies on gender and development were started. The Philippine Statistical Authority (2016) notes that since 2007, the wages of women workers have risen. In 2014, women earned more than men. According to many indicators, the Philippines has seemed to have addressed the fundamental problems that hinder women in other countries from achieving inclusive growth *vis-à-vis* gender and development.

The paradoxical reality of Filipino female migrant workers, however, renders the impression described above as problematic. The problem lies in the ideological façade that the Roman Catholic Church employs that continues the production and reproduction of imagery that depicts a weak, passive woman. This "good" woman finds her fulfillment of womanhood in mothering. The protest song, *Babae* (a woman), attempts to raise the consciousness of Filipinas by challenging them to answer the following questions[3]:

Kayo ba ang mga Maria Clara?	Are you the Maria Claras?
Mga Hule at mga Sisa?	Are you Hule and Sisa?[2]
Na di marunong na lumaban?	Do you know how to fight back?
Kaapiha'y bakit iniluluha?	Why do you only weep away your oppression?
Mga babae,	You women,
Kayo ba'y sadyang mahina?	Are you innately weak?[3]

From where I live in the Philippines, I can hear the resounding "no" of Filipino women who can be found in almost all corners of the world, with a majority of them toiling at jobs that are insecure. Yet many of them have found a sense of independence in these situations. Marian images that resonate with their independent nature and taste for wanderlust are just right. For Filipino women in the twenty-first century, particularly migrant workers, Mary has become a constant companion who just happens to be a miracle worker, and a goddess in her own right.

Thus, I find it deeply troubling that the Roman Catholic Church continues to lapse into dogmatic doublespeak when it comes to women and to women's bodies. It continues to uphold women's essentialist connection to reproduction. In the 1975 Pastoral Letter on Mary in the Philippines, specifically in paragraph 89, the prelates demonstrated a reasonable grasp of the rising feminist consciousness that was sweeping the globe:

> A revolution is going on which is woman's growing awareness of what she is. Previously consigned to roles defined for her by a mancontrolled society, woman is now questioning the structures of such a society. Agencies all over the world are taking cognizance of this phenomenon. The United Nations, for one, has designated 1975 as International Year of Woman. If the Church is to be faithful to her call, she must look at this phenomenon and question herself regarding her own attitude towards women. This is not a problem only for women, but a profoundly human one (CBCP 1975, par. 89).

---

3. Maria Claras is a reference to characters in Jose Rizal's novel, *Noli me Tangere* Hule and Sisa are characters in Jose Rizal novels; Translation in English mine. The song, "Babae Ka," is written by Karina Constantino and performed by a duo singing group, Inang Laya (Mother Freedom).

In a moment of great clarity, the Filipino Catholic bishops in this instance self-reflexively questioned the Church's part in the subjugation of women, which still remains a reality in many parts of the world. Nevertheless, the local Catholic Church's vacillation between the recognition of Filipino women's worth as women in their own right and the demand to be faithful to the dogmatic demands of upholding an image of the Virgin Mary is an impasse. The qualities of weakness and passivity do not speak today for the overseas Filipino women workers as these characteristics undermine the real transformative power of Mary as it influences the lives of contemporary Filipino women.

Their lived experiences continue to inform the liberal rights discourse now heard in the Philippines. Although the vehement opposition of the local Roman Catholic Church to the Magna Carta Law of Women had made some Filipino women abandoned their faith in the Church, the far-reaching success of the Magna Carta Law of Women has shown that it is an inspired piece of legislation because it is culled from Filipino women's realities, issues and concerns. These realities reveal that the image of the Virgin Mary of the Catholic Church is an impossible image. For the Church to deny this truth is for it to succumb to a gender impasse and deny the female faithful of the opportunity to be listened to on issues surrounding gender justice. Consequently, it excludes as well as alienates from the Church's pastoral care, those who whose realities are not considered because they are rendered obscure or invisible.

Contemporary Filipino women's growing independence; their heightened sense of rights to self-determination; and their resistance to impossible representations of ideal woman, can all help to introduce a bigger space for rights language to thrive in the Philippines. A bigger space means Filipino women are no longer invisible.

References

Bräunlein, Peter J. 2014. "Who defines 'the Popular'? Post-Colonial Discourses on National Identity and Popular Christianity in the Philippines." In *Religion, Tradition and the Popular: Transcultural Views from Asia and Europe*, edited by Judith Schlehe and Evamaria Sandkühler, 75–80. Bielefeld: Germany: transcript. https://doi.org/10.14361/transcript.9783839426135.75

Brazal, Agnes. 2010. "Harmonizing Power-Beauty: Gender Fluidity in the Migration Context." *Asian Christian Review* 4(10): 32–46.

Carandang, Ma. Lourdes. 2007. *Nawala Ang Ilaw Ng Tahanan-Case Studies of Families Left Behind*. Quezon City: Anvil.

Catholic Bishops' Conference of the Philippines (CBCP). 1975. "Ang Mahal na Birhen Mary in Philippine Life Today." A Pastoral Letter on the Blessed Virgin Mary by the Catholic Bishops' Conference of the Philippines. https://doi.org/10.1057/9780230371262_6

———. 2005. "With Mary, the Migrants and Their Families Find Life in the Eucharist." A Message for the Nineteenth National Migrants' Sunday by the Catholic Bishops' Conference of the Philippines. http://www.cbcponline.net/ecmi/letters/19th%20National%20Migrants%20Sunday.htm

Cruz, Gemma. 2007. "Em-body-ing Theology: Theological Reflections on the Experience of Filipina Domestic Workers in Hong Kong." In *Body and Sexuality*, edited by Agnes Brazal and Andrea Si, 60–74. Quezon City: Ateneo de Manila.

Constantino, Karina. 1983. "Babae." *Kalayaan: Isang Daang Taong Paggunita.* CD-ROM.

De la Cruz, Deidre. 2015. *Mother Figured Marian Apparitions and the Making of a Filipino Universal.* Chicago. University of Chicago Press. https://doi.org/10.1111/aman.12737

Fiorenza, Elisabeth Schüssler. 2013. "Critical Feminist Studies in Religion." *Critical Research on Religion* 1(1): 43–50. https://doi.org/10.1177/2050303213476112

Furusawa, Yuria. 2013. "Image and Identity: A Study on the Images of the Virgin Mary Clad in a Local Dress in the Philippines." In *The Work of the 2011/2012 API Fellows*, 88–97. Japan: Nippon Foundation.

General Secretariat of the Synod of Bishops. 2014. *Lineamenta: The Vocation and Mission of The Family in the Church and Contemporary World.* http://www.vatican.va/roman_curia/synod/documents/rc_synod_doc_20141209_lineamenta-xiv-assembly_en.html

John Paul II. 1981. *Laborem Exercens: Encyclical Letter on Human Work.* http://w2.vatican.va/content/john-paul-ii/en/encyclicals/documents/hf_jp-ii_enc_14091981_laborem-exercens.html

Joy, Morny. 2004. "Postcolonial and Gendered Reflections: Challenges for Religious Studies." In *Gender, Religion and Diversity: Cross-Cultural Perspectives*, edited by Ursula King and Tina Beattie, 28–39. New York: Continuum.

Kawahashi, Noriko. 2013. "Gendering Religious Studies: Reconstructing Religion and Gender Studies in Japan." In *Gender, Religion and Education in a Chaotic Postmodern World*, edited by Zehavit Gross, Lynn Davies, and Al-Khansaa Diab, 111–123. New York: Springer. https://doi.org/10.1007/978-94-007-5270-2_8

Mactal, Roland. 2007. "Mariological Developments after Second Vatican Council and the Impact of Marian Devotion in the Philippines." *Philippiniana Sacra* XLD (25): 249–300.

Mabanglao, Ruth E. 1997. "Liham ni Pinay Mula sa Brunei" (Pinay's Letter from Brunei). In *Philippine Literature: History and Anthology* (revised edition), edited by Bienvenido Lumbera and Cynthia Lumbera, n.p. Pasig City, Philippines: Anvil Publishing. https://www2.hawaii.edu/~mabanglo/engPinay_brunei.htm

Peracullo, Jeane. 2012. "A Filipino Feminist Perspective On The Rh Bill Debates." *SDRC Occasional Paper Series* 2 (2012-B): 1–10.

———. 2015. "Kumakalam Na Sikmura: Hunger as Filipino Women's Awakening to Ecofeminist Consciousness." *Journal of the Feminist Studies of Religion* 31(2): 25–44. https://doi.org/10.2979/jfemistudreli.31.2.25

Philippine Statistics Authority. 2013. "Total Number of OFWs is Estimated at 2.2 Million (Results from the 2012 Survey on Overseas Filipinos)." 11 July. http://web0.psa.gov.ph/content/total-number-ofws-estimated-22-million-results-2012-survey-overseas-filipinos

Parmanand. Sharmila. 2014. "Mapping the Path to Philippine Reproductive Rights Legislation Signs of Progress Amidst Obstacles." *Social Transformation* 2(1): 61–80. https://doi.org/10.13185/st2014.02104

Reyes, Melanie. 2008. *Migration and Filipino Children Left-Behind: A Literature Review*. Miriam College/UNICEF.

Soriano, Cheryll Ruth R., Sun Sun Lim, and Milagros Rivera-Sanchez. 2015. "The Virgin Mary with a Mobile Phone: Ideologies of Mothering and Technology Consumption in Philippine Television Advertisements." *Communication, Culture and Critique* 8: 1–19. https://doi.org/10.1111/cccr.12070

Tanyag, Maria. 2015. "Unravelling the Intersections of Power: The Case of Sexual and Reproductive Freedom in the Philippines." *Women's Studies International Forum* 53: 63–72. https://doi.org/10.1016/j.wsif.2015.10.002

8

The Reconstruction of Muslim Women's Property Rights in the Twenty-first Century

Sri Zaleha Kamaruddin was the fifth Rector at the International Islamic University of Malaysia (2011–2018), the first woman to hold this position. She is both a lawyer and an academic, having earned her PhD in Comparative Laws at University College, London. An expert on Family Law, she was appointed as a member of the National Women Advisory Council. She holds a number of other prestigious appointments. Since 2017 she has been Judge of the Sharī'ah Court of Appeal of Terengganu, a position she will hold until 2020. Her contribution to this volume addresses the position of women and her concern to help them achieve economic empowerment so as to thwart discrimination and exploitation.

Introduction

In the quest towards empowering women, different societies have introduced phenomenal reforms over the centuries but there still exist significant limitations in certain communities across the world. The Muslim world has been a focal point for most human rights activists.[1] The general perception persists regarding equal access and opportunities for women in their pursuit of property rights. The frequently headlined point of ratio two to one in the Muslim inheritance share of men and women has been overstretched without any meaningful consideration to how women access other property rights through legitimate means provided under the Islamic law as well as other seemingly Sharī'ah-compliant provisions in

---

1. Human rights are rights that belong to an individual or group of individuals as a consequence of being human. Once an individual happens to be a member of humankind, human rights are demands and claims that he can make on the society. However, it is generally perceived that the women folk have been deprived of such values in many respects simply by virtue of being women. As such, the idea of personal autonomy of women's property rights have become a significant means of curtailing "the oppression of individual women within the family unit where women's human rights are frequently violated through domestic violence, restrictions on access to resources and in matters of [...] property rights." See Fox (1998, 5).

conventional human rights instruments. The modern dynamics underlying women's property rights and the continued struggle towards securing such rights within complex societies that are tainted with pseudo-religious practices and mummified by deep-rooted cultural norms lead to two simultaneously deficient views with special reference to Muslim societies.[2] While the first view believes women's property rights are curtailed and excessively limited in Islam, the second position emphasizes the postmodernist approach, which tends to gravitate towards emancipating the modern day Muslim woman.

Against the above backdrop, this chapter seeks to address four pertinent questions:

1. What are other property rights Muslim women can acquire apart from inheritance, which is often perceived in some quarters as being discriminatory?
2. What are the obstacles and limits constraining the full implementation of property rights for Muslim women?
3. Can the international human rights instruments help in providing equal access to, and protection of, property rights of both men and women, and to what extent is such a legal framework accepted in Muslim states?
4. How can a fresh and balanced appreciation of Islamic principles as lobbying tools for positive interpretation be constructed in the modern world?

The legal status of women under the Sharī'ah has been a subject many Muslim jurists of the past have laboured on in their respective juristic treatises. This same concept has touched off a maelstrom of controversy across the Muslim world and beyond, particularly when it comes to the strict interpretation of the inheritance rights in Islam. While one might not need to delve into the arena of controversy among some contemporary Muslim jurists, an endeavour to look inwards within the general Sharī'ah framework reveals a plethora of neglected Islamic legal rules that may be closely studied to evolve a new integrated and holistic transformative property regime. This will re-emphasize the relevance of Islamic legal principles in the twenty-first century, which is expected to lead to some sort of convergence of laws in an increasingly globalized world. Therefore, it is high time people took a step further from the culturally denied gender

---

2. The generic term "women's property rights" contains women's rights to own, acquire (through purchase, gift, or inheritance), manage, administer, enjoy, and dispose of tangible and intangible property, including land, housing, money, bank accounts, livestock, crops, and pensions. These are human rights that women by virtue of being human are entitled to enjoy. These rights are guaranteed under international human rights law as well as, though with some variation, under the Sharī'ah.

land rights and the perceived gender discrimination in inheritance rights in Islam. This chapter focuses on some of these potential concepts within the Islamic framework that would promote unhindered access to property rights by way of recompense bearing in mind the increasing responsibilities shouldered by women in Muslim societies across the world.

Muslim women and property

Different paradoxes emerge in the quest for property rights for Muslim women in the modern world. When one glosses through annals of Islamic history, with specific reference to precedents set during the early days of Islam, one can easily establish the fact that Muslim "women were property holders, a fact which has been pointed out for various Islamic societies and should be reiterated here [...] that this certainty was not the case in many other civilizations, including many Western societies" (Baer 1983, 9). From the idealistic standpoint, this explains why the right to property is granted to all regardless their gender or racial background in Islam. Property rights constitute one of the foundational bases of any Muslim society and in most cases there is no distinction on the basis of gender.

Thus, what went wrong along the way is a matter of concern that requires further expert explorations, wider deliberations, and well-reasoned resolutions. Though this chapter does not intend to fully adopt a socio-legal approach to Muslim women's property rights, an investigative foray into the prophetic precedents and the cornucopia of the *fiqh* books reveals the real legal status of women with regards to property and property acquisition. From the classical provisions of Islamic law, there is no restriction on women's right to property and land ownership. The basis of this form of protection for all individuals regardless of their sexual orientation is firmly rooted in the Islamic legal sources. Given the fact that the focus of this chapter is Muslim women's property rights, Islam originally considers women as a special class of people who require maximum protection in all forms. This does not portend the culturally tainted practices of divesting women of their property rights as being experienced in many Muslim societies today.

Being the main source of Islamic legislation, the Qur'an clearly provides for women's property rights as it confers on women an independent legal and economic status. Before the advent of Islam, women were unjustly deprived of their property rights as they themselves were considered part of the property of the patriarchal system that prevailed in the then Arabia and elsewhere. The often-labelled discriminatory textual evidence in the Qur'an, including the verses that relate to share of inheritance of women as compared to their male counterparts, are themselves revolutionary, considering the way women were treated as objects rather than independent human beings who can acquire and enjoy basic rights like any other human being.³ This informs the corrective measures taken by the Qur'an to right the prevailing wrongs through revolutionary provisions such as women "shall be legally entitled to their share" (Qur'an 4:7).⁴ Apart from such testamentary entitlements, the right to acquisition and ownership of property is granted equally to men and women: "To men is what is allotted what they earn, and to women what they earn" (Qur'an 4:7). Men are not in whatever capacity or under any circumstance allowed to take over the ownership of property that belongs to women around them.⁵ There

---

3. An important aspect of women's property rights is the right of inheritance – a right which Sharī'ah accord to women. This aspect of Islamic law has created controversy especially among the non-Muslims and human rights activists simply because it provides for a son's share to be twice that of the daughter's. The Qur'an states: "Allah (thus) directs you as regards your children's (inheritance): To the male, a portion equal to that of two females." See Qur'an 4:11. In the opinion of non-Muslims, the Islamic Law of Inheritance is discriminatory and thus unjust. However, many writers on Islamic law have argued that this law does not discriminate against women. For instance, Perveen Shaukat Ali is of the view that: "in their opinion this is against the basic rules of justice to give women half of the male's share. It may, however, be pointed out that a woman is in no way a loser in this bargain. She gets her part of property from three different sources, i.e., father, husband and son, and this makes her share almost equal to man" (see Ali 1980, 120).

    The reasoning forwarded by Muslim jurists for the wisdom behind the inheritance law that is subject to criticism is the fact that in Islam, it is the man's responsibility to provide safety, protection and sustenance to women. As the Qur'anic verse quoted earlier says, "Men are the protectors and maintainers of women." Hence, even though the son's share is larger, he has to provide for and support his own family with his inheritance. On the other hand, the daughter has no such responsibility, thus, she is the sole benefactor from her inheritance. As a general rule, in Islam, a woman has full ownership of the property she acquired before and after, or during the marriage. There is no rule such as the old English doctrine of coverture where a woman's property is automatically transferred to the husband upon marriage.

4. In fact it was Islam that gave women the right to inherit, as the pre-Islamic custom excluded women from any form of inheritance, and improved their economic status by identifying their share of inheritance. The Qur'an 4:7 provides: "Unto the men (of a family) belongeth a share of that which parents and near kindred leave, and unto the women a share of that which parents and near kindred leave, whether it be little or much – a legal share."

5. This right and status was given to women in Islam at a time when women themselves (widows) were considered as inheritable objects, confining the right to inheritance only to male descendants. In fact, Islam prohibited the

must be a valid alienation or transfer of such property before men can legally acquire ownership of such. The foregoing Qur'an principles permeate numerous prophetic precedents where such basic principles were enforced. As it has been argued elsewhere, history may serve as a veritable springboard to achieve women's legal rights in modern Muslim societies. Such reiteration of Islamic history would enhance the property rights of modern Muslim women a great deal.

Modern realities: Revisiting the property rights of Muslim women

Throughout the world women, in comparison with men, endure a mediocre economic status – a status which is unequal, vulnerable to human rights abuses (Crimm 1995, 3–4) – a status that emanates mainly from the violations of the right to property.[6] Respecting women's right to property under international human rights law, irrespective of the approach one follows (i.e., gender-based or non-gender-based),[7] helps to enhance the economic status of women, raises their social standings and thus curbs violations of women's human rights in general. Moreover, property rights are part of the civil and political rights that are believed to be the first generation rights, but the attainment of such rights hinges more on the economic status of an individual (Claude and Weston 2006, 9).[8]

The overarching influence of cultural practices on some religious ide-

---

abominable practice of inheriting women. Qur'an 4:19 provides: "O ye who believe! ye are forbidden to inherit women against their will."

6. "Generally, the right of an individual to own some property and not be deprived of it arbitrarily is recognized as a human right" (Vogelson 1996, 210).
7. Some concerned groups have struggled for decades to improve the human rights conditions for women under international law using a gender-based approach, while some others advocated non-gender-specific in pursuing women's human rights, therefore bringing women's human rights into the mainstream under general human rights instruments. Those who adopted a non-gender approach reasoned that since women are human beings, they should defend their rights using general human rights treaties rather than separate gender-based initiatives.
8. It should be noted that the International Covenant on Civil and Political Rights has incorporated nearly all the rights that are proclaimed in the Universal Declaration on Human Rights, but it excludes the right to own property. The International Covenant on Economic, Social and Cultural Rights has provided for rights under which states are to take steps toward implementing them in a progressive manner through forward-planning. But it has made the obligation to prohibit discrimination in the enjoyment of property rights as an immediate obligation (Claude and Weston 2006, 21–22).

als, which were ordinarily non-discriminatory, justifies the need to revisit Muslim women's property rights in the light of modern realities. There has been increasing criticism against the prevailing practices in Muslim countries, which are somewhat contrived to represent Islam.

> Muslim feminists strongly argue that the current Islamic legal norms are based on a masculine and patriarchal interpretation of the Koran and suggest re-interpretation of the Koran from the perspectives of females. The development of the feminists' argument is motivated to achieve two main objectives. First, to redress gender inequality in the Islamic legal norms. Second, to represent authentic Islam. (Shah 2006, 882)

This line of argument has also been supported by people like An-Na'im, who believes the Sharī'ah needs reform and a new understanding to be able to address such elements of inequalities staring at the faces of onlookers (An-Na'im 1990, 171). An-Na'im contends that:

> In inheritance, a Muslim woman receives less than the share of a Muslim man when both have equal degree of relationship to the deceased person. [...] We are not concerned here with the historical justification of these instances of discrimination on grounds of religion or gender. Reasonable people may differ in their view of the historical sufficiency of any justifications that may be offered for any particular instance of discrimination. For example, it may be argued that economic and social conditions of seventh-century Arabia did not justify some or all of the discriminatory rules cited above. It is my submission, however, that regardless of differences over the historical sufficiency of justifications, these instances of discrimination against women [...] under Sharī'ah are no longer justified (An-Na'im 1990, 176–177)

An-Na'im is not alone in holding such a view. Shahrur believes the norms set by the Sharī'ah are not absolute and that what is provided by the law is just the maximum and minimum limits while the legislature is free to determine individual cases based on the specific needs of a particular era (see, generally, Browers 2004, 445–467). While these scholars may have their justifications for their standpoints, there are other Islamic legal materials that can be used to ensure access to property rights rather than stirring unnecessary controversy in the (re)interpretation of affirmative evidence in Islam.

Notwithstanding the above, the modern realities in Muslim societies conspicuously present a gloomy picture of discriminatory practices against women, particularly in their rights to property ownership. Figure 1 shows the extent of women's rights to property ownership and inheritance according to different regions across the world.

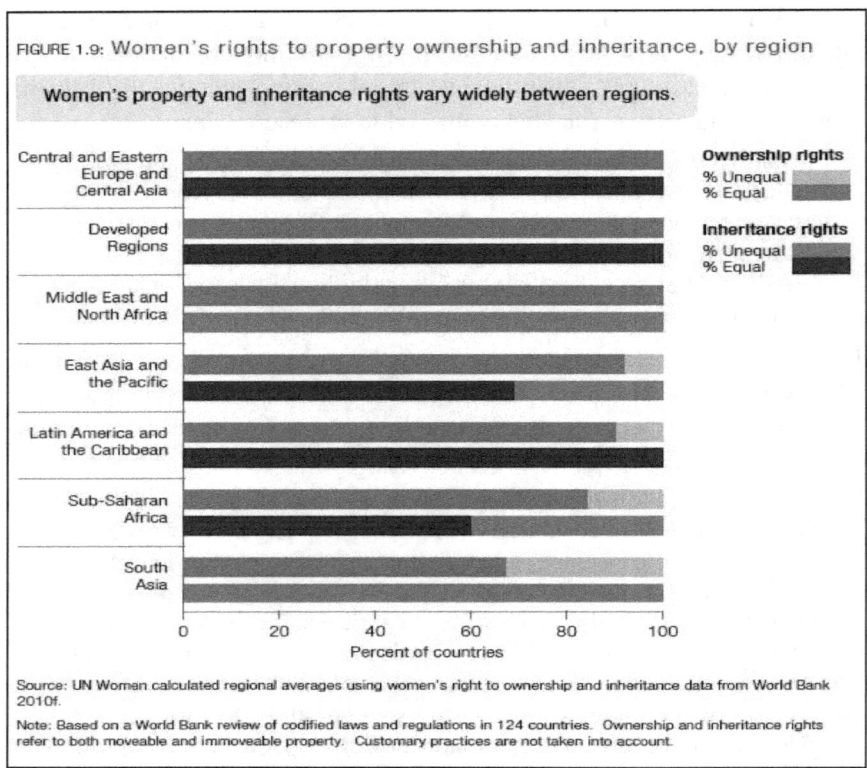

Figure 1. Women's rights to property ownership and inheritance. Source: United Nations Entity for Gender Equality and the Empowerment of Women (2011, 39).

Since the scope of this chapter relates to Muslims who constitute the majority in Middle East and North Africa, it thus appears that both property ownership and inheritance rights of women in Muslim-dominated regions are below a reasonable level.

Muslim women's property rights and the international human rights framework

International human rights law is a branch of public international law, and thus its sources are the same as those of international law, which include, *inter alia*, international conventions (treaties), custom, and general principles of law (Statute of the International Court of Justice 1945, Arts. 38 and 59). Women's right to property has been recognized by international human rights law, as is evident from the relevant provisions of the international human rights instruments, including the International Covenant on Economic, Social, and Cultural Rights,[9] the International Covenant on Civil and Political Rights,[10] the Platform for Action adopted at the 1995 Fourth World Conference on Women,[11] the United Nations Convention on the Rights of the Child,[12] the United Nations Commission on Human Rights resolution 2002/49, and the Convention on the Elimination of All Forms of Discrimination against Women.[13] A review by UN-Habitat of the international human rights instruments, resolutions, and documents within which women's rights to land, housing, and property are situated reveal that under the international human rights law system, women have the following rights (UNCHS 1999, 22):

1. The right to be free from discrimination[14];
2. The right to an adequate standard of living;
3. The right to adequate housing;
4. The right to enjoy financial independence and to earn a livelihood; and
5. The right to own, manage, enjoy, and dispose of property.

These are the core human rights of women, but the interpretation and realization of them remains unsettled due to variations in forms of law governing property issues and the ways in which domestic statutory and customary laws interact and conflict. Moreover, the right to land and the right to inheritance do not appear as independent rights in international human rights law, so progress toward the right to housing may inform the broader struggle for women's rights to land, housing, and property.

The rights highlighted above are interrelated and complementary to women's equal property rights – rights so fundamental that, if imple-

---

9. UNGA Res. 2200 (XXI), December 16. 1966, entered into force January 3, 1976.
10. UNGA Res. 2200A (XXI), December 16. 1966, entered into force March 23, 1976.
11. The Fourth World Conference on Women: Action for Equality, Development and Peace, Beijing, 4–15 September 1995.
12. UNGA Res. 44/25, 1989 (entered into force Sept. 2, 1990).
13. Adopted by the UN General Assembly at New York on December 18, 1979; Entered into force on 3 September 1981. UN GA Res. 34/180.
14. The Convention on the Elimination of All Forms of Discrimination against Women defines the right of women to be free from discrimination and sets the core principles to protect this right. It establishes an agenda for national action to end discrimination and provides the basis for achieving equality between men and women through ensuring women's equal access to, and equal opportunities in, political and public life as well as education, health, and employment. CEDAW is the only human rights treaty that affirms the reproductive rights of women.

mented, would ensure women's economic security, strengthen their social and legal status in the society, and possibly even guarantee their survival. It was observed that the structure supporting the conventional human rights instruments which address general rights without gender specification are stronger than those supporting women's rights. The specific international human rights instruments relating to women have fragile and weaker implementation mechanisms (Fox 1998, 4). Though an increasing number of countries around the globe have now recognized women's equal rights in their constitutions, in compliance with their international and regional human rights requirements and obligations, the impact of such legislations are not yet recorded as a result of lack of strong enforcement mechanisms (Benschop 2004, 4). Unavoidably, reference can be made to all the above interrelated rights, but an attempt is made in this chapter to concentrate on women's rights to property as contained under international human rights law with particular reference to the relevant provisions of the Convention on the Elimination of All Forms of Discrimination against Women (CEDAW). This is an important convention as far as women's equal property rights are concerned.

Women's Property Rights under CEDAW

CEDAW, adopted in 1979 by the UN General Assembly, is often described as an international bill of rights for women. CEDAW, one of the most ratified international treaties, has been ratified by 187 states including a significant number of Muslim states. Its primary purpose is to eliminate *de facto* and *de jure* discrimination and inequality on the basis of sex.[15] Consisting of a preamble and thirty articles, it defines what constitutes discrimination against women and sets up an agenda for national action to end such discrimination. It defines discrimination against women as: "any distinction, exclusion or restriction made on the basis of sex which has the effect or purpose of impairing or nullifying the recognition, enjoyment or exercise by women, irrespective of their marital status, on the basis of equality of men and women, of human rights and fundamental freedoms in the political, economic, social, cultural, civil or any other field." (Article 1, CEDAW). The implementation of CEDAW is overseen by the Committee on the Elimination of Discrimination against Women (CEDAW), which is a body of twenty-three independent experts.[16]

---

15. Comm. On the Elimination of Discrimination against Women, Report of the Committee on the Elimination of Discrimination against Women, p. 4, U.N. Doc. A/59/38.
16. On 6 October 1999, the UN General Assembly adopted a 21-article Optional

The Convention provides the basis for realizing equality between women and men through ensuring women's equal access to, and equal opportunities in, political and public life, including the right to ownership of property. Hence, discrimination is defined as an act that violates the principles of equality, and it recognizes women as equal to men in human dignity, establishing a concept of equality that is not andocentric but based on the protection of women's human rights (Facio and Morgan 2009). CEDAW implies that it is the concept of "equality" that is needed to end discrimination against women as opposed to "equity." Black's Law Dictionary (at 576) defines "equality" as "the quality or state of being equal; esp., likeness in power or political status." Hence, a woman has an equal right as a man to own property.

CEDAW in its Article 16 sets out equal rights of spouses in the enjoyment and disposition of property by obliging states to ensure "[t]he same rights for both spouses in respect of the ownership, acquisition, management, administration, enjoyment and disposition of property, whether free of charge or for a valuable consideration."[17] This equality of rights

---

Protocol to the Convention on the Elimination of all Forms of Discrimination against Women. The Protocol entered into force on 22 December 2000. By ratifying the Protocol, a state recognizes the competence of the Committee on the Elimination of Discrimination against Women – the body that monitors states parties' compliance with the Convention – to receive and consider complaints from individuals or groups within its jurisdiction. The Protocol contains two procedures: (1) A communications procedure allows individual women, or groups of women, to submit claims of violations of rights protected under the Convention to the Committee. The Protocol establishes that in order for individual communications to be admitted for consideration by the Committee, a number of criteria must be met, including that domestic remedies must have been exhausted. (2) The Protocol also creates an inquiry procedure enabling the Committee to initiate inquiries into situations of grave or systematic violations of women's rights. In either case, states must be party to the Convention and the Protocol. The Protocol includes an "opt-out clause," allowing states upon ratification or accession to declare that they do not accept the inquiry procedure. Article 17 of the Protocol explicitly provides that no reservations may be entered to its terms.

17. Article 16 of CEDAW provides: "States Parties shall take all appropriate measures to eliminate discrimination against women in all matters relating to marriage and family relations and in particular shall ensure, on a basis of equality of men and women: (a) The same right to enter into marriage;(b) The same right freely to choose a spouse and to enter into marriage only with their free and full consent; (c) The same rights and responsibilities during marriage and at its dissolution; (d) The same rights and responsibilities as parents, irrespective of their marital status, in matters relating to their children; in all cases the interests of the children shall be paramount; (e) The

to women is safeguarded and guaranteed through the principle of state obligation as provided in Article 2 of CEDAW.[18] This provision provides that states parties should eliminate discrimination against women in all its forms through appropriate legislation and repeal all national penal provisions as well as customary practices which are discriminatory to women.

The use of the equality principle in the CEDAW Convention was challenged by some Muslim States parties, the Vatican City, and the Latin American states. These states favoured the use of "equity" rather than "equality."[19] These states believe that the term "equity" goes beyond

---

    same rights to decide freely and responsibly on the number and spacing of their children and to have access to the information, education and means to enable them to exercise these rights; (f) The same rights and responsibilities with regard to guardianship, wardship, trusteeship and adoption of children, or similar institutions where these concepts exist in national legislation; in all cases the interests of the children shall be paramount; (g) The same personal rights as husband and wife, including the right to choose a family name, a profession and an occupation; (h) The same rights for both spouses in respect of the ownership, acquisition, management, administration, enjoyment and disposition of property, whether free of charge or for a valuable consideration. 2. The betrothal and the marriage of a child shall have no legal effect, and all necessary action, including legislation, shall be taken to specify a minimum age for marriage and to make the registration of marriages in an official registry compulsory."

18. Article 2 of CEDAW provides: "States Parties condemn discrimination against women in all its forms, agree to pursue by all appropriate means and without delay a policy of eliminating discrimination against women and, to this end, undertake: (a) To embody the principle of the equality of men and women in their national constitutions or other appropriate legislation if not yet incorporated therein and to ensure, through law and other appropriate means, the practical realization of this principle; (b) To adopt appropriate legislative and other measures, including sanctions where appropriate, prohibiting all discrimination against women; (c) To establish legal protection of the rights of women on an equal basis with men and to ensure through competent national tribunals and other public institutions the effective protection of women against any act of discrimination; (d) To refrain from engaging in any act or practice of discrimination against women and to ensure that public authorities and institutions shall act in conformity with this obligation; (e) To take all appropriate measures to eliminate discrimination against women by any person, organization or enterprise; (f) To take all appropriate measures, including legislation, to modify or abolish existing laws, regulations, customs and practices which constitute discrimination against women; (g) To repeal all national penal provisions which constitute discrimination against women."

19. "Although some feminists have attempted to go 'beyond equality' to a deeper analysis of what it means to say that men and women are equal, a few state actors in the international arena such as Sudan, have taken a different direction, one that threatens to restrict women's rights. They argue that the word

"equality." Equity requires that each person is given according to their needs. The object of using equity instead of equality is not to treat women the same as men but, more importantly, to give women what they need. The Convention, however, adopted the principle of equality between men and women.

The adoption of the equality principle dissuaded some Muslim countries like Sudan not to adopt CEDAW. Some Muslim countries adopted it without any reservation while some others made reservations on CEDAW's provisions,[20] which are not Sharī'ah compliance including the provisions on women property rights and equality excluding the application of the provisions upon themselves. The concept of reservation in the context of CEDAW will be discussed shortly after a brief discussion on women's property rights under Sharī'ah, as this will put the discussion on "reservations" in perspective.

Reservations to CEDAW by Muslim State Parties

Reservations are "unilateral statements, however phrased or named, made by a State, when signing, ratifying, accepting, approving or acceding to a treaty, whereby it purports to exclude or modify the legal effect of certain provisions of the treaty in application to the State."[21] Reservation, as a legal regime,[22] provides a compromise allowing states to become parties

---

'equality' be replaced with the word 'equity' with respect to gender-based issues. Equality is not seen as desirable. Rather, equity and fairness, as more abstract and flexible provisions that could readily depart from the principle of formal equality, should guide state action toward women. Of course such provisions would likely draw on contextual mores and particular traditions to develop their meaning and guide their applications" (Coomaraswamy 1997, 1258).

20. "Of the fifty-seven OIC member countries, all but Iran, Sudan and Somalia have ratified the CEDAW Convention. Twenty-nine ratified without reservations, mostly African and Central Asian countries. Yemen and Indonesia are the only two countries outside of Africa and Central Asia that ratified without reservations. Turkey removed all its reservations later. Mauritania and Niger are the only two sub-Saharan African countries which ratified with reservations" (Sisters in Islam 2011).

21. Vienna Convention on the Law of Treaties, opened for signature May 23, 1969, 1155 U.N.T.S. 331, 8 I.L.M 679 (entered into force 27 January 1980) Article 2, p. 1.

22. The legal regime of reservations has been codified in the Articles 19 to 23 of the Vienna Convention on the Law of Treaties (VCLT). Article 19 provides that a State may, when signing, ratifying, accepting, approving or acceding to a treaty, formulate a reservation unless: The reservation is prohibited by the

to the treaty without accepting all of the provisions therein or limiting the application of certain provisions. CEDAW as a special Convention has enjoyed ratification from many countries of the world with reservations of certain significant provisions of the Convention.

Among the 187 states that ratified or acceded to CEDAW are all Muslim states except Iran, Sudan, and Somalia.[23] However, many Muslim states made reservations under Article 28 of the Convention on certain core articles, such as Articles 2, 16, 9, etc., of the Convention on the grounds that they conflict with certain provisions of Sharī'ah (Bangladesh, Egypt, Iraq, Maldives, Mauritania, Morocco), the Act on Personal Status (Jordan), the Family Code (Algeria) or the Personal Status Code (Tunisia). Malaysia is also a party to CEDAW, but it declares that its accession is subject to the understanding that the provisions of the Convention do not conflict with the provisions of Sharī'ah and the Federal Constitution of Malaysia. With regards thereto, further, the Government of Malaysia does not consider itself bound by the provisions of articles [...] 9(2), 16(1)(a), 16(1)(f) and 16(1)(g) of the CEDAW.[24] Similarly, Egypt while ratifying CEDAW made a declaration that: "The Arab Republic of Egypt is willing to comply with the content of this article (2), provided that such compliance does not run counter to [...] Sharī'ah." This reservation applies to Article 2 of CEDAW. Germany, Mexico, the Netherlands, and Sweden all entered objections to the reservation made by Egypt, stating that it was contrary to the object and purpose of the treaty (Nicolai 2004).

---

treaty; (b) The treaty provides that only specified reservations [...] may be made; or (c) The reservation is incompatible with the object and purpose of the treaty.

23. Interpretation of the Islamic Jurisprudence in the Spirit of the International Human Rights Norms and the Convention on the Elimination of All Forms of Discrimination against Women, Ferdous Ara Begum. http://www.wunrn.com.

24. CEDAW, Article 9 (2) provides: "States Parties shall grant women equal rights with men with respect to the nationality of their children." The relevant part of Article 16 of the same Convention reads: "1. States Parties shall take all appropriate measures to eliminate discrimination against women in all matters relating to marriage and family relations and in particular shall ensure, on a basis of equality of men and women: (a) The same right to enter into marriage; [...] (f) The same rights and responsibilities with regard to guardianship, wardship, trusteeship and adoption of children, or similar institutions where these concepts exist in national legislation; in all cases the interests of the children shall be paramount; (g) The same personal rights as husband and wife, including the right to choose a family name, a profession and an occupation."

In fact, it is glaring that most of the Muslim states have maintained reservations on the Convention on Article 2 (state obligation) and Article 16 (property rights) subject to the applicability of Sharī'ah (Article 9 (2), CEDAW). The reservation made by Muslim states allows Sharī'ah to take precedence over the implementation of legislation to eradicate discrimination against women within the said states. However, as in the case of Egypt, such reservations are heavily criticized as undermining the object and purpose of the treaty. Article 28 of CEDAW allows reservation provided that the reservation is not "incompatible with the object and purpose" of the Convention. But the Muslim states have justified the reservation on traditional and religious grounds.

Muslim women's property rights: A transformative property regime through microfinance

While the Muslim states reserve the prerogative to stipulate certain reservations in the international human rights instruments that ostensibly seek to promote women rights, including their property rights, it is pertinent to look inwards into some models of economic empowerment driven by the transformative property regime in Islamic law. What we present here is a case study of such modern initiatives in some Muslim states which, apart from the inherent principles in Islamic law that can be used to empower women such as *wasiyyah*, *hibah*, and even *waqf al-ahli*, may be utilized in reconstructing the Muslim women's property rights. There is a need for a paradigm shift to some socio-economic models that are based on communal efforts to ensure and recognize property rights for all, especially women. In some Muslim communities, the microfinance model has been successfully utilized for this purpose which has invariably recorded far-reaching results. Though the Grameen bank model in Bangladesh has been largely criticized as a result of the interest rate charged, it however spurred further development of Sharī'ah-compliant microfinance models in the Muslim world. In the Grameen model, over 95 per cent of the borrowers are women, and most of them got economically empowered and self-reliant after some time. It is believed women are more reliable than men as borrowers in most microfinance initiatives (Rahman 2007, 38–53).

Some other Sharī'ah-compliant microfinance schemes introduced include Hodeidah microfinance program in Yemen, Amanah Ikhtiar Malaysia in Malaysia, UNDP Murabahah-based microfinance in Jabal al-Hoss in Syria, Rural Development Scheme of the Islami Bank Bangladesh Limited, and Baittul Maal wa Tamwil (BMT) microfinance system in Indonesia. Through some of these laudable initiatives, millions of women have been economically empowered through well-thought-out transformative regimes. Such empowerment stems from the unique nature of Islamic microfinance, which primary relies on profit and loss sharing models in some of its financing models. This gives an uncommon opportunity to rural women to become micro-entrepreneurs. So from micro-entrepreneurs, they may transform their businesses to small and medium enterprises (SMEs) (Oseni *et al.* 2013, 153–80).

These are practical initiatives that transcend mere academic narratives, which are often unproductive in the final analysis. Moving on, there is a need to focus more on these practical initiatives to reconstruct Muslim women's property rights in the 21st century rather than waste time and resources debating the reinterpretation of Islamic legal principles on the ratios of heirs and the wrongly perceived discriminating tendencies in Islamic law.

Conclusion

This paper's outline of the dynamics of Muslim women's property rights and human rights demonstrates the inherent regulatory and transformative regime of Islamic law. Such a framework is often buried in the treasure-trove of Islamic jurisprudence, which requires a clear understanding and reinterpretation in line with modern exigencies. With the foregoing analysis, it is crystal-clear that there is an Islamic dimension to the modern world debate on women's property rights vis-à-vis modern human rights instruments. So, rather than considering the additional access to boundless property rights for Muslim women as a transformative property regime, it might just be possible to have a more general perception about the increasing gulf between ideals and realities in Muslim societies. This therefore makes a case for an integrated and holistic approach towards access to property rights through the exploration of the Islamic mechanisms highlighted in the chapter that are geared towards ensuring sustainable practices in the wider Muslim societies across the world.

Given the fact that the modern Muslim women are taking up more responsibilities, rather than calling for the reinterpretation of the applicable original sources of Sharī'ah, a better approach is to explore those other mechanisms through which women's rights to property could be enhanced. Though legal heirs are not entitled to *wasiyyah* (bequest), a gift (*hibah*) made *inter vivos* by a testator to any of the legal heirs provides a solution (Mokhtar 2007). Similarly, in order to ensure the sustainability of a family, a testator may make a family endowment (*waqf al-ahli*) *inter vivos*, which takes effect during the lifetime of such testator (Powers 1990,

22). Some of these testamentary dispositions taking effect during the lifetime of the testator are being widely used in Muslim communities in India and Southeast Asia.[25]

Finally, while one cannot totally throw away the baby with the bathwater, it is pertinent to implement some Sharī'ah-compliant provisions of both international and domestic human rights instruments in the light of modern realities. This suggests a proactive human rights approach that would enhance the economic status of women in order to boost their financial strength to acquire and own property. It will further give women the opportunity to exercise their rights to property. This can be achieved through strengthening the gender-specific instruments dealing with the rights of women and the mechanism for their enforcement by harmonizing the provisions of the conventional laws, as represented by CEDAW, and Islamic law. While there should not be any controversy about the exercise of some reservations by some Muslim countries, taking the harmonization path would be more sustainable in the long run. Rather than coming up with a convention that has the inherent character of generating unwieldy controversies, it is better to consider the values and legal culture of the major world legal systems, where the Islamic legal system occupies a front stage.

References

Ali, P. S. 1980. *Human Rights in Islam*. Lahore: Aziz.

An-Na'im, Abdullahi Ahmed. 1990. *Toward an Islamic Reformation: Civil Liberties, Human Rights, and International Law*. Syracuse, NY: Syracuse University Press. https://doi.org/10.1017/s0034670500017265

Baer, Gabriel. 1983. "Women and *waqf*: an analysis of the Istanbul *Tahrir* of 1546," *Asian and African Studies* 17: 9–27.

Benschop, M. 2004. "Women's Rights to Land and Property," Commission on Sustainable Development, Women in Human Settlements Development – Challenges and Opportunities. 22 April. www.unhabitat.org/downloads/docs/1556_72513_CSDwomen.pdf

Browers, Michaelle L. 2004. "Shahrur's Reformation: Toward a Democratic, Pluralist and Islamic Public Sphere." *Historical Reflections / Réflexions Historiques* 30(3): 445–467. http://www.jstor.org/stable/41299318

---

25. However, there is a legal restriction in such disposition of property particularly when such is done during the death sickness of the testator. Such disposition must not be more than one-third of the estate of the testator in order to protect the rights of the legal heirs.

Claude, R. P., and Burns H. Weston, eds. 2006. *Human Rights in the World Community: Issues and Action*. Philadelphia: University of Pennsylvania Press.

Coomaraswamy, Radhika. 1997. "Reinventing International Law: Women's Rights as Human Rights in the International Community," *Commonwealth Law Bulletin* 23: 1249–1262. https://doi.org/10.1080/03050718.1997.9986487

Crimm, Nina J. 1995. "Introductory Remarks: Women's Rights as International Human Rights." *St. John's Law. Review* 69(1): 3–4.

Facio, Alda, and Martha I. Morgan. 2009. "Equity or Equality for Women? Understanding CEDAW's Equality Principles" [Morgan Symposium on the Gender of Constitutional and Human Rights Law]. *Alabama Law Review* 60: 1133–1170. https://doi.org/10.2139/ssrn.1469999

Fox, Diana, J. 1998. "Women's Human Rights in Africa: Beyond the Debate over the Universality or Reality of Human Rights." *African Studies Quarterly* 3(3): 3–16. http://sites.clas.ufl.edu/africa-asq/files/ASQ-Vol-2-Issue-3-Fox.pdf

Mokhtar, Mohd. Kamil. 2007. *Al Hibah: The Principles and Operational Mechanism in the Contemporary Malaysian Reality*. Master's thesis, Universiti Teknologi Malaysia, Faculty Geoinformation Science and Engineering.

Nicolai, Caroline E. 2004. "Islamic Law and The International Protection of Women's Rights: The Effect of Sharī'ah in Nigeria." *Syracuse J. International Law and Commerce* 31: 299–327.

Oseni, Umar A., M. Kabir Hassan, and Dorsaf Matri. 2013. "An Islamic Finance Model for the Small and Medium-Sized Enterprises in France," *Journal of King Abdul Aziz University, Islamic Economics* 26(2): 153–180. https://doi.org/10.4197/islec.26-2.5

Powers, David S. 1990. "The Islamic Inheritance System: A Socio-historical Approach." In *Islamic Family Law*, edited by Chibli Mallat and Jane Frances Connors, 11–29. London: Graham & Trotman. https://doi.org/10.1163/1568519972599888

Rahman, Abdul Rahim Abdul. 2007. "Islamic Microfinance: A Missing Component in Islamic Banking." *Kyoto Bulletin of Islamic Area Studies* 1–2: 38–53.

Shah, Niaz A. 2006. "Women's Human Rights in the Koran: An Interpretive Approach." *Human Rights Quarterly* 28(4): 868–903. https://doi.org/10.1353/hrq.2006.0053

Sisters in Islam. 2011. *CEDAW and Muslim Family Laws: In Search of Common Ground*. Malaysia: Sisters in Islam (SIS Forum Malaysia). http://www.musawah.org

Statute of the International Court of Justice. 1945. Articles 38 and 59. Entered into force 24 October. http://www.icj-cij.org/en/statute

United Nations Centre for Human Settlements (UNCHS). 1999. *Women's Rights to Land, Housing and Property in Post-conflict Situations and During Reconstruction: A Global Overview*. Nairobi: United Nations.

United Nations Entity for Gender Equality and the Empowerment of Women (UN Women). 2011. *Progress of the World's Women: In Pursuit of Justice*. https://doi.org/10.1093/law-epil/9780199231690/e2195

Vogelson, Jay M. 1996. "Women's Human Rights," *The International Lawyer* 30(3): 653–663.

9

Charity and Justice:
A Conversation with Evangelical Christian Women Serving Marginalized Populations in British Columbia

Kathryn Chan is an Associate Professor at the University of Victoria Faculty of Law, where she teaches and researches in the areas of non-profit law, public law, and law and religion. She previously practiced law at a boutique charity law firm in Vancouver and completed her doctoral research on comparative charity regulation at the University of Oxford as a Trudeau Foundation and SSHRC-funded scholar. Her first book, *The Public-Private Nature of Charity Law*, was published by Hart Bloomsbury in November 2016.

Erin Thrift is a PhD candidate in Educational Psychology at Simon Fraser University. She attained an MA in Counselling Psychology from Simon Fraser University in 2004 and has worked as a counsellor and sessional instructor at numerous universities. In this time, she has also served as a board member of non-profit organizations that develop social enterprises, supportive housing projects and promote sport for children. Her current scholarly interests include critical and historical analysis of charitable institutions, social movements, and social justice practices and rhetoric in education and psychology.

Introduction

Charity and justice are central concepts in most religious and ethical traditions. However, the precise meaning of each concept, and the nature of their interrelationship, has varied between cultures and through time. Contemporary liberal societies tend to associate "justice" with duty, with our collective moral obligation to ensure that all members of a society have a fair share of social goods (Kymlicka 2001). The discourse of "rights" has been prominent in this conception of justice. "Charity," on the other hand, is associated with voluntariness, with individual choices to act generously that materially improve the situation of a stranger in need. Charity and justice are thus portrayed as dichotomous concepts within a liberal paradigm, with justice being ascribed significantly more normative weight (Kymlicka 2001).

The normative universes of many religious traditions paint a more complex picture of the relationship between justice and charity. Islamic law, for example, counts *zakat* (obligatory alms-giving) among the five pillars of Islam, and instructs the Muslim in great detail about the circumstances in which *zakat* is payable, the rate at which *zakat* is payable, and the categories of needy persons who are entitled to receive it (de Zayas 2003). Judaism, for its part, situates the act of giving to the needy within a broader jurisprudence of *mitzvot* or obligations, and ranks different forms of almsgiving in accordance with a particular vision of economic justice.[1] The narratives of charity and justice vary *within* as well as *between* religious traditions: indeed, the meaning and relative importance of charity and justice may be subject to contestation even within a particular faith community. This exploratory study examined how a group of evangelical Christian women are seeking to define and live out these concepts in the various contexts of their work with marginalized populations in British Columbia.

The evangelical tradition in North America has tended to either adopt an individualistic notion of justice that is closer to liberal conceptions of charity, or to relegate justice to a sphere outside the church's core concerns.[2] Evangelical institutions have supported "charitable" projects that are aimed at alleviating the needs of individuals, but have not traditionally supported "justice" projects aimed at addressing systemic inequalities (Offutt *et al.* 2016). Previous research has shown that while mainstream evangelical churches are engaged in supporting certain political causes (e.g., opposing abortion and promoting socially conservative candidates), they have been reluctant to engage in social analysis or political activism aimed at fixing structural injustices (Conradson 2008; Delahanty 2016; Offutt *et al.* 2016; Thacker 2015). Delahanty (2016) argues that this tendency is the result of "a highly individualistic political theology" (p. 43) in which social issues and religious obligations are understood in individu-

---

1. The great medieval Jewish scholar Maimonides famously ranked almsgiving in eight different categories, with the highest being the formation of a partnership with, or the provision of a loan, grant or job to a person in need: see Maimonides (1979) and Cover (1992).
2. The contested meaning of the term "evangelical" is not a central focus of this piece. We adopt here the approach of John Stackhouse, using the term to denote a group of movements in church history that look back to the Protestant Reformation to emphasize the unique authority of Scripture and salvation through faith alone in Christ. The group includes the Puritans of England and America, Methodists, Baptists, Pentecostals, and others.

alistic terms. The "comfortable church culture" that is associated with this theological position both reinforces and is reinforced by the wider cultural context. Within this culture, "charity and volunteering [are considered to be] appropriate activities for church life [...] [but] collective analysis of systemic social problems [is] something to do elsewhere, if at all" (Delahanty 2016, 43). "Justice" efforts are considered to be, at best, outside of the purview of religion, and, at worst, a direct (possibly Communist) threat to Christianity (Delahanty 2016; Offutt *et al.* 2016).

The evangelical church is not univocal, however, and there is an important counter-current within the evangelical community that considers advocacy efforts aimed at changing unjust systems and structures to be central to the Christian faith. In North America, this counter-current has been sustained most consistently by the Black evangelical church in the United States, which has long married a concern with social justice issues with more traditional evangelical concerns such as personal conversion, discipleship, and service provision (McNeil 2011; Berk 1989). This counter-current has also made small inroads into mainstream white evangelical churches and non-profit organizations in recent years. For example, Conradson (2008) describes how four mainstream faith-based organizations in New Zealand adopted a more explicit social justice orientation between 1996 and 2006. These four large organizations – Anglican Care, Methodist Mission, Presbyterian Support and the Salvation Army – transitioned from engaging primarily in social support and provision activities to engaging in social analysis and advocacy, in a very intentional way. This transition was, in part, a response to the increased social inequality the leaders of these organizations recognized as resulting from the neoliberal turn in politics during the 1990s in New Zealand.

As Delahanty's (2016) paper illustrates, there are also activist clergy and community organizers embedded within evangelical churches in the United States. Delahanty describes leaders in the American faith-based community organizing (FBCO) movement who endeavour to establish social justice activism as "an essential part of the mission to which God calls followers" (49). These FBCO leaders have two aims: they aspire to achieve political and social change but also to achieve "a deeper cultural change in what *church* and *religion* mean to religious Americans" (53, italics in original). One of the leaders sums up the challenge in this way: "We must no longer be chaplains to an empire. We must be the prophets of resistance" (53–54).

Evangelicals who privilege justice efforts in their work are very clear that they are motivated by theological frameworks that understand correcting socioeconomic injustices to be a central tenet of the Christian faith. There are several of these justice-privileging frameworks, including liberation theology (e.g., see Thacker 2015), Anabaptist theology (e.g., see Finger 2004), kingdom theology (e.g., see Wright 2012) and the social gospel movement (e.g., see Deichmann 2015; Marsh 2008). Recently, there also have been efforts to develop a uniquely evangelical theology that places activism and advocacy at the centre of Christian life (e.g., see Offutt et al. 2016). For evangelicals who embrace these theologies, issues of social justice are primary, not tangential, issues for the church (Conradson 2008; Delahanty 2016). Nonetheless, leaders with a commitment to social justice and political advocacy still represent a minority or "counter-current" within the evangelical tradition.

In British Columbia, these evangelical counter-currents are identifiable among female evangelicals who work with marginalized populations and are committed to addressing both the individual and systemic dimensions of the challenges faced by those populations. This study sought to explore these counter-currents, engaging with a group of female evangelicals who are actively pursuing "justice-oriented" models of non-profit service provision in spite of the dominant "charity-oriented" paradigm of evangelical charitable organizations. The researchers wanted to document the experiences and perspectives of these individuals – as service providers, as women, and as persons of faith – as they swim against a number of powerful institutional currents.

Research goals and methodology

For purposes of this work, we defined "justice-oriented" models of service provision as models that either blurred the lines between service-provider and beneficiary, and/or gave political voice to those they represented. (e.g., by advocating on behalf of refugees or trafficked persons). Our participants all worked for registered charities or other non-profit groups that pursue such a "justice-oriented" model and are affiliated with an evangelical church. We invited fourteen women to participate; seven ultimately took part in the group interview. Both of the researchers had worked with non-profit organizations in British Columbia and as a result the study participants were known to the researchers. Thus, care was taken during recruitment and data collection to ensure that participants did not feel obligated to participate as a result of prior relationships.

They women ranged in age from thirty to fifty-three, with a mean age of 40.7. All had a post-secondary degree, and four of the seven participants had graduate degrees. All of the participants had personal connections to evangelical churches; some had pastoral roles.

This research was exploratory and had three broad goals. The first was to gain insight into the different models of non-profit service provision that are currently being pursued by evangelical Christian organizations in British Columbia. Although we perceived these women to be "justice-oriented" from a distance, it was not clear to us from the outset whether they were justice-oriented *because of* or *in spite of* the service provision model of the organization for which they worked. As such, the first goal was simply to gather information about their working contexts. The second goal was to identify whether the women perceived regulatory or institutional obstacles to their efforts to provide justice-oriented services to marginalized populations. Our third goal was to explore how these women understand the concepts of charity and justice, and the relationship of those concepts to their work, gender, and faith.

As this was an exploratory study, we used a group-interview, which was recorded, transcribed and analyzed thematically. We began with a few planned open-ended questions and spent most of the conversation listening to participants and asking for further clarification of ideas they introduced. Both researchers were involved in analysis of the transcripts – first independently and then together. Similar themes emerged from the independent analyses; we discuss three of these themes below.

Thematic analysis

The complex relationship between justice and charity

A first theme that emerged from the discussion was the complex relationship between justice and charity. Although participants distinguished between charity and justice, it became apparent that a dualistic understanding of these two concepts was problematic for the participants, particularly as they tried to pursue these aims in their work.

In general, the participants envisaged a distinction between justice and charity. One participant stated that justice involved "working against systems" while charity was about "addressing the results of those systems." Another painted an image of justice and charity as "upriver work [and] downriver work [...] if you don't do the upriver work, you're going to have the wreckage constantly that you're dealing with." The participants were all involved in non-profit models of service provision that intentionally sought to blur the lines between service-provider and beneficiary, for example through the development of personal relationships with persons who might elsewhere be described as "clients." One participant described this blurring of boundaries as "a movement from charity towards justice."

Another discussed the negative connotations that charity held for her, and her desire to privilege justice in her work with marginalized communities.

> I think, for me, when [...] just this whole conversation of charity and justice, automatically, I'm like, "Charity is bad and justice is good." ... charity is, like, pitying or belittling people, and justice is, like, empowering or understanding people more [...] it often feels like they're against each other; one is better than the other; and hopefully, you're on the justice side, something that's cooler [...] or more, like, forward-thinking.

Many of the participants understood their own movement towards more justice-oriented models as a response to a mainstream evangelical perspective that minimized the importance of justice:

> [...] in a large part of North American [...] a good portion of the churches, there is no systemic understanding of justice. So I think we've had, in a sense, to do that kind of separating-out for it to be seen. And maybe we still need to because that's ... the winds are so strong in that direction; but I think maybe we've skewed it a little bit as well, in terms of how that happens.

In another exchange, the group's perception of the dominant position of the evangelical church emerged even more starkly:

> So, certainly for denominations and churches, there's more this sense that charity is good and justice is
>
> [...] Communist.

However, this group of women also acknowledged the close connection between justice and charity and the difficulty of teasing the two concepts apart, particularly in practice. One pastoral participant noted that Jesus Christ was engaged in both "charity" (helping individuals) and "justice" (challenging systems) during his time on earth:

> If I look at the example of Christ, some of the work that Christ did looked like maybe charitable work in some ways, but it was challenging systems. And so, I think, although I would probably still define charity and justice the way you do [speaking to another participant], I think that I'm maybe seeing that there's ways that you can do charity work that then challenges justice. And there's also ways that you can do justice work that maybe sometimes seems to undermine it.

The discussion took an interesting turn and some members of the group postulated that living in community might be the nexus between justice and charity. One participant wondered out loud "if there's another level in there. There's charity, large systemic change, and then there's community."

The group emphasized that living in community is difficult, particularly when community includes people who have a high degree of stress and trauma in their lives. Identified challenges included vicarious trauma, overwork, and performing tasks that at times felt beyond their areas of competence. One participant who worked with homeless women stated:

> There's such a high degree of trauma that I'm seeing the staff be very seriously traumatized [...] not very seriously, but pretty seriously traumatized. I'm experiencing trauma there like I've not experienced ever.... And so I don't know how sustainable that'll be in the long run, offering that kind of intensive trauma care where, many days, it feels like you're working in the Psych Ward. And we do have women from Psych so it is kind of like that. But it's kind of in this Christian-do-gooder kind of mode; so you're not really sure, "Am I actually equipped to do this? Well, here I am, so let's do it," you know. But not having ... we don't have a lot of ways to debrief that or hold that together.

Another participant suggested that living in community might be more difficult than practicing either justice *or* charity:

> It can be hard to be sustainable when I become friends with everybody who's living at [X charity], whether that's just like, expectations of birthday parties, going to events or, just like, "Oh, you don't come visit me anymore at my house." Oh, like, I just don't have the capacity; and then, also the trauma that you were talking about. It's like hearing the reality of so many people and such stressful environments, over time, it's so exhausting. And so I feel like that blurring of boundaries, in my mind, is what leads towards that justice model, and it helps us and it hinders us, and it's very complicated.

Social architecture of charity

A second set of themes that emerged from the discussion related to the effects that the "social architecture" of charity had on the participants' attempts to implement justice-oriented models of service provision. The participants discussed what one participant called the "non-profit industrial complex," at some length, identifying several elements of that complex that limited their ability to pursue justice in their work. These limiting elements included the Canada Revenue Agency rules on registered charities, the policies and attitudes of funding bodies, and the internal policies of the organizations for which the participants worked.

The participants were all aware of Canada Revenue Agency's role as the regulator of registered charities in Canada, and of the existence of special rules governing charities and other non-profit organizations. However, several participants were confused about the content of those rules, and what they meant for the activities of their organization. At one point a participant suggested that her organization was not allowed to do something because of its charitable status, prompting a humorous exchange.

> What? They're not allowed to by who?
>
> I don't know, the charity [...] [Laughter] [...] The charity rules [...] The charity police. [A lot of laughter] [...] Maybe the lawyer knows why. I don't know why.

The participants also joked about the confusion was exacerbated by the regular turnover on non-profit boards.

> And it feels like, even if you sometimes get it explained, then you've got boards that constantly turn over. So people don't always keep up or know [...] and then the law changes, too, it seems like.
>
> But the fear remains the same.
>
> Yeah [laughs].
>
> The fear passes on [...] [A lot of laughter] [...] even if the understanding of the [...] the basis of the fear does not pass on.

If the participants were able to laugh about their confusion over the CRA's regulatory policies, however, it was also evident that those policies created fear and uncertainty for their organizations. One participant described people's perceptions or misperceptions of charity law as "a big boogeyman that keeps a lot of organizations from fulfilling what they even are convinced is their mandate because they feel like they don't have that freedom." Another described how the CRA's rules on political advocacy for registered charities limited her organization's ability to challenge the status quo:

> There's a fear related to charitable status, "Oh, are we doing too much advocacy? Would we lose our charitable status?" Like, what are [...] we don't have legal consultation or someone that can sometimes guide us through kind of what are some of the lines that we can push. And when you're a pretty small [...] stable, but fragile organization, I think there's [...] I know, with all the cuts to healthcare for refugees and all the changes to legislation around the system, it was [...] like, there was such a need for advocacy, but there was a real challenge to, "What are you allowed to do and what can we do kind of safely that's not going to prevent us from being able to provide the direct care to families that are arriving on our doorsteps?"

Participants also described being oriented away from "justice" activities and towards "charity" activities by their interactions with charitable foundations and other funding organizations. "When [non-profit organizations] are financially in trouble," one participant asserted, "they move conservative." The participants associated this move towards conservatism with the little-understood CRA rules and the fear of losing charitable status. However, the participants also stated that the challenges of finding and retaining donors created pressures for their organizations to help people on an individual level rather than challenging systems.

The participants identified a number of possible reasons why donors were more comfortable with "charity" than "justice" initiatives. A first was that funders understood charity better than they understood justice. As one participant explained:

> charity seems like it can be funded. Like, it exists in people's imaginations and it kind of [...] once you can set a compelling vision out, it kind of goes. Justice doesn't feel that way and as you set out a justice vision, it's like, sometimes you can catch this little moment, but it doesn't [...] it isn't sustained,

Another participant linked this difficulty in understanding justice initiatives to established patterns of assistance within the Christian church.

> I think it's a huge challenge to try to sort of like, open up the Christian imagination to the fact that, in the church's history, what we have been doing [...] is sort of these individualistic, like, helping people on an individual level or giving money to charities who are helping people on an individual level. Instead of asking the question, "Why are these individuals in this place . . . ?" And it's hard to get people to move to the systemic understanding because it's so vague, it's so big, it's so overwhelming. People don't even know where to begin.

Donors like measurables, the participants suggested, and it is easier to measure individual acts of charity than systemic change. When their organizations did receive funding from donors, that funding often came with conditions or requirements that inhibited the beneficiaries of the funding from exercising collective agency. In order for justice-oriented initiatives to flourish, one participant suggested, marginalized communities needed to have the space to develop agency and treat the donated funds as collective assets.

> But this model where funding means you have a certain amount of control, [and] you get to say how things happen; and that might not be the best thing for that community [...] so the people who are most affected are also the most [expels breath] [...] not the least [...] I don't want to say, "The least reliable," but [...] their lives are chaotic.... So they take more time and it requires more protection around them for them to move where they need to go [...] So, [...] I see myself as this sort of protector of that process. And often, supporters, then, of various sorts feel like they're being held off – and they are being held off – in order to allow this process to develop. But I think that dynamic is both one of the most beautiful things...

like, when it can happen and when that community can speak for what they want and kind of come into the fullness of themselves, then that's really beautiful and powerful. But the dynamic of creating the space that can allow that to happen and sustain that, is really complicated.

The participants put forward a further reason why donors were more comfortable with "charity" than "justice" initiatives: justice implicates donors in unjust systems, while charity feels good. "One of the reasons why we don't talk about justice so much," one participant stated, "is that it implicates us." The participant pointed out that for people of relative privilege, confronting unjust systems often produces uncomfortable feelings of guilt.

> we've never taken the time to think about it [systems of power], because, when you think about it, then you have all of that guilt. And I mean, I still struggle with so much white colonial guilt, you know; and then, "what do I do with that guilt?" And [...] then you're in this other place of struggle, which can feel really overwhelming, and it's exhausting. And why not just donate to [X charity] and then "Let's go out to dinner." And, you know, like [...] you've done your charitable thing and you can feel really good about that; and we'll send you a picture of me taking the ladies to [X] Gardens – not of us doing a smudge[3] – but taking them to the Gardens, which is very nice and white and civilized.

Finally, the participants expressed the view that in seeking to carry out justice-oriented programs of service provision, they often had to confront unjust practices *within* their own organizations. One participant who worked for a well-established and well-funded religious charity related this to the very low wages the charity paid to its workers:

> the reason I keep bringing up the alleviation of poverty is that they [X charity] pay poverty wages to most of the staff that I work with. [one person laughs] [...] So I think that's problematic. That goes against your Mission Statement. So [...] when we were talking about working against systems [...] I think the system that I work against there is the organization itself. That is the system that I'm working to transform.

The same participant also identified racism and patriarchy as injustices that were reinforced by the charity's practices:

---

3. KiiskeeNtum [She Who Remembers] (1998) describes the practice of smudging in the following way: "The burning of various medicine plants to make a smudge or cleansing smoke is used by the majority of Native North American peoples. It is a ritual cleansing. As the smoke rises, our prayers rise to the Spirit World where the Grandfathers and our Creator reside. Negative energy, feelings, and emotions are lifted away. It is also used for healing of mind, body and spirit, as well as balancing energies."

One of the things that I try to do there internally is my own commitment to Indigenous sovereignty – and that's playing out in all kinds of different ways in the organization – and ending racism and patriarchy. And so I am fighting those systems but within the organization, but I try to organize people in the organization to then change, and, hopefully, that change will ripple out [...] a group of us [...] have been doing trainings with the senior leadership team at [X charity] around Indigenous issues.

The participant noted that when she was younger, and working for organizations that were less a part of the non-profit establishment, she would have criticized the charity she now worked for "until the cows came home." Over time, she had become more familiar with "the ways you can act [to combat injustice] within the systems." However, she noted that because the establishment charity she worked for was such "an intense power and principality, it's very hard not to get coopted there and kind of fall asleep."

Finally, participants noted that the growth of charitable institutions has had the effect of displacing community organizing. The decline of community organizing is exacerbated by the fact that many charities, even those whose mission is poverty reduction, pay poverty wages and expect much of their staff. As a result, as is recounted in the following exchange, those who work for non-profit organizations have little energy left over for community organizing or participation in community advocacy:

You see, this is a huge thing that has shifted [...] from people doing grass-roots, social-change work, to [...] working for a non-profit in order to try to do ... make change. So it's like this non-profit-industrial complex... where ... [people] only have the energy for their work. [...] whereas, before, I think, most social change that has taken place has been through. [...] broad-based community organizing. [One person agrees] And that's not to say that what the non-profits are doing is wrong, or that what charities are doing should [...] that all should stop. Because if that stopped, well, yeah, people would be screwed.

I think it's that community organizing isn't happening as much now...

Right, right [...] you don't have the energy for it.

and in the past, I think you had the charity and then you had the community organizing [...] but I also think there's less broad-based community organizing that's going on now. So the community organizing that I've seen here is like [...] I can name, you know, I., W., [...] you know, we could list off all the people on two hands, kind of thing. So I think that's another issue.

Justice/charity and women

A final theme that emerged from the discussion was the relationship between justice, charity and gender. Several participants expressed the view that marginalized women experience unique forms and layers of oppression that are often embodied and invisible. This oppression is society-wide, but may also be experienced *within* religious contexts and charitable organizations. As one participant stated:

> I think the stakes are much higher [for women] because the women have so much less power – socio-economic power, spiritual power – in society, that they're so much more marginalized, that it's just got – [...] I mean, I think about the difference in our work between men's A&D recovery – which is what receives the lion's share of the funding, and what we've mostly done – and [X program for women]. And it's very hard for the organization even to understand – the leadership on the men's side – to understand how our programs are so very different. Because the kinds of trauma and the levels of the trauma, the layers of the trauma, that the women have experienced is so much deeper, is so much more layered; and they've been so much more disempowered. And I think so many of them also have been sexually abused or sexually assaulted that they have so much trauma that they carry within their bodies, and their trauma is so relational; the trauma plays out in these relational ways. So I think that they just have more at stake, and it's much more challenging working with them.

Another participant identified patriarchy as a form of oppression that distinguished the position of marginalized women and marginalized men.

> the invisibility issue, because [another participant] mentioned the physicality in-the-body things for women, that trauma is in their physical – [...] – well, you didn't say that – but it's in their physicality, it's in their bodies. And, also the socio-economic realities for women, partly because of the whole children thing, because they are often the ones taking care of children and so forth. But then there's the invisibility thing, of how we actually [...] patriarchy is invisible to us, so is its own system. So, even though women are dealing with all these other systems – as are the men – but the women are dealing with this one system that no one even acknowledges.

The layered trauma and disempowered state of marginalized women made it especially important that non-profit initiatives seek to address unjust systems rather than simply providing individual aid. As one participant put it:

> I think that women know that what they're experiencing is a broader political issue that other women are experiencing. And so I think it would be important to them that people are working on justice as well as [...] so, providing care, but also working to change systems at the same.

Interestingly, the participants noted that it is women who are pushing justice issues within these institutions, perhaps because women often recognize the systemic nature of trauma and marginality as a result of their experience of patriarchy:

> And we've only just now, after all this pushing for like, four years, have gotten smudges – I've already been smudging, but they didn't know that – but allowing smudges to happen on our side […] it's only the women's side that's even talking about this. And they're saying the women's side is so pioneering, they're pushing the envelope all over the place.

Participants in this study were very clear that although downriver charity for individual women is important, it is equally necessary to connect individual stories to broader structures such as patriarchy. Thus, charity for women must be closely connected to justice.

Discussion

The themes that emerged from this study point to the complexity of the concepts of charity and justice. The participants valued individual aid but also were acutely aware of the role of systems and structures in perpetuating injustice. Their awareness of structural forces seemed to come, at least in part, from their experiences as women. Their efforts to connect individual acts of charity to wider systems of justice were often carried out *in spite* of church, government and fundraising institutions that promoted charity, not justice. The themes that emerge from their conversation suggest that for certain evangelical women, charity and justice are not disparate concepts or actions, but rather dual commitments of the Christian faith that ought to be held together.

The perspective that the female participants provided on charity/justice has parallels to the anti-dualist view of an ethic of rights and ethic of care advanced by Kroeger-Mappes (1994).[4] Kroeger-Mappes (1994) argues that the dichotomy between an ethic of rights (sometimes called the "justice" ethic), associated with the research of Kohlberg, and an ethic of care, associated with the work of Gilligan, is problematic in that it places

---

4. Participants did not use the language of "rights" in their descriptions of their work, even though the term is commonly associated with challenges to unjust systems. Instead they framed their actions and perspectives as examples of "justice," perhaps because this is the language we introduced at the outset of the research project. The absence of the mention of "rights" could also have been a reflection of their religious backgrounds. An area for further research would be to explore how evangelical women understand the concept of "rights" and how the language of rights aligns with and/or differs from their views on justice and charity.

women in the challenging position of being accountable to two moral systems whose requirements often are contradictory. Men, particularly men who are privileged, in contrast, are primarily held to an ethic of rights, which also is considered to be the superior ethical position. Kroeger-Mappes is critical of efforts to subsume one ethic into the other, pointing out that this has the result of making invisible certain types of work and morality. Thus, she advocates that both ethics be understood as being part of the same system, with an ethic of care providing the foundation for an ethic of rights (Kroeger-Mappes 1994). The critique of an ethic of rights/ethic of care offered by Kroeger-Mappes has implications for the way justice/charity is understood. The women in this study, like Kroeger-Mappes, understood charity and justice as being part of the same system and at least some expressed discomfort at having to parse their actions into categories of "charity" and "justice" (as we asked them to do, implicitly, through our questioning). Dichotomizing charity and justice is problematic, but particularly so for women who are often involved in both "care" and "justice" work, as Kroeger-Mappes discusses.

Parallels may also be drawn between the experience of the participants in this study and the experience of the activist clergy and community organizers described in Delahanty's study. Both sets of participants are engaged in challenging systems that perpetuate inequalities within society *and* within church institutions (Delahanty 2016). Delahanty states that activist clergy and organizers that challenge "comfortable church culture" ideology in their own evangelical churches face the added obstacle of having their efforts framed "as challenges to established cultural orthodoxy or profane intrusions into sacred church spaces" (Delahanty 2016, 43). Although we did not ask participants in the present study whether their particular church culture was impeding their activist efforts, several participants did mention ways in which they were seeking to bring justice to the Christian organizations in which they worked and numerous comments were made regarding the way the general theological stance of the Evangelical church and, especially, conservative funders, impeded their efforts.

Conclusion

Our exploratory study provides just one snapshot of the various counter-currents within the Canadian evangelical community that consider activities aimed at changing unjust systems to be central to the Christian faith. Further research would be required to determine the strength of this counter-current, the range of theological positions that support it, and the extent of the institutional obstacles that it faces. What is clear, however, is that there are people (women, in this case) within the evangelical religious tradition who are very cognizant of systemic contributors to wellbeing and are committed to helping individuals, but also connect individual stories of pain to larger structures that maintain inequality and injustice and work to change these structures. This is in contrast to the stereotypical evangelical response, which has been noted as individualistic in its focus (e.g., see Offutt *et al.*'s description of evangelicalism). Although this group is a statistical minority within this Christian tradition, it seems, from the testimony of these women, that they are having a powerful effect not only on larger societal issues of injustice, but also on the evangelical institutions in which they work.

The following points emerged strongly and may provide directions for future study:

1. The evangelical women that we interviewed had a robust sense of social justice that was deeply rooted in their Christian faith. All of our participants were acutely aware of the ways in which the institutions of the "non-profit industrial complex" could (either deliberately or inadvertently) produce injustice. While these evangelical women were committed to challenging unjust structures, however, they also saw the value of individual acts of mercy. Although there was some evidence of justice "displacing" charity as the normative framework for their work, what emerged overall was an understanding of the interrelatedness of the two concepts: what one participant described as a "need for justice to be married with the charity side." A future study might explore further the multivocal nature of the concepts of charity and justice within or between religious traditions. It might look more closely at how particular groups within evangelicalism understand and act on the dual requirements of charity and justice, paying particular attention to the ways in which acts of charity and justice are in some instances mutually reinforcing and, in others, contradictory or opposing.

2. While the researchers did not directly raise the issue of the participants' *own* marginalization, the discussion suggested that "justice-oriented" female evangelicals may experience marginalization in a number of different ways. Their religious beliefs situate them as Evangelical Christians, but their feminism and political views place them at the margins of this broader community of faith. Their work situates them as social activists, but their religious and social views may place them on the margins of this broader community as well. The comments of participants in this study seemed to suggest that as a result of experiences of marginalization (e.g., as women in a tradition that has been very patriarchal, historically) they were attuned to the way structural injustices contributed to individual experiences of pain. A future study might confirm this experience of double

marginalization, and explore whether it has an impact on these women's faith and work.

3. The way in which the practices of religious and government/regulatory institutions influence understandings and actions of charity and justice merits further exploration. The participants in this study indicated that the institutions that have arisen around non-profit organizations tend to support a very traditional, individualistic understanding of charity, which tends towards the maintenance of the status quo. Future studies might examine how institutional practices influence the development of models of non-profit service provision, and how views of charity and justice differ amongst funders and front-line workers in Christian organizations.

References

Berk, S. E. 1989. "From Proclamation to Community: The Work of John Perkins." *Transformation* 6(4): 1–7.

Conradson, D. 2008. "Expressions of Charity and Action towards Justice: Faith-Based Welfare Provision in Urban New Zealand." *Urban Studies* 45(10): 2117–2141. https://doi.org/10.1177/0042098008094876

Cover, R. 1992. "Obligation: A Jewish Jurisprudence of the Social Order." In *Narrative, Violence and the Law: the Essays of Robert Cover*, edited by M. Minow, M. Ryan, and A. Sarat, 239–248. Ann Arbor: University of Michigan Press. https://doi.org/10.2307/827615

Deichmann, W. J. 2015. "The Social Gospel as a Grassroots Movement." *Church History* 84(1): 203–206. https://doi.org/10.1017/s0009640715000050

Delahanty, J. D. 2016. "Prophets of Resistance: Social Justice Activists Contesting Comfortable Church Culture." *Sociology of Religion* 77(1): 37–58. https://doi.org/10.1093/socrel/srv054

Finger, T. N. 2004. *A Contemporary Anabaptist Theology: Biblical, Historical, Constructive*. Downers Grove, IL: InterVarsity Press. https://doi.org/10.1177/004057360606300220

KiiskeeNtum (She Who Remembers) 1998. "Gifts from the Creator for Man's Use ... The Smudging Ceremony." *Aboriginal Multi-Media Society* 16(2); retrieved from: http://ammsa.com/node/12407.

Kroeger-Mappes, J. 1994. "The Ethic of Care vis-à-vis the Ethic of Rights: A Problem for Contemporary Moral Theory." *Hypatia* 9(3): 108–131. https://doi.org/10.1111/j.1527-2001.1994.tb00452.x

Kymlicka, W. 2001. "Altruism in Philosophical and Ethical Traditions: Two Views," in *Between State and Market: Essays of Charities Law and Policy in Canada*. Edited by J. Phillips, B. Chapman and D. Stevens, 87-126. Montreal: McGill-Queen's University Press.

Maimonides. 1979. *The Code of Maimonides (Mishneh Torah), Book VII, The Book of Agriculture*. Translated by Isaac Klein. New Haven, CT: Yale University Press. https://doi.org/10.1163/19606028_015_02-16

Marsh, C. 2008. *The Beloved Community: How Faith Shapes Social Justice, from the Civil Rights Movement to Today*. New York: Basic Books. https://doi.org/10.2307/27649218

McNeil, G. R. 2011. African American Church Women, Social Activism, and the Criminal Justice System. *Journal of African American History* 96(3): 370–383. https://doi.org/10.5323/jafriamerhist.96.3.0370

Offutt, S., F. D. Bronkema, K. Vaillancourt Murphy, R. Davis, and G. Okesson. 2016. *Advocating for Justice: An Evangelical Vision for Transforming Systems and Structures*. Grand Rapids, MI: Baker Academic. https://doi.org/10.1111/rsr.13079

Thacker, J. 2015. "From charity to justice: Revisited." *Transformation* 32(2): 112–127.

Wright, N. T. 2012. "Imagining the Kingdom: Mission and Theology in Early Christianity." *Scottish Journal of Theology* 65(4): 379–401. https://doi.org/10.1017/s0036930612000178

de Zayas, Farishta G. 2003 [1960]. *The Law and Institution of Zakat*. New York: The Other Press.

10

Women, Rights Talk, and African Pentecostalism

Rosalind I. J. Hackett is Distinguished Professor in the Humanities and Professor of Religious Studies at the University of Tennessee. In fall 2018, she was the Gerardus van der Leeuw Fellow, Faculty of Theology and Religious Studies, University of Groningen. Her recent (co-edited) books are *New Media and Religious Transformations in Africa* (2015) and *The Anthropology of Global Pentecostalism and Evangelicalism* (2015). She is Past President and Honorary Life Member of the International Association for the History of Religions (IAHR).

Introduction

In this essay, I seek to bring a rights perspective to women's religious leadership and agency in Africa, notably in the case of the newer forms of Pentecostal-charismatic Christianity that now predominate in many parts of the continent. Rather than adopting a legal approach, I focus on the concept of "rights talk" (*cf.*, Glendon 1991) which provides a more productive and inclusive way to approach ideas about women's leadership in locally grounded (and often transnationally connected) African Christian communities. Such a line of inquiry shifts the emphasis from analyzing the impact of the newer generation churches (as the Pentecostal-charismatic churches are sometimes termed) on women's rights—however narrowly or broadly conceived. It focuses on the women church founders and leaders who have publicly addressed the emancipation of women in the varying contexts of gender inequality. Sources for their discourses of freedom may be traditional, biblical, or theological, as well as government policy, and international human rights instruments. The discourses are increasingly tinged with neoliberal conceptions of individual freedom. I contend that the way modern Pentecostal-charismatic women leaders argue for equality, justice, and dignity in their religious communities can also be traced back to their forbears in the African-initiated or independent churches that date from the seventeenth century onwards. There are interesting parallels, as well as some differences, in the ways that they frame, explicitly or implicitly, their understandings of equality and freedom from oppression, and balance compliance and resistance to perduring patriarchal limitations on their religious agency.

Women, culture, and rights in Africa

There is no shortage of studies of women's rights in Africa (Cole *et al.* 2007; Kevane 2014), or of initiatives to promote gender equality (Otas 2015; "African Leaders" 2013). Similarly, women's roles in Africa's three main religious traditions, indigenous, Christian, and Muslim, have been examined from a range of angles (e.g., Olademo 2003; Hodgson 2008; Badru and Sackey 2013; Olajubu 2005; Sackey 2006; Phiri 2012). Fewer are those that investigate the imbrications of religion, rights, and women in African contexts (Abusharaf 2011; Badran 2011; Akintunde 2001). Often, reports and scholarly works revolve around controversial issues such as female genital cutting (Horn 2010), land rights (Wanyeki 2003), marriage (Kisaakye 2002), and conflict and peace-building (Yusuf and McGarvey 2015; Hayward and Marshall 2015). Or, they may be concerned with a particular country, such as Nigeria (Abdullah 2002) or religion (Elmadmad 2002). They vary in their degree of engagement of religious influences.

As part of my research on religion in Africa over the last few decades, I have conducted research on women, religious independency, and self-determination in Africa, notably in the context of African initiated or independent churches and the newer forms of Pentecostal-charismatic Christianity (Hackett 1995; 2000). However, I did not explicitly explore the rights dimension. I touched on this with an earlier piece (Hackett 2007), where I compared Pentecostal deliverance ministries and human rights organizations in terms of their emancipatory rhetoric – but gender questions were under-analyzed. The present essay, therefore, represents an effort to draw some of these strands together and point to areas of future research.

A significant part of the scholarship on Africa's ever-burgeoning sector of new religious movements, particularly Christian movements and churches, addresses their continuity and discontinuity with local indigenous forms of religious belief and practice. The Pentecostals and newer charismatic or neo-Pentecostal movements are generally at pains to "make a break with the past" (Meyer 1999) and demonize those who are not "born-again," whether mainline Christians or traditionalists. In contrast, some observers and scholars are keen to point out the continuities and similarities (Coleman and Hackett 2015; Bateye 2007). With their involvement in healing practices and spirit possession, women bridge the worlds of both traditional or indigenous religion and Christianity are thus caught up in these arguments (*cf.*, Sackey 2006). Before discussing the burgeoning Pentecostal scene, I revisit some of the earlier African initiated church founders to consider whether their acts of resistance or independency were articulated in terms that could be considered precursive to more explicit human, civil or constitutional rights language of the modern era.[1] This move also parallels the work of some African theologians, such as John Mbiti and Kwame Bediako, who argued that traditional religions contained the seeds of the Christian Gospel.

African independent church movements: Pioneering resistance, envisioning new futures

It seemed only appropriate to begin with one of the earliest recorded independent church movements in Africa, the Antonians, since it grew out of the remarkable activities of a young Kongo woman, Kimpa Vita, known by her baptismal name, Dona Béatrice (Thornton 1998; Hastings 1994). Born around 1684, she claimed that she was possessed by St. Anthony and that Christ was born in the Kingdom of Kongo (Central Africa). While her message was not directed at women, her mass movement was aimed primarily at ending a long civil war in the region, and constituting a protest against slavery. Revered as a saint, Dona Béatrice promised a new era of wealth: her followers would discover European treasures, luxury goods, and mines hidden around and under the city. Because she preached a form of anti-Catholicism, infused with Kongo ritual and symbolism, and an increasingly politicized message, the Kongo king, Pedro IV, had her burned at the stake as a heretic in 1706. Her nationalization and democratization of Christianity, according to Wyatt MacGaffey, "threatened all the existing hierarchies" (MacGaffey 1986, 210). He underscores the continuity between the Antonians and the later, modern Kongo prophets such as Simon Kimbangu. Adrian Hastings notes that while the missionaries considered her declarations "blasphemous nonsense, much of it might well be regarded as a remarkably acute judgement upon the externalism of Kongolese Christianity" (1994, 107).

Around the time of independence in Zambia there arose one of Africa's best-known independent churches. Known as the Lumpa Rising or Lumpa Church, it became renowned, not just because it was founded by a woman, the prophetess Alice Lenshina Mulenga Mubisha, but also because of its

---

1. This is somewhat akin to the debates over whether there were conceptions and protections of rights in the precolonial era in Africa. See, e.g., An-Na'im and Deng (2010).

eventual rejection of secular authority and clashes with the new government (Hinfelaar 1991; Roberts 1970). Born around 1920 among the Bemba of northeastern Zambia, Lenshina began receiving visions in 1953. She was associated with a Presbyterian mission at the time but was not yet baptized. She claimed to have died several times and returned from the dead. According to one of her visions, Christ had ascended on a white cloud but would return at the Last Judgment on a black one (Shepperson 1970, 157). She began attracting many thousands of former Catholics and Presbyterians because of her healing rituals, simple evangelical liturgy, and popular hymns. After she began baptizing her mainly rural followers, the movement assumed independent status in 1959 and became known as the Lumpa Church (*lumpa* means "best" or "highest" in Bemba). At its inception, there were no separatist aspirations. As with other Central African movements, such as the Bamucapi of the 1930s, she propagated a message of witchcraft eradication but did not call for a revival of traditional religious beliefs and practices (Bond 1979). In its earlier phase, the movement was nationalist and anticolonial (van Binsbergen 1981, 288–291; Bond 1979, 158–159). But, inspired by chiliastic teachings, Lenshina advocated the construction of new social and economic relations, along theocratic lines. This put the community (about twenty thousand after many defections in the early 1960s) (van Binsbergen 1981, 306) at odds with nationalist leaders, as well as local chiefs, and, in the face of attacks in 1963–1964, it became increasingly intransigent and withdrawn from the state. Lenshina rejected the registration of her church and the payment of taxes (Garvey 1994). During police and army attacks over three months, seven hundred church members were killed. The church was eventually banned and Lenshina was arrested. She eventually died under house arrest in December 1978.

Just as many stories circulated about Lenshina's powers and exploits, so too have interpretations differed among the various analysts over the nature of Lenshina's message and the orientation of her movement. Brian Garvey (1994) observes that while the Lumpa Church was generally seen as an outgrowth from the Livingstonia Mission, the appeal of its founder was to all those Bemba who retained a fear of witchcraft, whatever their religious affiliation. Hugo Hinfelaar highlights the way in which Lenshina restored women's religious roles as intercessors, and the significance of the firm foundation of family life. It was the married woman who was the "mediatrix of the divine" (1991, 123). Wim van Binsbergen (1981, 312) views her as an innovator who opposed peasantization, while George C. Bond (1979, 159) puts her in the Christian reformist tradition in that she sought to restore fundamental Christian (Free Church) values. He also underscores the appeal of Lenshina's egalitarian and otherworldly message for such a subordinated social group as the Lumpa Church members, who were both the laboring poor of the towns, mines, and plantations of east, central, and southern Africa, as well as the least prosperous and educated of the peasantry when they returned home

Feminized or feminist churches?

In the view of Adrian Hastings, "Lumpa appears as a feminist Church, not only led by a woman but expressing feminine aspirations, a woman's view of the ideal society, more than others" (1994, 525). The opposition to polygamy was one of the primary aspirations, along with the clusters of symbols deployed in the hymns that contained Lenshina's vision and religious ideology. Hugo Hinfelaar, who conducted a thorough study of the hymnology, considers that these surpassed any oral teaching. His analysis reveals that "the Prophetess wished to restore the dogma of her traditional religion between the human and the divines as the Priestess of the home-shrine (*Nachibinda*)" (1991, 116). However, her religious cosmic position shifted to seeing herself as the medium between humankind and the joyous light of the future Christ. This served to liberate women from undue concern for the old taboos. In the words of one of their songs, "our Savior has positioned us the poor people, in front. Christians, do not look anywhere else" (Hinfelaar 1991, 116).

In her study of the Roho Movement or Holy Spirit churches in Western Kenya, Cynthia Hoehler-Fatton acknowledges that, during the early period especially, "women were able to achieve autonomy and mobility and to exercise leadership generally denied them in Luo society at that time" (Hoehler-Fatton 1996, 209). They played a major role in the establishment of the church in the 1930s and some even took vows to postpone marriage to serve as missionaries and went around the region singing militant hymns (Hoehler-Fatton 1996, 113). Roho oral tradition describes the founding women as "strong-willed and defiant" (Hoehler-Fatton 1996, 103). Significantly, Hoehler-Fatton reports that older women members maintained that what attracted them to Roho religion in the first place was that they had the freedom to preach, a ritual activity forbidden them in mission churches during that period (Hoehler-Fatton 1996, 103). This freedom of self-expression was not without suffering as they had to endure beatings from their menfolk and loss of reputation. Hymn singing helps keep these memories alive, as in the case of the song, "We are Women of War" (Hoehler-Fatton 1996, 103), and provides inspiration for some (particularly older) women to resist their social subordination.

As Hoehler-Fatton rightly notes, the earlier charismatic fervor of this period known as the East African Revival was not conducive to the assignment of religious roles to different gender roles (1996, 105). However, from the 1960s onwards, the confluence of social, political and economic trends, notably Western-style institutionalization and education, resulted in the increasing marginalization of women within the church. Hoehler-Fatton contends that this process of disempowerment or "defeminization model" (1996, 208), which occurred in many other African independent churches in the region and beyond, could be explained by the Weberian notion of the rationalization of charismatic authority (1996, 111).[2]

African Pentecostalism and Its paradoxes for women

Pentecostalism is the one of the world's fastest growing religious movements and academics are lining up to account for its successes and its paradoxes. Africa is one of the prime sites of Pentecostal expansion. Ruth Marshall, who has written on the political agency of Nigerian Pentecostals, attributes their growth to not just an ability to compete in the religious field by providing spiritual and material benefits others did not provide (especially in a context of crisis), but more so to their "reconceptualization of the moral and political order representing a vision of citizenship in which the moral governance of the self is linked to the power to influence the conduct of others" (Marshall 2009, 125). However, she contends that there is an "internal instability" that troubles Pentecostal theology and practice which is occasioned by the oscillation between two conceptions: first, Born-again techniques of self-edification and second, the intervention of supernatural power (Marshall 2009, 13). She also adds that the new emphasis on wealth in post-colonial Nigeria has created further instabilities. While Marshall's study does not factor in the gender question, her thesis of political agency among modern-day Nigerian Pentecostals is apposite in the present context.

A similar argument about internal tensions within Pentecostalism is advanced by Musa Dube who, unlike Marshall, relates this to gender issues (Dube 2014). She talks about the tensions between the theological space of the Word and the democratic space of the Spirit. She maintains that the space between the Word and the Spirit is where the perpetual battle for gender justice is fought. Perhaps this can explain in part why there is no consistency on rights talk among Pentecostal-charismatic women leaders

---

2. *Cf.* Crumbley (2008) who discusses how women exercise leadership and agency in the face of taboos and restrictions on ordination in Aladura churches in Nigeria.

or male leaders about women for that matter. Akosua Adomako Ampofo, writing about Ghana's new Pentecostal-charismatic mega-churches, attributes the problematic discourses on women (e.g., the "weaker sex" needing male protection and guidance; necessity of marriage for women to be valued) to the particular brand of masculinity expounded by the "Men of God" in these churches (Ampofo 2017). A case in point would be the influential Mountain of Fire and Miracles Ministries (MFM), a deliverance-oriented Pentecostal movement headquartered in Lagos, Nigeria, that talks about the "unique" role of women who have been "specially endowed" for "specific assignment." The anthem of the MFM Women Foundation, Let the Beauty of Jesus Be Seen in Me, reminds women to "strive to keep sweet" in their words and deeds.

Bargaining with patriarchy, resisting oppression

Tapiwa Praise Mapuranga, writing about the rise of women leaders in the second wave of Pentecostalism in Zimbabwe, observes that the majority are married to founders of Pentecostal-charismatic ministries (Mapuranga 2013) (which, in the case of the Zimbabwe Assemblies of God [ZAOGA] entails their being addressed as "mai pastor" [mother, who is a pastor's wife] rather than just "pastor" (Bhatasara *et al.* 2017). These women leaders are therefore unwilling to challenge patriarchy, but rather "bargain" with it, promoting instead a position on biblical hermeneutics that is subservient and moderate on feminist issues (*cf.*, Oduyoye 1995). Along the same lines, sociologist Kelly Chong, who has done extensive research on women in South Korean Pentecostalism, contends that ultimately the newer churches serve to refeminize, redomesticate, and depoliticize women (Chong 2007).

Kenyan religion scholar Philomena Mwaura (2007) offers a slightly more positive assessment of the capacity of Pentecostal churches to transform women's lives.[3] She acknowledges that the founding of churches by women in Africa is the ultimate act of religious independency and self-determination. She claims that they are "promoting the inculturation of Christianity by interpreting the Gospel message in a new perception that is both liberating and empowering especially to their female colleagues and followers" (2007, 423). In addition to breaking the patriarchal barrier they are also engendering a more inclusive concept of Church. She rightly

---

3. Afe Adogame (2008), writing on the growing leadership opportunities afforded to women in diasporic Pentecostal-charismatic churches (that he refers to as "feminization"), cites the case of a pioneering pastor who was referred to by a member as a "**she-man**, a no-nonsense leader with a clear vision of leadership" [emphasis added].

notes that women's involvement is more prominent in churches with a pneumatic emphasis. Moreover, Mwaura claims that the healing metaphor in the churches enables women to gain social recognition and then to fight oppression. Both the newer Pentecostal-charismatic and the older spiritual churches, in her view, "reclaimed the pneumatic and charismatic experience that was suppressed by mainline Christianity and that resonated well with African spirituality" (Mwaura 2007, 416–417). They provided opportunities for women to recover their traditional status and positions as diviners, mediums, prophets, herbalists, priestesses, healers and owners of shrines that had been undermined by the teachings of the mission churches (Mwaura 2007, 420). As women became more familiar with the scriptures through their vernacularization, they became aware of the discrepancy "between the missions' rigidity and the New Testament vision of the freedom of women in Christ" (Barrett 1968, 147 qtd. in Mwaura 2007, 421). In both the older and newer African churches, the latter has been understood as liberation from the ever-present fears of witchcraft, burdens of traditional customs and tensions in the home (Mwaura 2007, 421–422).

This is well evidenced in the case of Rt. Rev. Margaret Wanjiru, the founder of Jesus Is Alive Ministries (JIAM), a neo- Pentecostal-charismatic church that started in 1993. Mwaura (2012) studied this well-known Kenyan movement in terms of its conception of human rights. The founder's biography provides some insights into her rights talk as both religious leader and politician. Given Wanjiru's involvement with the "devil's kingdom" as a young woman, it is not surprising that, following her conversion to Christianity, she put her efforts into a deliverance ministry. She was ordained a Bishop in 2002 and in 2006 became a Member of Parliament of Starehe Constituency, Nairobi and an Assistant Minister for Housing. Following the 1998 bomb blasts in Nairobi that killed several of her church members, she launched a successful media ministry. This included a national television program entitled *Healing the Nation* which was later renamed *The Glory is Here* (Mwaura 2012, 25). According to Mwaura, all their departments and ministries are

> geared towards shoring up individual and community resources for human empowerment, growth and dignity. It is the concern for peoples' total well being that motivates the church to engage in these ministries. In their own understanding, this is a recognition and promotion of people's human rights. (2012, 26)

The church emphasizes success and modernity, teaching its members how to prosper and be delivered from the evil forces they believe are responsible for poverty, illness misfortune, social, economic and political problems (Mwaura 2007, 39). While Wanjiru has been criticized for emphasizing the spiritual roots of evil rather than structural causes, Mwaura notes that the church promotes good governance and speaks out against social injustice, while manifesting intolerance toward Muslims and gays.

New generation Pentecostals revisit empowerment

Bolaji Bateye, in her study of one of the most successful new generation churches in Yorubaland, Nigeria, Agbala Daniel Church, discusses how its founder, Archbishop Dr. Dorcas Siyanbola Olaniyi, encourages women to be self-reliant in life and to join the ordained ministry (Bateye 2007). She uses various biblical passages to "authenticate their right to preach and teach" (Bateye 2007, 5). For example, regarding Paul's command that women keep silent in the house of the Lord (such as 1 Timothy 2.11–12), Dorcas Olaniyi argues that it was addressed to unruly women and not to the "godly" and virtuous (Bateye 2007, 8). She claims that her mission (revealed to her in a vision from Jesus and articulated in her publication, *Woman, I Condemn You Not*) is "to promote the attitude, especially among women, that discrimination or subordination of women with regard to leadership roles in the church is not by divine mandate" (Bateye 2007, 8; cf. 2002). However, Olaniyi, along with other Pentecostal women leaders studied by Bateye, is reluctant to be branded as a feminist even though she has advocated the liberation of women in general.[4]

Entrepreneurial and professional skills may be extolled in these newer Pentecostal-charismatic organizations, as in the case of Girl Power Ministries in Uganda, the international movement created by Pastor Jessica Kayanja, the wife of Pastor Robert Kayanja, founder of Miracle Centre Cathedral, Rubaga, Uganda. The biblical notion of the woman as "helper" is central to their publicity, rather than a more politicized message of equality: "women were uniquely fashioned by God to play a complementary rather than a competitive role alongside the men to achieve greater good of the society" (www.girlpowerministriesinternational.org/). Biblical role models are invoked to inspire some of the most vulnerable women in society, single and widowed women, in Rev. Elizabeth Wahome's Single Ladies Interdenominational Fellowship in Nairobi, Kenya. However, United Nations functionaries may also be invited to come and encourage women "to rise above victimhood and to value themselves" (Parsitau

---

4. But, see Mikell (1997) for the argument that African understandings of feminism differ from Western interpretations in that it is "is distinctly heterosexual, pronatal, and concerned with 'bread, butter, and power' issues" (book summary).

2011, 141). While uplifting the lives of Kenyan single women through spiritual, social, and economic empowerment, this female-led ministry, according to Parsitau, also "addresses critical issues around inadequate healthcare, poverty, low self-esteem, loneliness, and marginalization" (Parsitau 2011, 139).

In their research on perceptions of women's health and rights in contemporary Kenyan Pentecostal-charismatic ministries, Parsitau and Mwaura (2012) argue that these ministries are ultimately inimical to women's well-being despite their modern, international image. Due to their focus on biblical inerrancy and personal holiness they fail to address broader issues of structural inequality. Despite acceptance of education and employment for women they continue to promote images of the submissive wife and loving mother, rejecting the types of emancipation advocated by the feminist movement (Parsitau and Mwaura 2012, 178–179). Mwaura and Parsitau argue strongly that this ideology exposes women to exploitation and potentially abusive relationships and limits their reproductive health. They note that Bishop Margaret Wanjiru of Jesus is Alive Ministries International has strongly opposed the inclusion of abortion legalization and same-sex unions in the new Kenyan constitution (Parsitau and Mwaura 2012, 183). They conclude their article by stating that the empowerment of women articulated in the newer Pentecostal and charismatic churches "does not translate into an acceptance of women's moral agency in matters of reproductive health and rights over their own bodies" (Parsitau and Mwaura 2012, 183).

Strategizing between the spiritual, the social, and the state

Jane Soothill's book, *Gender Social Change and Spiritual Power: Charismatic Christianity in Ghana*, provides one of the few monographs on the contemporary period (Soothill 2007). Her work is germane to the present essay as she assesses three major charismatic churches in the Ghanaian capital, Accra, for the ways in which they reflect or challenge the gender ideology and politics of the day (Soothill 2007, 101–102). She talks about the impact of state feminism on the churches and how this and the economic downturn of the 1980s led to the increasing marginalization of women. There is now an emphasis in state discourse on "gender complementarity" along with "national development" (and she also includes reference to the impact of international discourses and movements such as the UN Decade for Women [1975–1985] or the UN Convention on the Elimination of all Forms of Discrimination against Women [CEDAW]

Soothill 2007, 93–94). Citing Gwendolyn Mikell's work from the late 1990s (1997, 96–123), she notes a significant trend of women in Accra turning to legal processes to meet their domestic needs, although such processes may not factor in the influence of custom and tradition (Soothill 2007, 99). Soothill is keen to underscore the "complex dialectic between the social and the spiritual," with the spiritual (and its roots in African religiosity) constituting the primary source of attraction to the charismatic churches (2007, 224). Importantly, she further contends that "the use of spiritual power to negotiate gender relations may be a lower risk strategy than an appeal to the structures of state feminism" (Soothill 2007, 225).

Conclusion: Mixed blessings in African women's quest for freedom and equality

In the words of Isabel Phiri, "African women's discourse has pointed out that the coming of Christianity to Africa brought mixed blessings for African women" (2012, 255). Arguably these paradoxes have been heightened in the case of the burgeoning Pentecostal-charismatic movements. Damaris Parsitau attributes the contradictions in part to the fact that "the democratizing ethos of Pentecostalism coexists with hierarchical leadership based on charisma" (2011, 143). As adumbrated above, despite the exhortations of self-empowerment for their female congregants by African Pentecostal women leaders and church founders, patriarchal attitudes perdure, notably in the way that women's roles continue to be framed as complementary, supportive, and/or limited to women's and children's groups.

While trying to avoid the imputation of Western rights talk to contemporary African women Pentecostal-charismatic leaders and their forerunners in the African initiated churches, we have noted recurring themes in their discourses on freedom for women: the freedom to preach, lead, and enjoy access to spiritual power, the freedom to develop as individuals and communities, as well as freedom from witchcraft and abuse, and recognition of their human dignity, notably in the context of the family. In this essay, I have argued that it is instructive to consider the continuities and discontinuities of broadly conceived rights talk by African women leaders in both the earlier African independent and initiated Christian movements and the newer general Pentecostal-charismatic churches. In both instances, socio-historical context and state/global initiatives regarding women, rights, and development must be taken into consideration. Undoubtedly, there is ample room for more research on these questions as gendered rights discourse continues to be both expressed and resisted in Africa's ever-evolving Pentecostal-charismatic communities.

References

Abdullah, Hussaina J. 2002. "Religious Revivalism, Human Rights Activism and the Struggle for Women's Rights in Nigeria." In *Cultural Transformation and Human Rights in Africa*, edited by Abdullahi A. An-Na'im, 151–191. London: Zed.

Abusharaf, Rogaia Mustafa. 2011. "Gender Justice and Religion in Sub-Saharan Africa." In *Religion and the Global Politics of Human Rights*, edited by Thomas Banchoff and Robert Wuthnow, 129–155. Oxford: Oxford University Press. https://doi.org/10.1093/acprof:oso/9780195343397.003.0006

Adogame, Afe. 2008. " 'I am Married to Jesus' The Feminization of New African Diasporic Religiosity." *Archives de Sciences Sociales des Religions* 143: 129–149. https://doi.org/10.4000/assr.17133

"African Leaders Reaffirm Commitment to Prioritize Women's Rights." 2013. *Africa News Service*. 11 October.

Akintunde, Dorcas Olu, ed. 2001. *African Culture and the Quest for Women's Rights*. Ibadan: Sefer.

Ampofo, Akosua Adomako. 2017. "Africa's fast-growing pentecostal mega churches are entrenching old injustices against women." *Quartz Africa*.

Badran, Margot, ed. 2011. *Gender and Islam in Africa: Rights, Sexuality, and Law*. Stanford, CA: Stanford University Press. https://doi.org/10.1017/s2151348100056512

Badru, Pade, and Brigid M. Sackey, eds. 2013. *Islam in Africa South of the Sahara: Essays in Gender Relations and Political Reform*. Lanham, MD: Scarecrow.

Barrett, David B. 1968. *Schism and Renewal in Africa. an Analysis of Six Thousand Contemporary Religious Movements*. Oxford: Oxford University Press. https://doi.org/10.1016/0048-721x(71)90027-3

Bateye, Bolaji Olukemi. 2007. "Forging Identities: Women as Participants and Leaders in the Church among the Yoruba." *Studies in World Christianity* 13(1): 1–12. https://doi.org/10.3366/swc.2007.13.1.1

Bhatasara, Sandra, Rumbidzai Shamuyedova, Choguya Naume Zorodzai, and Manase Kudzai Chiweshe. 2017. "Women and Pentecostalism in Zimbabwe: Negotiating Leadership in the Zimbabwe Assemblies of God 'Forward in Faith' (ZAOGA FIF) Ministry, Harare." In *Annual Review of the Sociology of Religion*, edited by Michael Wilkinson and Peter Althouse, 291–306. Leiden: Brill. https://doi.org/10.1163/9789004344181_017

Bond, George C. 1979. "A Prophecy that Failed: The Lumpa Church of Uyombe, Zambia." In *African Christianity: Patterns of Religious Continuity*, edited by George C. Bond, Walton Johnson and Sheila S. Walker, 137–160. New York: Academic. https://doi.org/10.1525/ae.1981.8.2.02a00190

Chong, Kelly H. 2007. *Deliverance and Submission: Evangelical Women and the Negotiation of Patriarchy in South Korea.* Vol. 309, *Harvard East Asian Monographs.* Cambridge, MA: Harvard University Press. https://doi.org/10.1111/j.1748-0922.2012.01618_2.x

Cole, Catherine M., Takyiwaa Manuh, and Stephan F. Miescher, eds. 2007. *Africa after Gender?* Bloomington: Indiana University Press. https://doi.org/10.1086/ahr.112.3.973-c

Coleman, Simon and Rosalind I. J. Hackett, eds. 2015. *The Anthropology of Global Pentecostalism and Evangelicalism.* New York: New York University Press. https://doi.org/10.1558/ptcs.34838

Crumbley, Deidre H. 2008. *Spirit, Structure, and Flesh: Gendered Experiences in African Instituted Churches among the Yoruba of Nigeria.* Madison: University of Wisconsin Press. https://doi.org/10.1353/arw.0.0272

Dube, Musa. 2014. "Between the Spirit and the Word: Reading the Gendered African Pentecostal Bible." *Hervormde Teologiese Studies* 70(1): 1–7. https://doi.org/10.4102/hts.v70i1.2651

Elmadmad, Khadija. 2002. "Women's Rights under Islam." In *Human Rights of Women: International Instruments and African Experiences*, edited by Wolfgang Benedek, Ester M. Kisaakye and Gerd Oberleitner, 245–268. London: Zed. https://doi.org/10.2307/3559359

Garvey, Brian. 1994. *Bembaland Church: Religious and Social Change in South Central Africa, 1891–1964.* Leiden: Brill.

Glendon, Mary Ann. 1991. *Rights Talk: the Impoverishment of Political Discourse.* New York: The Free Press. https://doi.org/10.2307/1964145

Hackett, Rosalind I. J. 1995. "Women and New Religious Movements in Africa." In *Gender and Religion*, edited by Ursula King, 257–290. Oxford: Blackwell.

———. 2000. "Power and Periphery: Studies of Gender and Religion in Africa." *Method and Theory in the Study of Religion* 12(1–2): 238–244. https://doi.org/10.1163/157006800x00148

———. 2007. "Competing Universalisms: New Discourses of Emancipation in the African Context." In *La rationalité, une ou plurielle?*, edited by Paulin Houtondji, 163–171. Paris: UNESCO.

Hastings, Adrian. 1994. *The Church in Africa 1450–1950.* New York: Clarendon.

Hayward, Susan, and Katherine Marshall, eds. 2015. *Women, Religion and Peacebuilding: Illuminating the Unseen.* Washington, DC: US Institute of Peace.

Hinfelaar, Hugo. 1991. "Hinfelaar, Hugo." *Journal of Religion in Africa*. Special Issue: Women's Revolt: The Lumpa Church of Lenshina Mulenga in the 1950s. 21: 99–129. https://doi.org/10.1163/157006691x00258

Hodgson, Dorothy L. 2008. *The Church of Women: Gendered Encounters between Maasai and Missionaries*. Bloomington: Indiana University Press. https://doi.org/10.2979/aft.2006.53.2.120

Hoehler-Fatton, Cynthia. 1996. *Women of Fire and Spirit: History, Faith, and Gender in Roho Religion in Western Kenya*. Oxford: Oxford University Press. https://doi.org/10.2307/3169573

Horn, Jessica. 2010. Christian Fundamentalisms and Women's Rights in the African Context: Mapping the Terrain. Toronto: Association of Women in Development (AWID).

Kevane, Michael. 2014. *Women and Development in Africa: How Gender Works*. Second edition. Boulder, CO: Lynne Rienner. https://doi.org/10.1017/s1743923x05252017

Kisaakye, Esther M. 2002. "Women, Culture, and Human Rights: Female Genital Mutilation, Polygamy and Bride Price." In *Human Rights of Women: International Instruments and African Experiences*, edited by Wolfgang Benedek, Ester M. Kisaakye and Gerd Oberleitner, 268–285. London: Zed. https://doi.org/10.2307/3559359

MacGaffey, Wyatt. 1986. *Religion and Society in Central Africa*. Chicago: University of Chicago Press.

Mapuranga, Tapiwa Praise. 2013. "Bargaining with Patriarchy? Women Pentecostal leaders in Zimbabwe." *Fieldwork in Religion* 8(1): 74–91. https://doi.org/10.1558/firn.v8i1.74

Marshall, Ruth. 2009. *Poltical Spiritualities: The Pentecostal Revolution in Nigeria*. Chicago: Chicago University Press.

Meyer, Birgit. 1999. *Translating the Devil: Religion and Modernity Among the Ewe in Ghana*. Trenton, NJ: Africa World Press.

Mikell, Gwedolyn, ed. 1997. *African Feminism: The Politics of Survival in Sub-Saharan Africa*. Philadelphia: University of Pennsylvania Press. https://doi.org/10.9783/9780812200775

Mwaura, Philomena Njeri. 2007. "Gender and Power in African Christianity: African Instituted Churches and Pentecostal Churches." In *African Christianity: An African Story*, edited by Ogbu U. Kalu, 410–445. Trenton, NJ: Africa World Press. https://doi.org/10.3366/swc.2004.10.2.160

———. 2012. "Concept of Basic Human Rights in African Independent Pentecostal Church of Africa and Jesus Is Alive Ministries." *Journal of World Christianity* 5(1): 9–42. https://doi.org/10.5325/jworlchri.5.1.0009

Oduyoye, Mercy Amba. 1995. "Calling the Church to Account." *Ecumenical Review* 47 (4): 479–489. https://doi.org/10.1111/j.1758-6623.1995.tb03742.x

Olademo, Oyeronke. 2003. *Women in the Yoruba Religious Sphere, McGill Studies in the History of Religions*. Albany, NY: State University of New York Press. https://doi.org/10.1017/s0041977x05640050

Olajubu, Oyeronke. 2005. Gender and Religion: Gender and African Religious Traditions

Olaniyi, Dorcas S. 1988. *Woman, I Condemn You Not*. Ibadan: Agbala Daniel Church Ministry.

Otas, Belinda. 2015. "Empowering African Women: Gender is the Agenda." *NewAfrican*. 10 April. http://newafricanmagazine.com/empowering-african-women-gender-agenda/

Parsitau, Damaris. 2011. "'Arise, Oh Ye Daughters of Faith': Women, Pentecostalism, and Public Culture in Kenya." In *Christianity and Public Culture in Africa*, edited by Harri Englund, 131–145. Athens, OH: Ohio University Press. https://doi.org/10.1353/chapter.236179

Parsitau, Damaris S. and Philomena N. Mwaura. 2012. "Perceptions of Women's Health and Rights in Christian New Religious Movements in Kenya." In *African Traditions in the Study of Religion in Africa: Emerging Trends, Indigenous Spirituality and the Interface with other World Religions*, edited by Afe Adogame, Ezra Chitando, and Bolaji Bateye, 175–186. Abingdon: Routledge. https://doi.org/10.1163/15700666-12340017

Phiri, Isabel. 2012. "The Church and Women in Africa." In *The Wiley-Blackwell Companion to African Religions*, edited by Elias Kifon Bongmba, 255–268. Oxford: Blackwell. https://doi.org/10.1002/9781118255513.ch17

Roberts, Andrew D. 1970. "The Lumpa Church of Alice Lenshina." In *Protest and Power in Black Africa*, edited by Robert I. Rotberg and Ali A. Mazrui, 513–570. Oxford: Oxford University Press. https://doi.org/10.1177/030639687101300212

Sackey, Brigid M. 2006. *New Directions in Gender and Religion: The Changing Status of Women in African Independent Churches*. Lanham, MD: Lexington. https://doi.org/10.1353/arw.0.0037

Shepperson, G. 1970. "The Comparative Study of Millenarian Movements." In *Millennial Dreams in Action: Studies in Revolutional Religious Movements*, edited by Sylvia L. Thrupp, 44–54. New York: Schocken.

Soothill, Jane E. 2007. *Gender, Social Change and Spiritiual Power: Charismatic Christianity in Ghana*, vol. 30, *Studies of Religion in Africa*. Leiden: Brill. https://doi.org/10.1163/18712411-0x542888

Thornton, John K. 1998. *The Kongolese Saint Anthony: Dona Beatriz Kimpa Vita and the Antonian Movement 1684–1706*. Cambridge: Cambridge University Press. https://doi.org/10.1017/cbo9780511572791

van Binsbergen, Wim M. J. 1981. *Religious Change in Zambia: Exploratory Studies*. Boston: Kegan Paul. https://doi.org/10.2307/3166780

Wanyeki, Lynne Muthoni, ed. 2003. *Women and Land in Africa: Culture, Religion and Realizing Women's Rights, Black women writers series*. London: Zed. https://doi.org/10.1017/s0021855303002146

Yusuf, Bilkisu and Sr. Kathleen McGarvey. 2015. "Women, Religion, and Peacebuilding in Kaduna State, Nigeria." In *Women, Religion, and Peacebuilding: Illuminating the Unseen*, edited by Susan Hayward and Katherine Marshall, PAGES. Washington, DC: US Institute of Peace. https://doi.org/10.1111/pech.12249

11

Politicizing Piety: Women's Rights and Roles in the *Tarbiyah* Movement in Indonesia

Diah Ariani Arimbi is Dean of the Faculty of Humanities at the Faculty of Humanities, Airlangga University in Surabaya, Indonesia. She received her Ph.D from The University of New South Wales, Australia in 2006. Her interests include Islamic feminisms, Indonesian women in post-colonial Indonesia with current research focusing on the portrayal of women in popular culture. The focus of this Chapter is women in the Indonesian *Tarbiyah* movement. Her publications include *Reading Contemporary Indonesian Muslim Women Writers* (2009), translated into Indonesian in 2018, and *Tradition Redirecting the Present: A Survey of Modern Indonesian Cultural Productions* (2017).

Introduction

The *Tarbiyah* (education) movement in Indonesia today is the best known and has the largest number of members amongst groups in the *Dakwah* (proselytising) movements that mostly work in Indonesian campuses. Using the notion of Islamic feminism, this study aims to explore the numerous varieties of women's activities in this movement, especially in relation to the ways women see their rights and roles within their notion of piety. Female and male activists of the *Tarbiyah* movement in six state universities in East Java were interviewed to obtain data. Participant observations and in-depth interviews were used as approaches for data collection. This was undertaken from April 2015 to September 2016. One important finding indicates that the *Tarbiyah* members acknowledge that male and female are segregated in nature (biological construction). At the same time, however, they subscribe to concepts of women's rights and equality while maintaining a form of sexual segregation.

Islamic feminism in Indonesia

The Islamic feminist movement in Indonesia, which started in the 1990s (Istiadah 1995), was not the only Islamic movement in the New Order period. The 1980s marked the revival of an Islamic movement that had existed earlier. One of them is the *Dakwah* (proselytising) movement that began in secular university campuses, such as at ITB (Institut Teknologi Bandung [Bandung Institute of Technology]). The *Dakwah* movement itself is not a homogeneous movement as there are other sections, such as *Hizbut-Tahrir, Darul Arqam*, and *Tarbiyah* (education) centred in university campuses.

It is, however, the *Tarbiyah* movement that is most widely known and has the most members, especially students who are actively involved in the campus mosque activities or SKI (Sie Kerohanian Islam [Islamic Spirituality Section]). *Tarbiyah*, or better known as "Islamic Campus," consists particularly of students and graduates who started their education or "persuasion" at the Salman Mosque, ITB (Van Bruinessen 2002, 117) in the 1980s. The movement later inspired similar activities in various places, both in Islamic-affiliated campuses such as in State Islamic Institutes and particularly in "secular" campuses (Van Bruinessen 2003). This phenomenon, in the words of Machmudi who wrote his dissertation on *Jamaah Tarbiyah*, indicates the emergence a new type of devout Muslims who are different from their parents in terms of religious ideology and traditions.

> Inspired by a religious movement in the Middle East, the Egyptian Muslim Brothers, *Jemaah Tarbiyah* has played a role as the agent of religious reform and at the same time has embarked on political activities to present itself as a united force of *ummah* regardless of individual religious orientations within its ranks. In carrying out its reform, *Jemaah Tarbiyah* has shown an accommodative strategy in order to avoid religious disputes and resistance among Indonesian Muslims in general. (Machmudi 2006, 4)

Some groups in this movement call for Indonesia to be more Islamic – in the Middle Eastern way – with religious clothing and segregation and limitation on women's role. Many see the *Tarbiyah* movement as mirroring the *Ikhwanul Muslimin* (Muslim Brotherhood) of Egypt set up by Hassan Al-Banna in 1928. They are also afraid that this movement might steer Islam toward radical revisionism and revival, which is potentially dangerous for the moderate form of Islam in Indonesia. However, in contrast to other Islamic revivalist organizations, the *Tarbiyah* movement is reformist and relies heavily on modern interpretations of Islam concerned with democracy, civil society, human rights, and equality of women, although these values are understood differently from common Western notions.

Unlike most social movements in the world, or in Indonesia in particular, the *Tarbiyah* movement does not only revolve around a social movement, but the movement also includes religion or piety. It is essential to see that, in addition to the social mobility that occurs through this movement, the area of religion or piety becomes a very important marker of the politicization. This involves external relations, not only between individuals and religion in the private sphere, but also individuals, religion, and social dimensions in the public sphere. The *Jilbabisasi*[1] movement in secular campuses, for example, is seen as a form of freedom and expression of religion both in the private sphere (one's private right in showing piety to the religion that she embraces) and the public sphere as women wear the veil when they are in a public area. Women wear the veil by choice; it is not compulsory (Brenner 1996; El Guindi 1999; Cooke 2001; Carpenter 2001). This example shows that the politics of piety are active in Muslim society.

In this movement, many women become activists, although in every meeting women and men are separated by different entrances. Women sit in ranks parallel to men, although they are separated. In the parliamentary election in 2004, PKS (*Partai Keadilan Sejahtera* [Prosperous Justice Party]), whose main members were also members of the *Tarbiyah*, the highest number of women were elected as parliamentary members, in comparison with other parties (both Islamic and non-Islamic ones). The numbers were even more than the 30 per cent required quota *(Pikiran Rakyat*, January 17, 2004).

Although many are afraid that female activists in the *Tarbiyah* movement are accepting more rigid interpretations of gender roles, in my opinion, such a fear is exaggerated. I would argue that women's roles in this movement share some similarities with other Muslim women in contemporary Islam. Islam is still highly respected as providing guidance for religious and social life:

> Muslim women see no contradiction between democratic values and religious principles. [...] According to the survey conducted by Gallup, Muslim women with some education and awareness of their rights are not hostile to Islam, they do not see in Islam an obstacle to their progress. Thus, supporting women's progress, rather turning to account *Shari'a* values than eliminating them, is a recurring theme on the agenda of contemporary Muslim societies. (Chirleşan and Cîrneanu 2011, 292–93)

The emergence of the *Tarbiyah* movement increasingly shows the complexity of the issues about women and their roles in Islam in Indonesia. Unfortunately, there are very few reviews as yet or research and writing

---

1. *Jilbab* in Indonesia means to veil. *Jilbabisasi* was a veiling movement in the 1980s and 1990s where some girls from public schools chose to don veiling as a sign of religious expression. In Indonesia, there are different ways to wear the veil. *Kerudung* is a form of veiling usually worn by older women, *jilbab* refers to the veil popular in 1980s to 1990s, and *hijab* a more fashionable veil referring to more glamorous and haute couture styles as an up-to-date veiling.

on women's roles in the *Tarbiyah* movement. Material is more commonly found about the relationship of women's roles and Islamic guide manuals. These are books that provide models or tips on how to be a virtuous Muslim woman or *Sakina* woman, without providing any deeper insights into the complexities of women's roles in Islam (Abubakar 2002, 135; Meuleman 1993, 177). Most of the writings on the movement simply discuss the movement in general, and virtually none of them discuss in detail the views of women and their roles in the *Tarbiyah* movement.

This study aims to observe women members of the *Tarbiyah* movements and the discourse of piety that they believe in, especially concerning the politics of religion in their daily lives and during their college years. "Politics of religion" as a term in this study indicates an examination of the discourse of Islam in the *Tarbiyah* movement and how it influences the concept of gender, and also the role of gender in constructing women's lives. Since politics embodies relations and relations generate legitimizing power, it is clear how the concept of gendered behavior is crucial for members of *Tarbiyah* as it legitimizes the reason or their piety. In the *Tarbiyah* movement, the most frequent question asked in relation to women's piety is the actual meaning of a virtuous woman? Being such a pious woman or a pious girl would normally be the ultimate purpose for members of the *Tarbiyah* movement. In the study that follows, comparison with Western and other forms of Islamic feminism will be discussed.

In this study, the construction of gender and the emerging gender relations for women in the *Tarbiyah* movement, particularly in Indonesia, will be the major focus. Questions that arise as to the meaning of the *Tarbiyah* movement as part of the Islamic youth movements, will be investigated. A short historiography of the *Tarbiyah* movement in Indonesia, women's roles, women's issues, as well as insights into gender equality in the discourse of this movement, will be addressed through analyzing in-depth interviews with 90 activists both women and men in Surabaya, Malang, and Jember, in East Java. The interviews and observations were conducted from April 2015 to September 2016. Each interview lasted approximately sixty to ninety minutes; they were recorded and later transcribed. Transcripts and recordings are the primary data source, while the secondary data sources were books, online resources, etc. These will all be examined through the lens of Islamic feminism.

Islamic feminism

In general, Islamic feminism deals with the private realm, but practical Islam, i.e., Islam and its teachings, which are implemented in daily life, cannot be separated from political and socio-cultural situations of the society (Risalah Gusti 2000). Therefore, the definition of Islamic feminism is not monolithic:

> Such feminism is unique in conjuring up delicate and challenging issues for political and religious authorities as well as for scholars in a world of a billion Muslims. Within that new overarching background which deals with Islamic laws and traditions, the category of "Islamic feminism" may stand its ground by the sheer diversity it includes: contributors to the debate have been considered "new feminist traditionalists, "pragmatists," "secular feminists," "neo-Islamists," and so forth. For all these thinkers, however, there is a common concern with the empowerment of their gender within a rethought Islam. (Yamani 1996, 1)

Yamani's quote above shows that feminism in Islam has multiple meanings. Islamic feminisms, similar to other feminisms, are never meant to be simple or one-sided. Feminism is always contextually grounded as women are always historically located.

Today, in certain Muslim countries where strong Islamic values influence the context of feminism, it is not surprising that Islamic feminism is also associated with feminist theology, as described by Riffat Hassan of Pakistan:

> The importance of developing what the West calls "feminist theology" in the context of the Islamic tradition is paramount today in order to liberate not only Muslim women, but also Muslim men, from unjust social structures and systems of thought that make a peer relationship between men and women impossible. It is extremely important for Muslim women activists to realize that in the contemporary Muslim world, laws instituted in the name of Islam cannot be overturned by means of political action alone, but through the use of better religious arguments.... [B]y means of feminist theology it is possible to equip and empower women to combat gender-inequality and injustice to which they have been subjected for a very long time. (Hassan 1996, 52–53)

With the strong religious element in its women's movements, Islamic feminism also marks the emergence of a politics of piety because through religious piety, justice, freedom, and equality can be achieved. Most important is to give women space for them to make their own choices on the basis of self-awareness, as stated by Didin Syafrudin of UIN Syarif Hidayatullah Jakarta:

> The drive in interpreting Al Qur'an is not to interpret women in male interpretations in biological, psychological or sociological meaning, but to make possibilities for women to act in their own free and conscious choices just like men. That women have traditional role or completely new role

is not the problem. What matters is that women are free to choose and have their own decision. (1994, 10)

Analogous to women in other Muslim countries, Indonesian *muslimah* (Muslim women) have long demanded a claim to participate in public life. Although Indonesian Muslim women traditionally enjoyed more freedom compared to their sisters in the Arab world, this does not automatically mean that they are granted equal access and authority in public realms. Still, changes are definitely taking place.

Defenders of women's rights from the Indonesian older generation of *ulama* (religious clerics), such as Ali Yafie, Quraish Shihab, Abdurrahman Wahid, Zakiyah Daradjat, Aisyah Hamid Baidlowi, and Maftuchah Yusuf, and certainly other Muslim feminists of the younger generations, such as Masdar F. Mas'udi, Zainatun Subhan, Siti Nurhayati Dzuhayatin, and Nursyahbani Katjasungkana agree that women's rights are to include women's place in the public sphere. They also agree that the exclusion of Indonesian women from the public arena was a product of socially and culturally constructed interpretations of the *Qur'an* and *Hadith*. Women are today encouraged to become political actors by becoming town mayors and members of city councils, as well as leaders in the economic field. Indonesian feminists also believe that gender is a matter of social construction. From this perspective, they state that supposed women's domesticity must not hamper women's involvement in public participation. It is for women themselves to decide which sphere they want to inhabit. Whatever their choice, it is an indication of women's liberation in social, political, and economic life. Dzuhayatin writes:

> Being married or single, willing to have or not to have children, choosing a career or being housewives are all issues that should be resolved on the basis of women's own choices. No one has the right to interfere in these decisions. Not even the husband or the state has the right to assert control over a woman's body or mind. (Dzuhayatin 2001, 205)

The ideas and practices that Dzuhayatin and other feminists of her generation offer is vital as it exemplifies a paradigm shift in the notion of women and their public positions. The growth of global discourses on women and development has had a strong influence on women's movements in Indonesia. This has resulted in the fact that the younger generation no longer sees domesticity as an obligation for women. For them, the notion of motherhood becomes less important in shaping women's status, and a woman's decision to get married or to stay single is not determined by women's *kodrat* (destiny).

Mahnaz Afkhami identifies twelve issues in a platform for action that need attention in order to improve the situation of women's human rights: poverty, education, health, violence against women, effects of armed conflict, economic structures and politics, inequality of men and women in decision-making, gender equality, women's human rights, media, environment, and the girl child (Afkhami 1997, 109). In her well-crafted "Platform for Action," she argues that one major way to help women realize that their rights are being denied is through education. Afkhami is correct. Education is an essential means through which women can gather experience and knowledge so as to implement gender equality. Education is a powerful means for social transformation. The state policy of implementing *wajib belajar* (an obligation for all Indonesian children – male and female – to enter elementary education at least from year 1 to year 12) is critical in the drive for education as a way to social transformation, especially for women. However, for a number of reasons, including poverty, geographical isolation and the persistence of child labour, a sizeable number of Indonesian youth are still denied their right to education. Thus, this research is very important to investigate whether the patterns or models of the roles of women in the *Tarbiyah* movement in Indonesia are the same or different from comparable movements elsewhere.

The *Tarbiyah* movement in Indonesia

The *Tarbiyah* movement, as described by one respondent, is a movement of education and, as in other movements, primarily aims to provide education, particularly Islamic education, to its followers (members of *Tarbiyah*). The movement that initially began in a campus community at a mosque in ITB in the early 1990s eventually spread to various campuses throughout Indonesia.

The *Tarbiyah*[2] movement is an educating movement. According to K.H. Rahmat Abdullah in the publication of National Seminar, "*Tarbiyah* in the

---

2. *Tarbiyah* came to Indonesia more than two decades ago. However, Ustadz Rahmat Abdullah, known as the *syaikhut* of *tarbiyah* in Indonesia, claimed that the process of *tarbiyah* has been going on for centuries in Indonesia and not only in the past two decades. The spread of Islam in Indonesia has worked for centuries, and the process of *tarbiyah* has taken a long time already. If the term *tarbiyah* is used to describe a movement that recently entered Indonesia for about two decades, then Ustadz Rahmat Abdullah requires to replace the lowercase '*t*' in the word *tarbiyah* with the uppercase '*T*'. It is intended to show that *Tarbiyah* is not *tarbiyah*. *Tarbiyah* refers to certain rules, system, and ideology coming to Indonesia within the past twenty years, not to the meaning of *tarbiyah* commonly used by most Muslims.

New Era," at the Mosque of Indonesia University, Depok Campus, the meaning of *tarbiyah* (education) does not negate the process of *tarbiyah* that has been present in Indonesia for a long time. Without the process of *tarbiyah*, *walisongo* (the nine Javanese saints) could never have disseminated Islam in Java. In sum, *tarbiyah* with capital "T" or with lower "t" obviously refers to a process of education. *Tarbiyah* is also commonly associated with a study group teaching three levels of Islamic education. First is the education of *dzikir* (worshipping) or educating the spiritual aspects. Second is the education of *fikriyah*, the scientific aspect. Third is *dakwah*, the *harakiyah* aspect, namely the implementation of the first and the second levels. Members of *tarbiyah* are taught in these levels consecutively, and when they finish their education, they will have the necessary education to go back to the community where they live. Here they can create changes (Tarbiyah 2007). Basically, *Tarbiyah* educates its member how to be "a good Muslim" (Anismar 2014).

Many have said that the *Tarbiyah* group in Indonesia is inspired by the ideas and ideology of the *Ikhwanul Muslimin* (IM), founded by Hasan Al Banna in 1928, with the special aim of training cadres. The *Tarbiyah* group conducts its cadres' training through cell forums called *liqo'*. (In the 1980s and early 1990s, such a forum was called *usrah*). A forum is usually held on a weekly basis and led by a *murabbi* (teacher) and attended by about ten *mutarabbi* (education participants). Such a coaching model is the characteristic of the *Tarbiyah* group, both in Indonesia and other parts of the world.

By using the slogan "establishing brotherhood, expanding the horizons," the movement, through its vision and mission, claims that it is a civil movement very closely related to the formation of civil society. When examined more deeply, this movement is not different from other humanist movements because, in terms of language discourse, the choice of words used are words that are very common to all such movements in the world – both those with religious affiliation and the secular ones, whose aim is equality. Words such as "peaceful," "friendly," "merciful," "great," "harmonious faith," "science and technology," "alignment with the marginalized," "fight against crime," demonstrate that this movement also contains universal values. Like other Islamic movements, words in Arabic are very prominent in this movement. Almost all the main terms are in Arabic, indicating the proximity of this movement to the Arab world (i.e., *Ikhwanul Muslimin* from Egypt). Yet they do have differences from other humanist movements, e.g., the feminist movement or the civil rights movement.

The *Tarbiyah* movement embraces religious (Islamic) values and is oriented toward the past. The present-day context appears to be no longer important for the movement's aim, vision, and mission. Nevertheless, it recognizes that the development of science and technology is something that should be embraced and not be regarded with hostility. The golden age of the Islamic Caliphate (8th to 14th century C.E.) became a model for the creation of a civil society wherever this movement exists. Although its strong focus is on the golden age of Islam, this movement does not include the conflicts and the dynamics that occurred in the golden age. Again, the context of universal values that *tarbiyah* supports refers to those of the golden age of Islam and not to the present. Perhaps, in this movement, the dynamics of a society, with its contestations, negotiations, and hegemony, are no longer important, especially when related to the context of an event and the confines of time and space. It is as if the context of time and place is lost (in the sense of Indonesian-ness or the time and place in Indonesia/context of locality). This is in line with the opinion of Damanik Ali Said, stating that in Indonesia, although it can be classified as part of the Islamic modernism movement, it is rather difficult to find the roots of the relation between the group that started as "Gerakan Dakwah Kampus" (GDK [Campus Proselytizing Movement]) with any Islamic religious movements that may have existed in Indonesia. The existence of this movement is closely related to the influence of the International Islamic movement that thrived in Egypt, *Ikhwanul Muslimin* (the Muslim Brotherhood). The influence of this movement in the last two decades of the 20th century was observed in many countries of the world. During this period, the movement, led by urban-based, young educated people, was able to contribute to the process of opinion formation in public religio-cultural areas. Widespread acceptance of religious symbols, such as the wearing of Muslim clothing (veil), was one of the successes of this movement. After being engaged for more than a decade in this field, creating a momentum of reform, this movement aimed to engage at the state level by establishing Partai Keadilan (Justice Party). Since then, the party has become a phenomenon in Indonesian politics (Damanik 2002).

As explained above, the followers of this movement are mostly members of campus communities (college students). They are usually addressed as *akhwat*, which means "sister," and *akhwan*, which means "brother," without any differentiation in age, social background, etc. Individual identity (gender, class, race and others) is merged into the single form of address: sister or brother. This marks a democratization in greeting the followers of this movement, even though they are separated by their different roles and tasks.

Often women sit behind men in meetings, but this only applies when the room size is not large enough for women to sit parallel to men, although they are separated by a room-divider. The key tenet of this movement is that men's space is public space, and women's space is domestic space. Men sitting in front and woman behind indicates that this movement is still connected to a patriarchal ideology with which Islam is always associated. However, this separation is not without challenge. There are occasions when men and women sit in the same room and are separated by a *hijab* or separator. They are separated but sit parallel with each other.

Given that the framework of this movement is highly patriarchal, the following questions inquire about the existence of women's rights in this movement: Do they have rights at all? If they do, what kind of rights? Are these rights in conflict, or are they in support of these devout Muslim women who are taught democracy and equal rights in their secular schools or universities? These questions will be discussed in the following analysis, based on interviews with the followers of this movement, which is part of the Islamic Youth Movement. Most of its members are of school age or are college students.

Women in the public sphere

According to the *Tarbiyah* movement members, a woman's main place is in the domestic sphere, although there are a lot of female members involved in public activities. Such a contradiction does not seem to be a problem, because, according to *halaqah* or studies that they carry out on a regular basis, women are an appendage of men. Women may lead, but men are preferred as leaders. Leading women are those who reach the top, but they are never in the highest rank. It is still men who hold the highest leadership positions, especially when the leadership is related to religion:

> The man, a leader, whatever his position is, he remains a leader. While a woman is the companion of a man. No matter how high the woman's position is, the boss is still the man. (Interview with LLF, March, 2015)

> It's recommended in Islam that men are leaders. But in a democratic society, men may not be leaders. (Interview with RTO, April, 2015)

Men must be leaders in religious matters, while women can be leaders in worldly duties. Men and women sit in a different room or in the same room, divided by a *hijab* or barrier. Men sometimes sit in front of women. Sometimes they sit equally, though separated. Male space is public space, and the space of women is domestic space: this is a key tenet of this movement. This separation between maleness and femaleness resonates strongly with the notion of difference feminism of the 1980s to 1990s, suggested by Carol Gilligan's *In a Different Voice* (1993). This notion of feminism follows a form of biological essentialism that states men and women are different biologically. Thus, they are regarded as incomparable, and so they should be treated equally. However, this type of feminism gradually fell out of favour with later feminists.

The quotations above from women activists signal a contradictory view of how *Tarbiyah* women see themselves. It seems that they make a distinction between their life as *Tarbiyah* members within the *Tarbiyah* movement and their life outside it. It perhaps correlates with their position as devout Muslim women within the movement, yet different outside the movement when they are students at secular universities. This discrepancy is reinforced in their statements, affirming their public lifestyle, while at the same time they follow the teachings of *Tarbiyah*.

The sense of being both "in" and "out" must be continuously negotiated by these members. One activist even said that being in the movement simply did not stop her from practicing her rights to join a *karate* club. When doing her *karate* exercises, she chose to wear a loose skirt and not pants (Interview with FWP, May 2016). This negotiation of being in and out of the movement is crucial for the female members. It demonstrates that they have the right to choose and thus to be able to express themselves. When they are outside the movement, they behave in accordance with common decency and in accordance with rights. One activist said, "When I am with other members, I would behave accordingly (following the rules in the movement), but when I am outside the movement, I would mingle with men, working together, presenting our paper together, just like any other girl." Here there appears to be no separation from the boys (Interview with INS, June 2016). I would argue that the right of the girls to choose, is a basic right. These university girls understand that, when women are allowed to choose, they are exercising a fundamental human right. The girls' right to choose might be well uniquely Indonesia's Islam in favouring of girls being educated.

In relation to female leadership, the *Tarbiyah* movement does refer to women activists. The book *Keakhwatan* (femaleness) (1. 2010) is written mostly by male writers: Cahyadi Takariawan, Abdullah Sunono, Wahid Ahmadi, and Ida Nur Laila. They state that women are active citizens, not only in the private sphere, but also in the public sphere. The difference is that women's involvement in the public roles is limited to leading other women and not men. In this case, seemingly women have no right to be leaders. Women can lead men only when no man is capable. Nevertheless, based on the interviews, some activists admitted that they often became leaders of both men and women in activities outside the movement. Again, within the movement, women can be leaders of a small group, such as the head of the Student Executive Board or the commander of a ceremony, but only when no man is capable. Outside the movement, women can freely lead. One activist admitted that, when she was in the movement, she was never a leader, but outside *Tarbiyah* participation, she was a leader of extracurricular activities at her school (Interview with FWEP, May 2016). Activists have also expressed their role model Aisyah, the wife of the Prophet Muhammad, who is also respected as one most reliable transmitters of *Hadith* (the sayings of the Prophet Muhammad). Aisyah was also a leader and a commander in the Battle of Camel (AD 656) when she waged war against Ali Ibn Abi Talib's troops. With her role in this battle, combined with her intelligence as transmitter of thousands of *Hadith*, Aisyah is a model of gender equality and leadership within the *ummah* (community of believers). Aisyah was indeed a "feminist" when the word "feminism" was not yet known. It is no surprise to know that some of the *Tarbiyah* female activists and members idolize her. These girls want to follow the examples that Aisyah has provided.

Gender relations in the public sphere

Spatial separation is important for *Tarbiyah* activists. One activist said that *Hijab* (a veil) is often understood to be a separation, whether the actual division exists or not, but separation does not automatically mean subordination (AM, April 2015). In the *Tarbiyah* movement, spatial separation between men and women is never an opposition between superiority and subordination. Although women should sit separated from men, women may express their opinion in a forum with men. It is indeed clear for the *Tarbiyah* activists that men are companions of women. Gender relations between them are not enacted in the form of superiority/subordination, where men are believed to be superior to women. The following excerpts from an interview best describe the gender relations in the public realm between women and men in this movement.

> As I said earlier, the man is the leader, he who leads us, while the woman is the companion of a man, but she also cannot be ruled out, meaning she is not in the lower position, but actually in a term of position. We are parallel as we accompany each other mutually. (Interview with LLF, March 2015)

The interviewee indicates that women and men are biologically different, but that biological difference does not automatically create inequality. In fact, many activists believe that men and women are companions of each other, and they regard this as equality. An activist described that in an activity, if a male was the leader, the secretary then had to be the female because male and female complement each other (Interview with NNS, May 2016). A man and a woman already are each created with their specific distinctions in their own spheres. An activist declared: "Because men were physically strong, they took care of physical activities, such as moving and arranging chairs for meetings. In contrast women, because of their delicate nature, took care of logistic needs" (Interview with NNS, May 2016).

In the movement, although women seem to have a lower status than men, this should not be understood that women disappear from public sphere. One activist admitted the importance of gender equality: "Knowing gender relations is very important. Because it talks about difference in terms of roles and responsibilities. Surely men must have commitment and trust. There are many female leaders now.... Gender equality is needed. Now it's different era" (Interview with ZIN, June 2016).

Women as community members

Women's membership in this movement also indicates other interesting developments. The *Tarbiyah* movement makes women work in accordance to their reproductive function. Married women are taught to have as many children as possible (Interview with SMP, October 2011). This is a strategy of the members of this movement to increase the population numbers. The need to increase the number of members in this movement is one of the answers to the question why the brothers and sisters in this movement tend to get married as soon as possible after graduating from university, and also why they tend to have many children. Increasing the population becomes a very important strategy in the development of this movement. Although this policy does not seem to be in line with the family planning program, which is the government's agenda, it seems that the government does not do anything to interfere in this matter.

As a community member, it seems that women in this movement have, again, a contradictory role. On the one hand, their membership is seen only from reproductive needs, but, on the other hand, they are considered as cadres, who are as disciplined as male members. As members of the community, the roles of women are quite significant in this movement. Women are cadres. As cadres, in addition to being responsible for improving the quality of the members being trained, they are also responsible for the quantity or growth in membership. In this case, women are equal to men in their function as community members. Regeneration is the duty of each member of this movement. Together with this emphasis on having children, a strong sense of discipline is also introduced. *Halaqoh* (circle) and *liqo'* (meeting) are very effective forums in the spread of this movement. This is because it is through these forums that both the doctrine of faith and the personality formation of the members are instilled (*Program dan Solusi Kaderisasi*, Andul Hamid Al-Bilali, Era Media, 2000). In this formation, female and male cadres have the same responsibility as members of the wider community and members of the *Tarbiyah* movement.

Being highly disciplined is a requirement for both male and female activists. Such disciplined activism is no longer the sole possession of men but of women as well. Women also have the right to this strict self-discipline. Despite the fact that most activists believe ideal female characters are pious, soft-spoken, and well mannered, they must be disciplined too. The resultant activism is a characteristic that is mainly associated with being masculine, but, in this movement, strict discipline is also an integral part of being feminine.

As a religious movement, the *Tarbiyah* movement definitely centres its main direction within the religious realm. These activists believe that if women become leaders, their strong commitment to being good Muslims will direct them to the ultimate goal: to be pious women. Being pious means a woman should be virtuous, and being educated is an important quality of being virtuous. As educated women, they will contribute their work to the society, especially when they become mothers. This is because mothers are respected as the primary educators of the society. One female activist asserts that, in today's digital era, women in *Tarbiyah* will have more demanding roles, one of which is for the advancement of civilization. Women must thus contribute, not only at the state and national level, but also the world at large (Interview with NNS, May 2016). These activists are typical of the millennial generation; because of speedy and instant connectivity to the world, the millennials are well aware of their position in the global scene.

Conclusions and suggestions

A number of findings can be concluded from this study. One is that a form of segregation remains in force in the teachings of this movement, although its members are quite familiar and supportive of the values of civil society. What is more important, however, is that female activists are highly aware of their negotiations as they transfer in and out of the movement, with the rights and roles this entails. Female activists are allowed to choose their commitments both inside or outside the movement. Being inside and outside comes with different responsibilities and roles. Freedom to choose for these members signals their fundamental rights of beings. Their awareness of such rights for women is a result derives not so much from the movement itself, but the fact that at schools, especially at university levels, women are taught strong feminist awareness and encouraged to take part in public roles. Since Indonesian independent movement (1908 – 1945) women had always been actively participating in the movement. Furthermore, the 1945 Constitution of the Republic of Indonesia guarantees gender equality by saying that all citizens are equal accorded by law and by the government (Article 27 of the 1945 Constitution). This constitution basically protects and support women's rights and women's participation in all sectors of life.

The segregation of women and men indicates only a separation of space but not of piety. Women are active in both the domestic and public sphere. When it comes to piety, these activist women believe that equality rules. When faith matters, equality is also in play, meaning that piety is the same for both women and men, regardless of gender difference.

In addition to women's piety, female members of *Tarbiyah* do traits of Islamic feminism that allow them to appear in public spaces. Women can indeed be leaders in Indonesia, though not religious leaders. Women are equal to men when they are cadres or activists. Strong discipline is required for both men and women. Such discipline is mostly associated with men, but it is also embraced by the women of the *Tarbiyah* movement, especially in connection with piety.

One final remark on women's piety, rights, and roles in the *Tarbiyah* movement is that it needs to be understood that these versions of piety, rights, and roles are not, by any means, monolithic or inflexible. There may be alternatives and many more variations of ways these activists understand and negotiate their position as Muslim women, especially when different contexts, locations, and spaces apply. What is written here is a small effort to voice women's position in Indonesia's Islam. It remains dominated by men, though there are many strong feminists who are both aware of their rights and demand them.

References

Abubakar, I. 2002. "Islam and Gender Books Published in Indonesia (1990–2003)." *Kultur: The Indonesian Journal For Muslim Cultures* 2(2): 131–148.

Afkhami, M. 1997. "Claiming Our Rights: A Manual for Women's Human Rights Education in Muslim Societies." *Muslim Women and the Politics of Participation: Implementing the Beijing Platform*, edited by Mahnaz Afkhami and Erica Friedl, 109–120. Syracuse: Syracuse University Press. https://doi.org/10.1017/s0026318400037597

Anismar, Elsi. 2014. *Kaderisasi Pada Basis Sosial Parkai Keadilan Sejahtera (PKS) di Perguruan Tinggi (Studi Kasus Jamaah Tarbiyah UI)*. Unpublished manuscript. http://www.digilib.ui.ac.id/naskahringkas/2016-08//S56416-Elsi%20Anismar

Brenner, S. 1996. "Reconstructing Self and Society: Javanese Muslim Women and "the Veil." *American Ethnologist* 23(4): 673–695. https://doi.org/10.1525/ae.1996.23.4.02a00010

Carpenter, M. 2001. "Muslim Women Say Veil is more about Expression than Oppression." *Post-Gazette*. 28 October. http://www.post-gazette.com

Chirleşan, G. and Adelina Cîrneanu. 2011. "Effects Of The Religion Upon The Democratic Affirmation Of Muslim Women. *Revista Academiei Forţelor Terestre* 3(63): 287–295.

Constitution of the Republic of Indonesia. 1945. https://www.ilo.org/wcmsp5/groups/public/---ed_protect/---protrav/---ilo_aids/documents/legaldocument/wcms_174556.pdf

Cooke, M. 2001. *Women Claim Islam Creating Islamic Feminism through Literature*. Abingdon: Routledge.

Damanik, A. S. 2002. *Fenomena Partai Keadilan Transformasi 20 Tahun Gerakan Tarbiyah di Indonesia*. Jakarta: Penerbit Teraju.

"Dilema Para Caleg Perempuan." 2004. *Pikiran Rakyat*. 17 January. http://www.pikiran-rakyat.com/cetak/0104/17/hikmah/lainnya04.htm

Dzuhayatin, S. R. 2001. "Gender and Pluralism in Indonesia." *The Politics of Multiculturalism: Pluralism and Citizenship in Malaysia, Singapore and Indonesia*, edited by Robert W. Hefner, 253–267. Honolulu: University of Hawai'i Press. https://doi.org/10.1515/9780824864965-011

El Guindi, F. 1999. *Veil Modesty Privacy and Resistance*. Oxford: Berg.

Geertz, C. 1976. *The Religion of Java*. Chicago: University of Chicago Press.

Hassan, R. 1996. "Feminist Theology: The Challenges for Muslim Women." *Critique* (Fall): 52–65.

Istiadah. 1995. *Muslim Women in Contemporary Indonesia: Investigating Paths to Resist the Patriarchal System*. Working Paper No. 91. Clayton, Victoria, Australia: Monash University.

Machmudi, Y. 2008. *Islamising Indonesia The Rise of Jemaah Tarbiyah and the Prosperous Justice Party (PKS)* Canberra: Australian National University Press. https://doi.org/10.22459/ii.11.2008

Meuleman, J. 1993. "Analisis Buku-Buku tentang Wanita Islam yang Beredar di Indonesia." *Wanita Islam Indonesia Dalam Kajian Tekstual dan Kontekstual*, edited by Lies M. Marcoes-Natsir and Johan Hendrik Meuleman, 175–206. Jakarta: INIS.

Risalah Gusti, Tim. 2000. *Membincang Feminism: Diskursus Gender Perspektif Islam*. Surabaya: Risalah Gusti.

Syafrudin, D. , 1994. "Argumen Supremasi atas Penafsiran Klasik QS al-Nisa': 34." *Ulumul Qur'an*. Special Edition 5–6 (V): 4–10.

Tarbiyah, Syaikhut. 2007. "Ikhwanul Muslimin Inspirasi Gerakan Tarbiyah." 10 October. http://syiar.wordpress.com/2007/10/27/ikhwanul-muslimin-inspirasi-gerakan-tarbiyah/

Yamani, M. 1996. "Introduction." *Feminism and Islam: Legal and Literary Perspectives*, edited by Mai Yamani, 1–29. Reading, UK: Itacha.

Van Bruinessen, M. 2002. "Genealogies of Islamic radicalism in post-Suharto Indonesia." *South East Asia Research* 10(2): 117–154. https://doi.org/10.5367/000000002101297035

———. 2003. "Post-Suharto Muslim engagements with civil society and democracy." Paper presented at the Third International Conference and Workshop "Indonesia in Transition." Organized by the KNAW and Labsosio, Universitas Indonesia, August 24–28. Universitas Indonesia, Depok. https://doi.org/10.1111/j.1478-1913.2009.01302.x

Interviews

Interview with SMP, Universitas Airlangga, October 11, 2011.

Interviews with members or activists of *Tarbiyah* movement at Universitas Airlangga, Institute Teknologi Surabaya, Universitas Negeri Surabaya, Universitas Brawijaya, Universitas Negeri Malang and Universitas Jember from April 2015 to September 2016.

12

Women's Freedom of Religion Claims in Canada: Assessing the Role of Choice

Jennifer Koshan is a Professor in the Faculty of Law at the University of Calgary. Previously, she worked for several years as a Crown prosecutor in the Northwest Territories, and as Legal Director of West Coast LEAF (Women's Legal Education and Action Fund). Her research and teaching focuses on constitutional law, human rights, legal responses to interpersonal violence, and feminist legal theory. Jennifer regularly contributes to the legal work of LEAF and The Equality Effect, in the context of rights to address violence against women and girls in Canada, Ghana, Kenya and Malawi. Jennifer frequently collaborates with her colleague Jonnette Watson Hamilton on Charter equality rights, and more recently, on domestic violence and residential tenancies.

Jonnette Watson Hamilton is a Professor in the Faculty of Law, University of Calgary. Her research focuses on property law and theory, equality rights, access to justice, and discourse analysis. Her recent teaching includes property law, property theory, law and literature, legislation, and research methodologies. The paper in this volume is the tenth collaborative publication with her colleague Jennifer Koshan. Her most recent publications are 2018. "Colour as a Discrete Ground of Discrimination." *Canadian Journal for Human Rights* 7(1): 1–33 (co-authored with Joshua Sealy-Harrington) and 2019. "Reforming Residential Tenancy Law for Victims of Domestic Violence." *Annual Review of Interdisciplinary Justice Research* 8: 245–276.

Introduction

In this essay, we explore whether religious women's reliance on choice as the basis for their rights claims in Canada may undermine the success of those claims. Religious freedom under section 2(a) of the *Canadian Charter of Rights and Freedoms* has been interpreted to include a strong element of choice. People's choices about the religious beliefs they hold (or do not hold), and how they manifest those beliefs, are generally protected from state interference. In some cases, however, religious choices – particularly those perceived to be the cause of the claimant's harm and those identified as causing harm to others. Some cases, however, have not received protection under section 2(a), nor under section 15's guarantee of equality, particularly those choices that are seen to be the cause of the claimant's harm or that cause harm to others. Choice may also be seen as inconsistent with section 15, which focuses more on group- and identity-based harms. Our analysis centres on a case examining a Muslim woman's freedom to wear a *niqab* during citizenship ceremonies, situating this case in the broader context of decisions involving women, religious freedom, equality, and choice. We conclude that a de-emphasis on choice may be strategic for religious women's rights claims.

The Canadian context is crucial for this paper. Canada is a liberal constitutional democracy and the *Charter* is a liberal constitutional document. Liberalism is committed to the primacy of the autonomous individual. The individual is also the dominant unit of the *Charter* and law must conceive of religion in a way that is coherent with its analytical structure. As Berger (2008, 265) has argued, Canadian constitutional law has no choice but to "cast religion in terms compatible with its own assumptions, which are influenced not only by liberalism by also by Judeo-Christian religions." While feminists have critiqued the individualizing, de-contextualizing and privatizing nature of the liberal paradigm, particularly in the context of choice and autonomy (e.g., Majury 2006; Hong 2011), it is nevertheless the framework for rights arguments in Canada.

We begin with a brief review of an issue of women's religious freedom and equality rights that rose to prominence in the fall of 2015 during the Canadian federal election: whether Muslim women are free to wear a *niqab* while swearing an oath of citizenship. Then, we briefly canvass the Supreme Court of Canada case law to see what claimants must prove when claiming violations of their freedom of religion and equality rights, touching as well on what the government must prove to justify such violations. Our focus is on the Court's freedom of religion decisions and what they say about the role of choice. Then we narrow our attention to two cases involving women, freedom of religion, equality, and choice in order to identify the issues and themes that emerge. These cases illustrate the tensions created by the notion of choice in the context of religious women's rights claims. Throughout the paper, we attend to three topics from the feminist literature about religious women and choice: the relationship between choice, agency and autonomy; the role of individualization; and the public/private dichotomy. We conclude by suggesting that a decreased reliance on choice may be strategic for religious women's rights claims.

The Ishaq case

The issue of women's religious freedom and equality rights that rose to prominence during the 2015 Canadian federal election was whether Zunera Ishaq, a Muslim woman, was at liberty to wear a *niqab* while participating in a citizenship ceremony. The *niqab* is not the only religious head wear that has been controversial in Canada,[1] and the 2015 federal election is not the only or even the most recent time that *niqab* wearing has led to public debate and court cases (Bakht 2015).[2] Nevertheless, we have chosen this controversy as our focus because veiling and the state-required removal of veils raises questions at the intersection of women, religion and rights. The rhetoric around Ms. Ishaq's case raised the issue of choice in ways that provide good examples of the competing roles that choice can play in freedom of religion and equality claims, the two grounds of Ms. Ishaq's appeal. In addition, Ms. Ishaq did speak publicly about the controversy, allowing us to hear from the woman at the heart of this particular debate (although we recognize there are many different discourses around different veiling practices [Bakht 2012; Hafez 2015]).

Zunera Ishaq was a permanent resident of Canada, originally from Pakistan. She wears a *niqab*, a veil covering all of her hair and face except her

---

1. Turbans worn by Sikh men have also attracted controversy. See for example Bhinder *v.* CN (1985), finding the application of an employer's hardhat requirement to a Sikh employee who wore a turban was justified as a *bona fide* occupational requirement, and Grant *v.* Canada (Attorney General) (1995), denying an application for an order prohibiting the Commissioner of the Royal Canadian Mounted Police from allowing the wearing of religious symbols as part of the RCMP uniform. More recently, in 2013, the Quebec Soccer Federation banned turbans on soccer fields, but lifted the ban following its suspension and a ruling by FIFA (CBC News 2015a).
2. There have been many instances just in the last decade. For example, in 2007, the then federal government proposed an amendment – Bill C-6, Act to amend the Canada Elections Act (visual identification of voters) – which would have prevented *niqab*-wearing women from voting unless they removed their veils. In Quebec in 2010, after a woman was barred from a French-language class for refusing to remove her *niqab*, the then provincial government's proposed Bill 94, which targeted only *niqab*-wearing women and would have required a "naked face" in order to provide or receive a state service (Chung 2010; Hong 2011; Thomas 2015). During a provincial election in 2013, the then Quebec government tried to introduce the Charter of Quebec Values Bill, which would have prevented all people who wore conspicuous religious symbols from working in the public service (Global News 2013). In 2015, after an election and a change in the governing party, the new premier of Quebec proposed to bar that province's public servants from wearing the burqa or *niqab* at work (Authier 2015).

eyes. Late in 2013, Ms. Ishaq became eligible for Canadian citizenship, but she could not become a citizen until she took the oath of citizenship in a public ceremony. Federal government policy required her to remove her *niqab* for that ceremony. Ms. Ishaq had no problem removing her *niqab* in private before a female immigration official to write her citizenship exam, but she was unable to comply with the policy during the public ceremony without betraying her faith as a Sunni Muslim. She asked the Federal Court to enjoin the government from applying the policy to her, arguing, first, that the policy conflicted with the requirements of the *Citizenship Act*, and second, that it violated her freedom of religion and right to equality under the *Charter*.

In Federal Court in February 2015, Ms. Ishaq succeeded on her first argument that the government's policy contradicted its own regulations, and the Court did not discuss her *Charter* claims. The government appealed and the order was upheld by the Federal Court of Appeal on September 15, 2015. Ms. Ishaq became a Canadian citizen two weeks later at a citizenship ceremony during which she wore her *niqab*, just in time to vote in the October 19, 2015 federal election.

In the interval between the two court decisions, Prime Minister Stephen Harper, then the leader of the Conservative Party, called a federal election and, after the Federal Court of Appeal ruling, Ms. Ishaq's case became a controversial issue in that election. The Conservative government said that it would appeal that ruling to the Supreme Court of Canada and that, if re-elected, it would pass legislation requiring women to remove all face coverings during citizenship ceremonies. The issue was credited with increasing electoral backing of Prime Minister Harper's Conservative government, which supported the ban, and eroding electoral support for the New Democratic Party, which opposed the proposed ban. According to one poll, ninety-three per cent of electors in the province of Quebec supported the Conservative position on the *niqab*, as did eighty-two per cent of all Canadians (Andrew-Gee 2015). The Conservative government was not re-elected, and the issue faded from the public consciousness – for a while.[3]

---

3. In 2016 a new Liberal government in Quebec put forward a bill to force people offering or receiving a public service to do so with their face uncovered (Valiante 2016). Quebec courts suspended the effect of that bill before it became law on the basis that "irreparable harm will be caused to Muslim women" (National Council of Canadian Muslims 2019). Then, after decades of failed attempts to impose "secularism" legislation, the National Assembly of Quebec passed Bill 21, An Act respecting the laicity of the State, which came into force June 16, 2019. The Act bans teachers, police, government lawyers and other civil servants in positions of authority from wearing religious symbols such as

Ms. Ishaq was interviewed after her victory in the Federal Court of Appeal and stated that "it is a religious duty of mine to cover my face in public at all times," while acknowledging that she was aware there are differences of opinion among Muslim scholars about whether there is a religious requirement to wear the veil (CBC News 2015b). In that same interview, she also stated: "I would only say that in my case, it was my personal choice. Nobody has ever forced me." These two quotes illustrate an interesting relationship between choice and obligation – about a choice to be obligated – rather than the usual dichotomy. They also indicate an individualized take on religion as the veiling arises from personal conviction and the exercise of agency (Afshar 2008; Burke 2012; Hong 2011). All of these themes are supported by Canadian case law, as we shall see, as well as by Canadian scholarship (e.g. Clarke 2013; Razavy 2015).

On the topic of her head covering as a heated election issue, Ms. Ishaq said "It is a little sad, as well as a little disappointing for me as well, that this personal choice of mine has nothing to do with anyone, and it ... has been take[n] to this political game" (CBC News 2015b). This points to a public/private dichotomy, with religion in the private sphere and politics in the public sphere (Berger 2008, 280–281; Ryder 2008, 88–89; Fournier and See 2012), as well as to the individual nature of choice. In another interview, Ms. Ishaq indicated that the *niqab* protected a woman from being judged by her appearance rather than by her actions or intellect; wearing the *niqab* made her appearance "a private matter" (McKeon 2016).

We note that in a recent study of eighty-one Ontario women who wear the *niqab* – the only Canadian study on the topic – Clarke concluded that the adoption of the *niqab* "is always and without exception represented as a momentous choice made on the basis of personal considerations" (2013, 45). Indeed, Ms. Ishaq's statements echo points that other *niqab*- and

---

the *kippah*, turban or *hijab*, and it also requires that government services be delivered and received with faces uncovered (Authier, 2019). The Act invokes the "notwithstanding clause" in section 33 of the Charter, which permits legislation to override certain rights, including freedom of religion under section 2(a). Nevertheless, the Act is seen as unfairly targeting Muslim women who wear *hijabs* or other head-coverings. The National Council of Canadian Muslims and the Canadian Civil Liberties Association have challenged the Act on the basis it is criminal legislation beyond the jurisdiction of the provinces and also impermissibly vague (Montpetit, 2019). It is also expected that the Act's targeting of religious women will be challenged for violating the Charter's "equal rights amendment," section 28 (Alam and Froc, 2019). That provision guarantees that the rights and freedoms of the Charter apply equally to male and female persons "notwithstanding" anything else, including the override powers of section 33.

hijab-wearing Canadian women have made (e.g., Clarke 2013; Eid 2015). For many Muslim women, veiling is important to women's rights because it represents freedom of choice, i.e., autonomy and agency (Afshar 2008; Hong 2011).

Ms. Ishaq also described her personal research into religious texts, an example of a woman claiming the freedom to interpret her own traditions. Her interviewer summarized her study of scholarly texts: "After a year, she decided women were meant to wear it as an expression of their faith. More than that, she felt that it was an obligation designed to protect them" (McKeon 2016). This statement also illustrates autonomy and agency, two concepts raised by the use of choice and two values important to freedom of religion and to women's rights in Canada.

What of the rhetoric of the federal politicians? The then Prime Minister had stated in the House of Commons that the practice of covering one's face with a *niqab* was "rooted in a culture that is anti-women," claiming a need for laws to ensure women's equality (Chase 2015). This remark positions veiled women as lacking agency and in need of rescuing (Bakht 2015, 16). The Minister of Immigration had protested that "a huge number of Muslims have reminded me that the face covering is not a religious obligation" (Geddes 2015) – one of the standard arguments for banning the *niqab* (Bakht 2012, 76). This argument is a claim that only religious duties recognized by established religious leaders are protected by religious freedom, a claim that has been rejected by the Canadian courts. That same Minister also declared a *niqab* at a citizenship ceremony to be "un-Canadian," explaining that "[a]llowing a group to hide their faces while they are becoming members of our community is counter to Canada's commitment to openness and equality and social cohesion" (Goodman 2015). He thus asserted that religion belongs in the private sphere because it is incompatible with other values in the public realm (Bakht 2012), and trivializes, with his "hide their faces" comment, the role that religion plays in identity and belonging.

While these are but a small sample of the statements made by Ms. Ishaq and politicians during the election campaign, they do raise the issues that we will see in the case law.

The basic structure of *Charter* claims

Under the *Charter*, there is a two-step process for analyzing rights claims. First, the claimant bears the burden of proving that one of their rights or freedoms has been violated by state action. For the purposes of this paper, the relevant rights-conferring provisions of the *Charter* are:

> Section 2(a): Everyone has the following fundamental freedoms ... (a) freedom of conscience and religion [...]
>
> Section 15(1): Every individual is equal before and under the law and has the right to the equal protection and equal benefit of the law without discrimination and, in particular, without discrimination based on race, national or ethnic origin, colour, religion, sex, age or mental or physical disability.

Intersectional claims, or claims of discrimination based on multiple overlapping protected grounds, are possible under the equality provisions of section 15, which lists various grounds of discrimination, including sex and religion. Also relevant is section 27 of the *Charter*, which requires the *Charter* to be interpreted "in a manner consistent with the preservation and enhancement of the multicultural heritage of Canadians."

Second, if the claimant meets their burden of proving a violation of rights or freedoms, the government then has an opportunity to justify the violation under section 1 of the *Charter*, which provides that the *Charter* "guarantees the rights and freedoms set out in it subject only to such reasonable limits prescribed by law as can be demonstrably justified in a free and democratic society." Under section 1, it is up to the government to prove its side of the case.

Freedom of religion

What is protected by section 2(a) of the *Charter*? In the first case in which the Supreme Court considered that section, R *v.* Big M Drug Mart Ltd (1985, 336–337), the Supreme Court defined freedom of religion to include both beliefs and practices, holding that "no one is to be forced to act in a way contrary to his beliefs or his conscience." R *v.* Big M Drug Mart Ltd also explicitly stated that it is "the right of every Canadian to work out for himself or herself what his or her religious obligations, if any, should be" (351). Thus, from the beginning, freedom of religion included the opportunity for women to interpret their own tradition.

One of the subsequent leading cases, Syndicat Northcrest *v.* Amselem (2004) held that the belief or practice in question can be either objectively or subjectively obligatory, or customary. A particular practice or belief need not be "required by official religious dogma" nor be "in conformity with the position of religious officials" (para 56). Claimants must show that the practice or belief for which they seek protection from state interference has a nexus with religion and is based on beliefs that are sincerely held. The claimant must also prove that the violation is more than trivial and insubstantial (Syndicat Northcrest *v.* Amselem 2004, para 59)

This approach provides for "an expansive definition of freedom of religion, which revolves around the notion of personal choice and individual autonomy and freedom" (para 40). Thus, choice is at the core of freedom of religion in Canada (Berger 2008, 272–73; Moon 2008, 58; Razavy 2015, 170).

Equality rights

Section 15(1) of the *Charter* provides a guarantee of substantive equality, embracing the idea that "equality does not necessarily mean identical treatment and that the formal 'like treatment' model of discrimination may in fact produce inequality" (R *v*. Kapp 2008, para 15). In other words, section 15(1) requires that differences — including religious differences — be accommodated.

R *v*. Kapp (2008, para 17) established a two-part test for proving a violation of section 15. First, does the law create a distinction based on a ground enumerated in section 15 or analogous to those grounds? Second, does the distinction create a disadvantage by perpetuating prejudice or stereotyping? The equality guarantee protects against both direct distinctions drawn by laws or government policies, as well as adverse impacts flowing from laws or policies that are neutral on their face, provided the distinctions or impacts relate to the enumerated, or analogous, grounds.

The second step of the test focuses on whether the distinction shown in the first step results in discrimination. It was recently expanded in Quebec (Attorney General) *v*. A (2013, paras 325–332) to recognize that perpetuation of historical disadvantage, regardless of whether stereotyping or prejudice are present, may be sufficient to prove discrimination.

Government justifications of rights violations

If a claimant meets their burden of proving a violation of rights or freedoms, the burden shifts to the government to justify the violation under section 1 of the *Charter*. As interpreted first in R *v*. Oakes (1986, para 69), section 1 requires the government to satisfy "two central criteria." First, the government's objective for violating a *Charter* right or freedom must "relate to concerns which are pressing and substantial in a free and democratic society." Second, the government must show that the means it used to implement the pressing and substantial objective are proportional. If the government proves both of these things, the claim will be dismissed. If the government cannot meet its justificatory burden, the claimant is entitled to a remedy (Schachter *v*. Canada 1992).

This analytical structure makes it clear that the court's scrutiny of government justifications under section 1 is to be kept separate from analysis of whether there is a violation of rights or freedoms. However, section 1 considerations sometimes creep into the analysis of section 2(a) and section 15 claims. This is especially the case where there is seen to be a potential conflict between the exercise of religious freedom and the rights of others. When justifications for violations slip into analyses of rights violations, courts place internal limits on freedom of religion. The placement of internal limits on section 2(a) and 15(1) of the *Charter* can also arise through a consideration of choice, as we will discuss.

The jurisprudence on freedom of religion and choice

The Supreme Court's case law on women, equality rights and religion reveals two major and potentially conflicting trends on the role of choice. First, choice is often seen as a value or interest underlying particular rights and freedoms, and is therefore itself seen as deserving of protection. Second, choice is used as the basis for denying a claim where it, rather than government action, is seen as the cause of the harm suffered by the claimant. We will examine these trends in turn, and then consider their application in two cases involving the rights and freedoms of religious women.

Choice as an underlying value

In a series of cases, the Supreme Court has referenced the notion of choice as one of the values underlying freedom of religion. In R v. Big M Drug Mart Ltd (1985) – a case considering a mandatory Sunday closing law – the Supreme Court defined freedom of religion as "the right to entertain such religious beliefs as a person *chooses*, the right to declare religious beliefs openly and without fear of hindrance or reprisal, and the right to manifest religious belief by worship and practice or by teaching and dissemination" (336–337, emphasis added). The Court also held that, if Parliament could compel adherence to the day of rest preferred by the majoritarian religion, its power would be inconsistent with section 27 of the *Charter* and its requirement that the *Charter* be interpreted so as to preserve and enhance Canada's multicultural heritage. However, in spite of the reliance on section 27 in that case, the Court has rarely tied notions of race, ethnic origin or culture to religion, even when we might have expected to see some references because the claimants were disadvantaged by more than their religion (Eid 2015, 1915). This approach is in keeping with the individualization of freedom of religion claims, as race, ethnicity and culture are tied to group membership (Kislowicz 2012).

In *Syndicat Northcrest v. Amselem* (2004) the majority upheld the freedom of Orthodox Jewish condominium residents to build succahs on their balconies, regardless of conflicting expert evidence on whether this practice was objectively obligatory according to rabbinical authority. In doing so, they held that it is "central to [the] understanding of religious freedom that a claimant need not show some sort of objective religious obligation, requirement or precept to invoke freedom of religion. Such an approach would be inconsistent with the underlying purposes and principles of the freedom emphasizing personal *choice*" (para 48, emphasis added). The majority focused on the individual, personal and subjective nature of the rights protected by section 2(a), rejecting the dissenting justices' focus on a collective and objective conception of what beliefs and practices are required (para 46).

These cases illustrate that the concept of choice generally plays a positive role in freedom of religion claims, where it is seen as an underlying value meriting protection from state interference or coercion. Emphasizing autonomy and individuality, the Court has also recognized that religious beliefs and practices may be subjectively obligatory, as was Ms. Ishaq's belief and practice with respect to the *niqab*.

Choice as the basis for denying rights claims

Despite the relatively expansive role choice plays in the first set of cases, religious choices are not absolute and may be overridden by the state where the exercise of those choices might be harmful to the claimant or others, or simply made more costly to exercise by state action.

An example of choice playing both roles can be seen in the Supreme Court's consideration of the constitutionality of another Sunday closing law in *R v. Edwards Books and Art Ltd.* (1986). A majority of the Court found that "legislative or administrative action which increases the cost of practising or otherwise manifesting religious beliefs is not prohibited if the burden is trivial or insubstantial" (para 97). While the impact of the Sunday closing legislation was seen by the majority to "significantly impinge" on the freedom of Saturday observers to manifest or practice religious beliefs, this violation of section 2(a) was justified under section 1 of the *Charter* because it was enacted for a secular purpose and included exemptions that "substantially reduc[ed] the impact of the Act" on Saturday observers (paras 102, 131). According to the majority, the religious practices were made more costly by state action, but not costly enough for the violation to be unjustifiable. In a judgment concurring in the result, however, two justices found that "[t]he economic harm suffered by a Saturday observer who closes shop on Saturdays is not caused by the *Retail Business Holidays Act.* [...] It results from the deliberate choice of a tradesman who gives priority to the tenets of his religion over his financial benefit" (para 168). Because the claimants' choices, rather than government action, were seen as the cause of their losses, there was no violation of section 2(a) of the *Charter* in the minds of these justices.

In a more recent example, Alberta *v.* Hutterian Brethren of Wilson Colony, the Court dealt with a claim brought by the Anabaptist sect, who argued that Alberta's requirement for photographs on drivers' licenses violated their section 2(a) and 15(1) *Charter* rights. This claim was based on the belief of some members of the Hutterian Brethren that the Second Commandment prohibits them from having their photographs willingly taken. In finding that the conceded violation of section 2(a) was justified under section 1 of the *Charter*, Chief Justice McLachlin, on behalf of the majority, accepted the government's argument that the claimants' exercise of religious freedom undermined the goal of preventing identity theft through a mandatory photograph requirement – i.e. it caused harm to others. She also stated that "it may be more difficult to measure the seriousness of a limit on freedom of religion where the limit arises not from a direct assault on the right to choose, but as the result of incidental and unintended effects of the law.In many such cases, the limit does not preclude choice as to religious belief or practice, but it does make it more costly" (para 93).

Writing in dissent, Justice Abella disagreed with that characterization, stating that, "[w]hen significant sacrifices have to be made to practise one's religion in the face of a state imposed burden, the choice to practise one's religion is no longer uncoerced" (para 167).

This jurisprudence indicates that framing a rights claim in the language of choice may have adverse results for the claimant when her choices, rather than state action, are seen as the cause of her harm, or her choices cause harm to others. This may be particularly true where the choice is constructed as a personal or private one, as we shall see in the next part, although our analysis also shows that religious choices exercised in the public sphere can be viewed as problematic. Alternatively, the claim may also be undermined when the Court sees the practice as a choice that is merely made more costly by the state.

The role of choice at the intersection of women, religion and equality

How do these understandings of choice play out in cases involving women, religion and equality? The Supreme Court has heard only two such cases to date: Bruker v. Marcovitz and R v. NS.

Bruker v. Marcovitz

Bruker v. Marcovitz (2007) involved a dispute between a Jewish couple over the husband's repeated refusals to give his wife a *get*, contrary to an agreement they had entered into at the time of their civil divorce. The claim was not a *Charter* claim, but an action for damages against Mr. Marcovitz, alleging that his breach of their agreement deprived Ms. Bruker of the opportunity to re-marry. Mr. Marcovitz responded that the agreement was a religious one that was unenforceable at law and, alternatively, that his freedom of religion protected him from the consequences of breaching the agreement.

The dissenting Supreme Court justices believed that the agreement was unenforceable, based on the edict in Syndicat Northcrest v. Amselem (2004) that "the State is in no position to be, nor should it become, the arbiter of religious dogma" (paras 37, 131). The dissent also invoked the notion of choice, stating that "[w]here religion is concerned, the state leaves it to individuals to make their own choices" (para 131). This characterization coincides most closely with the first trend we noted, where choice is a value underlying religious freedom. Here, denying a role for the state privatizes the parties' agreement and gives effect only to Mr. Marcovitz's choices.

Writing for the majority, Justice Abella disagreed with this approach, finding that the religious element of the couple's agreement "does not thereby immunize it from judicial scrutiny" (para 47). She focused on the fact that the couple's agreement was negotiated between two consenting adults, each represented by counsel, and the provision of the *get* was part of a voluntary exchange of commitments. This reasoning is also consistent with the first trend, although in a more comprehensive way than the dissent, as Justice Abella considered both parties' choices.

On the question of whether Mr. Marcovitz's freedom of religion protected him from a claim for damages, Justice Abella relied on R v. Big M Drug Mart Ltd and Syndicat Northcrest v. Amselem for the point that religious freedoms are not absolute. She balanced his freedom of religion against equality, religious freedom and autonomous choice in marriage and divorce. In this part of Justice Abella's judgment, choice seems to

R v. NS

The only other Supreme Court case involving women, religion and equality to date is *R v NS* (2012), where the Court considered the freedom of a Muslim woman to wear a *niqab* while testifying in a sexual assault matter. The Court split three ways in its handling of this issue.

Chief Justice McLachlin, for the majority, established a framework of four questions to be asked and answered on a case-by-case basis (para 9). First, would requiring the witness to remove the *niqab* while testifying interfere with her religious freedom? Second, would permitting the witness to wear the *niqab* while testifying create a serious risk to trial fairness? Third, is there a way to accommodate both rights and avoid the conflict between them? And fourth, if no accommodation is possible, do the salutary effects of requiring the witness to remove the *niqab* outweigh the deleterious effects of doing so?

In her judgment, the Chief Justice variously described NS's wearing of the *niqab* as a "requirement" (paras 1, 4, 14), a "wish" (paras 3, 4, 11, 29), and a "desire" (para 13). She did note, however, that "[t]he value of adherence does not depend on whether a religious practice is a voluntary expression of faith or a mandatory obligation under religious doctrine" (para 36). She sent the matter back to the preliminary inquiry judge for final determination on the sincerity of NS's beliefs and the balancing of salutary and deleterious effects. Commentators have predicted that the majority's approach will almost never allow women to testify in "high stakes" cases such as sexual assault proceedings while veiled. (Bhabha 2012, 876).

In a judgment concurring in the result only, two Justices placed much less weight on the rights of NS They balanced her rights against those of the accused, and "also with the constitutional values of openness and religious neutrality in contemporary democratic, but diverse, Canada" (para 60). Construing NS's wearing of the *niqab* as a subjective requirement, they advocated for a "clear rule," holding that "the wearing of a *niqab* should not be allowed" when a complainant is testifying in a criminal matter (paras 59, 69). Effectively, these justices found that NS's choice to wear a *niqab* harmed the rights of the accused and society.

Writing in dissent, Justice Abella took an approach that weighed NS's rights more heavily. She framed the question as: "Where identity is not an issue, should a witness' sincerely held religious belief that a *niqab* must be worn in a courtroom, yield to an accused's ability to see her face" (para 80). In this framing, and elsewhere in her judgment, Justice Abella saw the *niqab* as a subjectively obligatory requirement, "not providing a genuine choice to the religious believer" (para 93).

This characterization raises the question of whether wearing a *niqab* or other head covering would be protected when it is presented simply as a voluntary choice. It is true that practices that "subjectively engender a personal connection with the divine or with the subject or object of an individual's spiritual faith" are protected under section 2(a) according to Syndicat Northcrest v. Amselem (2004, para 56). However, when the court takes a balancing of rights approach, particularly if the strength of the belief is considered, one might reasonably predict that voluntary choices would weigh less heavily in the balance when up against interests such as the right to a fair trial. Cases involving choices that are constructed as voluntary run the risk of engaging the second trend, where claimants's (poor) choices are seen as the cause of their harm, rather than any state action.

The right to equality was not considered by any of the justices. NS did put forward arguments based on equality rights, as did the Women's Legal Education and Action Fund (LEAF), which intervened. According to LEAF, "[p]rioritizing freedom of religion would overlook the totality of the *Charter* rights advanced, including the complainant's rights to equality and to physical and psychological integrity. This would do a grave injustice to the rights asserted" (LEAF Factum 2011, para 4). Attention to equality rights may have led the Court to focus more on the intersections between gender and religion and possibly on ethnic origin as well, and on the corresponding identity and group-based dimensions of NS's claim, rather than the individualized focus provided by freedom of religion and its underlying value, choice.

When the NS case returned to the preliminary inquiry judge for a decision on the merits, he was satisfied that what he called NS's "wish to wear" her *niqab* in court was based on a religious belief that was both sincere and strong (R v. S(M), 2013, para 1). But he also indicated that "[s]he could have had her day in court back in 2008. She has chosen, however, to spend the last five years fighting for her right to freedom of religion, all the way to the Supreme Court of Canada" (para 8). NS's decision to wear the *niqab* – and to fight for her freedom to do so in the public sphere of a courtroom – is again construed as a (poor) choice not deserving of constitutional protection.

Ishaq v. Canada

How might these trends in the case law have played out in Ishaq *v.* Canada if the courts had considered the *Charter* issues Ms Ishaq raised? It is unlikely that the courts would have taken a balancing of rights approach, as they did in NS, because Ms. Ishaq's freedom to wear her *niqab* did not harm the rights of specific others, such as an accused. Nor did the government raise concerns related to security, credibility or identity; its justification was based on abstract references to (other) women's equality, as well as "values of openness and social cohesion" (Fine and Galloway 2015).[4] Ms. Ishaq's *Charter* arguments presented what should have been a fairly easy claim for freedom from state interference with her religious practices. Therefore, it may be that, even though her claim was articulated as being grounded in her choice to wear the *niqab*, it would have been protected, in keeping with the first trend we have identified. Indeed, Ms. Ishaq presented her claim as involving the sort of paradigmatic state-coerced choices that freedom of religion protects against, with her counsel arguing:

> [S]he must abandon either her religious beliefs or her dream of becoming a citizen, for which she has already made significant sacrifices. Offering citizenship as a prize for such a *choice* is a significant violation since it denigrates her deeply-held beliefs. (Ishaq *v.* Canada, 2015 FC, para 23, emphasis added)

However, the government's arguments in *Ishaq* invoked part of the second trend with their suggestion that religious choices can be overridden by government where they are not particularly strong or are simply being temporarily suspended by state action, a justifiable cost for citizenship. The government argued:

> Wearing the *niqab* is just a personal *choice*, not a basic sacrament. Indeed, the Respondent contends that it is unclear why a citizenship ceremony, which happens once in a lifetime, is not one of those rare instances where it is absolutely necessary for the Applicant to remove her *niqab*. (Ishaq *v.* Canada, 2015 FC, para 38, emphasis added)

The case law supports our thesis that framing freedom of religion or religious equality claims in the language of choice may have adverse consequences for claimants where choices are constructed as poor or overly personal ones, or as choices that harm others. However, at least when there

---

4. Although security concerns were not argued as a basis for denying Ms. Ishaq's freedom to wear her *niqab* in the citizenship ceremony, in other contexts the government has defended bans on *niqabs* for identification, security and communication reasons (Chung 2010).

are no competing rights of other individuals to be balanced, whether a choice to wear the *niqab* is free or constrained seems irrelevant. The protection of section 2(a) would not be withheld from Ms. Ishaq if wearing a *niqab* embodied her submission to men rather than God. How could it be if the *Charter* protects religious belief and not merely choice itself?

Conclusion

The implications of construing the protection of freedom of religion as the protection of individual's private religious choices are numerous and we have mentioned them throughout this paper. We will close with a few additional concerns about the way freedom of religion is understood in Canada's *Charter* jurisprudence.

First, the decisions of some Muslim women to wear the *niqab* in public challenges the public/private dichotomy by placing women's religious beliefs in the public sphere (Bakht 2012). The law's conception of religion as belonging in the private sphere makes it difficult for religious individuals to participate equally in Canadian society without abandoning their beliefs and practices (LEAF 2011). But the more closely *niqab*-wearing is connected to citizenship – to equal religious citizenship (Ryder 2008) – the more likely it is to be seen as worthy of protection.

The tenuous connection between religion and group-belonging when choice, rather than identity, is paramount in understandings of freedom of religion may have an adverse effect on equality rights claims, which are based on group membership (Berger 2008, 268). As Berger has warned, equality, with its focus on identity, appears to be in tension with the focus on autonomy and choice under freedom of religion (2008, 276).

Freedom of religion claims are also weak on intersectionality. The fixation on gender as the sole locus of oppression by those who support *niqab* bans ignores the fact that in the West, *niqab*-wearing Muslim women are discriminated against as Muslims, as women, and typically as members of visible minorities (Eid 2015, 1915). To the extent that the case law focuses on freedom of religion and choice rather than equality and identity or group membership, these intersectionalities are not captured. Can the values underlying religion be more explicitly recognized as those of cultural identity, in addition to those of choice, as Ryder (2008), Kislowicz (2012), and LEAF in NS (2011) argued?

The case law and literature also raise the issue of what is to be gained by showing religious women as having agency and exercising choice (Burke 2012). Characterizing religion as choice may restrict women's ability to articulate what it means to wear the veil not as a personal choice or preference but as a religious duty (and perhaps, as an aspect of group identity) (Burke 2012, 124). For many scholars and activists (e.g. Afshar 2008; Bilge 2010; Cader 2013; Campbell 2009; Deckha 2004, 2007; Eid 2015; Hoodfar 1992; Narain 2014; Singh 2015), and for the many devout women belonging to a conservative religion, their participation in practices such as the *niqab* is how they constitute themselves as ethical subjects, a characterization that "choice" fails to capture. In cases where the rights of religious women must be balanced with the rights of others, construing claims in the language of duty rather than choice may be a more successful strategy.

Even if the language of choice continues to predominate in freedom of religion claims, what is needed is a more complex understanding of choice, including recognition of gendered and systemic constraints and reservations that haunt many of our "choices" (Majury 2006, 213). We also need to be talking about choice_s_ rather than choice and recognizing the multiplicity of choices as well as the factors that limit them (Majury 2006, 215; Abrams 1990, 795–801).

References

Abrams, Kathryn. 1990. "Ideology and Women's Choices." *Georgia Law Review* 24: 761–801.

Afshar, Haleh. 2008. "Can I See Your Hair? Choice, Agency and Attitudes: The Dilemma of Faith and Feminism for Muslim Women Who Cover." *Ethnic and Racial Studies* 31(2): 411–427. https://doi.org/10.1080/01419870701710930

Alam, Samer A. and Kerri A. Froc. 2019. "Quebec's secularism bill violates Canada's 'equal rights amendment.'" 17 April. https://nationalmagazine.ca/en-ca/articles/law/opinion/2019/quebec-s-secularism-bill-violates-canada-s-equal-r

Alberta v. Hutterian Brethren of Wilson Colony, [2009] 2 S.C.R. 567, 2009 SCC 37.

Andrew-Gee, Eric. 2015. "Conservatives vow to establish 'barbaric cultural practices' tip line." 2 October. http://www.theglobeandmail.com/news/politics/conservatives-vow-to-establish-barbaric-cultural-practices-tip-line/article26640072/

Authier, Philip. 2015. "Proposed legislation would ban *niqabs*, burkas in Quebec's public sector." 10 June. http://montrealgazette.com/news/quebec/proposed-legislation-would-ban-niqab-burka-in-quebecs-public-sector

———. 2019. "Bill 21: Quebec passes secularism law after marathon session." 17 June. https://montrealgazette.com/news/quebec/quebec-passes-secularism-law-after-marathon-session

Bakht, Natasha. 2012. "Veiled Objections: Facing Public Opposition to the *Niqab.*" In *Reasonable Accommodation: Managing Religious Diversity*, edited by Lori Beaman, 70–108. Vancouver: University of British Columbia Press.

———. 2015. "In Your Face: Piercing the Veil of Ignorance About *Niqab*-Wearing Women." *Social and Legal Studies* 24(3): 419–441. https://doi.org/10.1177/0964663914552214

Berger, Benjamin L. 2008. "Law's Religion: Rendering Culture." In *Law and Religious Pluralism in Canada*, edited by Richard Moon, 264–96. Vancouver: University of British Columbia Press.

Bhabha, Faisal. 2012. "R. v. NS: What Is Fair in a Trial: The Supreme Court of Canada's Divided Opinion on the *NIQAB* in the Courtroom." *Alberta Law Review* 50: 871–892. https://doi.org/10.29173/alr79

Bhinder v. CN, [1985] 2 S.C.R. 561.

Bilge, Sirma. 2010. "Beyond Subordination vs. Resistance: An Intersectional Approach to the Agency of Veiled Muslim Women." *Journal of Intercultural Studies* 31: 9–28. https://doi.org/10.1080/07256860903477662

Bruker v. Marcovitz, [2007] 3 S.C.R. 607, 2007 SCC 54.

Burke, Kelsey. 2012. "Women's Agency in Gender-Traditional Religions: A Review of Four Approaches" *Sociology Compass* 6(2): 122–133. https://doi.org/10.1111/j.1751-9020.2011.00439.x

Cader, Fathima. 2013. "Made You Look: *Niqabs*, the Muslim Canadian Congress, and R v NS" *Windsor Yearbook of Access to Justice* 31: 67–93. https://doi.org/10.22329/wyaj.v31i1.4311

Campbell, Angela. 2009. "Bountiful Voices" *Osgoode Hall Law Journal* 47: 183–234.

Canadian Charter of Rights and Freedoms, Part I of the *Constitution Act, 1982*, being Schedule B to the *Canada Act 1982* (UK), 1982, c 11.

CBC News. 2015a. "5 head-covering controversies in Canada." 27 February. http://www.cbc.ca/news/canada/5-head-covering-controversies-in-canada-1.2975181

CBC News. 2015b. "Zunera Ishaq, who challenged ban on *niqab*, takes citizenship oath wearing it." October 5. http://www.cbc.ca/news/politics/zunera-ishaq-niqab-ban-citizenship-oath-1.3257762

Chase, Steven. 2015. "*Niqabs* 'rooted in a culture that is anti-women,' Harper says." 10 March. http://www.theglobeandmail.com/news/politics/niqabs-rooted-in-a-culture-that-is-anti-women-harper-says/article23395242/

Chung, Andrew. 2010. "Quebec *niqab* bill would make Muslim women unveil." 25 March. https://www.thestar.com/news/canada/2010/03/25/quebec_niqab_bill_would_make_muslim_women_unveil.html

Clarke, Lynda. 2013. *Women in Niqab Speak: A Study of the Niqab in Canada.* Gananoque, ON: Canadian Council of Muslim Women.

Deckha, Maneesha. 2004. "Is Culture Taboo - Feminism, Intersectionality, and Culture Talk in Law." *Canadian Journal of Women and the Law* 16: 14–53.

———. 2007. "(Not) Reproducing the Cultural, Racial and Embodied Other: A Feminist Response to Canada's Partial Ban on Sex Selection." *UCLA Women's Law Journal* 16: 1–38.

Eid, Paul. 2015. "Balancing Agency, Gender and Race: How Do Muslim Female Teenagers in Québec Negotiate the Social Meanings Embedded in the *Hijab*?" *Ethnic and Racial Studies* 38(11): 1902–1917. https://doi.org/10.10 80/01419870.2015.1005645

Fine, Sean and Gloria Galloway. 2015. "Ottawa asks for stay on *niqab* ruling pending Supreme Court appeal." September 18. http://www.theglobe-andmail.com/news/national/ottawa-asking-for-stay-on-citizenship-ceremonies-pending-niqab-appeal/article26421828/

Fournier, Pascale and Erica See. 2012. "The Naked Face of Secular Exclusion: Bill 94 and the Privatization of Belief." *Windsor Yearbook of Access to Justice* 30: 63–76. https://doi.org/10.22329/wyaj.v30i1.4360

Geddes, John. 2015. "Interview: Jason Kenney responds to Justin Trudeau's speech." 10 March. http://www.macleans.ca/uncategorized/interview-jason-kenney-on-justin-trudeaus-speech/

GlobalNews.2013."Read:FulltextofBill60–Quebec'sCharterofValues."November 7. http://globalnews.ca/news/952478/read-full-text-of-bill-60-quebecs-charter-of-values/

Goodman, Lee-Anne. 2015. "Jason Kenney defends *niqab* ban at citizenship ceremonies on Twitter." October 17. http://www.cbc.ca/news/politics/jason-kenney-defends-niqab-ban-at-citizenship-ceremonies-on-twitter-1.2803642

Government of Canada. 2008. "Bill C-6: Act to amend the Canada Elections Act (visual identification of voters)."

Government of Canada. *Citizenship Act*, [1985] RSC c C-29.

Grant *v.* Canada (Attorney General), [1995] 1 FC 158 (TD).

Hoodfar, Homa. 1992. "The Veil in Their Minds and On Our Heads: The Persistence of Colonial Images of Muslim Women." *Resources for Feminist Research* 22(3–4): 5–18.

Hong, Caylee. 2011. "Feminists on the Freedom of Religion: Responses to Quebec's Proposed Bill 94." *Journal of Law & Equality* 8: 27–62.

Ishaq *v.* Canada (Citizenship and Immigration), [2015] FC 156.

———, [2015] FCA 194.

Kislowicz, Howard. 2012. "Freedom of Religion and Canada's Commitments to Multiculturalism." *National Journal of Constitutional Law* 31: 1–23.

Majury, Diana. 2006. "Women are Themselves to Blame: Choice as a Justification for Unequal Treatment." In *Making Equality Rights Real: Securing Substantive Equality under the Charter*, edited by Fay Faraday, Margaret Denike and M. Kate Stephenson, 209–243. Toronto: Irwin Law.

McKeon, Lauren. 2016. "Zunera's War." March 8. http://torontolife.com/city/toronto-politics/zunera-ishaq-niqab-ban/

Montpetit, Jonathan. 2019. "Court challenge, protest greet day one of Quebec's anti-religious symbols law" 17 June. https://www.cbc.ca/news/canada/montreal/quebec-religious-symbols-legal-challenge-1.5178503

Moon, Richard. 2008. "Bruker v. Marcovitz: Divorce and the Marriage of Law and Religion." *The Supreme Court Law Review* 42: 37–62.

Narain, Vrinda. 2014. "Taking Culture out of Multiculturalism." *Canadian Journal of Women and the Law* 26: 116–152.

National Assembly of Quebec. An Act respecting the laicity of the State, SQ [2019] c 12.

National Council of Canadian Muslims (NCCM) c. Attorney General of Québec, [2018] QCCS 2766

Quebec (Attorney General) *v.* A, [2013] 1 S.C.R. 61, 2013 SCC 5.

R *v.* Big M Drug Mart Ltd, [1985] 1 S.C.R. 295.

R. *v.* Edwards Books and Art Ltd., [1986] 2 S.C.R. 713.

R *v.* Kapp, [2008] 2 S.C.R. 483, 2008 SCC 41.

R *v.* NS, [2012] 3 S.C.R. 726, 2012 SCC 72.

R *v.* S(M), 2013 ONCJ 209.

Ryder, Bruce. 2008. "The Canadian Conception of Equal Religious Citizenship." *Law and Religious Pluralism in Canada*, edited by Richard Moon, 87–109. Vancouver: University of British Columbia Press.

Schachter *v.* Canada, [1992] 2 S.C.R. 679.

Singh, Jakeet. 2015. "Religious agency and the limits of intersectionality." *Hypatia* 30(4): 657–674. https://doi.org/10.1111/hypa.12182

Syndicat Northcrest *v.* Amselem, [2004] 2 S.C.R. 551, 2004 SCC 47.

Thomas, Jasmine. 2015. "Only If She Shows Her Face: Canadian Media Portrayals of the *Niqab* Banned during Citizenship Ceremonies." *Canadian Ethnic Studies* 47(2): 187–201. https://doi.org/10.1353/ces.2015.0018

Women's Legal Education and Action Fund (LEAF). 2011. Factum of the Intervener in R *v.* NS. http://www.leaf.ca/wp-content/uploads/2012/12/NS-SCC.pdf

Valiante, Giuseppe. 2016. "Quebec government blasted on Day 1 of hearings into bill on religious neutrality." 18 October. http://www.cbc.ca/news/canada/montreal/bill-62-day-1-1.3811260

13

Women, Rights and Religion in India: Questioning the Tradition

Asha Mukherjee (Dubey) is Professor in the Department of Philosophy and Comparative Religion; Dean, Institute of Humanities and Social Sciences (Principal, Vidya-Bhavana); Present Chair, Department of Philosophy and Religion; Founder Director of the Women's Studies Centre, 2009–2012, and also from July, 2018, at Visva-Bharati Central University, Santiniketan, West Bengal, India. Dr. Mukherjee has published more than seventy articles in Indian and international journals and anthologies. Her publications include "Comparative Religion as an Academic Study in Contemporary India" (*Argument* 2016) and "Religion as a Separate Area of Study in India" (*Issues in Religion and Education, Whose Religion?* 2015).

Introduction

It is often suggested that human rights and duties are two sides of the same coin. Yet in the Indian context, traditionally there is *dharma* discourse, which, with its rules of conduct, is obligation-based. As such, the issue of human rights has never been at the centre of discussion. Nor it has posed a "problem" for the Indian masses. In modern India, human rights and women's rights have been reconciled with, or made meaningful within Hinduism. At the same time, however, it is the caste system in India which necessarily generates tension and conflict, due to its complexity and multi-layered dimensions. Questions such as: "Who deserves what?" and 'Who decides this? are extremely important. I would argue that, in India today, the most difficult question to be addressed is: "How to include the excluded and how to exclude the included?" At the core of the women's rights debate there lies a need to interrogate the very being of an individual, person, self, or "other," in order to accommodate the claims and the counter-claims of rights. This is necessary in order to be creatively human, as the promise of humankind is often threatened by the destructive activities of the few who are in power, whether they be connected with political, social, economic, or religious matters.

What is apparent in India today is more and more a division between the "self" and the "other" in the name of democracy and secularism. There is no automatic guarantee of success by the mere existence of democratic institutions. Democratic institutions, like those of all other institutions, depend on the interpretation and activities of human agents in utilizing opportunities for reasonable realization. Furthermore, Indian civilization, based on *dharma*, has often been claimed as creative and communicative. *Dharma* can be understood as recognizing human dignity and worth in terms of justice, unity, and benevolence, as a virtue of human fulfilment. It is accompanied by its theological insights and metaphysical doctrines.

Dharma has both descriptive and prescriptive contents. It encompasses the way things are and the way things ought to be – involving the nature of human beings and their obligations or duties. The concern for gender justice and women's rights, however, has also been an extremely important area in the Indian Constitution, right from the *Independence Act* of 1947. In examining the way that *dharma* is practiced in Indian society as part of gender justice, however, one finds a paradox in the urge to change and accept Western progressive and democratic values. This is because such a change also needs to be rooted in the past achievements of Indian society. This is highly problematic, particularly as the past has become interpreted by the contemporary Hindutva (Hindu right wing) advocates of social justice.

This paradox, to a large extent, influences the way that women's issues are being developed. There are two conflicting images of women in India, that of *devī* (goddess) or that of *dāsi* (servant). It is difficult for the middle class, educated, working women to be either one of these two roles. Each woman wants to be treated as a human being, as a dignified person who would have the power to decide what *to be* and *to do*. Yet to attain this, she would have constantly to face a struggle, which is often very difficult. In this paper, I will focus on the different layers of struggles that women in contemporary India have to face to negotiate both freedom and dignity.

In this way, at the root of the feminist concern lies a critique of the traditions described above, and a search for ways that women can assert their own identity as human beings. One way, surely, would be the assertion of women's rights. There may well be differences between Indian feminism and Western feminism, but the fundamental concern for both is a moral imperative to achieve well-being and dignity. Well-being, in this context, is to be understood as having real opportunities for individuals "to do and to be." The situation in a society becomes complicated when such opportunities are denied women by the patriarchal structure. Yet such discrimination is apparent in all religious traditions, such as Hinduism, Islam, Christianity, as well as in caste and tribe.

In this chapter, I will raise some fundamental questions regarding individual rights in relation to religion, such as: Does an individual have a right to interpret one's own religion and tradition? Do individuals have the right to interpret other religious tradition(s)? If they do, to what extent, and who decides which interpretation is correct? These are the most important questions from a feminist perspective, specifically in the contemporary Indian context. Interpretation of religion, as living religion, is an essential part of everyday life of every woman and, for that matter, of every individual. In addition, tradition, culture, religion, and philosophy are inseparable in the everyday life of every individual in India (Mukherjee 2015).

Women in Indian history

The majority of religions in the world have a history of excluding and devaluing women, and Hinduism is no exception. Religion is basically regarded as a cultural phenomenon which is embedded in multiple cultural contexts. In most religions, women and marginalized others have been excluded by methods and practices of their tradition. Some of the basic reasons that have been advanced for the exclusion of women mention their body and their bodily functions, irrationality, passivity, weakness, deception, and dependency. These characteristics deem female persons to be ethically and politically inferior (Sharma 2002). As a result, they have not been allowed to hold any authority in religious matters. Other reasons proposed are that women, due to their limited knowledge, and their impure body, do not deserve to be granted the title of 'personhood' or to be regarded as "human beings." Furthermore, within the established hierarchy in India, women are considered as lower, lesser human beings, similarly to the *śūdras* or the lowest caste. Clearly, in such a framework, women have hardly any opportunity to be recognized as 'persons' or "human," for that matter. They do not fulfil the required relevant criteria on many counts.

Why are women also excluded from having access to divine knowledge? Why must women believe in what they are told? As a cognitive disposition, this assigned behaviour is associated with a sensibility that develops in keeping with their upbringing and education. In order to remove such unfair, stereotypical prejudices, reflective, critical openness and scrutiny needs to be developed in each individual. Emotions, love, care, beauty, birth, and justice, which are deemed as feminine perspectives, have been omitted from the main discourses of religions (see Dalmiya 2001, 293–306.)

From early Vedic days, the Indian tradition has demonstrated a marked preference for males over females. It is a part of respected scriptures, e.g., *ManuSmṛti* (*Manu's Laws*) and Kauṭilya's *Arthaśāstra*. One obvious demotion of women is that no individual is allowed entry into heaven unless a male child performs his or her funeral rites. From the beginning, Hinduism teaches young girls to be like *Sītā*, wife of mythological hero Rama (in the epic *Rāmāyaṇa*), who always followed her husband. To a large extent, such religious teachings are responsible for the low status of women in society. The *ManuSmṛti* defined the social role of a women as one who, in childhood is subject to her father, in youth to her husband, and when her husband is no more, to her sons. The only aim of her life is to obey and follow the commands of her lord. The place of women is always "inferior" and "subsidiary" to that of a man in Indian society. Her life is full of trials, turbulence, pain, and suffering from birth to death. In contrast, the birth of a male child, the son, is a matter of celebration in any Indian family even today.

A woman has no choice of her own. She is compelled to marry the boy of her father's or elder's choice. After marriage, she does not have her own identity; she has to change her name and surname. Her honor lies in that of her husband. Women are thus considered as a commodity – a possession within a patriarchal tradition that has existed since the days of the Hindu scripture as, for example, in the Mahābhārata. Women who feature in Hindu epics and tales, such as Draupadī, Damayantī, and Taramati, have been treated as the possessions of their husbands in Indian history. A male, in contrast, is respected as 'superior' to a woman in every sense and is supposed to protect women by 'controlling' them. A woman must be submissive, remaining within the four walls of her house, bearing responsibility for the whole family. Her husband and his family determine her identity, and marriage is considered as the most important and determinative event of her life.

On the other hand, Indian cultural symbols glorify the women's role as mother-goddess. She is the symbol of productivity and welfare. She is Durgā, Kālī, Saraswatī and Lakṣmī, destroying all evils and spreading all goodness, nullifying wrong and the wrong-doer. She is the divine energy, power, and fertility. Women, as incarnations (swaroop) of Śakti, curse all wrongdoers. She is a creator like Śivanī, and a protector like Bhavanī. In modern India, women also figure as symbols, an instrument for nationalism and patriotism such as *Bhārat Mātā* (Mother India). Ultimately, however, a woman's status is determined by her ability to produce male heirs and to perpetuate her husband's lineage.

Traditionally a woman is thus denied any individuality of her own. Her identity is always determined by the roles assigned to her in society. In medieval Indian history, and the introduction of the there was a further visible decline in the status of women. The age of marriage was lowered; there was less and less access to education; widow marriage was prohibited, and *satī* became a common practice. Women's status became equivalent to that of a *śūdra* – the lowest category in the *varṇa* hierarchy, as prescribed by *Manusmṛti*. Then came the *purdah* system with seclusion, and veiling, which was another constraint on women's freedom. The practice of child marriage increased, defining social prestige and disgrace. All this was admitted into Indian society in the name of *dharma* (law).

Women in modern India

In the beginning of the twentieth century, a number of women's organizations began to emerge, such as the Indian Women's Association in 1917; the Council of Women in India in 1926; and the All India Women's Conference in 1927. In these organizations the major issue was to establish a relation with the national movements. Very often there was a sharp division on issues such as whether to treat women's issues as primarily welfare issues, or to work together with the government on political development. The differences became clear after independence when it was a question of translating the principles of equality into legislation, especially in regard to marriage, inheritance, and guardianship. After long and serious debates, the Constitution of India was adopted in 1950. It provided ample space for reforms based on democratic principles of human liberty and dignity. It is considered as perhaps one of the most rights-based Constitution in the world, with rights here being equivalent to claims for justice. The Indian Constitution was strongly influenced by the Universal Declaration of Human Rights (1948), and it guarantees the fundamental principles of human rights. It also provided a solid foundation for equality, except in terms of providing reservation clauses 3–5 of Article 15. Article 46 of the *Indian Constitution* protects educational and economic interests of the weaker sections of society. These peoples belong to the lower castes and are called scheduled castes (SC) and scheduled tribes (ST). Their status is unique to India due to its manifold social and cultural conditions.[1]

---

1. Article 15 (1) and (2) prohibit the state from discriminating any citizen on ground of any religion, race, caste, sex, place of birth or any of them. These articles provide there shall be no restriction on any person on any of the above bases to access and use the public places such as shops, restaurants, hotels, places of public entertainment etc. or use of wells, tanks, bathing ghats, roads and places of public resort maintained wholly or partly out of State funds or dedicated to the use of the general public. From article 15(3) onwards,

In one way, Article 15 has provided an immense advantage to women's issues, as women are regarded as the 'weaker section of society' and, as such, are 'marginalized.' Since its establishment, other extremely important changes have also taken place. Since then, other extremely important changes have also taken place. For example, the *Scheduled Caste* [SC] *and Scheduled Tribe* Act [ST] were established in 1989. There is a thirty per cent reservation of seats for women in the *panchayati* (Local Councils in villages). In addition, the *National Commission for Women* was established in 1992. In addition, The *National Human Rights Commission* was established under the *Protection of Human Rights Act* (1993). This body also protects the *Right to Information Act* (2005), the *National Rural Employment Guarantee Act* (2005), and the *Right to Food Act* (2013). The concern for gender justice and women's rights has been an extremely important area in the Indian Constitution. For almost two decades, women in India have been demanding reservations at every level, similar to the reservations for SC and ST and other minority classes (OBC) at different levels. Until now, however, this movement has not achieved any major success.

Women's rights were first recognized as human rights during the world conference on human rights held in Vienna in 1993. It declared the full and equal participation of women in civil, political, economic, social, and cultural life, at the national, regional, and international levels. It also proclaimed the eradication of all forms of discrimination on the grounds of sex as priority objectives of the international community. The Indian constitution also prohibits any discrimination on grounds of religion, race, caste, sex, or place of birth. The Convention on the Elimination of All Forms of Discrimination against Women, (CEDAW 1976) acknowledges that discrimination against women violates the principles of equality or rights and respect for human dignity. As such, discrimination is an obstacle to the participation of women on equal terms with men in the political, socio-economic, and cultural life of their countries. This, in turn, affects the development of family and society as a whole. CEDAW has been ratified by India and utilized by the Indian judiciary in order to direct the state to take action at various levels.

---

the constitution covers protective discrimination. Article 15(3) empowers the state to make special provisions for women and children. Article 15(4) empowers the state to make special provisions for advancement of socially and educationally backwards or SC/STs. Article 15(5) goes one step further and empowers the state to make reservation in admission into education institutions including private schools or colleges. Thus, article 15(3) and 15(4) are foundational bricks of reservation in the country.

Unfortunately, however, in independent India, equality of the sexes has not been a topic of serious debate until recently. Despite women's participation in all kinds of movements, women's issues are neglected. One example is the women's labour movement, which did not fight for the rights of women on all levels. This was because they had been led and guided by either elite women or men. The National Federation of Women, which was formed in 1954, was militant in the beginning, but in the post-1952 period, social work and development work such as health, education, childcare, and family planning became their major preoccupation. As a result, there was an overall neglect of women's aspirations for political recognition.

The International Decade for Women (1985–1995) infused a new spirit and awareness among women, as Western feminism and feminist debates, together with the media, playing an important role in a growing awareness. Increased participation of women was evident in various aspects of life. The Muslim Women's Bill, anti-*satī* demonstrations, and their united efforts started to affect social and political actions. Sadly, despite this activity, little has been translated into genuine equality between Indian men and women. All the changes in social attitudes have become available only to a few privileged sections, i.e., influential politicians and the elite class. This does not ensure equality on a universal, cross-class basis of women. 'Woman' remains the custodian of a tradition that confines her within the walls of the house or office with a false sense of security and of power.

As a result, there are two conflicting pictures of women in India. On the one hand, the mythological image of women establishes her as an all-powerful entity. Yet a more realistic image of women considers her as '*parai*' ('not one of ours'). This term indicates one who has to go away (by death as an infant, by malnutrition, by marriage, or finally by death in old age). She always has to submit to someone. Nonetheless, there are contemporary women who are well aware that they no longer want to be Kālī or Durga, nor do they want to be Roop Kunwar (an infamous case of *satī* in 1987),[2] or the victim of the Nirbhaya gang-rape case in Delhi in 2012.

---

2. Roopkuvarba Kanwar was a Rajput woman who was immolated at Deorala village in 1987 of Sikar in Rajasthan, India. At the time of her death, she was eighteen years old and had been married for eight months to Maal Singh Shekhawat, who had died a day earlier. Several thousand people attended the event. After her death, Roop Kanwar was hailed as a "*satī mātā* – "*satī*," being a mother goddess. The incident led first to state level laws to prevent such incidents, of burning or burying widows alive, which was followed by The Commission of Sati (Prevention) Act, 1987.

Women today want to be acknowledged as human beings who can decide for themselves who they want *to be* and what they want *to do*.

Feminist discourse and women's rights

It is often argued that human rights discourse destroys interpersonal relationships, as it divides a society rather than uniting it. Rights can also separate people from their communities, emphasizing individual self-interest over collective goods. In India, it is often claimed that Indian culture has always been *dharma*-based rather than rights-based. It is also claimed that human rights talk ignores how our identity and agency arise from a group membership. Feminist theorists have added that the focus on rights can detract from attention to our responsibilities to other human beings. This is because such responsibilities require more sensitivity to a specific context and to individual experience than rights-based theories allow. In a more recent controversy, at the 1993 World Conference on Human Rights, delegations from Asian countries declared that human rights reflect a Western cultural bias by promoting individualism. In contrast, 'Asian values' are regarded as favouring the rights of communities over individuals. A fundamental question nevertheless remains, given the diversities within Asian citizens: "How can it be determined whether Asian values express the basic ideas of an everyday person or do they exemplify the views of the political elites?"

Basically, rights are analyzed as consisting mainly of four components: claims, liberties (or privileges), powers, and immunities. In this system, every claim or right has a corresponding duty toward at least one other person. Such a claim could create duties that require that a particular action should not be performed. The fundamental right to life entails an obligation that people refrain from (an unjustifiable) killing of a girl child (feticide). The justification for rights is derived from two sources. These are will-based theories and interest-based theories. Will-based theories hold that the purpose of rights is to protect people's autonomy, and the freedom to exercise their choices. The interest-based theories (which are basically utilitarian or consequentialist) place an emphasis on rights as grounded in people's fundamental interests. Both approaches have limitations and debates continue. Yet it is clear that 'positive' rights as claims are often ambiguous as who has the duty to fulfil them. Guaranteeing these rights can require coercion, such as paying taxes towards social programs. Many positive rights, however, remain an ideal to strive toward, rather than an immediate goal. They thus appear to be of less urgent implementation as, for instance, gender equality has been in India.

Hermeneutics and feminist interpretations of religious texts

In Hinduism the self of ordinary experience (*jīva*) is unique, whereas the *atman* or the deep self is the same in all. In this non-dual perspective of the *Upaniṣads*, the self, persons, and the world, as experienced, are grounded in *Brahman*, the unity. *Brahman* transcends the world as well as being immanent in it. The world thus represents only a partial reality. At a deeper level, *atman* is identical with *Brahman*. Therefore, on the ontological level, there is no distinction between the self, persons, plants, animals, the world, and *Brahman*. The distinctions are perceived only at the level of everyday experience and are mistaken as real. *Mokṣa*, or the ultimate identity of the self with *Brahman*, is attained when oneness is experienced – self and the other become one, as "I am Brahman" (*aham brahmāsmī*). God is not separate from the self; God is one's deepest self.

In such metaphysics of the self and the other, how do we justify basic rights for women? Each self at the deeper level is connected with the other. Thus, acting out of compassion and non-violence is not just a duty towards the other but harming the other is to harm oneself. The *Īśa Upaniṣad* states: "He who sees all beings in his own self and his own self in all beings does not feel hatred because of this" (The Principal *Upaniṣads*, 572). In practicing compassion one is driven closer to the other, experiencing suffering of the other as one's own. One thus comes closer to the experience of the identity of the self with the other, or *Brahman*.

Dharma values such as compassion and non-violence also serve as ideals in the realm of political justice for Hindus. Gandhi's struggle for *swaraj* (self-rule), and opposition to the caste system, to the oppression of women and lower castes, was based on *ahiṃsā* (non-violence) and grounded in an *advaita* (non-dual) mode of reasoning.[3] This is clearly a very different approach to inequality and injustices in comparison to the Western model. One individual's freedom may infringe on others. Thus there is a need to establish social norms, values, and human rights, that are meant to protect one's self from the other, for the sake of mutual self-interest. But, in the *dharma* model, basic human rights and the social conditions required to live a good life are rooted, not on separateness and the potential threat that others represent, but on identity. They flow from one's interconnectedness to others and imply a unity. Consequently, one cannot deny others their basic human rights because, ultimately, their suffering is one's own

---

3. The Advaita (non-dual) mode of reasoning supports the view that everything in the universe is manifestation of one reality called Brahman, self and the other are not two but one.

suffering. Rabindranath Tagore proposed that such an ethic has much to offer the West; seeing the other as entirely separate being brings with it indifference and callousness, or a "dark world, where passions of greed and hatred are allowed to go unchecked" (Tagore 1917, 122).

Clearly, the caste system and the oppression of women is inconsistent with the fundamental spirit of Hinduism. Gandhi, Rammohan Roy, Śri Aurobindo and Tagore have each, in their own way, tried to interpret the principle of moral, social, and political equality. Yet the caste system in India can be compared to racism in America. Stringent constitutional laws against discrimination exist in India and America, yet still the discrimination exists in society. In India, it continues to get more and more complicated with new reservation laws, in addition to globalization and plurality.

In the patriarchal ideology of Hindutva (Hindu right-wing movement), the patriarchal arrangement, norms, and behaviours are viewed as both "natural" and "moral." The women's movement, by questioning them, can thereby only be regarded as 'unnatural' and "immoral." As a result, any radical mode of critique of traditional marriage and religion as patriarchal by feminists alienates a large section of middle-class women. These women may feel more comfortable with a "patriarchal" version of women's issues, especially because they see no existing 'easy' and 'secured' alternatives to it. When women question prevailing social norms which requires breaking existing structures and building anew, they create a situation which cannot be very reassuring when contrasted with a conventional life in a patriarchal framework. Patriarchy is oppressive in many ways, yet it rewards women who conform to its norms and penalizes the ones who do not. If women choose to conform to patriarchy, they believe obtain power and so remain relaxed.

Feminists have mainly critiqued religious texts which are anchored in unequal gender relations. By thus linking religion to politics, feminists have faced criticism for equating religious faith and spirituality with religious fundamentalism. They are accused of being unable to seriously engage in the religious life-worlds of their fellow citizens. An important question that arises is: 'How does Hindutva ideology and "Hindutva Gender Rhetoric" affect the ways in which women, religion, and politics are interlinked?"

Hindutva gender rhetoric and secularism: The impact on women's rights

The rise of the Hindutva movement and its proclaimed love for the Hindu tradition and culture in recent times is a serious concern. There are conflicting versions everywhere, depending on a narrow or a more expansive viewpoint. According to certain scholars, the history of India is a history of assimilation of all cultures and religions, as well as a history of violence and wars against others. According to some, India is a land of peaceful co-existence of different religions which have integrated over the centuries into today's society. This means that one can observe cultural harmony among the communities in the sense that they live, share, and react in a friendly way in day-to-day living. Their linguistic behaviour, expressions, clothes, beliefs, values, and social behaviour, in addition to religious beliefs and practices are viewed as similar. This is largely due to a mutual influence on each other. People of different faiths even participate spontaneously in each other's religious ceremonies. India does not have any one religion as dominant; yet the rise of Hindutva is a challenge for India's religious diversity.

The process of mainstreaming of the Hindutva movement first occurred in the mid-1980s. This was a time when the liberal and secular-minded persons could not respond to incidents of large-scale sexual and communal violence which occurred in the country after the assassination of Indira Gandhi in 1984.[4] The demand for a Universal Civil Code (UCC) and the subsequent debate initiated a process of right-wing appropriation of slogans from the progressive women's movement. Feminists were accused of being anti-national, western, and elitist. One of the reasons for this is that women's movements had strategically used Hindu religious symbols of female power such as those of the goddess *Kālī*.

The Supreme Court's emphasis on the Universal Civil Code raised old fears that it would become an instrument for imposing Hindu hegemony, which led feminists to retract to their demand for a UCC. The controversies over the *Muslim Women's Act* (Protection of Rights upon Divorce) in the 1980s, and the Women's Reservation Bill in 1990's, affirm the importance of caste and community.[5] They also illustrate the difficulty of artic-

---

4. Major incidents occurred, such as 1.The Godhra train burning on the morning of 27 February 2002, in which fifty-nine people died in a fire inside the Sabarmati Express train near the Godhra railway station in the Indian state of Gujarat. The victims included Hindu pilgrims who were returning from the city of Ayodhya after a religious ceremony at the disputed Babri Masjid site.

5. The Shah Bano case, was a controversial lawsuit in which a supreme court delivered a judgment favoring that maintenance be paid to an aggrieved divorced Muslim woman. The judgment in favour of the woman in this case evoked criticism among Muslims, some of whom cited the Qur'an to show that the judgement was in conflict with Islamic law. It triggered controversy about the extent of having different civil codes for different religions, especially

ulating a politics of gender that is commensurate with these identities. Women started uniting together, e.g., "*dalit* women" (a term for lower caste women), also Muslim women, and working-class women, as distinct from simply "women." The paradox here is that a feminist emphasis on a categorical appeal to all women as potential participants in a single movement then leads to negating the heterogeneity and differences in India.

This is evident when the movements of different women such as *dalit* women, Muslim women, and tribal women are definitely distinct, yet there is a trend to count them all as feminist. Often, however, they do not want to identify themselves as feminist. Thus, questions such as "who is part of the feminist movement and who is not?" and 'are all movements led by women feminists?' become important. Moreover, a further question arises as to whether an action can be called 'feminist' if those who perform these actions are not actually feminists.

At this stage, it is also relevant to discuss briefly the rhetoric of secularism and its relation to women's rights. 'Secularism' is seen as one of the prime concerns in Indian democracy. It needs to be observed that 'secularism' has a very different meaning in the Indian context, as distinct from the Western understanding of the term. Much has been written on this topic in last two decades. Interestingly, *Sangh Parivar* (Indian Nationalist Organization) also support some forms of secularism. It is thus worth focussing on the way "feminism" and "secularism" are practised by *Sangh Parivar* and Hindutva advocates within their respective women's organizations. The Hindutva ideology affects ways in which women, religion, and politics are interlinked. Kapur describes how secularism has become the central and powerful weapon in Hindu Rights' quest for discursive and political power (1999, 323–328).

The basic idea of secularism in India is that of equal respect for all religions. It does not require a wall of separation between religion and politics or state; rather, it promotes equal respect of all religions within both public and private spheres. This concept of secularism is largely based on the meaning that is assigned to the "equality" of religions. If it is taken in an Aristotelian sense of "treating likes alike," then secularism will insist on treating India's various religious communities similarly. By contrast, if equality is understood in a more substantive sense, such as that of address-

---

for Muslims in India. This case, however, caused the Congress government, with an absolute majority, to pass the Muslim Women (Protection of Rights of Divorce) Act, 1986, which diluted the judgment of the Supreme Court and restricted the right of Muslim divorcées to alimony from their former husbands for only ninety days after the divorce.

ing disadvantages, then secularism will allow for an accommodation of differences between religious groups and protection of the rights of religious minorities.

The Hindu right-wing has increasingly been trying to cast itself as the true inheritor of India's secular tradition that indicates they are the promoters of a genuine or "new" mode of secularism. In its formal approach to equality, then, all religious communities are to be treated the same. Any protection of the rights of the religious minorities is deemed as an "appeasement" and a violation of the "true spirit" of secularism. Within this formal approach to equality, the majority becomes the norm against which all others are to be judged. Secularism, then, is no longer about the protection of the rights of religious minorities, but, rather, becomes the assimilation of minorities. In this sense, the discourse of equality and secularism is an unapologetic appeal to brute majoritarianism and an assault on the very legitimacy of minority rights. Thus, the Hindutva movement regards special protection for the rights of minorities as a violation of secularism. They argue that democracy in normal parlance means the rule of the majority and that no religious group can claim any exclusive rights or privileges to itself.

By this same logic, secularism, based on formal equality, advances the project of the Hindu right wing in relation to women's rights. It has have taken on board a broad range of women's rights issues, both within the majority community as well as the minority community. Election promises in the Hindutva movement included the following projects: ensuring women's rights; putting an end to polygamy; enforcing the principles of equal wages; passing anti-sexual harassment codes; enacting criminal laws against domestic violence; preventing media projections of women in any manner that demeans or hurts their dignity; and passing a bill that reserves seats for women in all elected bodies, including the National Parliament. It reads like an ideal feminist wish list!

These promises, however, need to be understood in the context of their broader political program of cultural nationalism regarding both the role of family and their targeting of the Muslim minority community. Strategically, the Hindu right wing has attempted to position itself as the guardian of the rights of women from minority religious communities as part of its more general project of undermining the very legitimacy of these communities. This is evident in their trying to develop the Universal Civil Code as applicable to all communities in the same way, with the intention of civilizing the "uncivilized" Muslims who are viewed as discriminating against women. Ironically, however, within this project, all women are to be treated as equal, and all women deserve to be treated differently than men. As a result, problematically, Hindu men retain their position and status and are never required to concede anything to the regulations of the UCC.

"New Indian women"

If marriage is accepted as a natural, eternal unit of society, and the family as a primary unit to impart good *sanskars* (sacraments of life), things become extremely problematic. *Sangh Parivar*, as described above, also poses new problems for feminism in India. This is because they support globalization and liberalization, and retain the title of "new Indian women." These women are middle class and their values have been defined by economic liberalism and sexual illiberalism. Television representations have helped to shift their focus from social development and nationalism to a politics of family, sexuality, and intimacy. One example of this "new Indian woman" is Smriti Irani, who was a television star of a very popular serial, *Main Tulsi Teri Angan ki*. She symbolizes the traditional ideal woman who now holds a cabinet minister's position in present ruling Bharatiya Janata Party (BJP party) in India. Other women, like Uma Bharati, Susma Swaraj, also hold very important positions in the present BJP rule. The fundamental questions now become: "In what sense are these 'new Indian women' feminists?" and "How, and on what grounds, can we say that *Sangh Parivar* and their organizations are misusing feminism as a tool, if indeed they are?"

The fact remains that most Indian women have a connection with Hindutva ideology. They live and lead their lives within this ideology, even if they are not Hindu. This situation is due to the close affinity of the different religions in India. The media projects the women's connectedness with their traditions and then manipulates this bond for promoting a form of "purported feminism" which, with its restrictions, protects the traditional roles of women in the society. Critique and questioning of the tradition, culture, and the natural will always be a difficult path. Feminism, as a critique of tradition and patriarchy, is also bound to be a demanding path. If it is adopted, it can often lead to bitter consequences and uneasy relations in society and state.

The "new Indian women" are also exploring various kinds of power, although within a limited space. New women's movements have also been able to achieve certain intellectual, institutional, and political transformations that are perceived as feminist goals. Therefore, at first glance, there does not seem to be anything wrong in welcoming this change. Surely, however, much more action is required to take these movements forward toward the requisite end of gender justice. In my opinion, the 'strategic' gender interests would work differently for women from different castes, classes, communities, sexuality, etc. It all depends on the context. The individual agent would know what works for her in a particular context. It should be left to each woman to work out the best strategies for her specific feminist goals.

If "freedom to achieve well-being" were to be understood in terms of people's capabilities, that is, of peoples' real opportunities "*to do and to be,*" they could be aligned with the conceptual foundations of justice and theories of capability, as presented in the work of Amartya Sen (1992) and Martha Nussbaum (2000). Nonetheless, many questions remain. As there are many differences in their respective theories of capability.) What happens when opportunities are being denied by the state? In particular, is this refusal due to a particular religious belief in Hindutva? Unfortunately, theories of justice do not cover the entire spectrum of moral and religious issues. It is also generally agreed that some components of morality and religiosity fall outside the scope of justice.

Justice is a property that has also been ascribed to both individuals and institutions. Justice is both a virtue of that individual exercises in their interactions with others, and justice is also a virtue associated with social institutions. But, if gender is naturalized and attributed to an individual (due to faith in a particular religion, in this case, Hindutva) so that this individual and others cease to see any distinction between just and unjust, how can the idea of justice be implemented? The foundational question: 'How do we obtain justice in a society like India?' remains unanswered. This crucial issue seems to be the main concern for all of us who identify ourselves as feminists.

In agreement with Mary E. John (2004), one could say that "no non-contradictory" or "pure" feminism is possible in India, as tribal as well as *dalit* feminisms are products of critique in mainstream feminism. As a result, critiquing feminism itself does not defeat its purpose or make the whole exercise futile. However, one needs to be more self-reflective about one's objectives, methods of critique, and their politics of alliance. Furthermore, women, with their particular identities, become especially important in the present context because of the growing fragmentation of the universal category of "woman." This makes it impossible to speak of women without reference to their class, caste, and community. One needs to address the challenges posed by "Hindutva New Feminism" to the Indian women's movements and the limited space provided for women to explore their identities within "Hindutva New Feminism." One has also to examine seriously the answers to questions such as: 'If Hinduism is also full of diversity and plurality, is there any grand narrative of an Indian Hindu tradition?" (Lorenzen 2006, 1–2).

Let me conclude this section on an optimistic note, with a list of recent victories of women's rights movements. In the district of Maharashtra, Vanita Gutte sucessfully appealled to authorities to overcome obstacles for women seeking to enter the *garbha griha* (*sanctum sanctorum*) of the Trimbakeshwar temple; this occured thirteen days after protesters, organized by Trupti Desai, had been allowed into the Shani Shingnapur temple (FP Staff 2016). Another victory was obtained by the Indian Muslim Women's Movement, also known as the Bharatiya Muslim Mahila Andolan (BMMA). In this instance, India's Supreme Court banned the controversial Islamic divorce practice known as *"triple talaq"*[6] in a landmark of ruling, announced on Tuesday, 22 August 2017. Much of the legal argument in this case hinged on the question of whether striking down the practice would violate religious freedom. However, the judges in the majority ruling concluded that, on the basis of an act passed in 1937, enshrining Muslim legal beliefs and traditions into law, anything that was "anti-Qur'anic" was therefore banned and didn't deserve constitutional protection.

Conclusion

The rights of women, as part of human rights discourse, are related to the ideal of social justice. Deciding on the question of secular justice in accommodating diversity, however, has been a major challenge for India's democracy. The task of where to draw the line between competing constitutional claims in such a diverse democracy does not provide easy resolution. Often the democratic ideal of legitimacy and the liberal demands of egalitarian justice are associated with tolerance and liberal pluralism. The democratic ideal also demands religious liberty and freedom of speech, but this leads to tension between group rights and individual rights. For example, the issue of the rights of Hindus leads to tension between upper caste and lower caste individuals to enter a temple. Such tensions lead to many equalities, not only one. They pose a serious dilemma of conflicting

---

6. *Triple Talaq*, a form of instant Islamic divorce, was practised frequently by Muslim men in India. It permitted a man to divorce his wife legally by repeating the word *talaq* three times, be it by verbal or electronic means. In August 2017, the Supreme Court of India declared it as unconstitutional. Then, in December 2017, Lok Sabha (the Indian Government) passed the Muslim Women (Protection of Rights on Marriage) Bill, deeming that *talaq* was void. This has permitted Muslim women to live with equality and self-respect. The Muslim Women (Protection of Rights on Marriage) Bill, 2017.

equalities for advocates of secular justice. This is made especially complicated in the Indian context because of India's vast mosaic of caste, creed, religion, ethnicity, and political ideologies, to name just a few examples. How do contemporary feminist Indian scholars respond to such challenges?

A number of attempts have been made to meet such challenges. These can be found for example, in Vedanta and inclusive Hinduism; in the secular made sacred in the Bhagavad Gita; in Buddha's humanism; in Vivekananda's bold embrace of progressive Hinduism; in Gandhi's celebration of all religions in his social utopia; in Nehru's secular liberalism (almost Rawlsian in its implications); in Tagore's civic religion; and in Śri Aurobindo's integral approach.

In contrast to the standard divide within liberalism in articulating a global dimension of justice, Indian scholars have been arguing in favour of bridging this divide. The Indian approach may help in understanding that the narrow conundrum of statism versus globalism in justice literature need not pose an irreconcilable dilemma. The Indian ideal of unity in diversity can demonstrate that cultural or political divisions need not be viewed as conflicting loyalties, but rather as nested multiple loyalties that are frequently negotiated. The liberal commitment to pluralism still displays an uneasy alliance with diversity, generating tension and confusion among liberals and non-liberals alike. This is clearly evident in the social and political scenes of contemporary India. The Indian brand of liberalism is extremely complicated. Often Indian scholars shun the image of liberalism as a Western import, yet embrace liberal pluralism as the normative foundation for justice in India. Interestingly, liberalism is both substantive and negotiable as it faces continuous challenges of diversity in India and this opens up a great front for dialogue between the Indian and Western scholars.

References

Dalmiya, Vrinda. 2001. "Dogged Loyalties: A Classical Indian Intervention in Care Ethics." In *Ethics in the World Religion*, Volume III, edited by J. Runzo and N. Martin, 293–308. Oxford: One World.

FP Staff. 2016. "Another gender equality win: Women allowed to enter Trimbakeshwar temple." *Firstpost*. 21 April. http://www.firstpost.com/india/another-gender-equality-win-women-allowed-to-enter-trimbakeshwar-temple-2740960.html

John, Mary. 2004. "Feminism in India and the West – Recasting a Relationship." In *Feminism in India*, edited by Maitreyee Chaudhuri, 52–68. New Delhi: Kali for Women.

Kapur, Ratna. 1999. "Fundamentalist Face of Secularism and its Impact on Women's Rights in India, Joseph C. Hostetler-Baker and Hostetler Lecture." *Cleveland State Law Review* 47(3): 323–333.

Lorenzen, David. 2006. *Who Invented Hinduism: Essays on Religion in History.* New Delhi: Doda Press.

Mukherjee, Asha. 2015. "Religion as a Separate Area of Study in India." In *Issues in Religion and Education: Whose Religion?*, edited by Lori Beaman, 83–103. Leiden: Brill. https://doi.org/10.1515/zfr-2019-0010

Nussbaum, Martha. 2000. *Women and Human Development – The Capability Approach.* Cambridge: Cambridge University Press.

Sen, Amartya. 1992. *Inequality Reexamined.* Oxford: Clarendon.

Sharma, Arvind, ed. 2002. *Women in Indian Religions.* Oxford: Oxford University Press.

Tagore, Rabindranath. 1917. *Nationalism.* San Francisco: Book Club of California.

14

Caring Detachment in Buddhism and Implications for Women's Rights

Suwanna Satha-Anand's interests cover the fields of Buddhist Philosophy, Confucian Ethics, Women and Buddhism, and Religion. Currently she is invited Professor, Philosophy Department, Chulalongkorn University and Senior Research Scholar, *The Buddhist Pluralism Project*. Her major publications include *Faith and Reason: A Philosophical Dialogue on Religion and Ethics of Reciprocity in Confucius's Philosophy*. She wrote the first philosophical translation into Thai of the *Analects of Confucius*. Besides being the first woman President Philosophy and Religion Society of Thailand, at the Twenty-fourth World Congress of Philosophy in Beijing 2018, she was elected Secretary General of the International Philosophical Societies.

Introduction

Despite its seemingly limiting force for women's liberation, caring is a core value that defines various key relationships in human co-existence. On the other hand, detachment is an illustration of spiritual liberation in Buddhism. These two aspects of human experience seem to cancel each other out.

This paper is an attempt to illustrate and investigate "caring detachment" in Buddhism by exploring and analyzing the ways in which the Buddha deals with two cases of women who are in deep and extreme sorrow, namely the cases of Paṭācārā, the mad and naked woman who lost all her family members in one day of storm and torrential rain, and Kisā Gotamī the mother who cannot come to terms with the fact that her dear son had died. It will be argued that, for the Buddha, detachment does not cancel out caring. In these two cases, the Buddha shows great compassion in his positive engagement in the emotional turmoil of Paṭācārā and Kisā Gotamī, while simultaneously instructing them out of the entrapment of deep and extreme sorrow. Implications for the respect of human rights for women in Buddhism will be discussed.

Compassion and caring detachment

There is no controversy in saying that the philosophical, spiritual project of Buddhism is the transcendence of suffering. Suffering is generally explicated in terms of the inevitable process of birth, old age, sickness, and death. Negatively, it indicates psycho-physical pain and attachment to sense pleasures, and ontologically it indicates the universal condition of impermanence.[1] Due to this universal condition of being, a key Buddhist ethical value is compassion (*karuṇā*), meaning the desire to help beings out of suffering. And yet, an ideal state of mind in Buddhism is expressed in such terms as "detachment" and/or "equanimity." This means that in Buddhism, spiritual liberation is the recognition of the universal condition of impermanence, in a detached state of mind or a mind of equanimity.

However, it is interesting to note that these two discourses of compassion, on the one hand, and the other discourse of detachment or equanimity, on the other, seem to go their separate ways. Very few Buddhist scholars pay close attention to the tension or the possible conflict between the two.[2] This paper is an attempt to put these two ideals of Buddhism in close proximity and investigate them together. This paper argues that an adequate discussion of detachment in Buddhism needs to incorporate the emotional dimension of caring. This paper illustrates this point by analyzing two cases when the Buddha exercises his great wisdom in healing the wounds of deep sorrow for two women. I would argue that the Buddha is illustrating an attitude of "caring detachment," and not simply a "balanced state of mind" without any emotional concern. In this close reading of the two cases, I would argue that the Buddha is demonstrating a deep respect for human dignity for the two women strangers. An analytical discussion of this concept of caring detachment is needed as it would enrich a more nuanced understanding of both suffering and detachment in Buddhism and thus would help bring into Buddhism a more embodied sense of suffering. It would also illustrate more concretely in what way the Buddha exercises his deep respect for human dignity. It is believed that this close and sensitive reading of caring detachment of the Buddha could serve as

---

1. Rahula (1959) and Kalupahana (1976) are two widely referenced examples of this approach to explaining suffering in Buddhism.
2. One exception is found in Aronson (1980). It is interesting to note that, in many publications on the compassion of the Bodhisattvas in the Mahayana tradition, the scholarly tension tends to be posited between emptiness and compassion, not between compassion and detachment. It should also be noted that William Theodore de Barry (1969, xx) mentioned a Buddhist spirit of "at once detached and compassionate," but there was no elaboration.

a viable ground for future dialogue between Buddhism and human rights, especially women's rights.

Embodied suffering

Perhaps one of the reasons why caring detachment has escaped most Buddhist scholarly attention is because suffering itself tends to be explicated in broad, abstract terms of the general, inevitable, universal and thus impersonal condition of existence. While this kind of framing of the issue serves well a philosophical approach of the understanding of suffering, it tends to eclipse the real, painful embodied dimension of suffering. This paper tries to fill this gap by going back to the thick narratives of real people with drastic and dramatic experiences of great loss and who came to seek solace from the Buddha. There are numerous instances of such cases. I will deal with only two paradigmatic and relatively well-known episodes in the life of the Buddha.

Encountering deep sudden sorrow

Case 1. Paṭācārā: Preserver of the Vinaya[3]

> Paṭācārā was the daughter of a very wealthy merchant of Sāvatthī. When she was sixteen years of age her parents had her confined to the top floor of a seven-story high mansion, where she was surrounded by guards to prevent her from keeping company with young men. In spite of this precaution, she became involved in a love affair with a servant in her parents's house.
>
> When her parents arranged a marriage for her with a young man of equal social standing, she decided to elope with her lover. Having escaped from the tower by disguising herself as a servant girl, she met her lover in town, and the couple went to live in a village far from Sāvatthī. There the husband earned his living by farming a small plot of land, and the young wife had to do all the menial chores, which formerly had been performed by her parents's servants. Thus, she reaped the results of her deed.
>
> When she became pregnant she begged her husband to take her back to her parents's house to give birth there; for, she said, one's mother and father always have a soft spot in their hearts for their child and can forgive any wrongdoing. Her husband refused, however, afraid that her parents would have him arrested or even killed. When she realized that he would not yield to her entreaties, she decided to go by herself. So one day, while her husband was away at work, she slipped out the door and set out down

---

3. Quoted from Nyanaponika and Hecker (2003, 293–298). For reasons of brevity, I have omitted parts of this story.

the road to Sāvatthī. When her husband learned from the neighbors what had happened, he followed her and soon caught up with her. Though he tried to persuade her to return, she would not listen to him but insisted on continuing. Before they reach Sāvatthī the birth-pain started and she soon gave birth to a baby son. As she had no more reason to go to her parents's house, they turned back.

Sometime later she became pregnant a second time. Again, she requested her husband to take her home to her parents, again he refused, and again she took matters into her own hands and started off, carrying her son. When her husband followed her and pleaded her to return with him, she refused to listen. After they had traveled about halfway to Sāvatthī a fearful storm arose quite out of season, with thunder and lightning and incessant rain. Just then her birth-pains started.

She asked her husband to find her some shelter. The husband went off to search for material to build a shed. As he was chopping down some saplings a poisonous snake, hidden in an anthill, came out and bit him. Its poison was like molten lava and instantly he fell down dead. Paṭācārā waited and waited for him, but in vain. Then she gave birth to a second son. Throughout the night both children, terrified by the buffeting of the storm, screamed at the top of their lungs, but the only protection their mother could offer them was her body, lean and haggard from her tribulations.

In the morning she placed the new-born baby on her hip, gave a finger to the other child, and set out upon the path her husband had taken, saying: 'Come, dear child, your father has left us.' As she turned the bend in the road she found her husband lying dead, his body stiff as a board. She waited and lamented, blaming herself for his death, and continued on her journey.

After some time, they came to the river Aciravatī. On account of the rain the river had swollen and was waist-high, with a violent current. Feeling too weak to wade across with both children, Paṭācārā left the older boy on the near bank and carried the baby across to the other side. Then she returned to take the firstborn across. When she was in midstream, a hawk in search of prey saw the newborn baby. Mistaking it for a piece of meat, the hawk came swooping down, pounced on the child, and flew off with the baby in its talons, while Paṭācārā could only look on helplessly and scream. The older boy saw his mother stop in midstream and heard her shouts. He thought she was calling him and started out after her, but as soon as he stepped into the river he was swept off by the turbulent current.

Wailing and lamenting, Paṭācārā went on her way, half-crazed by the triple tragedy that had befallen her: the loss of her husband and both her sons in a single day. But more misfortune lay ahead. As she approached Sāvatthī she met a traveler who was coming out from the city, and she asked him about her family. 'Ask me about any other family in town but that one,' he told her. 'Please don't ask me about that family.' She insisted, however, and thus he had to speak: 'Last night, during the terrible storm, their house collapsed, killing both the elderly couple and their son. All three were cremated together just a short while ago, there,' he said, pointing to a wisp of pale blue smoke swirling up in the distance, 'if you look where I'm pointing you can see the smoke from the funeral pyre.'

When she saw the smoke, instantly Paṭācārā went mad. She tore off her clothing and ran about naked, weeping and wailing. 'Both my sons are dead, my husband on the road lies dead, my mother and father and brother burn on one funeral pyre!' Those who saw her called her a crazy fool, threw rubbish at her, and pelted her with clods of earth, but she continued on until she reached the outskirts of Sāvatthī.

At this time the Buddha was residing at the Jetavana monastery surrounded by a multitude of disciples. When he saw Paṭācārā at the entrance to the monastery he recognized her as one who was ripe for his message of deliverance. The lay disciples cried out, 'Don't let that crazy woman come here!' But the Master said 'Do not hinder her; let her come to me.' When she had drawn near, he told her, 'Sister, regain your mindfulness!' Instantly, she regained her mindfulness. A kindly man threw her his outer cloak. She put it on, and approaching the Enlightened One, she prostrated herself at his feet and told him her tragic story.

[…]

The Teacher listened to her patiently, with deep compassion, and then replied, 'Paṭācārā, do not be troubled any more. You have come to one who is able to be your shelter and refuge. It is not only today that you have met with calamity and disaster, but throughout this beginningless round of existence, weeping over the loss of sons and others dear to you, you have shed more tears than the waters of the four oceans.' As he went on speaking about the perils of samsara, her grief subsided.

[…]

This exposition of the Enlightened One penetrated her mind so deeply that she could completely grasp the impermanence of all conditioned things and the universality of suffering. By the time the Buddha had finished his discourse, it was not a lamenting mad woman that sat at his feet but a stream-enterer, a knower of the Dhamma, one assured of final liberation.

Immediately after attaining stream-entry Paṭācārā requested the going forth and the higher ordination, and the Buddha sent her to the bhikkhunis. After entering the Bhikkhuni Sangha, the order of nuns, Paṭācārā practiced the Dhamma with great diligence. Her efforts soon bore fruit and she attained her goal.

[…]

During her career as a Bhikkhunī, Paṭācārā achieved the distinction of being designated by the Buddha as the foremost among the bhikkunīs who are experts in the Vinaya.

[…]

It is perhaps natural that Paṭācārā should have been particularly concerned with discipline, since in her earlier years she had experienced so keenly the bitter fruit of reckless behavior.

Later on, we are told that Paṭācārā attained her goal, Nibbāna, the permanent quenching of the fires of greed, hatred, and delusion.

This story is selected here because of the rather long and thick narratives of a series of tragic events that affect the life of a run-away daughter of a wealthy family in the ancient great city of Sāvatthī. It illustrates well how suffering is embodied in the life of Paṭācārā. The abstract philosophical framing on the universal condition of suffering comes at the very end of the story, and only in a brief statement by the Buddha. This story is selected not because it is an exception but because stories like this are quite common in the *sutta*, one of the three baskets of the Tripitaka, the Buddhist Bible. Too often, these narratives are cited as an illustration of the philosophical teaching of Buddhism, indicating the Three Characteristics of Existence, namely, impermanence, suffering, and non-self.[4] As an alternative, this paper views this story as indicating the concrete manifestation of how the Buddha operates when he encounters extreme suffering of people around him. This is intended not to lessen the sacred image of the Buddha in the minds of many Buddhists but to pay respect to the Buddha as someone "real" *to* and *for* the people around him as recorded in the Tripitaka. Our approach starts from the real-life experience of people who "suffer" in body and mind, as indicated in the term "embodied suffering." Once the suffering of people is sensitively narrated in the thickness of tragic loss and deep sorrow, the detachment or equanimity of mind of the Buddha would not be seen as neutral, non-concerned, or totally detached from other people. As one leading scholar of Buddhism puts it:

> Whatever (English) term we adopt (for *upekkhā*), something of its quality is evident: Controlled balanced of mind, emotional non-attachment or neutrality, and 'beyondness' with regard to the ordinary ethical uncertainties and struggles. It is seemingly a calm detachment of eternity mindedness that has little interest longer in the ordinary affairs of men; […]

---

4. See scholarly works on Buddhism or Buddhist philosophy. A key example is Harvey (2000).

the possessor of equanimity goes on, completely unshaken emotionally or mentally by the world's mental, moral or social disturbances.[5]

The following critical discussion hopes to illustrate a different picture of the way the Buddha with his equanimity of mind seems to be sympathetically engaged with the emotional turmoil of the suffering people who come to seek solace from him. He may be "unshaken," but he is certainly not unconcerned. He might not be emotional about the situation, but he is certainly caring. He cares about the emotional turmoil of other people without being emotionally entangled himself. This is an attitude of caring detachment. In detachment, the Buddha cares. His caring for the deep, total, and sudden loss of Paṭācārā does not point to a state of "beyondness" with regard to ordinary ethical uncertainties and struggles. On the contrary, his caring in detachment creates a leap of moral imagination that punctures a hole in the neat rules of convention regarding mad and naked woman. The caring attitude and action of the Buddha crossing over the certainty of moral rules and rituals provide a new platform for a reinstatement of Paṭācārā's dignity as a human person. But first, the Buddha, as the only possible refuge for her, seeing beyond the physical appearance of madness and nakedness, renews and refocuses the suffering of this woman. In recognition of that deep suffering, the Buddha revives her dignity as a person.

It is interesting to note that the people of the great city of Sāvatthī had shown no sympathy for this naked and mad woman (Nyanaponika and Hecker 2003, 295). (Is it not possible to imagine that some of these people might have recognized her and known her as a daughter of one of the wealthy families of the city?) When they saw her, some threw dirt and dust at her; others threw earth at her. Even the people in the Jetavana where the Buddha was residing, who were listening to the sermons of the Buddha, did not behave that much differently from the city people. When the latter saw her, their first reaction was to try chase her away from their sight. At the sight of a mad naked woman, these people, both those in the city and those close to the Buddha, seemed to lose their sympathetic sensitivity and no longer were able to recognize the "dignity" of this woman. They had to protect themselves and their family from the sight and proximity of madness and nakedness. This woman was a threat to their "cleanliness" and their "civility." She could "defile" them. Paṭācārā's body of madness and nakedness had eclipsed her body of extreme suffering in the eyes of the people. But the eyes of the Buddha could clearly see Paṭācārā's body of suffering. The Buddha took a different approach to her body of madness

---

5. Winston King, as quoted in Aronson (1980, 89).

and nakedness. Perhaps his caring detachment provides him this extraordinary vista to "see into" and "beyond" her physical condition and thus create a possibility of restoring her human dignity hidden in plain sight in her naked madness.

The reaction of the Buddha was totally different. He told the people not to forbid her from coming closer, but to let her "come to me." He showed sympathy to the people's aversion to Paṭācārā at that point, by letting her come closer to him and not to "us." They needed not to be close when they were not yet ready. At the same time, he instructed the people not to chase her away. For the Buddha, Paṭācārā's body of madness and nakedness was not to be feared or rejected. In closer proximity, he opened a way for her suffering body to speak. He gave her suffering body a voice. He spoke to her first, telling her: "Sister, regain your mindfulness." In the Pali Text Society's translation, it was the 'supernatural power of the Buddha' that caused her to be become aware that her clothing had fallen off her body. Is it beyond reason to suggest that this "supernatural power" does not indicate a divine source of power of the Buddha, but it points to an extraordinary compassion and wisdom of the Buddha. The Buddha used the term, "Sister," to call her. This is a term that showed human civility in addressing a woman and a term of relatedness that fate has cruelly taken away from her in the last day. This gesture of caring kindly welcomes her back to the human community, going beyond her physical nakedness, which is repulsive to civilized society. Through the Buddha's kindness, she became aware of her own nakedness. Her first reaction was to prostrate herself at the feet of the Buddha. This sign of modesty could be seen as a restoration of forthcoming civil interaction.

Then a "kindly" man threw her his outer cloak. He was cautiously kind. He was giving her a garment to restore her dignity, but he threw the cloak to her. In throwing (as a gesture of kindness), he did not have to get too close to her. After covering up her body, she could approach the Buddha and prostrated before his feet. She then was able to ask the Buddha to be her refuge. She began to tell her tragic story of the repeated loss of all her family members within one stormy day. Her being able to tell her story was the beginning of a return of senses as now she could "make sense" to other people. These tragic turns of events were like the "storm" that had swept her whole life away in the aftermath of one night of torrential rain. When a whole life is swiftly swept away, madness lurks around the corner. One could imagine that in many ancient societies, when all family members of a woman are gone, she is left metaphorically "naked," vulnerable, and exposed to the cruel world without protection. Paṭācārā beseeched the

Buddha to be her last refuge for her life. The Buddha assured her that now she had met someone who would be her refuge.

At the moment of the encounter between this mad naked woman and the Buddha, the Buddha, unlike other people, is fully mindful of the sorry state of this woman. He does not react from the basis of social convention, which would solicit a reaction of rejection. Neither does he react from a psychology of fear, which would solicit a reaction of chasing her away. On the contrary, he calmly tells the people not to forbid her from coming closer. In my view, the decisive moment is when the Buddha *welcomes her back into human embrace*. She does not need another rejection and disdain. It would only be like pouring boiling water onto a deep wound. When she is welcomed back into human embrace, her humanity is restored. She comes to her senses. She can speak. She can tell her story. In narrating her great loss in life, she is regaining her former decisive self. She used to have a mind of her own, choosing her own partner, disguising herself as servant so that she could run away. We cannot say she makes all the right and wise decisions, but we cannot fail to see her as a strong, hard-headed woman who goes through incredible tragic turns of events within such short time. She gambles her life with this man; she loses everything.

Reading this episode from the perspective of the Buddha, we can imagine the "risks" he takes in order to help Paṭācārā. As the great teacher of the community of monks, he allows madness and nakedness and a woman to come near. Is it beyond imagination to think that this could be seen as a violation of social convention, not to mention the rules of conduct for monks? He lets his mind of equanimity and heart of compassion take hold of the event. He does not follow "proper" code of conduct laid down by society. This initial "violation" of expectation could cause a shock or surprise among his followers. But something human is already taking shape. Paṭācārā seems calm. She begins to talk. She might be "normal" after all.

It is also important to note that when Paṭācārā is asking the Buddha to be her last refuge, as she has lost everyone she can rely on, the Buddha assures her he will be her refuge. Anyone familiar with Buddhism would recognize the importance of the concept of "refuge." Buddhism encourages people to rely on the Triple Gem of the Buddha, the *Dhamma*, and the *Saṅgha*. The triple gem is a refuge in the sense of showing the way to a system of practice that will ultimately lead one to the cessation of suffering. It could be said that the Buddha is using the term "refuge" both in the human sense of someone to rely on for help, as well as in the *dhammic* sense of a spiritual anchor for practice.[6] Later on in the story, this

---

6. Buddhadasa's theory of "Human Language Dhammic Language" is the basis

Paṭācārā, having embraced the practice of Buddhism, becomes a *"Therī,"* which indicates she is a senior, well-accomplished, fully ordained nun in Buddhism. She became an expert in the Vinaya, comparable to the Elder Upāli, the chief Vinaya specialist among the bhikkhus.

What does this story tell us about caring detachment? Harvey B. Aronson offers several examples and a good discussion of the sympathy of the Buddha and his disciples and argues that that same spirit is alive and well in Theravada Buddhism (Aronson 1980, chapters 1 and 2). He also offers an interesting discussion of the Buddhist concept of equanimity and argues for an emotional dimension of this concept (Aronson 1980, chapter 6). He argues that equanimity should be understood, not only as a meditative or balanced state of mind, but also as working together with loving-kindness, compassion, and sympathetic joy, "outside of meditation" (Aronson 1980, 90). He criticizes Spiro for giving a misleading impression of Theravada Buddhism in identifying "detachment" as the destruction of all emotion (Aronson 1980, 95).

I agree with Aronson on most of his accounts, and I think his position could even be stronger had he paid closer attention to the narratives of the sufferings of people who come to seek help from the Buddha. It is clear from our analytical discussion on the tragic story of Paṭācārā that the Buddha is very sensitive to the plight of this woman. He illustrates great sensitive imagination of the sorrow of Paṭācārā and the rejection she has received thereof. The Buddha's tender caring approach to Paṭācārā, not only gives her an intimate space where she could feel human warmth again in being allowed close proximity to the Buddha, but she can speak freely about her great tragic losses and feel reassured of having someone as her last refuge. I, of course, cannot claim to know the mind of the Buddha, but from a close reading of this touching story, we can detect both the mind of equanimity of the Buddha as well as his caring compassion in the way he gently approaches and welcomes Paṭācārā back to the human circle. Her human dignity is thus restored.[7]

While Paṭācārā is a woman from a wealthy family whose life decisions lead her to face tragic events and who met her last refuge in the Buddha at Jetavana, Kisā Gotamī, our next selected case was born into an impoverished family whose intense suffering led her to the Buddha and was healed by his compassion.

---

of my analytical discussion of this point in the story.

7. Somehow this story reminds this author of the encounter between Jesus and the woman accused of adultery in John 8. Both the Buddha and Jesus "turn around" a critical, controversial moment and transform it into a restoration of human dignity.

Case 2. Kisā Gotamī: The Mother with the Dead Child

There lived in Sāvatthī a girl named Gotamī, in poor circumstances, the daughter of an impoverished family. Because she was very thin and haggard (*kisā*), everyone called her Kisā Gotamī, (Haggard Gotami). When one saw her walking around, tall and thin, one could not fathom her inner riches.

[...]

Due to her poverty and unattractiveness Kisā Gotamī was unable to find a husband, and for her this was a cause of deep dejection. One day, however, it suddenly happened that a rich merchant chose her as his wife, for he appreciated her inner wealth and considered it more important than her family background or outer appearance. However, the other members of her husband's family despised her and treated her contemptuously. This animosity caused her great unhappiness, especially because of her beloved husband, who found himself caught between love for his parents and love for his wife.

But when Kisā Gotamī gave birth to a baby boy, the husband's whole clan finally accepted her as the mother of the son and heir. Her relief was immense and she felt that a great burden had fallen from her back. Now she was totally happy and contented. Beyond the usual love of a mother for her child, she was especially attached to this infant because he was a guarantee of her marital bliss and peace of mind.

Soon, however, her happiness showed itself to be built on an illusion, for one day her little son suddenly fell ill and died. The tragedy was too much for her. She worried that her husband's family would again despise her, saying she was kammically unable to have a son, and other people in town would say, 'Kisā Gotamī must have done some very despicable deeds to merit such a fate.' Even her husband, she feared, might now reject her and seek another wife from a more favourable background. All such imaginings revolved in her mind and a dark cloud descended upon her. Refusing to accept the fact that the child was dead, she convinced herself that he was only sick and would recover if she could find the right medicine for him.

With the dead child in her arms, she ran away from her home and went from house to house asking for medicine for her little son. At every door she begged: 'Please give me some medicine for my child.' And always people replied that medicine was useless, for the child was dead. She, however, refused to accept this, and passed on to the next house, still convinced that the child was only ill. While many scorned her and others mocked her, at last she met, among the many selfish and unsympathetic people, a wise and kind man who recognized that she had become mentally deranged because of her grief. He advised her to visit the best physician, the Buddha, who would surely know the right remedy.

She immediately followed his advice and hurried to Jetavana, Anāthapiṇḍika's monastery, where the Buddha was staying. Arriving in renewed hope, with the child's corpse in her arms, she ran up to the Buddha and said to him, 'Master, give me medicine for my son.' The Awakened One replied kindly that he knew of a medicine, but she would have to procure it herself. Eagerly, she asked what it could be.

'Mustard seeds,' he replied, astounding everyone present.

Kisā Gotamī inquired where she should go to obtain them and what kind to get. The Buddha replied that she need bring only a very small quantity from any house where no one had ever died. She trusted the Blessed One's words and went to the town. At the first house she asked whether any mustard seeds were available. 'Certainly,' was the reply. 'Could I have a few seeds?' she inquired. 'Of course,' she was told, and some seeds were brought to her. But then she asked the second question, which she had not deemed quite as important: 'Has anyone ever died in this house?' 'But of course,' the people told her. And so it was everywhere. In one house someone had died recently, in another house a year or two ago; in one house a father had died, in another a mother or a son or a daughter. She could not find any house where no one had ever died. 'The dead,' she was told, 'are more numerous than the living.'

Towards evening she finally realized that she was not alone in being stricken by the death of a loved one: This was the common human fate. What no words had been able to convey to her, her own experience of going from door to door had made clear. She understood the law of existence, the law of impermanence and death within the ever-recurring round of becoming. In this way, the Buddha was able to heal her obsession and bring her to an acceptance of reality. Kisā Gotamī no longer refused to believe that her child was dead: She understood that death is the destiny of all beings.

[…]

After Kisā Gotamī had emerged from her delusion, she took the child's lifeless body to the cemetery, buried it, and then returned to the Enlightened One. When she came to him, he asked her whether she had gotten the mustard seeds. 'Done, venerable sir, is the business of the mustard seeds,' she replied, 'only grant me a refuge.'

[…]

As her mind had matured in the course of her ordeal, on hearing this one verse she won insight into reality and became a stream-enterer. Thereupon she asked for admission into the order of nuns. The Buddha gave his consent and sent her to the nuns's quarters, where she received the going forth and the higher ordination as a bhikkhunī.[8]

---

8. *Great Disciples of the Buddha* (2003, 273–282). This author is responsible for

In the story of Paṭācārā, the Buddha restores her dignity by letting her "in" human embrace, giving her a shocking chance to re-instate her sanity. In this story of Kisā Gotamī, the Buddha uses a "gradual" approach. First, he accepts her request of reviving her son. Then he sends her off on an impossible task of collecting mustard seeds from a household where no one has died. Any sane person would have seen the impossibility of the task from the very beginning, but not Kisā Gotamī. It takes her one whole day, coming in and going out of many households before she realizes the futility of her efforts. Her suffering is not just about the death of her son; her suffering is about her attachment to her son who dies. The death of her only son does not only take away her beloved, it also threatens her long-sought acceptance from her husband's family. After much difficulty, she finally had a son whose birth has been the key to her family's harmony. In this sense, her son's death is a particularly devastating experience for her. She needs more time and a "task" to digest the more universal aspect of this personal experience. Once she realizes this "parting" in a context of the rest of all other people, the severely "particular" experience is transformed by the "general" experiences of all others. She can then "distance" herself from her sorrow by letting in the "reality" of so many other "partings" she encounters during the day. This *distancing* creates a condition of detachment for her. She is healed.

From one perspective, this story of Kisā Gotamī is typical of the Buddhist approach to suffering. That is, one's intense suffering is transcended once one can see the "universal" condition of impermanence and suffering of life. On the other hand, is it beyond possibility to read this story from the perspective of Confucian ethics? A leading scholar of Confucius's philosophy who is interested in Buddhism once added an interesting twist to this story.[9] He proposes to read the return to normality of Kisā Gotamī, not only from the fact that she finally "sees" the universal condition of death as part of any life, but that the very process of entering and departing many households in the village is in and of itself, a "return" to human relationships. She is probably called "mother," or "aunty," or "sister," or "daughter" by the villagers whom she meets. Perhaps they console her. They share with Kisā Gotamī their stories of losses. Kisā Gotamī is restored back to the human community, perhaps not substituting, but filling in the painful gap left vacant by the unexpected departure of her son.

---

condensing and slight editing the long story while trying to keep the details of the original.

9. I learned of this way of reading the Kisā Gotamī story from Professor Roger T. Ames, a leading scholar of Confucian philosophy, University of Hawaii, and Beijing University.

From the perspective of the Buddha, perhaps he can see that "talking" would not help in this case. It is better to give her a "task" to perform. At least her sorrow will be directed towards a task, a task that could help "heal" her dead son. Initially, her great efforts are seen as part of the "cure" promised her by the Buddha. But the task itself is the cure. The suffering self is diverted and invested in the tiring task, a task of despair. That despair would terminate the sense of the task and thus the sense of her attachment and suffering. We can see how the Buddha wisely uses the doomed task to "get Kisā Gotamī out" of her own psychological entrapment. She needs to be pushed to the end of the road before she can realize that the road leads nowhere. The medicine from the Buddha is healing her and thus her deep sorrow of her lost son is healed.

Again, we can see in this story as well, how the dhammic sense of "cure" used by the Buddha can be communicated to Kisā Gotamī only later on in the story. It is not yet possible at the beginning, when her mind is fixed only on the "human" sense of "cure." Once the cure in the *dhammic* sense is achieved, the cure in the human sense of a medicine is no longer needed. From this story, we can see the compassion of the Buddha, who accepts the original emotional entrapment of Kisā Gotamī. At the first moment, language would not work; healing words or words of consolation would not be feasible. The sympathy and the equanimity of the Buddha work together, devising a task for her to do. The realization of her condition would come about as a result of her task, not from a verbal exhortation. The Buddha can see her clearly with his mind of equanimity. His heart of caring compassion solicits a gentle, gradual approach.

Caring in detachment

A general observation can be made that most Buddhist scholars have paid careful attention to expunge "emotion" from the discussion of spiritual liberation. Over the decades, Buddhist scholars, including key figures such as Walpola Rahula, David J. Kalupahana, Peter Harvey, and Milford Spiro, all explicate detachment in non-emotional terms[10] This has given rise to a general image of Buddhism as a religion of other-worldly concern, and perhaps even an "unfeeling" religion. However, more recent Buddhist scholarship has raised issues relating to sexuality, the family, and love and sympathy in Buddhism. Take, for example, a ground-breaking book, *Family Matters in Indian Buddhist Monasticisms* by Shayne Clarke, which argues that, contrary to the previous image of the Buddhist monk as a "rhinoceros roaming alone" in the forests, studies of the

---

10. On Buddhist ethics, see Kalupahana (1995) and Harvey (2000).

Vinayas have given rise to a very different picture. According to Clarke, a detailed study of the Vinayas brings out many rules and regulations that are "family friendly." There are injunctions for monks visiting their family, of nuns nursing infants (Clarke 2014, 155–162). In a concluding note, Clarke offers this picture:

> These monastics were not ascetic forest dwellers wandering alone like rhinoceroses; they were most likely slightly portly, homely, easygoing family men and women who had chosen to wander down the religious path and seek spiritual betterment and (on occasion, perhaps perfection) as they knew it; they had come to the realization that family matters in Indian Buddhist monasticisms. (Clarke 2014, 155)

Different but relevant studies of Buddhism and ethics of wealth, of Buddhism and business practices, on sexuality and gender in Buddhism all point to recent scholarship that offers a more complex and humanistic portrayal of the original path of the Buddhist monks during the time of the Buddha and in later Buddhist historical developments (Sizemore and Swearer 1990; Faure 2003).

The focus of this paper on caring detachment goes further in this direction of offering a context-sensitive way of reading and understanding the original situation where and when *Brahmacariya* (Noble Life) of the Buddha thrived and had a great transformative impact on the lives of peoples during the time of the Buddha. It seems to this author that the yawning gap between religion and human rights discourse is not so much a matter of the "essence" of Buddhism as a spiritual project that tries to transcend suffering by transcending emotions. The emphasis on detachment, on equanimity without deep engagement with the virtue of loving-kindness, compassion, and sympathetic joy, all help create a misleading image of Buddhism as a spiritual practice that aims to leave the emotional life behind. The Buddhist ideal is not an aspiration for a life without emotion. The problem is how to be caring and compassionate without being attached to emotional entanglement.

Implications for women's rights and dignity

Women scholars and Buddhist activists have expressed concerns about problems in building a firm basis for respect of women's rights in many societies where religion looms large in women's lives and identity. Publications of sound scholarship and discussions of case studies of Christian, Muslim, and Buddhist societies all testify to the limits and potentials of implementing international guidelines to respect the human rights of women (e.g., Howland 1999; *Religious Activism and Women's Develop-*

ment in Southeast Asia 2011). Oftentimes, the call for fruitful dialogue is encouraged so that the legal overtones of international human rights language can sit well with a more moralist language of many religious traditions.

From my own experience, I note that, too often, many religious women are immediately turned off by the language of "rights." Sometimes, they feel this discourse is based on making demands, coming from Western and foreign-domineering powers and imposing a responsibility on others. The very dialogue, so desirable as a path to conversation and communication between religion and human rights, presupposes common ground for communication. A basic challenge is to establish some kind of common ground that would help facilitate the possibility and viability of that communication.

It seems to me a promising and viable approach would be to build up close and sensitive readings of religious canons that offer rich and varied narratives of real human encounters between suffering people and the religious founders themselves. This close reading of the "embodied suffering" of people who come to seek refuge in the Master, and detailed and sensitive readings of the ways the Master approaches these suffering people with great caring wisdom, could serve as a common ground, generated within each religious tradition; that is, Buddhism in this paper. Once this common ground is identified, a dialogue platform for possible fruitful communication between religions and human rights discourse can be established. In these narratives, the Buddha himself takes great measures to restore the dignity of these two women. This kind of analysis and argument is badly needed as it identifies the very basis of respect for human dignity within Buddhism itself.

Conclusion

From my close reading of the two cases here in this paper, I hope to establish a glimmer of that possibility. In the context of Buddhism, suffering is no longer an abstract philosophical ontology of human existence devoid of any touch with real life. The Buddhist concept of detachment is less of a neutral state of mind with no emotional content, but is filled with compassion and caring. This analysis of caring detachment aims to bridge not only between the intellectual and the emotional gaps, but also between the emotional and psychological attachment indicating suffering of the unenlightened minds and the mind of caring concern of the detached minds of those with spiritual liberation. Moreover, this kind of language could rediscover the deep respect for human dignity that lies at the very basis of

Buddhism. If a Buddhist can be convinced to be sensitive to the Buddha's respect for women's dignity, it would not be impossible to participate in a discourse of human rights that is also based on a deep concern for respect of human dignity. Once this common ground is highlighted, a bridge for dialogue between human rights discourse and Buddhism could more readily be built.

References

Aronson, Harvey B. 1980. *Love and Sympathy in Theravada Buddhism*. New Delhi: Motilal Banarsidass.

Clarke, Shayne. 2014. *Family Matters in Indian Buddhist Monasticisms*. Honolulu: University of Hawaii Press. https://doi.org/10.1080/0048721x.2014.931181

Faure, Bernard. 2003. *The Power of Denial: Buddhism, Purity and Gender*. Princeton: Princeton University Press.

Harvey, Peter. 2000. *An Introduction to Buddhist Ethics*. Cambridge: Cambridge University Press.

Howland, Courtney W. 1999. *Religious Fundamentalisms and the Human Rights of Women*. New York: St. Martin's Press.

Kalupahana, David J. 1976. *Buddhist Philosophy: A Historical Analysis*. Honolulu: University of Hawaii Press.

———. 1995. *Ethics in Early Buddhism*. Honolulu: University of Hawaii Press.

Nyanaponika, Thera and Hellmuth Hecker, trans. 2003. *Great Disciples of the Buddha: Their Lives, Their Works, Their Legacy*. Boston and Kandy, Sri Lanka: Wisdom and the Buddhist Publication Society.

Rahula, Walpola. 1959. *What the Buddha Taught*. New York: Grove.

Rahman, Noor Aisha Abdul. 2011. *Religious Activism and Women's Development in South East Asia*. Singapore: RIMA Centre for Research on Islamic and Malay Affairs.

Sizemore, Russell, and Donald Swearer, eds. 1990. *Ethics, Wealth and Salvation: A Study of Buddhist Social Ethics*. Columbia: University of South Carolina Press. https://doi.org/10.1017/s0036930600038813

Afterword:
Women and Religion in Global and Local Perspective

Paul Bramadat is Professor and Director of the Centre for Studies in Religion and Society at the University of Victoria, British Columbia, where he also holds a teaching appointment in the Religious Studies Program. His research interests include religion and public discourse, public health and safety. His articles have appeared in *Studies in Religion, Ethnicities*, the *Journal of the American Academy of Religion*, the *Journal of Religion, State, and Society*. His books include several co-edited volumes, including *Religious Radicalization and Securitization in Canada and Beyond* (University of Toronto Press, 2014), and *Public Health in the Age of Anxiety: Religious and Cultural Roots of Vaccine Hesitancy* (University of Toronto Press, 2017).

Introduction

Let me begin with some remarks that are both personal and professional: I am acutely aware that I am the only male scholar associated with this project. I wish the pioneering women of religious studies had been treated as well as I have been during our project. None of my colleagues in this work ever gave me the impression that my questions and comments were obtuse or without merit, even when indeed they were often the flat-footed questions of an amateur. I have been honoured by this kind of treatment and wish more men could have the experience of being outnumbered, decentred, and yet fully included.

Writing the afterword for this volume might become an opportunity to indulge in academic "mansplaining," as though I might provide a synoptic sense of intellectual closure. I am probably predisposed – by my culture, my privilege, my profession – to think this might be my appropriate role, but in my brief contribution to this volume, I have more modest ambitions. In the following reflections, I would like to identify and critically engage three of the common themes that appear in these chapters, or at least that occur to me in my reading.

Caretakers or critics?

Throughout the chapters of this book, these writers provide unique insights into the broader politics of gender, sexuality, and religion that inflect their cases. These studies are distinctive because in many (but not all) cases the scholars are either critical insiders of the traditions and topics that interest them, or sympathetic to the women or groups being addressed. Scholars of religion who are also part of the communities about which they write often – though perhaps not often enough – reflect on whether or not they think of themselves as rescuing their own or their admired traditions from patriarchal or otherwise stultifying social forces. Is the intellectual "endgame" in fact the liberation of their beloved communities from these corrosive influences and thereby the establishment of the conditions needed for these traditions to flourish in some imagined egalitarian or authentic manner? If one does adopt such an approach, what might one not be inclined to see, or to problematize? This is not a question of specific relevance to this volume or this topic – it reflects issues all scholars of religion ought to consider.

By way of two illustrations, in this book[1] Buddhist theologian, Carola Roloff, observes that it is necessary "to appeal to the repository of the very texts themselves, and to dismantle erroneous views, by means of hermeneutics, in order to promote progress." She uses Elisabeth Schüssler Fiorenza's (1984) model of feminist hermeneutics, one plank of which is "the hermeneutic of creative actualization." Suwanna Satha-Anand uses an ancient story of the Buddha's interaction with women to argue that "If a Buddhist can be convinced to be sensitive to the Buddha's respect for women's dignity, it would not be too impossible to participate in a discourse of human rights which is also based on a deep concern for respect of human dignity." I do not doubt that there are or could be positive "knock-on" effects for the traditions or societies involved were scholars to use this hermeneutic of creative actualization. Nonetheless, we need to ask: whose definition of creative, progress, erroneous, dignity, and rights are being "read in" to the texts, tensions and phenomena?

To pose the challenge another way: are scholars caretakers or critics, to use Russell McCutcheon's helpful alliteration. Does this matter – to the writers, or readers? In my view, a similar spirit of self-inquiry should guide not just the way we write but the way readers read, too. That is, when we read, are we reading to find a way to rescue this or that community

---

1. All authors mentioned in this chapter are contributors to this volume. For the sake of the fluidity of the piece, in subsequent paragraphs, I will avoid indicating this.

from some real or imagined enemy (within or without)? If this is the case, are there insights – in this volume, for example – the full implications of which readers might actively avoid? Are there analyses of the patriarchal or misogynistic elements of a religious community that might not just destabilize these specific elements but in fact the (read: "authentic" or essentially "egalitarian") religious communities themselves? If so, what then? When Rosalind Hackett observes that "These [African Pentecostal] women leaders are therefore unwilling to challenge patriarchy, but rather 'bargain' with it, promoting instead a position on biblical hermeneutics that is subservient and moderate on feminist issues," do readers who prefer stories that might end with the overthrow of a restrictive ideology, or evidence of the ongoing ossification of a patriarchal social system, look away from the ambiguous implications of this conclusion?

Of course, just as Morny Joy observes that the "religion vs. women's rights" dyad (as though the two are somehow naturally in tension) often constrains our thinking, sometimes the caretaker-critic binary is excessively stark. Some of the authors here reflect what political theorists refer to as a respectfully "agonistic" approach to the communities and claims they interrogate. For example, Pamela Dickey Young clearly demonstrates that scholars need to maintain a thoroughly critical perspective *vis-à-vis* all discourses and contexts, even those with which we might feel a strong sympathy. She is not alone: Many of these writers show us that it is possible to approach one's subject matter in a manner that is both fully rigorous and compassionate toward the individuals, families, ideas, texts, rituals, and institutions being studied. Here I use compassionate rather literally, as many of these authors are willing to "suffer with" the communities and traditions they engage, a posture that requires them to be severely critical at times.

Bodies

Morny Joy observes that "invariably when religion and rights clash, all too often it is control of women's bodies that is at stake." These bodies serve as stages on which religious and political communities perform dramas that tend to cement – and sometimes to trouble – certain local, global, and even cosmic roles and rules. The ways ideas and practices related to female virginity, chastity, and motherhood are expressed and policed within religious texts and traditions offer obvious examples. The pressure to perform in certain ways in such dramas is acute, since women are told implicitly and explicitly that their families, religious traditions, and entire societies will suffer or even perish if they do not comply. Indeed, the anxiety – here,

I use the term narrowly to refer to a free-floating fear – that patriarchal religious communities and societies often displace through the control of women's bodies is never finally eradicated. However, the authors in this volume lay bare the many ways narratives and norms of domination are sustained by men and women and yet also troubled – mostly by women.

It is nonetheless important to attend to the geographical and political location of these narratives about women, sex, and gender. The thinking about women, rights, and religion in this book does not come out of thin air: place, space, maps, and territory matter. Sylvia Marcos contends that "gender, in the indigenous worlds of Mesoamerica, is primarily conceived within the framework of a concept of duality, as distinct from Western notions of dualism. The entire universe is governed in these terms: male and female are regarded as complementary. In claiming, as part of their rights, the right to be guided by the manner in which their worldview conceives of gender, indigenous women reveal the place from which their struggles emanate." This problematization of this term is a useful critique of a certain kind of liberal – and often hegemonic – feminism associated with western Europe, Canada, and the United States. As a further illustration of an attentiveness to location, Jeane C. Peracullo expresses her frustration over the way the Catholic church "continues to lapse into dogmatic doublespeak when it comes to women and to women's bodies," a counter-productive trend poignantly evident in what she describes as the conflation between the Virgin Mary and the iconic and passive Maria Clara figure from Filipino literature and popular culture.

Beyond the value of thinking through the social contexts in which we all work on the issues that interest us, we need to think about the real and imagined bodies of our audience. Even though the analytical gaze in this volume is turned towards the experiences and challenges of women and girls, the phenomena being analyzed impact, and the audience for the volume includes, men and boys, too. Indeed, it seems clear that all of us – boys, girls, men, women, and those whose gender and sexual identities are more fluid – are diminished when women's autonomy is rigidly circumscribed. Decades of feminist research and activism have demonstrated that identifying the hegemonic pressures and consequences of patriarchy can help women achieve greater latitude, but it is my impression that the implications of such scholarship and political shifts for men and boys have yet to be fully defined. Again, that is not the central objective of this volume even if this work makes quite clear that we are all born into religious, cultural, and political systems sustained through the creation and sometimes violent imposition of gendered epistemic and political norms. In this sense, we are all subject to and subjects of these limiting and often highly spiritualitized (or perhaps we should say religionized) ideas about gender and sexuality. As scholars and others attend more fully to the many ways in which men *and* women receive and challenge the gender and sexual norms of their communities, we may see a clearer route toward more just societies.

Local and Global

One of the other interesting themes linking many of these chapters is the attention they pay to the "intersectional" and "glocal" nature of identities. What it might mean in a particular time and place to be a woman, a man, a cleric, a lay person, a Buddhist, a lawyer, an African, and so on, cannot be understood outside of what it means in those societies for these same individuals to be, *also*, members of the middle class, able-bodied, Taiwanese, white, Jewish, Dutch-speaking, or elderly communities. It is no longer novel to observe this heterogeneity, but often it seems to me that the disciplinary boundaries of our analytical training and the opportunity structures of the academy still drive us to seek singular explanations for complex polysemic phenomena. In other words, while we might understand that the subjects and social forces we examine are typically best grasped through an interdisciplinary approach, we tend to act as though the underlying issue determining a particular social field or quandary (a caste conflict in India or the tolerance for the male-only priesthood in the Roman Catholic community) must be *actually* one other force (class or race or gender or colonialism or capitalism or . . .).

We are often in the business of correcting false consciousness, but in fact this study demonstrates that it is the rule rather than the exception that people and societies are multi-layered and women find "counter-hegemonic" ways to assert their interests. As Diah Ariani Arimbi notes in her chapter on a movement within Indonesian Islam, "while the male and female members of the *Tarbiyah* movement are segregated in accordance with nature, they nevertheless subscribe to concepts of women's rights and equality while observing a form of sexual segregation." As well, as Kathy Chan observes, women use the groups she studies creatively to promote justice and charity work even though the groups themselves pay (usually women) workers very low wages.

We struggle to identify how the many variables at work in any identity-intersection interact largely because the interactions between individual subjects (a particular thirty-eight-year-old woman, named Fatima, in Winnipeg, for example) and larger especially global political forces are somewhat opaque. How, after all, might we see Fatima's choices as circumscribed not just by her own often quickly changeable inclinations and predilections but also by massive global forces that have clearly been developing across centuries and over the whole planet? Although Jonnette Watson Hamilton and Jennifer Koshan's observations concern the notion of choice in Canadian legal contexts, the broader implication of their chapter is that scholars would benefit from a reassessment on Fatima's choices, which are likely more complex than we imagine and unlikely to be entirely manageable by the current laws and norms of the dominant society.

These chapters offer readers a glimpse into the ways women around the globe live, on the one hand, in profoundly specific settings (British Columbia, Rwanda, Winnipeg, Indonesia, etc.), and, on other hand, in the welter of sweeping global forces. Of course, the imbrication of the individual within this much broader context takes its heaviest toll on the individual. As Louise du Toit reminds us, "the failure of African Christian churches to speak out against sexual violence and to address its causes, should be read on one level as in conformation with global patterns, especially patterns emanating from the centre of the global order." These political, economic, and legal forces do not just form a neutral or hegemonic context in which these women's subjectivities come into being. Rather, there is an active, creative, unpredictable, dialectical relationship between Fatima and the climate, social class, age, education, familial, religious, social and political spheres in which she moves. There is much to learn about how Fatima, as well as her grandmothers, mother, aunts, sisters, children, peers, and also her male kin, are shaped by, and move about within or negotiate these larger forces. This volume provides clear evidence of the creativity of these women, often against great odds. Moreover, these chapters and the community of scholars drawn together by this project have provided readers not just with a valuable account of some extremely interesting sites of struggle, but also a clear sense of the national, religious, and political spheres in need of critical inquiry in the future.

Index

A

Abella, Rosalie, 148, 250–252
Abocide Bill, 104
Aboriginal Women's Action Network (AWAN), 94, 101, 118
abortion, 37, 158, 216. See also reproduction, issues of women's rights around
Abya Yala, 51n3
ACHA Tibetan Sisterhood, 79
Act for the Better Protection of the Lands and Property of the Indians in Lower Canada, 90
Act for the Gradual Enfranchisement of Indians (1869), 92
Act on Personal Status, 184
Adomako Ampofo, Akosua, 213
affirmative action, 16
Afkhami, Mahnaz, 20
"Platform for Action," 229
African independent church movements, 209–211
Antonians, 209
Lumpa Rising or Lumpa Church, 209–11
African men as sexually deviant, 35, 38–39
African Pentecostalism, 212–13, 215–216. See also Pentecostal-charismatic Christianity in Africa
African woman as pure victim, 34
Agbala Daniel Church, 215
agency, 26, 241, 244
agunah, 142, 151
agunah activism, 150–152
agunot, 142, 146
Ahmadi, Wahid, 233
Al-Dien, Zain, 130
Alberta v. Hutterian Brethren of Wilson Colony, 250
Ali-Faisal, Sobia, 125, 130
All India Women's Conference, 264
Amanah Ikhtiar Malaysia, 185
American faith-based community organizing (FBCO), 192
Amirpur, Katajun, 83
An-Na'im, Abdullah Ahmed, 177
Anabaptist theology, 193
Anghie, Antony, 36
Anglican Care, 192
Anishinabek Nation, 109
Anti-Photo and Video Voyeurism Act (2009), 157
Anti-Child Pornography Act (2009), 157

anti-Semitism, 139, 151–152
Anti-Violence against Women and their Children Act (2004), 157
Antonians, 209
Appleby, Scott, 2n2
Arbitration Act of Ontario (1991), 8, 11
"Are religions a place of emancipation for women? Progress and setbacks," 68
Arimbi, Diah Ariani, 26, 299
"Women and the Politics of Piety," 25
Arjomand, Homa, 8
armed conflict, effects of, 229
armed conflict in Africa, 21, 38
Aronson, Jarvey B., 287
Asiyah, wife of the Prophet Muhammad, 234
assimilation policy. See under Indian Act
Atlantic Policy Congress of First Nations Chiefs, 118
atman, 268
Aurobindo, Śri, 269, 276
Australian Saṅgha Association, 80
autonomy, 26, 241, 244
autonomy and self-determination, 159
autonomy of indigenous peoples, 53–54

B

Baidlowi, Aisyah Hamid, 228
Baittul Maal wa Tamwil (BMT) microfinance system in Indonesia, 185
Bakht, Natasha, 10
"Family Arbitration: Using Shari'a Law," 9
Bakhtin, Mikhail, 50
balance, 57
balancing of rights approach, 253
Bangladesh, 184–185
Al Banna, Hasan, 230
Basic Law, 65, 69
Basic Law for the Federal Republic of Germany, 81
Basu, Amrita, 3–4
Bateye, Bolaji, 215
Beaman, Lori, 19
Béatrice, Dona, 209
Bedard, Yvonne, 96, 99, 118
Bediako, Kwame, 209
Beijing World Conference on Women (1995), 4
Benedict XVI, Pope, 164
Berger, Benjamin L., 241, 255
Bhagavad Gita, 276
Bharati, Uma, 273

Bharatiya Muslim Mahina Andolan (BMMA), 275
bhikkhunīs, 67–68
bhikshuni ordination, 80
Bill C-3, 89, 112–113. See also Indian Act
post Bill C-3 amendments, 114–117
Bill C-31, 89, 100
gender discrimination, 94, 105, 110–111
registrar's control under, 100–102, 104
second-generation cut-off rule, 104
Bill S-3, 89, 109–110, 116
gender discrimination, 110
Binsbergen, Wim M.J., 210
Black evangelical church, 192
black female victim, 39. See also African woman
blaming the victim, 33, 39, 44, 151
'Blessed Mother,' 159
Boden, Alison, 19
Bodhgayā ordination, 67
Bodies that Matter (Butler), 14
Bond, George C., 210
born-again, 208, 212
Boulous Walker, Michelle, 35, 41–42, 45
Boyd, Marion, 8, 11
Brahman, 268
Bramadat, Paul, 2
Brazal, Agnes, 164–165
British Columbia Court of Appeal, 102, 112
British Columbia Supreme Court, 111
British North America Act (1867), 90, 92
Brown, Wendy, 13
"The Most We Can Hope For…," 13
Bruker v. Markovitz, 147, 251
Buddhism
caring detachment, 27, 278–79, 284–85, 287, 291–292
caste system and, 75, 77
compatibility with Basic Law, 65
compatibility with Universal Declaration of Human Rights, 65
enlightenment, 75
equanimity, 73–74
gender discrimination, 22, 65
gender equity, 80
human equality and dignity of the individual, 75
and human rights, 28, 280
humanism, 276
law and religion closely linked, 68

respect for women's dignity, 296
subordination of women, 66, 77
women's potential for enlightenment, 75–80
Buddhist concept "Equanimity or Lack of egocentricity," 73
Buddhist principle of non-violence, 22, 65
Buddhistdoor Global, 80
Buen Vivir, 62
"Building our History," 48
Bush, George W., 13, 58
Butler, Judith, 4, 13
Bodies that Matter, 14
"The End of Sexual difference," 14
Gender Trouble, 5, 14

C

Cambodian Buddhist Saṅgha, 81
Campaign Live Coalition, 126
Canada Christian College and the Institute for Canadian Values, 126
Canada Council of Muslim Women, 8
Canada Revenue Agency rules on political advocacy, 197
Canada Revenue Agency rules on registered charities, 196–198
Canadian Bill of Rights, 96–97
Canadian Charter of Rights and Freedoms, 8–9, 89, 100, 111, 114–115, 128, 132
equality rights under, 247
freedom of religion under, 26, 240, 246–247, 255
Hebrew translation of, 138–39
Ishaq case, 242–50
remarriage after divorce under, 147
individual is dominant unit under, 241
Canadian federal election (2015), 241–242
Cannon, Martin, 110
Caracol of La Garrucha (2007), 57
caretaker-critic binary, 296–297
caring detachment in Buddhism, 27, 278–279, 284–285, 287, 291–292
"Caring Detachment in Buddhism and Implications for Women's Rights" (Satha-Anand), 27
Carling, Joan, 61
caste system, 260, 262, 264, 269, 271
compared to racism in America, 269
Gandhi's opposition to, 268
Catholic Bishop's Conference of the Philippines (CBCP) 1975 Pastoral Letter, 159–161, 169
Catholic Bishop's Conference of the Philippines (CBCP) 2005 Pastoral Letter, 161–162
Catholic Church, 83, 155, 157, 298

fights between Filipino feminists and, 158
involvement in the genocide in Rwanda, 33
man is the primary breadwinner teachings, 164–165
on migrant female workers, 156
priesthood reserved for men, 71
"pro-life," 159
women's essentialist connection to reproduction, 168
Catholic School system in Ontario, 123–124, 126, 129, 131
Catholic tribunals, 8
CEDAW. See Convention on the Elimination of Discrimination against Women
Central Institute of Higher Tibetan Studies in Sarnath, India, 79
Chan, Kathryn, 299
"Charity and Justice," 25
Chanicka, Jeewan, 125
charismatic churches in Ghana, 216
charity, 190–191, 203
dual requirements of charity and justice, 204
faith-based charities, 25
negative connotations, 195
promoted over justice, 197, 202
social architecture of, 196
"Charity and Justice" (Chan), 25
charity and volunteering, 192, 197–198
Charter of Quebec Values Bill, 242n2
child marriage, 264
choice, 26, 241
in Canadian legal contexts, 300
religious, 240, 249 (See also freedom of religion)
choice, agency, and autonomy, 26, 241, 244
choice, language of, 256
choice and obligation relationship, 244
choice as an underlying value, 248–249, 251
choice as basic right, 233
choice as the basis for denying rights claims, 249–250
Chong, Kelly, 213
Christian churches in Africa, 37. See also names of particular churches
authority and social impact, 33
as Civil Society Organizations (CSOs), 21
complicity, 39
patriarchal teachings, 21, 33–34
reflection of community attitudes, 33
role in dealing with sexual violence against women, 21, 32–34, 37, 45
roles usually associated with the state, 32
Christian-patriarchal influence, 37
Christianity, 262

church/state separation principle, 146–149
Citizenship Act, 26, 243
civil divorce, 251
  religious remarriage of spouse after, 146
civil divorce courts, 142–143, 146
civil society, 26, 224, 230–231
Clarke, Shayne, 292
  Family Matters in Indian Buddhist Monasticisms, 291
class, 48, 71. See also caste system
class actions, 16
Coalition of Jewish Women for the Get, 146
Cohen, J., "Is Multiculturalism Bad for Women?," 7
collective, men and women working as, 54
collective consensus, 51–52
collective rights, 16
collective rights to the land, 60–61
colonial history, 34
cult of Mary, 161
colonial pattern
  narrative of violence against women, 36
  colonial tropes of black male rapist exploiting black female victim, 39
colonizing-civilizing mission of European imperialism, 36
communal framework for rights and freedoms, 139
communities
  rights of communities over individuals, 267
community
  living in community, 195–196
community organizing, 200
compassion, 279, 286, 292
complementarity between women and men, 57, 62, 215–217, 235, 298
Confucian ethics, 290
Conrad, Joseph, 34
Conservative movement (Jewish), 143
Constitution Act (1982), 89, 117
Constitution of India
  advantages to women's issues, 265
  educational and economic interests under, 264
  human rights under, 264
Continental Encounter of Indigenous Women, Quito, Ecuador (2002), 51
"Continued Discrimination under the Indian Act" (Jacobs), 22
Convention on the Elimination of Discrimination against Women (CEDAW), 3, 6, 60, 158, 179–180, 182, 185, 217, 265
convention regarding mad and naked woman, 284
Corbiere case, 91, 94
Corbiere-Lavell, Jeanette, 96, 98–99, 118

cosmovision, 56–57
Council of Europe (2005), 70–71
Council of Europe in Strasbourg (2016), 68–69
Council of Women in India, 264
Cover, Robert, 40
critical race theory, 15–16
critical theorists, 11–13
Cruz, Gemma, 163
cultural context, 50
cultural diversity, 138–139
cultural identity, 255
cultural rights, 58
custody of children, 6

D

Dakwah movement, 223–224
Dalai Lama, 74, 80–81
dalit (lower caste) women, 271
'dangerous victims,' 45
Daradjat, Zakiyah, 228
Darul Arqam movement, 224
De la Cruz, Deidre, 159, 166
Declaration of Elimination of Violence against Women, 4
Declaration of the Second Summit of Women of Abya Yala, 62
Declaration of the Third International Forum of Indigenous Women, New York (2005), 51
Delahanty, J. D., 191–192, 203
deliverance ministry, 214
democracy, 25–26, 224, 261, 275
Hindutva view of, 272
democratic institutions, 261
Democratic Republic of the Congo (DRC), 32, 34
conflict, 21
male impunity for sexual violence, 40
struggle for control of mineral resources (colton ore), 38
western economic interests, 35
democratization, 52
democratizing ethos of Pentecostalism, 217
dependent origination, 74
Descheneaux, Stéphane, 114–115, 118
Descheneaux case, 116
detachment, 279, 292–293
Dhamma, 286
dhammic sense of "cure," 291
dharma, 76, 264, 267–268

both descriptive and prescriptive contents, 261
human rights, 268
dharma discourse, 26, 260
dialogical theology, 84
Dickey Young, Pamela
"Examining Competing Claims ... ," 23
Different Voice (Gilligan), 233
dignity
equity and, 50
human, 217, 279, 285, 287, 293
of the individual, 72
women's, 56, 70, 75, 181, 207, 296
disability, 71
discipline in Tarbiyah movement, 236–237
discrimination against women. See gender discrimination
divorce, 6, 8, 23, 93, 102, 104, 270, 275
divorce in Judaism. See Jewish divorce
domestic violence, 50, 79. See also violence against women
Domestic Workers Act, 157
double blindness, 71
double marginalization, 204–205
double-mother clause, 95, 112
Du Toit, Louise, 300
"Sexual Violence, Rights and Religion in Africa," 21
dualism, 7, 20, 56, 65
duality as a theory, 56, 298. See also complementarity between women and men
Dube, Musa, 212
Duterte, Rodrigo
State of the Nation Address (SONA), 156
Dzuhayatin, Siti Nurhayati, 228

E

East African Revival, 212
East Asian Buddhism (including Zen), 66, 77
Eberts, Mary, 95–96, 112, 115
EDSA Revolution (1986), 161
education, 6, 52, 79, 212, 229–230, 264. See also sexual education curriculum in Ontario; women's ordination
Filipino women, 156
Indonesia's Islam favours girls being educated, 233
Orthodox Jews, 141
in Tarbiyah movement, 236
Women's Legal Education and Action Fund (LEAF), 253
educational and economic interests under Constitution of India, 264
embodied suffering, 280, 283, 293

Encounter of Zapatista Women with Women of the World (2007), 51
"The End of Sexual Difference" (Butler), 14
enfranchisement under the Indian Act (1876), 91–94, 96
Engaged Buddhism, 74
Enlace Continental de Mujeres Indigenes (Continental Network of Indigenous Women), 51
enlightenment, 75. See also European Enlightenment
attained through practice of ethics, concentration, and wisdom, 76
equality, 26, 75, 207, 224. See also gender equality
Buddhist principle of, 72–73
challenges to equality principle in CEDAW Convention, 182–183
as opposed to equity, 181–182
women's equality rights vs. freedom of religious practice, 11, 22, 69–71
equality rights
under Canadian Charter of Rights and Freedoms, 247
"western" or "global north" imposition, 6
equanimity, 73–74, 283–284, 286–287, 291–292
equity, 149, 152, 181–182
Ermineskin Band, 106
essentialism, 1, 12–13, 36, 163, 168, 233
Estimated GNI per Capita, 158
"Eternal Feminine," discourse on, 160
ethic of care, 202–203
ethic of rights, 202–203
ethnicity, 48, 71
European Council of Human Rights (ECHR), 81
European Enlightenment, 50, 66
European imperialism, 36
Evangelical Fellowship of Canada, 126
evangelical institutions
individualistic in focus, 204
low wages (unjust practices), 199
racism and patriarchy, 199
social justice and political advocacy, 191–193
support for charitable projects, 191
Evans, Carolyn, 19
"Examining Competing Claims … " (Dickey Young), 23
Expected Years of Schooling, 158
EZLN (Zapatista Army of National Liberation), 58

F

false consciousness, 299
"Family Arbitration: Using Shari'a Law" (Bakht), 9
Family Code (Algeria), 184
Family Court in Quebec, 11

Family Law 186 from the Arbitration Act of Ontario (1991), 11
Family Matters in Indian Buddhist Monasticisms (Clarke), 291
female chastity, 297
female evangelicals working with marginalized populations in B.C., 193
female half-breed, 93
female sexuality as symbol of the profane, 43
female virginity, 297
the feminine as target of violence, 44
feminism, 12, 23, 271, 298
ethnocentrism in, 165
Filipino feminist perspective, 159
"gender feminists," 5
Global North feminism, 55
HIndutva New Feminism, 274
Indian feminism, 261, 270
Indonesian feminists, 228
intersectionalities and plural feminisms, 132, 299
Islamic feminism, 83, 223–229
mainstream feminism, 70
second-wave feminists, 70
state feminism, 216–217
Western feminism, 10, 70, 73, 266, 298
feminist churches, 211–212
feminist critical approaches, 138, 140
feminist hermeneutics, 78–79
feminist immanent critique, 15–16
feminist legal theory, 15
feminist theology, 83, 227
feminist theory, 23, 70
Filipinas. See Filipino women
Filipinized Mother Mary, 161
Filipino women
cultural double-bind, 164
cultural mandate to marry and have children, 164
economic independence, 164
as "empowered" and "highly educated," 156
good woman as weak and passive, 155, 165, 168
resistance against "Virgin Mother" image, 157
struggle between Catholic heritage and Filipino women's autonomy, 24
wages, 167
who are not well-educated, 156
Filipino women as Overseas Filipino Workers, 156, 163
First Continental Summit of Indigenous Women of Abya Yala, Puno, Bolivia (2009), 51, 57
First Nations peoples of Canada. See also Indian Act

control of their membership, 90, 100, 104–106, 108–109, 118
gender discrimination, 93, 105, 107–108
human rights violations, 22
Indian status, 104–105
Indian status defined through male head of household, 91
Indian woman married to a non-status man, 93, 98
Indigenous and Northern Affairs Canada (INAC), 100, 108–110
matriarchal history, 92
pre-confederation relations with the Crown, 90–92
First Summit of Indigenous Women of the Americas, Oaxaca, Mexico (2002), 21–22, 51, 58–59
First Summit of Indigenous Women of the Americas (Memoria 2003), 55, 58
Foucault, Michel, 50
Fourth Conference of the Continental Network of Indigenous Women, Lima, Peru (2004), 51, 55
Fourth National Indigenous Congress in San Pedro Atlapulxo, Estado de México (2006), 62
Fourth World Conference on Women (1995), 179
Francis, Pope, 83, 163
Fraser, Arvonne, 3
freedom, discourses of, 207
freedom of choice, 244
freedom of conscience and autonomy, 158
freedom of religion, 23, 25–26, 69, 81, 128, 130, 147–148
in American constitution, 7
under Canadian Charter, 26, 240, 246–247, 255
choice as underlying value, 248–249
and gender equality, 65, 80–81, 84
if harmful to others, 149
niqab while testifying, 252–256
not absolute, 251, 254
and right of women to equality under the law, 7
Freud, Sigmund, 42
fundamental right to life, 267
Fundamentalisms Observed (Marty), 2n2
fundamentalist Christian religious groups in US, 5
fundamentalist religions, 2, 6, 14, 21
Furusawa, Yuria, 166

G

Gandhi, 268–269, 276
Gandhi, Indira, 270
Garden River Band, 107
Garvey, Brian, 210
Garza, Ana Maria, 52

Gautamī, Mahāprajāpatī, 66
Gehl, Lynn, 108–109, 118
Gehl v Canada (Attorney General), 108
gender, 14, 48, 53
in debate about sexual education curriculum debate, 126–129, 131
indigenous conceptions of, 55–56
stigmas on women who do not conform to gender expectation, 129
gender and sexuality, 299
"gender balance," 84
gender discrimination, 65, 90–91, 110
Bill C-31, 94, 103, 105
Buddhism, 22
Gradual Civilization Act, 91
Indian Act (1876), 92–93
Indian Act (1951), 93, 95–96
Indian Act (1970), 93
under Indian Act (C-31, C-3, Bill S-3), 117
gender equality, 66, 69–71, 74, 84, 229, 235, 267
gender gap, 167
inequality, 207
and religious freedom, 65, 80–81, 84
as term, 72
gender equity, 57
"gender feminists," 5
Gender from the Perspective of Indigenous Women, 59
"Gender from the View of Indigenous Women," 55
gender identity, diversity in, 141
gender justice, 56, 212
Indian Constitution on, 261
gender neutrality, 15
gender relations in the public sphere, 234–235
Gender Social Change and Spiritual Power (Soothill), 216
gender stereotypes, 163
gender studies as "religion blind," 71
"gender" term, 4–5, 83–84
Gender Trouble (Butler), 5, 14
Gerakan Dakwah Kampus (GDK), 231
get (Jewish bill of divorce), 142–144, 146, 251
Ghana
new Pentecostal-charismatic mega-churches, 213
Pentecostalism, 25
Gilligan, Carol, 202
In a Different Voice, 233
Girl Power Ministries in Uganda, 215
Gitxsan Nation, 118

global patterns of injustice, 38
global relations of domination, 41
Global Summit to End Sexual Violence in Conflict (London 2014), 37
glocal nature of identities, 299
The Glory is Here (TV program), 214
God
  ancient Tagalogs conception of, 166
  at centre of the conventions of rights and responsibilities, 139
  "Mother God," 160
  one's deepest self, 268
Goodman-Thau, Eveline, 83
Gotami, Mahāprajāpatī, 66, 76
government justifications of rights violations, 347–348
Gradual Civilization Act, 91
Grameen bank model of microfinance, 185
Grant v. Canada (Attorney General), 242n1
Grewal, Inderpal, 12
Grismer, Jacob, 111–112, 117
group rights, 16, 275
Guatemala, 48
gurudharmas, 76–78
Gutte, Vanita, 275

H

Hackett, Rosalind, 297
"The Impact of Pentecostalism on Women and their Rights," 25
Hadith, 228, 234
Hague, William, 37–38
halakha, 150–151
Harper, Stephen, 243–244
Harvey, Peter, 291
Hassan, Riffat, 227
Hastings, Adrian, 209
Haudenosaunee people, 92, 118
Health and Physical Education Curriculum (Ontario). See sexual education curriculum in Ontario
heart of darkness, 34–35, 37, 39
Heberle, Renée, 35, 41–43, 45
Herman, Judith, 40
hermeneutic of creative actualization, 78–79, 296
hermeneutic of proclamation, 78
hermeneutic of remembrance, 78
hermeneutic of suspicion, 78
hermeneutics, 19, 78–79, 213
hermeneutics of orality, 48

hierarchical leadership based on charisma, 217
hierarchy in India, 262. See also caste system
hierarchy of rights, 132
hijab (veil), 26, 234
hijabs and niqabs
debates over in Canada, 132
Hinduism, 262, 268–269, 276
history of excluding women, 262
human rights and women's rights in, 260
status of women under, 263
Hindutva, 261, 269, 271, 273–274
challenge to India's religious diversity, 270
targeting of Muslim minority, 272
HIndutva New Feminism, 274
Hinfelaar, Hugo, 210–121
Hizbut-Tahrir movement, 224
Hodeidah microfinance program in Yemen, 185–186
Hoehler-Fatton, Cynthia, 211–212
Hogben, Alia, 8–9
homophobia in sexual education debate, 128
homosexuality, 4, 125–126, 128, 164
honour killings, 42
hooks, bell, 61
Howard, M., 7
Howland, Courtney, 5, 19
Human Development Index, 157–158
human dignity. See dignity
human rights, 26, 35, 49, 55, 72, 214, 224, 229, 268. See also individual rights
discourse of, 51
international human rights law system, 178–179
not alien to Buddhism, 66
perspective on domestic violence, 50
re-conceptualization, 47, 57
regional or local context, 12
transforming the meanings of, 48
Western cultural bias promoting individualism, 267
for women in Buddhism, 278
women's rights as, 3, 13, 70, 260, 265, 275
human rights discourse
modern India, 26–27
human rights for women a "western," i.e. colonialist imposition, 4
human rights framework, 50
human rights violations, 76–80, 110
First Nation peoples of Canada (especially women), 22
violence against women as, 61, 70

I

"I am Brahman," 268
identity, 118, 133, 268
Ikhwanul Muslimin (Muslim Brotherhood), 224, 230–231
illegitimate children, 93, 108, 110, 115, 145
Independence Act (1947), 261
Indian Act
assimilation policy goal, 90, 94
civilization policy goal, 90
Indian Act (1876)
enfranchisement under the, 91–94, 96
foundations of gender discrimination, 92–93
Indian status determined through Indian men, 93
origins of, 90
Indian Act (1951)
enfranchisement provisions, 94, 96
gender discrimination, 93
patriarchal notions, 94–95
Indian Act (1970), 96
gender discrimination, 93
Indian Act amendments (1985). See Bill C-31
Indian Act amendments (2011). See Bill C-3
Indian Act amendments (2017). See Bill S-3
Indian Act (Post-McIvor amendments), 111–113
Indian feminism / Western feminism differences, 261
Indian feminists accused of being anti-national, western, and elitist, 270
Indian ideal of unity in diversity, 276
Indian Muslim Women's Movement, 275
Indian Women's Association, 264
Indigenous and Northern Affairs Canada (INAC), 100, 108–110
Indigenous and Tribal Peoples Convention 169, 60
Indigenous Bar Association, 112
Indigenous cosmovisions, 51, 59
Indigenous migrants, 54
indigenous peoples of Abya Yala, 58–59
indigenous spirituality, 48
recovery of sacred spaces, 58–59
indigenous women, 48, 298. See also First Nations peoples of Canada
Indigenous women from the Andean region in Peru, Bolivia and Colombia, 21–22
Indigenous women from the Mesoamerican region of Central America, 21
Indigenous women in the Americas, 47
right to inherit land, 49
individual, 12, 241
individual empowerment

European Enlightenment's notion of, 50
individual freedom, neoliberal conceptions of, 207
individual rights against the community, 20
individual rights and freedoms in Judaism, 23, 139
individual rights in relation to religion, 262
individual rights over land, 60–61
individualism, 15–16, 56, 191
individualistic focus of evangelical religious tradition, 204
Indonesian feminists, 228
inheritance rights in Islam, 173–174
Institute for Catholic Education (ICE), 123
integration, 147
"Integration and Religion as seen by People of Turkish origin in Germany," 80
Inter-American Convention on the Prevention, and Eradication of Violence against Women, 61
interdisciplinary research, 18–19, 299
interest-based theories, 267
"International Buddhist Confederation" in Delhi, India (2013), 73
International Buddhist Women's movement, 66
International Campaign against Shari'a Courts in Canada, 8
"International Congress on Buddhist Women's Role in the Saṅgha," 79
International Covenant of Civil and Political Rights, 178–179
Canada's Indian Act violated, 99
International Covenant on Civil and Political Rights (1967), 111
International Decade for Women (1985-1995), 266
international law, 12, 36
International Women's Year (Mexico City), 3
interreligious dialogue, 65
intersectionalities and plural feminisms, 50, 132, 299
intersectionality, theory of, 70–71, 133, 255
interventions (western into non-European states), 36–37
Iran, 184
Irani, Smriti, 273
Iraq, 13, 184
"Is Multi-culturalism Bad for Women?" (Moller Okin), 6–7
"Is Multiculturalism Bad for Women?" (Cohen), 7
Ishaq, Zunera, 26, 242–244
Ishaq v. Canada, 242–245, 254–255
Islam, 83, 262
Islam, modern interpretations of, 26
Islamic Bank Bangladesh Limited, 185
Islamic divorce practice known as "triple talaq" banned by India's Supreme Court, 275
Islamic feminism, 83, 223–229
Islamic law, 172, 186

classical provisions of, 174
on relationship between justice and charity, 191
Ismail'i Muslims
tribunals, 8

J

Jacobs, Beverly, 89
"Continued Discrimination under the Indian Act," 22
Jamaah Tarbiyah, 224
Jamieson, Kathleen, 96
Jesus Christ, 195
Jesus Is Alive Ministries (JIAM), 215–216
Jewish divorce, 23, 142–146
agunah activism, 150–151
Canadian context, 146–149
Canadian federal divorce law amendment, 146–147
extortion in get cases, 142–143, 146–147
inequality, 144–146
Jewish Solution, 149, 151
mamzerim Jews, 145
man must be the initiator, 142–144
within Ontario family law, 146
jilbab (veil) movement in secular university campuses, 26
Jilbabisasi movement in secular campuses, 225
John, Mary E., 274
John Paul II, Pope
Laborem Exercens (papal letter), 164
Jolie, Angelina, 37
Jordan, 184
Joseph, Norma Baumel, "Women's Rights and Religion Jewish Style," 23
Joy, Morny, 69, 83, 139, 297, 165
Judaism
individual rights and freedoms in, 23
Jewish take on rights and responsibilities, 138–140
Jewish woman's human rights, 142–143
Jewishness through maternal lineage, 140, 145
Jews of a haredi (ultra-pietistic) persuasion, 141
relationship between justice and charity, 191
Judaism as a legal entity
obligation, 139
Judeo-Christian religions, 241
justice, 190–192, 203, 207, 274–276
justice, charity and gender relationship, 201
justice and charity, relationship between, 191, 194–195, 201
justice ethic, 202

"justice-oriented" charitable models, 25
justice-oriented female evangelicals, 204
justice-oriented models, 195–199

K

Kalupahana, David J., 291
Kamaruddin, Zaleha, 25
"The Reconstruction of Muslim Women's Property Rights...," 24–25
Kapur, Ratna, 271
Katjasungkana, Nursyahbani, 228
Kayanja, Jessica, 215
Kimbangu, Simon, 209
King, Sallie, 81
King, Ursula, 71
kingdom theology, 193
Kirchbach, Agnes von, 68
Kisā Gotamī (the Mother with the Dead Child), 27, 278, 288–291
Koggel, Christine, 70–71
Kongolese Christianity, 209
Koran, 82, 177
Korea, 66, 80
Koshan, Jennifer, "Women's Freedom of Religion Claims in Canada," 26
Kroeger-Mappes, J., 40, 202–203
Kuester, Voker, 83

L

Lacey, Nicola, 2, 9, 15–20
Laila, Ida Nur, 233
Lavell and Bedard, 96–97
law as relational, 18
Law's Relations (Nedelsky), 17
Le Roux, Elisabet, 32–33, 40
'legitimate' violence, 35
Lenshina Mulenga Mubisha, Alice, 209–211
lesbian Filipinas, 164
Letter from Brunei, 164
LGBTTQI rights, 133
liberal feminism, 298
"liberal pluralism," 27
liberal project (globally dominant liberal project), 40
liberalism, 20, 241, 276
liberation theology, 193
Liberia, 32
conflict, 21
male impunity for sexual violence, 40

Life Expectancy, 158
Lineamenta, 163
living in community, 195–196
Livingstonia Mission, 210
Lovelace, Sandra, 98–99
Lovelace v. Canada, 98–99
low wages, 299
Lower Nicola Band, 111
Lumen Gentium, 160
Lumpa Rising or Lumpa Church, 209–211

M

Mabanglao, Ruth, 164
MacGaffey, Wyatt, 209
Machmudi, 224
Mactal, Rolan, 160
Madonna and Child images, 156
Madonna-Whore dichotomy, 155
Magna Carta of Women, 157–158, 169
Mahābodhi Society, 67
Mahāyāna Buddhist scriptures, 74
Maimonides, 144, 191n1
mainstream feminism, 70
mamzerim Jews, 145
Mananzan, Mary John, 165
Mansfield, Nick, 42
ManuSmṛti (Manu's Laws), 263–264
Mapuranga, Tapiwa Praise, 213
Marchand, Christine Joyce, 102–103
Marcos, Sylvia, 22, 298
"Understanding Human Rights from Indigenous Women's Perspectives," 21
marginalized populations in British Columbia, 191
marginalized women
charity must be closely connected to justice, 202
trauma, 201
Maria Clara figure, 155, 162–163, 167, 298
"Maria Clara in the Twenty-first Century" (Peracullo), 24
marriage, 6, 93, 98, 213, 263
child marriage, 264
monogamy, 33
religious remarriage of spouse after civil divorce, 146
same-sex marriage, 130, 216
tribunals to arbitrate, 8
women in India, 263
Marshall, Ruth, 212

Marty, Martin, Fundamentalisms Observed, 2n2
Mary, Blessed Virgin, Saint, 159–160, 298
Catholic feminist theology on, 160
cult of Mary, 161
Filipinized Mother Mary, 161
image of a "good" Filipina of Filipino woman, 155
reimagining Mary to reflect realities of Filipino women, 165–166
Virgen of Balintawak, 166
Virgin Mary / Maria Clara conflation of images, 167
Virgin Mother, 156–157
wandering virgin, Lady of Caysasay, 166–167
masculine psychosis (in dominant institutions), 35, 45
masculine psychosis in the western foreclosure of the mother, 42
masculine subjectivity, 42
Mas'udi, Masdar F., 228
maternal lineage, 140
matrilineal descent, 118
Mauritania, 184
Mayan women in Guatemala, 53
Mbiti, John, 209
McCutcheon, Russell, 296
McGuinty, Dalton, 11, 122
McIvor, Sharon, 111–112, 117–118
McLachlin, Beverley, 250, 252
McVety, Charles, 125–126, 130
Mean Years of Schooling, 158
Mesoamerican cultural universes, 50
Mesoamerican region in Central America, 48
Methodist Mission, 192
Mexico, 48, 184
microfinance, 185
migrant female workers, 156–157, 164–165
Mikell, Gwendolyn, 217
Mik'maq people, 92
minority religions, 7
Misquito people, 54
mitzvah, 140
mitzvot (or obligations), 191
modernity, 13, 214
Moffett, Helen, "These Women, They Force Us to Rape Them," 43
Mohagheghi, Hamideh, 82
mokṣa, 75, 268
Moller Okin, Susan, "Is Multi-culturalism Bad for Women?," 6–7
Montreal Charter of Rights and Obligations, 139
Monture-Angus, Patricia, 98–99

Morocco, 184
"The Most We Can Hope For..." (Brown), 13
"Mother Earth," 60
"Mother God," 160
mother-goddess, 263
motherhood, 4, 228, 297. See also reproduction, issues of women's rights around
Mountain of Fire and Miracles Ministries (MFM), 213
Mukherjee, Asha, "Women, Rights and Religion in India," 26–27
multiculturalism, 6–8, 147, 149
multiculturalism vs. assimilation, 1, 7
Muslim adolescents
on sex education, 131
sexual values, 131
Muslim clothing (veil), 26, 132, 231, 234, 241–142, 252–255
Muslim imams as "experts" in sexual education debate, 127, 130
Muslim parents (Ontario)
removal of children from public schooling, 132
Muslim societies, modern realities in, 177
Muslim women, 10, 255
freedom to wear a niqab during citizenship ceremonies, 241–242
participation in public life, 228
property holders in early days of Islam, 174
property rights, 176n8, 177
property rights (figure), 178
property rights (microfinance), 185–186
Muslim Women's Act (Protection of Rights upon Divorce), 270
Muslim Women's Bill, 266
Muslims for Ontario's Health and Physical Education Currriculum, 125
Mwaura, Philomena, 213–216

N

nation state, 13
National Commission for Women, 265
national development (or development), 216
National Meeting of Indigenous Women, Oaxaca, México (1997), 48–49
National Reform Council (NRC), 68
National Rural Employment Guarantee Act (2005), 265
Native Women's Association of Canada, 104–105
Nedelsky, Jennifer, 2, 16, 18–20, 39–40, 44
Law's Relations, 17
Neema, Kanyere, 35, 38
Nehru's secular liberalism, 276
Netherlands, 184
new generation Pentecostal churches, 215–216

"new Indian women," 273
Nigerian Pentecostals, 25, 212
niqab, 242, 253–254
freedom of a Muslim woman to wear a niqab while testifying on sexual assault, 252
removal during citizenship ceremony, 26
niqab wearing Muslim women
discriminated against as Muslims, as women and as visible minority, 255
nirvāna, 74–75
Noddings, Ned, Women and Evil, 44
Noli me Tangere (Rizal), 162
non-profit organizations, 194, 196, 200
non-treaty Indian, 93
non-violence, 22, 65, 268
North/South inequalities, 12
nuns' order, 76, 78
Nussbaum, Martha, 7, 274
"Religion and Women's Human Rights," 6

O

Obama, Barack, 37
obligation in dharma discourse, 260
obligation in Judaism, 23, 139
Olaniyi, Dorcas Siyanbola, 215
Woman, I Condemn You Not, 215
Ontario Health and Physical Education curriculum. See sexual education curriculum in Ontario
Ontario Human Rights Code, 123, 128, 132
ordination of nuns, 67, 76, 287, 289
Burma, 67
East Asian Buddhism, 66, 77
Western Buddhists, 66
ordination of nuns in the Tibetan tradition, 22
ordination of women as deacons, 83
ordination of women Bishops, 214–215
ordination of women rabbis, 142
Orthodox Jews, 143
expanding conceptions of women's rights and responsibilities, 141
transformation in Jewish education, 141
tribunals, 8
Other, 12, 42, 44–45, 261, 268–269
Overseas Filipino Workers, 24, 156, 162, 169

P

Paikin, Steve, 127, 130

parental rights to absent children from sex education classes, 128–129
Parents against Ontario Sex-Ed Curriculum, 126
Parents as First Educators, 126
parents as primary sex educators, 130
Parsitau, Damaris, 216–217
Partai Keadilan (Justice Party), 231
participatory democracy, 25
Paṭācārā, 27, 278, 280–287, 290
Pateman, Carole, 40
patriarchal attitudes, 217
patriarchal communities
anxiety or free-floating fear, 297–298
patriarchal ideology, 231, 269
patriarchal interpretation of Koran, 177
patriarchal laws, 92, 150, 174
in 1951 amendments to Indian Act, 94–95
patriarchal rabbinic system, 144, 150
patriarchal power, 21, 53
patriarchal practices, 11
patriarchal structure, 71, 261
patriarchal world-view of Indian society, 27
patriarchy, 35, 37, 128, 199, 201–202, 213, 298
Paul, Pam, 118
Peach, Lucinda, 19
Pentecostal-charismatic Christianity in Africa, 25, 207–208, 216
mixed blessings for African women, 217
new generation Pentecostal churches, 215–216
Nigerian Pentecostals, 25, 212
role of women, 213
second wave of Pentecostalism in Zimbabwe, 213
women's recovery of traditional status, 214
Peracullo, Jeane, 298
"Maria Clara in the Twenty-first Century," 24
Perfection of Wisdom Sūtras, 74
Perron, Connie, 103
personhood, 93, 262
Perveen Shaukat Ali, 175n3
Philipose, Elizabeth, 34–36, 41
Philippines
EDSA revolution, 157
laws beneficial to women, 157
ranking on Gender Development Index (GDI), 158
ranking on WEF Gender Gap Report, 156–157
philosophy, 19
Phiri, Isabel, 217

"Piercing the Veil" (Sunder), 19
"La Pieta," 155
La Pieta (Michelangelo), 156
piety, 237
PKS (Prosperous Justice Party), 225
"Platform for Action" (Afkhami), 229
pneumatic emphasis, 214
"political economy of rape," 41
politics of piety, 225, 227
politics of religion, 226
polygamy, 211
Posadskaya-Vanderbeck, Anastasia, 5
"positionality," 61
post 9/11 climate, 10, 13
postcolonial discourse, 157
postcolonial scholars, 6, 11
postmodern theories, 23, 173
poverty, 53, 216, 229
prenuptial agreements, 146
Presbyterian Support, 192
pro-life notion, 159
"Pronouncement of Women of Chiapas against Government Repression in San Salvador Atenco," 61
property rights, 16, 60–61, 90, 172, 174
for Muslim women, 173
for women in Islam, 24–25
women's property rights under CEDAW, 180–183
women's right to property under international human rights law, 176, 178
Protection of Human Rights Act (1993), 265
Protocol to the Convention of the Elimination of all Forms of Discrimination against Women, 181n16
public versus private, 1, 9, 11, 15, 20, 241, 244, 255
purdah system with seclusion, 264

Q

Quebec (Attorney General) v. A, 247
Quechua women of Peru, 53
Qur'an, 174, 228
Qureshi, Sameera, 125

R

R. v. Big M Drug Mart Ltd, 246, 248, 251
R. v. Edwards Books and Art Ltd, 249–250
R. v. Kapp, 246
R. v. Oakes, 247

R v NS, 252–253
race, 48, 71
racism, 40, 199
Rahmat Abdullah, K.H., Tarbiyah in the New Era, 229–230
Rahula, Walpole, 291
Rape Victim Assistance and Protection Act (1998), 157
Razack, Sherene, 10
"The Reconstruction of Muslim Women's Property Rights…" (Kamaruddin), 24–25
Reform movement (Jewish), 143
refuge, concept of, 286
religion / rights clash, 1–2, 11, 17, 19, 81, 293
religion and secularism dualism, 7, 65
"Religion and Women's Human Rights" (Nussbaum), 6
religious and secular law, tension between, 65, 80–81
religious freedom. See freedom of religion
reproduction, issues of women's rights around, 2, 4–6, 42–43, 157. See also motherhood; women's bodies
reproductive health debate, 158, 216
Filipino feminist perspective, 159
reservation laws, 269–270
Reservations to CEDAW by Muslim State parties, 183–185
responsibilities and rights within Indigenous communities, 48
Responsible Parenthood and Reproductive Health Act (2012), 157–158
Retail Business Holidays Act, 250
rhythm method of family planning, 159
Right to Food Act (2013), 265
right to health, 52
Right to Information Act (2005), 265
rights, 25, 213, 241
adoption of the dialogic language of "rights" by Indigenous women, 50
attack from postcolonial theorists and critical theorists, 11–12
in debate about sexual education curriculum debate, 128–129
human (See human rights)
individual (See individual rights)
language of rights, 49
political and religious pressure not to claim, 5, 14
prospective rather than a regulative role, 16
rights discourse, 133
women's (See women's rights)
rights advocacy, 25
rights and religion topic, 1–2, 11, 17, 19, 81, 293
rights as relational, 16–17
rights of communities over individuals (Asian values), 267
rights theory, feminist critiques of, 15

Ritchie, William Johnstone, 97
Rivera, Tarcila, 52–55, 60–61
Rizal, Jose, Noli me Tangere, 162
Robo Movement or Holy Spirit churches, 211
Roloff, Carola, 296
"Women, Ordination, and a Buddhist Perspective," 22
Rosalinda, Comandanta, 52
Rose, Jacqueline, 42
Women in Dark Times, 41
Roy, Rammohan, 269
Rukunghu, Neema, 32, 35–36
Rumsfeld, Donald, 13
Rwanda, 32–33, 38
conflict, 21
male impunity for sexual violence, 40
Rwandan Mother's Union, 33

S

Said, Damanik Ali, 231
Sakina woman, 226
Salman Mosque, ITB, 224
Salvation Army, 192
same-sex marriage, 130, 216
Sandals, Liz, 123, 127
Sangh Parivar (Indian Nationalist Organization), 271, 273
Saṅgha, 286
Saṅgharāja, 67
Sarcee Band, 106
Sarkhanian, Shanké, 116
Satha-Anand, Suwanna, 28
"Caring Detachment in Buddhism and Implications for Women's Rights," 27
Sawridge Band in Treaty Eight Alberta
gender discrimination, 106
scapegoating. See blaming the victim
Schedule Caste and Scheduled Tribe Act, 265
Schmidt-Leukel, Perry, 75
Schmitt, Carl, 36
Schüssler Fiorenza, Elisabeth, 160, 165, 296
Wisdom Ways, 78
Scott, Joan, 5
second-wave feminists, 70
second wave of Pentecostalism in Zimbabwe
rise of women leaders, 213
secular campuses, 224–225
secular justice, 275–276

secular/religious debate concerning women's rights, 24
secular values of the Ontario school system, 129
secularism, 7, 65, 261, 271–272
assimilation of minorities, 272
central in Hindu rights' quest for power, 271
equal respect for all religions, 271–272
self and the other, metaphysics of, 268
"self-imaged victim," 43–44
self-reflexivity, 160
Sen, Amartya, 274
Severiano, Yoloxóchitl, 54
sex and gender, division of, 55
sex workers and marginalized women in Vancouver, 25
sexual education curriculum in Ontario, 23, 122–123
Christian objections, 124, 126, 130
fearmongering, 126
masturbation, 123
misinformation on, 130–131
Muslim objections, 124–125, 130
Muslim support for, 125
protests over, 122–123, 126
"real" experts in the debate, 127–128
religious accommodation, 123–125, 128–129
women's involvement in debate, 127, 131
sexual orientation or gender identity, 71
freedom from discrimination on the basis of, 128
sexual segregation, 223, 225, 231–234, 236–237, 299
sexual violence. See also violence against women
after assassination of Indira Gandhi, 270
caused by economic war, 38
embedded in liberal project, 40
as global depths of human depravity, 35–36
male impunity for, 40
in the peripheries, 39, 41
political unwillingness to protect women and children, 39
psychological explanation of, 42
as simple expression of male dominance, 43
stigmatizing of survivors, 21, 33–35 (See also blaming the victim)
war and post-war rape, 32
as weapon of war, 37
"Sexual Violence, Rights and Religion in Africa" (Du Toit), 21
sexuality, demonization of, 45. See also women's bodies
sexuality of the African man as predatory, 34
Shaheed, Fareeda, 10
Shahrur, 177

Sharī'ah, 177
  CEDAW provisions and, 184–185
  inheritance rights for women, 175n3
  legal status of women under, 173
  son's share of inheritance, 175n3
Sharī'ah-compliant microfinance models, 185
Sharī'ah-compliant provisions in human rights instruments, 172–173, 185
Sharī'ah law, 8–11
Sharī'ah principles, 24
Shi'a Sunni and Sufi Muslim Women, 8
Shihab, Quraish, 228
Sierra, Maria Teresa, 52
"simultaneity" of rights (individual and collective), 61
singe parenting, 163
Single Ladies Interdenominational Fellowship in Nairobi, Kenya, 215
Sivaraksa, Sulak, 73
social gospel movement, 193
social justice, 27, 48–50, 192, 204, 261, 275
social justice and political advocacy
  within evangelical tradition, 193
social movement, Tarbiyah as, 224
sociology, 19
Solo Parent's Welfare Act (2000), 157
Soothill, Jane, 217
  Gender Social Change and Spiritual Power, 216
Speed, Shannon, 54
spiritual liberation, 279
Spiro, Milford, 291
Sri Lanka
  restoration of Buddhist nuns' order, 67
Stanton, Kim, 115
state feminism, 216–217
State Islamic Institutes, 224
state-required removal of veils, 242
"States must not accept any religious or cultural relativism of women's human rights," 70
status Indian, 93
status quo, 9, 205
structural inequality, 216, 229
structural injustices, 202, 204
structural violence, 35, 52
Subhan, Zainatun, 228
suffering, 279
  Buddhist approach to, 290, 293
  deep sudden sorrow, 280–287

embodied suffering, 280, 283, 293
Sullivan, Winifred Fallers, 19
Summit of Indigenous Women of the Americas, Oaxaca (2002), 56
Sunder, Mahavi, 20
"Piercing the Veil," 19
Sunono, Abdullah, 233
supernatural power, 212
Supreme Court of Canada, 91, 94–98, 112, 147–148, 241, 246, 253
case law on women, equality rights and religion, 248
Supreme Saṅgha Council, 67–68
Swaraj, Susma, 273
Syafrudin, Didin, 227
sympathetic joy, 292
Syndicat Northcrest v. Amselem, 246, 249, 251, 253

T

Tabatabaie, Alireza, 130
Tagore, Rabindranath, 269
civic religion, 276
Takariawan, Cahyadi, 233
Tanyag, Maria, 159
Tarbiyah in the New Era (Rahmat Abdullah), 229–230
Tarbiyah movement, 25–26, 223–224, 299
as civil movement, 230
as education movement, 229–230
female members sense of being both in and out, 233, 236
gender roles, 225
oriented toward the past, 231
reformist, 224
as religious movement, 224, 231, 236
spatial separation between men and women, 233
women are cadres, 235–236
women as community members, 235–236
women's role in, 226, 232–235
Tarbiyah movement in Indonesia, 229–232
tension between universal pronouncements and local conditions, 16
textual analysis, 19
Thailand
ordination of nuns, 67–68
Theravāda Buddhism, 66, 287
Theravāda nuns, 67–68
"These Women, They Force Us to Rape Them" (Moffett), 43
Third International Forum of Indigenous Women, New York (2005), 51
Third National Indigenous Congress, Nurío, Michoacán (2001), 53
Thorncliffe Parents Association, 126

Thrift, Erin, 25
Tibetan Buddhism, 66, 78
on gender equality, 71
leading offices held by men, 79
ordination of nuns, 22, 67, 80
women's rights in, 72
Time Magazine, 35
Tobique Reserve, 98–99
Torah (Bible and Talmud) study
women have gained entry to, 141
Toronto District School Board, 128–129
religious accommodation, 132
"tradition" or "culture," 4
traditional individualistic understanding of charity, 205
traditional practices, 49, 118
traditionalists, 138
tribunals to arbitrate family problems, marriage and business disputes, 8. See also shari'a law
Trudeau, Pierre, 133
turbans worn by Sikh men, 242n1
Turshen, Meredith, 41
Twinn family, 106
Tyendinaga reserve, 103

U

Uganda, 25, 38
UN Convention on the Rights of the Child, 179
UN Decade for Women, 217
UN Declaration of the Rights of Indigenous Peoples (UNDRIP), 119
UN Development Program statement on work, 164
UN Human Rights Committee, 98, 117–118
UN promotion of women's interests, 3–5, 60. See also names of UN organizations supporting women
"Understanding Human Rights from Indigenous Women's Perspectives" (Marcos), 21
Universal Civil Code, 270, 272
universal condition of suffering, 283
Universal Declaration of Human Rights, 5–6, 65–66, 69–70, 74–75, 79–81, 139, 176n8, 264
universality, 14, 50, 70, 81
unstated paternity (First Nations children), 108–110
Upaniṣads, 268
urban women's gender concepts, 56
U.S. global feminism. See Western feminism
U.S. Helms Amendment (1973), 37

V

Vatican, 5, 70
challenges to equality principle in CEDAW Convention, 182
on women's rights, 44, 69
Vedanta and inclusive Hinduism, 276
veil, 26, 132, 231, 234, 241–242
veiling as important to women's rights, 244
Venezuela, 48
Vienna Declaration, 3
Vienna Declaration on the Elimination of Violence against Women (1993), 70
Vietnam, 66, 80
Vinaya, 68, 76
violence against women, 4, 49, 53, 55–56, 157–158. 229. See also sexual violence
human rights violation, 61, 70
husband of the rape survivor, 35
narrative of inferiority and backwardness, 36
women in most danger of suffering acute battering or murder, 43
violent militia groups (Africa), 38
Virgen of Balintawak, 166
Virgin Mother discourse. See Mary, Blessed Virgin, Saint
virginity, 33
virtuous Muslim woman, 226

W

Wahid, Abdurrahman, 228
Wahome, Elizabeth, 215
wajib belajar, 229
Wanjiru, Margaret, 214–216
war and post-war rape, 32
"war on drugs," 155
"war on terror," 13
Watson Hamilton, Jonnette, 26, 300
"We are Women of War" (hymn), 211
Weberian notion of the rationalization of charismatic authority, 212
Well-being, 261
West vs. Muslims, 10
Western Buddhists
ordination of nuns, 66
role allocations, 66
western categories and ideals, imposition of, 12
western cultural bias, 267
western economic interests in Africa, 35
Western Enlightenment narrative, 35, 41
western feminism, 12, 70, 73, 266, 298

western linear view of progress, 12
western model, 268
western philosophical and socio-political tradition, 43, 50
western progressive and democratic values
dharma practice and, 261
western religion, 53
western secular liberalism, 35, 40
western-style institutionalization and education, 212
"White Lady," discourse on, 160
Whitney, Amy, 19
will-based theories, 267
Williams, Patricia J., 16
wisdom, 74, 76, 293
Wisdom Ways (Schüssler Fiorenza), 78
witchcraft, 210, 214, 217
Woman, I Condemn You Not (Olaniyi), 215
woman as helper, biblical notion of, 215
"Women, Ordination, and a Buddhist perspective" (Roloff), 22
"Women, Rights and Religion in India" (Mukherjee), 26–27
women and development, global discourses on, 228
Women and Evil (Noddings), 44
"Women and the Politics of Piety" (Arimbi), 25
women as community members, 235–236
women as full-obligated Jews, 141
women as leaders, 232–234
women as property, 174, 175n5
women in India, 264–266
conflicting images of devī (goddess) or dāsi (servant), 261
women in Indian history, 262–264
decline in status in medieval Indian history, 264
denied individuality of her own, 263
excluded from access to divine knowledge, 262
marriage the most important determinative event, 263
preference for males over females, 263
women in the public sphere, 228, 232–234
"Women Living Under Muslim Law" (WLUML) network, 10
women's bodies, 11, 43, 297–298
control of women's sexuality, 6
female chastity, 33, 297
right to make decisions concerning, 52
women's dignity, 56, 70, 296
"Women's Freedom of Religion Claims in Canada" (Koshan), 26
Women's Legal Education and Action Fund (LEAF), 253
women's religious roles as intercessors, 210
Women's Reservation Bill, 270

women's rights, 2, 4–6, 24, 44, 69, 157, 216, 228–229
impact of newer generation churches, 207
Indian Constitution on, 261
Islamic conservatives on, 69
recent victories in India, 275
"Women's Rights and Religion Jewish Style" (Baumel Joseph), 23
women's rights as human rights, 3, 13, 70, 260, 265, 275
women's rights vs. multiculturalism, 10
women's sexuality. See women's bodies
women's space is domestic space, 231–234
Women's World Conferences (Copenhagen, Nairobi, Beijing), 3
work as hanap-buhay (searching for life), 164
World Conference on Human Rights (Vienna, 1993), 3, 267
World Economic Forum (WEF) Gender Gap Report, 156–157
Wynne, Kathleen, 123, 126, 128, 131

Y

Yafie, Ali, 228
Yantha, Susan and Tammy, 115, 118
Young, Pamela Dickey, 297
Yusuf, Maftuchah, 228

Z

zakat (obligatory alms-giving), 191
Zapatista revolutionary movement
gender relations and, 49
opportunity to question "bad customs," 52
Zapatista women, 52, 62
encounter with Women of the World, 57
"The Zapatistas and the 'ConSciences' for Humanity," Chiapas, México (2017), 51

www.ingramcontent.com/pod-product-compliance
Lightning Source LLC
Chambersburg PA
CBHW050836230426
43667CB00012B/2027